S0-ADT-572

ECOFORESTRY

—————

A thing is right when it tends to preserve the integrity,
stability, and beauty of the biotic community.
It is wrong when it tends otherwise.

— Aldo Leopold, ecologist

—————

ECOFORESTRY

The Art and Science of Sustainable Forest Use

Edited by Alan Rike Drengson
and
Duncan MacDonald Taylor

NEW SOCIETY PUBLISHERS

Canadian Cataloguing in Publication Data:
A catalog record for this publication is available from the National Library of Canada and the Library of Congress.

Main entry under title:

Ecoforestry

Includes bibliographical references.
ISBN 0-86571-364-2 (bound) -- ISBN 0-86571-365-0 (pbk.)

1. Sustainable forestry. 2. Forest ecology. I. Drengson, Alan R., 1934- II. Taylor, Duncan M. (Duncan MacDonald)
SD387.S87E26 1997   333.75   C97-910311-8

Copyright © 1997 by Alan Rike Drengson and Duncan MacDonald Taylor.
All rights reserved.

Cover design by Val Speidel, from a photograph by Bo Martin.

Printed in Canada on acid-free, 100 percent recycled paper (using a minimum of 50 percent post-consumer waste) with soy-based inks by Best Book Manufacturers.

Inquiries regarding requests to reprint all or part of *Ecoforestry* should be addressed to New Society Publishers at the address below.
Paperback ISBN: 0-86571-365-0 Hardback ISBN: 0-86571-364-2

To order directly from the publishers, please add $3.00 to the price of the first copy, and $1.00 for each additional copy (plus GST in Canada). Send check or money order to:

New Society Publishers,
P.O. Box 189, Gabriola Island, BC V0R 1X0, Canada.

New Society Publishers aims to publish books for fundamental social change through nonviolent action. We focus especially on sustainable living, progressive leadership, and educational and parenting resources. Our full list of books can be browsed on the world wide web at: http://www.swifty.com/nsp/

NEW SOCIETY PUBLISHERS
Gabriola Island, BC, Canada and Stony Creek, CT, U.S.A.

DEDICATION

This book is dedicated to the memory of Dieter Deumling, formerly of Rickreal, Oregon, who was a devoted ecoforester, teacher, family member and friend. He sponsored the first gathering of ecoforesters of the Pacific Cascadia bioregion. This volume is given with thanks to the tireless people who have worked on behalf of ecologically responsible forest use. It is given in gratitude to the natural forest ecosystems and communities that sustain our lives and provide a rich diversity of values.

TABLE OF CONTENTS

PART ONE: Ecoforestry Principles and Practices

PART TWO: Maintaining the Ecosystem

PART THREE: Ecoforestry—Past and Current Examples

PART FOUR: Forestry For the Future—Community, Bioregionalism and Certification

PART FIVE: Lessons From the Forest—A Comprehensive Ecocentric Approach

ACKNOWLEDGMENTS

We are grateful for the support of the many organizations and people who made this anthology possible. This project began several years ago, and some support was provided by the Foundation for Deep Ecology. Support was also provided by the Ecoforestry Institutes of Canada and the U.S., and the SILVA Foundation of British Columbia. We are grateful to all contributors and photographers for their support of this project. Thanks to freelance photographers Bo Martin, Adrian Dorst, Bob Herger, Garth Lenz and Chip Vinai for permission to use their photographs. Special thanks to Jerry Valen de Morco, Sierra Club of Western Canada, and B.C. Forest Service photo archives. We thank Genie Computing for help with word processing, and Desk Top Publishing for their work on file conversion and formatting. Thanks also to the support and encouragement of Chris Plant at New Society Publishers. In turn, we are grateful for the countless hours of support given to ecoforestry by Doug Patterson, Lara Lamport, Sharon McCann, Ray Travers, Sharon Chow, Merv Wilkinson, Kirke Wolfe, Mike Barnes, Twila Jacobsen and Alan Wittbecker. Finally, we thank the many participants and practitioners who have helped us to understand better the practices of ecoforestry. We gratefully thank our loved ones for the time work on this anthology has taken from them.

We thank the following publishers for permission to use the articles and materials as cited below:

To the *International Journal of Ecoforestry* (IJE) we are grateful for the use of the following: "Critical Elements of Forest Sustainability," Orville Camp, IJE 10, 1, pp. 7-10; "Forest Practices Related to Forest Ecosystem Productivity," Alan Wittbecker, IJE 10, 4, pp. 174-183; "The Battle for Sustainability," James Drescher, IJE 10, 1, pp. 16-19; "Ecologically Responsible Restoration and Ecoforestry," Drengson, Stevens, et al., IJE 10, 4, pp. 206-210; "Monitoring for Ecosystem Management," Richard Hart, IJE 10, 2, pp. 74-75; "The Function of Snags," David Lukas, IJE 10, 1, pp. 27-28; "Forest Managers Focus on Fungi as Part of the Big Picture," Maggie Rogers, IJE 10, 3, pp. 138-141; "Water and Connectivity," Herb Hammond, IJE 11, 1, pp. 12-14; "Driftwood and How Forestry Affects the Ocean," Chris Maser and James Sedell, IJE 10, 1, pp. 32-34; "Fire in Our Future," James Agee, IJE 10, 4, pp. 184-193; "The Worth of a Birch," George Matz, IJE 10, 3, pp. 141-144; "The Affect of Nature-Oriented Forestry on Forest Genetics," Lutz Faehser, IJE 11, 1, pp. 8-11; "Respecting the Forest," Ruth Loomis, IJE 10, 3, pp. 102-103; "Sustainable Forestry in Switzerland: Hard Lessons for Canada," Monika Jaggi and L. Anders Sandberg, IJE 10, 4, pp. 166-173; "The Bradley Method of Brush Regeneration," John Seed, IJE 10, 3, pp. 127-129; "Special Forest Products," James Freed, IJE 11, 2/3, pp. 62-67; "The Earth's Blanket: Traditional Aboriginal Attitudes Towards Nature," Nancy J. Turner, IJE 10, 1, pp. 20-22; "The Fire Practices of Aboriginal North Americans," Stephen J. Pyne, IJE 10, 2, pp. 88-90; "Man of the Woods," Cheri Burda, IJE 11, 2/3, pp. 53-56; "What's Behind a Certified Label," Herb Hammond, IJE 11, 4, pp. 95-96; "What is Certification?" Herb and Susan Hammond, IJE 11, 4, pp. 102-103; "What is the Pacific Certification Council?" Walter Smith, IJE 11, 4, pp. 105-107; "Standards for Ecologically Responsible Forest Use," Herb Hammond, IJE 10, 1, pp. 11-15; "The Bioregional Basis of Forest Certification: Why Cascadia?" David Simpson, IJE 11, 4, pp. 140-143; "An Ecoforestry Stewardship Land Trust Model," Tyhson Banighen, IJE 10, 4, pp. 199-205; "A Model for Ecoforestry Community Economic Systems," Alan Drengson, IJE 10, 3, pp. 110-112; "The Movement to Ecologically Sustainable Forestry," Michelle Thom, IJE 11, 1, pp. 2-3; "Culture and Environment," Arne Naess, IJE 10, 4, pp. 158-161; "Forest Reflections," Gary Snyder, IJE 10, 1, pp. 29-31; "The Heart of the Forest," Arne Naess, IJE 10, 1, pp. 40-41; "Beyond Empire Resourcism to Ecoforestry: Applying the Principles of the Deep Ecology Movement," Alan Drengson, IJE 10,1, pp. 35-39.

We thank Island Press for permission to reprint the article by James Agee, which consists of excerpts from Chapter 13, "Fire in Our Future," of his book *Fire Ecology of Pacific Northwest Forests*, Covelo, California: Island Press, 1993. Thanks to the University of Washington Press for permission to reprint pages 71-83 from Stephen Pyne's *Fire in America*, Seattle: University of Washington Press, 1996. Thanks to the Canadian Forest Service for permission to reprint the figure on carbon retention curves used in Victoria Stevens' article. This figure originally appeared on page 33 in *The Carbon Budget of the Canadian Forest Sector*: Phase I, Report NOR-X-326. Thanks to Broadview Press for permission to reprint a revised version of our article (published herein as the introduction) "Shifting Values: Seeing Forests and Not Just Tree$," published in *Canadian Issues in Environmental Ethics*, Broadview, 1997. Thanks to Scottish Wildlife for permission to reprint Donald McPhillimy's article "A Forest for Scotland." Thanks to the editors of *Tree Rings: The Yuba Watershed Institute Newsletter* for permission to reprint the following pieces: "The Function of Snags," by David Lukas; "Forest Reflections," by Gary Snyder, which originally appeared as three short pieces under the separate titles of "Watershed Perspectives," "At Home in the Forest," and "Crawling". These papers all appear in a recent collection of Snyder's work called *A Place in Space*, pages 192-198, published by Counterpoint Press, Washington D.C., 1995. Reprinted with permission.

Thanks to *The Trumpeter: Journal of Ecosophy*, for permission to reprint: "Nature as a Reflection of Self and Society," by Duncan Taylor, which appeared in Vol. 7, No.

4, Fall 1990, pp. 174-176; "An Ecoforestry Stewardship Land Trust Model," by Tyhson Banighen, in Vol. 7, No. 2, Spring 1990, pp. 80-85.

Thanks to *Headwaters Journal* for permission to reprint "Monitoring for Ecosystem Management," by Richard Hart, which appeared in the Summer 1994 issue.

Thanks to *The Journal of Wild Mushrooming* for permission to reprint "Forest Managers Focus on Fungi as Part of the Big Picture," by Maggie Rogers, reprinted from 45, Vol. 12, No. 4, Fall 1994, pp. 9-12.

Thanks to *Alaska Geographic* for permission to reprint "The Worth of a Birch," by George Matz, Vol. 21, No. 2, 1994.

Thanks to Polestar Press for permission to reprint excerpts from *Seeing the Forest Among the Trees*, excerpts from "Water and Connectivity" pages 35-36, 27, and 36.

Thanks to St. Lucie Press in Florida for permission to reprint "Driftwood and How Forestry Affects the Ocean," by Chris Maser and James Sedell, excerpted from their book *The Forest to the Sea: The Ecology of Wood in Streams, Rivers, Estuaries and Oceans*, 1994.

Thanks to *Global Biodiversity* for permission to reprint "The Earth's Blanket: Traditional Aboriginal Attitudes Toward Nature," by Nancy Turner, Vol. 2, No. 4, 1994, pp. 5-7.

Thanks to *Gaining Ground* for permission to reprint "The Movement to Ecologically Sustainable Forestry," by Michelle Thom, which appeared in 1995.

Thanks to the *Humboldt Journal of Social Relations* for permission to reprint "Culture and Environment," by Arne Naess, which appeared in Vol. 20, No. 4, 1994. This article also appeared in the publication by SUM, University of Oslo, *Culture and Environment: Interdisciplinary Approaches*, edited by Nina Witoszek and Elizabeth Gulbransen, 1993. Permission from the editors and SUM is gratefully acknowledged.

Thanks to Gibbs M. Smith for permission to reprint the "Platform Principles of the Deep Ecology Movement," by George Sessions and Arne Naess, which appeared in *Deep Ecology* by Bill Devall and George Sessions, 1985, p. 10.

Thanks to *Ecoforestry Report I*, Spring 1993, for permission to reprint "A New Vision for Forest Ecosystems: An Interview with Herb Hammond," by Mitch Friedman. This interview originally appeared in the newsletter of the Greater Ecosystem Alliance, based in Bellingham, Washington, U.S.A.

Thanks to the B.C. Forests Ministry for permission to publish Victoria Stevens' paper "The Role of Coarse Woody Debris," several versions of which are part of a larger project on the ecology of woody debris supported by the Ministry.

ABOUT THE AUTHORS

JAMES AGEE is Professor of Forest Ecology at the College of Forest Resources, University of Washington, Seattle. He is the author of *Fire Ecology of Pacific Northwest Forests* published by Island Press, 1993, Covelo, California. The above article is from the last chapter of his book and is reprinted here with the permission of Island Press. All rights reserved.

TYHSON BANIGHEN is the founder and present Executive Director of Turtle Island Earth Stewards (TIES). He has taught in the Communications Dept. of Simon Fraser University and at the Okanagan University College in Salmon Arm. This article first appeared in *The Trumpeter* and has been adapted for this publication. This model was presented to the B.C. Forest Commission hearings and is the basis of a research project undertaken in Costa Rica, Nicaragua and Mexico with funding from CIDA.

MIKE BARNES is co-director, with Twila Jacobsen, of the Ecoforestry Institute at 785 Barton Road, Glendale, Oregon U.S.A. 97442, Phone: (503) 832-2785, Fax: (503) 832-2785 (call first), Internet: ecoforest@igc.apc.org. The EI is dedicated to protecting, maintaining, and restoring forests.

CHERI BURDA has been an environmental activist for many years and has worked for many environmental organizations, including the Ecoforestry Institute Society in Canada. She is also working for a masters degree in Environmental Studies at the University of Victoria.

ORVILLE CAMP is a consultant in Natural Selection Ecoforestry and the author of *The Forest Farmer's Handbook*. He is writing a new book called the *Ecoforester's Guide*. He has practiced ecoforestry on his forest near Selma, Oregon, for over 20 years.

BILL DEVALL co-authored the book *Deep Ecology: Living as if Nature Mattered*, one of the seminal writings in the deep ecology movement, with George Sessions in 1985. He wrote *Simple in Means, Rich in Ends: Practicing Deep Ecology* in 1988, and edited the book *Clearcut: The Tragedy of Industrial Forestry* in 1994. He teaches at Humboldt State University in California.

ALAN DRENGSON is an Emeritus Associate Professor of Philosophy at the University of Victoria, Victoria, B.C., Canada V8W 3P4. He is the editor of *The Trumpeter: Journal of Ecosophy*, and also *The Philosophy of Society*, as well as the author of

Beyond Environmental Crisis, The Practice of Technology, and *Doc Forest and Blue Mt. Ecostery*. He is one of the founders of the Ecoforestry Institute.

JIM DRESCHER is an ecoforester who practices his art in Nova Scotia. He is associated with Weathervane Institute at RR2, Germany, NS B0R 1E0. They certify forest materials for ecological responsibility under the label "ECOFOR." He calls his approach Natural Forestry: tending forests and harvesting forest products for the benefit of the natural ecosystem. The article printed here was first a talk given in Victoria, B.C., at Kindwood Forest, sponsored by the Ecoforestry Institute in November 1993.

LUTZ FAEHSER is the Director of the Forestry Office in Luebeck, the largest city in northern Germany. His article was presented at the workshop on "Preservation & Restitution of Biodiversity," organized by Max Mueller Bhavan, Forum of Environmental Journalists of India and the Ecological Society of Poona, in September 1991.

JAMES FREED is with the Extension Division of Washington State University in Pullman, Washington. He also works as a consultant and is an author. His speciality is special forest products.

MITCH FRIEDMAN is the executive director of the Greater Ecosystem Alliance based in Bellingham, Washington. He writes on topics relevant to ecosystem-landscale approaches to management.

HERB HAMMOND is a consulting ecoforester living in Winlaw, B.C. He is the founder of SILVA Forest Foundation and is the author of *Seeing the Forest Among the Trees: The Case for Wholistic Forest Use*, Vancouver: Polestar, 1991.

SUSAN HAMMOND works with the SILVA Forest Foundation in the West Kootenay region of southeastern B.C. and is active with the Slocan Valley Watershed Alliance. She consults on ecologically responsible forest use and forest certification.

RICHARD HART is research coordinator for the Headwaters project in southwest Oregon. He leads workshops in forest monitoring. His article is reprinted, with permission, from *Headwaters Journal*, Summer 1994. Headwaters, an environmental organization, and the journal can be contacted at P.O.B. 729, Ashland, OR U.S.A. 97520 (503) 482-4459.

TWILA JACOBSEN is co-director, with Mike Barnes, of the Ecoforestry Institute at 785 Barton Road, Glendale, Oregon U.S.A. 97442, Phone: (503) 832-2785, Fax: (503) 832-2785 (call first), Internet: ecoforest@igc.apc.org. The EI is dedicated to protecting, maintaining, and restoring forests.

MONIKA JÄGGI is a visiting scholar in the Department of Geography at York University. She currently does research on aboriginal forestry projects. She received her PhD from the University of Basel, Switzerland. Her dissertation research was conducted in Tunisia, North Africa, where she investigated resource conflicts between indigenous people and the tourism industry.

RUTH LOOMIS is a writer and editor with Reflections Publisher. She wrote *Wildwood: A Forest for the Future* and scripted the video *Thinking Like a Forest*, which describes the work of Merv Wilkinson and other ecoforestry workers. Her guide to the video, *Keeping The Forest Alive*, explains the biodiversity of our forests and is used by environmental groups and schools. Ms. Loomis' first book *Small Stories of a Gentle Island*, tells of her experiences living for 35 years on a small island in Georgia Strait.

DAVID LUKAS is a freelance naturalist, ornithologist and writer who lives in Lake Osewego, Oregon. He leads natural history tours and has a book on Portland birds in progress. The article in this book was originally published in the Yuba Watershed Institute journal *Tree Rings*. Reprinted here with permission of YWI and the author.

JERRY MANDER is a well-known author. He wrote *Four Arguments for the Elimination of Television* and *In the Absence of the Sacred*, and co-edited, with E. Goldsmith, *The Case Against the Global Economy, and for a Turn to the Local*. He is co-founder of the Public Media Center, which helps nonprofit groups with media campaigns.

GEORGE MATZ is a freelance consultant, writer and photographer who lives in Anchorage, Alaska. Most of his previous work has been with energy. He is interested in the ecology and economics of sustainable development, particularly forestry. A slightly shorter version of this article appeared in *Alaska Geographic*, Volume 21, Number 2, 1994.

CHRIS MASER is a freelance sustainable forestry consultant and author of numerous papers and books, such as *The Redesigned Forest, The Forest Primeval and The Global Imperative: Harmonizing Culture and Nature*. This article is excerpted from Maser and Sedell's book *The Forest to the Sea: The Ecology of Wood in Streams, Rivers, Estuaries, and Oceans*, Delray Beach, Florida: St. Lucie Press, 1994. Printed with permission of St. Lucie Press and the authors.

DONALD MCPHILLIMY is an independent woodland manager, consultant and lecturer. He is a director of Reforesting Scotland, an NGO (nongovernment organization) "working to restore the land and communities of Scotland through reforestation." This paper is a summary of key extracts taken from a report of the same name published by Scottish Wildlife and Countryside Link.

ARNE NAESS is Professor Emeritus at the University of Oslo, Norway. He is the author of many books and articles. He is best known for his work in ecophilosophy and his articulation of the principles for the deep ecology movement. He published an article in *Inquiry* in 1973 distinguishing between the deep ecology movement and the shallow ecology movement. He also coined the word "ecosophy." His most recent book is *Ecology, Community and Lifestyle*, published by Cambridge University Press.

STEPHEN J. PYNE is professor of History at Arizona State University West in Phoenix. This article was taken from his book *Fire in America: A Cultural History of*

Wildland and Rural Fire, Princeton University Press, 1982, pp. 71-83. Reprinted with permission. Prof. Pyne has a newer work entitled *World Fire*.

MAGGIE ROGERS is Coordinating Editor of *Mushroom: The Journal of Wild Mushrooming*. This article was reprinted, with permission, from Issue 45, Vol. 12, No. 4, Fall 1994, pp. 9-12. The Journal, $16 U.S. per year, can be ordered by writing to 861 Harold St., Moscow, ID 83843.

ANDERS SANDBERG teaches in the Faculty of Environmental Studies at York University, Toronto, Ontario, Canada.

JAMES R. SEDELL is a research stream ecologist who works with the U.S. Forest Service out of the Pacific Northwest Research Station in Corvallis, Oregon. He is the author of many articles, and co-author of *The Forest to The Sea*.

JOHN SEED is founder and director of the Rainforest Information Centre in Australia. Since 1979 he has been involved in the direct actions that have resulted in the protection of the Australian rainforests. He has travelled around the world raising awareness of the plight of rainforests and has created numerous projects protecting Third World rainforests. He has written and lectured extensively on the deep ecology movement, and coedited *Thinking Like a Mountain:Towards a Council of All Beings* (New Society Publishers).

DAVID SIMPSON is the former director of the Pacific Certification Council and also has been deeply involved in the Mattole Restoration Project in California.

WALTER SMITH is with the Institute for Sustainable Forestry in Redway, California. He also heads their Smartwood certification program for the west coast of North America. Smartwood is under the auspices of the Rainforest Alliance out of New York. He has been a practising forester for many years.

GARY SNYDER is a well-known poet and author. He is active in the Yuba Watershed Institute. One of his most recent books is *The Practice of the Wild* and one of his older books of poetry is *Turtle Island*. He is also author of *The Old Ways*. His influence on bioregionalism and reinhabitation has been enormous. The pieces printed here appeared as three different articles in the Yuba Watershed Institute Journal *Tree Rings*. Reprinted with permission of the Institute, the author and Counterpoint Press.

VICTORIA STEVENS is a wildlife biologist who works as a consultant in British Columbia, Canada. She is the author of numerous reports and other publications about biodiversity and forest practices. She has a PhD from the University of Washington School of Forestry.

DUNCAN TAYLOR is an Assistant Professor of Environmental Studies at the University of Victoria. He is also an adjunct professor of Whole Systems Design at Antioch University in Seattle. In recent years he has written extensively on community forestry and changing social values. He is the author of the book *Off Course: Restoring Balance Between Canadian Society and The Environment*.

MICHELLE THOM is a former associate of the Institute for Agriculture and Trade

Policy's program on Agriculture and Biotechnology. She wrote this article for *Gaining Ground* magazine [(408) 457-0130], 740 Front St., Suite 355, Santa Cruz, CA 95060. Reprinted with permission of the author and *Gaining Ground*.

NANCY J. TURNER is a Professor of Biology and Environmental Studies at the University of Victoria, B.C. Canada V8W 2Y2. She is a well-known ethnobotanist who has published many books and articles. This article was previously published in *Canadian Biodiversity* 2 (4): 5-7. *Canadian Biodiversity* is now called *Global Biodiversity* and is published by the Canadian Museum of Nature. It is available from Don McAllister, CMN, Box 3443, Stn. D, Ottawa, ON K1P 6P4.

ALAN E. WITTBECKER is an ecologist and member of the board of directors of the Marsh Institute based in Idaho. He is Director of Distance Education for the Ecoforestry Institute and author of numerous publications including the work in progress *Eutopias: Making Good Places Ecologically*.

FOREWORD

Jerry Mander

The late French philosopher, Jacques Ellul, made the case that in technological society all forms of human activity, whether personal behavior or organized social and economic activity, are fundamentally adaptive to the dominant logic and form of the machine. Beyond adaptive, human beings and our political, social and economic expressions are at one with the machine, part of a seamless symbiotic product. Ellul offered the term *tecnic* (technique) as a way of encompassing the merger of humans with mechanical and industrial forms, and the human embodiment of industrial consciousness. He argues that the process is now ubiquitous, planetary. It is discoverable not only in the external forms of industrial expression, but also in the process of human co-evolution with the machines we use. (As we drive our cars, we merge with the machine and the road, becoming ultimately "car-like." As we "watch" TV, we actually ingest its images and store them and they become our consciousness; we begin to merge with the images we carry. As we use our computers, we are engaged in endless feedback cycles which bring our minds, hands and bodies in concert with the machine. As we work the assembly line, we are utterly subject to the external repetitive rhythms that the line imposes, but which are also internalized and carried by us beyond working hours.) On each side of the human-machine equation, there are adaptations to one another — the machine is adapted for human use, and we adapt to the machine — with the ultimate goal being merger. It is that merged symbiotic form that Ellul labels as technique, and applies as much to human behavior and consciousness and thought as he does to the metallic expressions of it. In fact, it has been a different co-evolutionary process, from times before the technological age, when evolution was strictly among living creatures and with the expression of nature. Now, increasingly, our co-evolution is with mechanical or electric forms, while non-human nature is dropped from the equation, and from consideration, with already evident disastrous consequences.

If this process of technique can be grasped, merging human thought and behavior ever more into industrial forms, then it is entirely obvious why the organizational forms that we invent and employ are even further expressions of technique, made more exquisite by the purity they can obtain. The corporation, for example, itself an example of technique, operates by a system of laws and inherent structural rules that leave it utterly and purely beyond the norms of human "morals" or concerns for community, or for the harms that may be caused by industrial activity to a world beyond the technological world — to nature and natural processes. The corporation operates by an internal logic containing certain guidelines: economic growth, profit, absence of ethics and morals, and the endless need to convert the natural world into industrial processes and commercial products, by the fastest, most "efficient" means possible.

All "values" aside from these become secondary; in fact, they do not enter the picture at all in most instances. Questions of community welfare, or environmental sustainability are only issues of public relations, under techno-corporate consciousness. And as for the intrinsic values of the creatures of the Earth — its wildlife, its forests — all are reduced to their objective commercial potential with their ultimate fate determined by what fits technological-industrial processes most neatly. In the case of forests, the picture is particularly grim as objectification of the sort above reduces the forests to so many "board feet", so many dollars per unit. Consideration of the entire forest biotic community is out of the picture; intrinsic values are never discussed; the spiritual emanations of ancient forests are not perceived; sustainable economic processes are "inefficient" and too slow for the market machine; and long-term planetary health becomes much too, well, long-term for a technical-commercial values construct.

So, in machine society, it becomes solely the values and forms of the technical instruments — including corporations — that finally determine the organization of human activity and our relationship to nature. This is now clearly evident in every area of economic endeavor, though especially in the areas that corporations have gathered under their control. Whether we speak of the agricultural sector, or manufacturing, or food delivery, or fishing industries, or as we see in this magnificent book, the care and use of forest communities of living organisms, from trees and humans, to insects and microbes, all are subject to the logic of the machine.

All of these economic areas now show the visible symptoms of industrialization, exemplified particularly as monoculture. In agriculture, where many families formerly grew diversified crops to feed themselves and their communities, we now see a global juggernaut of corporate massification: massive land buyouts, people driven from their farms and cultures to squalid urban situations, and vast farmlands converted to monocultures, using pesticide and machine-intensive means to care for plants that human beings once nurtured. Where once small farms fed many people and kept the land rich, now all production is in soybeans, or cattle, or coffee for export. This is industrial logic. Meanwhile, the poisons on the lands seep to the rivers and into the food and water. And the people driven to cities, jobless, join the hordes of hungry migrants moving across borders.

The situation with forestry is identical. Where once thriving biotic communities of life permitted a biodiversity rich and stable in its complexities, industrial forestry, following the dictates of the objective rules of technique and the corporate directors of the process, replaces diversity with emptiness: clearcut. Life removed. Sometimes the clearcut areas are replanted into the "tree farms" that corporations will trumpet in their advertising — long rows of single species of pine or eucalyptus or fir — looking just exactly like the assembly lines of other industrial processes, with all diversity of forest life wiped out: a forest community no more.

Similar instances can be cited in the industrialization of fisheries, the giant trawler sweeping quantities of ocean life thousands of times greater than the small fisher boats, killing the oceans and the traditional fishing practices alike. We could enumerate a hundred other areas of economic endeavor. In cities the forms of the industrial-technical process are especially clear: suburbs, freeways, high-rise buildings, concrete on the land, nature nowhere visible, humans moving via machines through industrial canyons at industrial speed.

This homogenizing, massifying process is now being globalized, as the corporate supervisors follow the inevitable growth and expansion dictates of their technological mandates. Technique goes global.

Today, it is only the very rare society that has managed to stay away from the subjugation of technique. There we can still see the application of some principles of a reciprocal relationship to the natural world and the application of non-machine formulas; reciprocal processes as determined by planetary nature-based logic not visible within technological forms. But once those societies succumb to the dictates of the machine, or are pressed to do so, all becomes uniform, at one with the rules of efficiency, objectivity, productivity, economic growth, and profit that are intrinsic to technique.

Only one century into this process, the result is apparent in the looming catastrophes of global warming, ozone depletion, loss of species, pollution of all waters, loss of ecosystem viability, massive loss of biodiversity and in the case of forests, their rapid elimination and replacement with vast wastelands of clearcuts, or monocultural industrialized tree farms. The combination of these and other goings-on have brought us directly to the brink of a terrible ecological Armageddon.

Are there beneficiaries? Not judging by what is also simultaneously happening among human populations being similarly industrialized, made to fit the rules of the corporate-industrial process. We now see a level of alienation, suicide, violence, and a growing gulf between rich and poor that bespeaks a society that has been as victimized nearly as much as the natural world it worked to destroy. As the industrial processes globalize, the devastation accelerates, as does the despair of human beings left even more powerless in their decimated, and increasingly jobless, communities. Only those few people who are at the driver's wheel of the global industrial machine will benefit, albeit briefly, though one wonders at their joy in drinking their

If our acceptance of the entire industrial experiment has been a mistake ... how do we escape from the mess?

champagne toasts on the decks of the Titanic.

But if our acceptance of the entire industrial experiment has been a mistake, whether viewed from the social or ecological perspective, how do we escape from the mess? It is not complicated.

The first step is to gain consciousness, and stop engaging in the process which is killing us and killing the planet. Then we need to recover viable practices to reverse it. In the case of forestry the immediate need is to abandon the industrial forestry model as quickly as possible, and seek to apply such principles and practices as express a reciprocal relationship with nature, beyond the rules of the machine; a human-nature collaboration rather than a human-machine one. *Ecoforestry: The Art and Science of Sustainable Forest Use* is a major step forward in the rejection of the failed system, and the articulation and embrace of a viable new one.

* * *

In some ways, this book furthers the work of the earlier *Clearcut: The Tragedy of Industrial Forestry*, edited by Bill Devall (1993). That work presented dozens of magnificent large size photographs, proving the extent and the brutality of clearcutting in the North American landscape. Accompanied with texts by many of the authors who also write here in *Ecoforestry: The Art and Science of Sustainable Forest Use*, that work was intended to shock an unknowing public and public policy community into a new realization of the truth behind the "beauty strips" along highways, the unconscionable, nearly unimaginable (until you see it) devastation that results from the industrial model, made all the more tragic for its ubiquity.

In *Ecoforestry*, the authors carry the argument many stages further. While reporting and up-dating much of the news from the earlier work, the concentration is now on how to move forward by defining clearly, as never before, the ecoforestry alternative.

Here we have the greatest collection of practitioners and theorists in the movement toward ecologically responsible and sustainable forest use gathered under one cover to present and explain every nuance and the new paradigms that are represented. The collective aim of these writers is preservation and restoration of forests throughout the world by clarifying that a forest is something far more than the trees within it; it is a community of hundreds of thousands of life forms that collaborate for sustainability. Humans are notable among them, but not dominant. Forests bring uncountable gifts to human society, material and spiritual, but this is surely not the primary point, as the value of forests is intrinsic to their existence. It does not depend on human opinion. This viewpoint as to intrinsic value instantly sets the ecoforesters apart from the industrial foresters caught within tecnic. Ecoforestry, in the end, is more than a good plan for sustainable use of forests, though it is that. It is also more than a good plan for ecological sustainability. It is above all a moral and spiritual undertaking and commitment at the highest level.

A forest is something far more than the trees within it; it is a community of hundreds of thousands of life forms that collaborate for sustainability.

The Ecoforesters who write herein express a vision of diversity as a primary value: the maintenance of the forest's miraculously diverse community of flora and fauna, and also its diversity of cultures and practices. Ecoforestry practice encourages us to merge with our forests, rather than our machines, in such a way that we become once again native to them, reinhabiting carefully where possible, learning to accept the forest's wisdom and live by its limits. Any relationship to forest other than such a reciprocal and respectful one, especially one based on human dominion and need, is doomed to fail, as we already see.

Finally, of course, human need is also served by respecting the forest's intrinsic value, though it may truly be the case that humans who have merged with technology may have lost the ability to grasp their alienation and its consequences. Like forest ecosystems suffering the ravages of technique, humans, too, can be saved. The human-nature synthesis as expressed by ecoforestry and described in this book has the potential for saving it all.

PREFACE

This anthology has been a long time in the making. It had its genesis, we suppose, when we both were young, in love with the forests and wildlands of Canada and the United States. During our development we both came to know the forests through firsthand experience by living and working in them. We also came to know many forest dwellers, both human and nonhuman, who live wisely in the forests of their home places. Such wise dwellers taught us much that we know of forests and their responsible use.

Over the years, we came to appreciate the degree to which wholesome human communities depend upon the Earth's natural forests and their integrity. It has taken a long time to realize the complexity of interdependencies that exist between forests and human civilization and life. Whether practising fishing, farming or forestry, all are, in the last analysis, dependent on forest ecosystems. We have seen fisheries in danger from not just overfishing in the oceans, but also from destruction of the upland and riparian systems that are intimately interconnected with the marine environment. We have come to see how the hydrological cycles involve the entire region and planet, and how cycles of carbon from standing tree to rotting log are part of the total forest ecological processes. The natural forests represent a multitude of biological communities that are intertwined with complex structures above and below ground, and were created by evolutionary processes through natural selection. To learn from these vast historical, biological and geological masterpieces is our basic need.

As debates raged in the West about industrial clearcut logging practices—rasing ancient forests to replace them with monoculture tree plantations, we both looked for better ways of using the forests, ways that preserve their ecological functions and integrity. We came to the conclusion that we had to change our basic ways of thinking. We learned ways of thinking and acting based on ecological values, values that are intrinsic to the ecological communities themselves. We learned both outside in and inside out. We not only learned the sciences and research of the scholars, we sampled the work of practitioners, many of whom have lived in the forests for generations, and others who appeared to be dwelling wisely in the forests. It was about this time that ecoforestry was emerging as a movement to a "kinder, gentler forestry."

We both participated in the development of ecoforestry and contributed our respective skills and resources to its development. In the course of the social and cultural evolution of the last 10 years the Ecoforestry Institutes in the U.S. and Canada were born. The *International Journal of Ecoforestry* absorbed *Forest Planning Canada*, and the *Ecoforestry Report* appeared. Many books and articles to which we contributed were published to aid in the fight to save the natural forests from destruction. During this same time we participated in courses, conferences, workshops, summer institutes and meetings. Both of us realized how important it is to draw together the material on ecoforestry presented in this anthology to be shared by a larger audience than that of the Pacific Cascadia Bioregional Ecoforestry Working Group. Throughout this educational process it became clear that we needed a collection such as the one we present here. This book is for the movement to ecoforestry in the belief that it will serve as a catalyst to further change of practices throughout the planet to place-specific ecoforestry that is based on ecological wisdom (ecosophy) learned through long-term commitment to the places wherein practitioners dwell, aging and seasoning with the forests themselves. In reality, this book has been the work of the contributors and practitioners themselves. While this book addresses the philosophy and practice of ecoforestry in broad terms, future volumes will focus more on the applied, day-to-day work of forest workers and users.

Ecoforestry: The Art and Science of Sustainable Forest Use can be considered a sequel to an earlier book *Clearcut: The Tragedy of Industrial Forestry*. In this earlier work many noted authors and photographers presented the case against placeless, industrial development paradigms as they are applied to natural forests. It shows the consequences of clearcutting and turning diverse natural forest communities into managed, tree plantations. The destructive results reverberate through every dimension since sustainable communities depend upon sustainable, self-maintaining ecosystems. The industrial models are human-centered and reduce everything to single quantitative measures such as quarterly profits. *Clearcut* provided a glimpse of the alternative to industrial development models. The alternative approach is called ecoforestry. *Ecoforestry* explores in greater depth the art, science, and practices of sustainable forest use, based on respect for all ecological values found in specific places.

We hope that the *Clearcut* book as critique, and this *Ecoforestry* book as an alternative vision, help others to see how the same critiques and alternatives can be worked out in all areas of resource use now dominated by industrial paradigms, such as fishing, mining, ranching, and farming. Ecoforestry is part of a larger movement toward sustainable, ecologically responsible practices in part known as the "deep ecology movement". Once this wider view is gained, it is far easier to translate support for these principles into other areas of action in specific places.

The collection of papers and photos presented in this book are not an exhaustive treatment of the diverse forms of ecoforestry. This anthology gives readers a basic introduction to the ecoforestry movement and its practices, arts and science as represented in the work of its diverse researchers and practitioners. The papers reflect the ongoing development of ecoforestry as a movement and practice over the last five years. The bibliography, references and contacts provide resources for readers who want to go further. And the Glossary is intended to explain terms that are not common knowledge.

An important note to readers: The authors in this book might not hold exactly the same views or express them in quite the same way as they did when their papers were written. We are after the sense of the historically dynamic ecoforestry movement. Many of the papers herein represent thinking and work in progress. Ecoforestry is a learning approach. This book provides a general introduction to it. Other books are in the works the focus of which is hands-on practices.

May all forest dwellers, beings and forests flourish and realize themselves!

INTRODUCTION

An Overview of Ecoforestry

Alan Drengson and Duncan Taylor

EARLY IN THE MORNING on August 9th, 1993, nearly 300 men, women and children, many of them chanting and singing, were arrested and hauled away by the RCMP for protesting clearcut logging in British Columbia's Clayoquot Sound. The morning's confrontation constituted the largest single mass arrest in B.C. history. By the end of the summer the number charged with obstructing the logging bridge across Clayoquot Sound's Kennedy River totalled 800. Many of the protesters arrested that morning had been camped in a clearcut that had become known throughout the province as the Black Hole. The slashed, burned, blackened and eroded hills surrounding the protest camp look down on that part of Highway 4 which divides in opposite directions at the point where it reaches the west coast of Vancouver Island: to the southeast the road ends at the town of Ucluelet, to the northwest it ends at the community of Tofino. The fact that these communities lie geographically at opposite ends of Pacific Rim National Park merely underscores the polarization that has arisen between the residents of Ucluelet and Tofino regarding the future of the 350,000 hectares of coastal temperate old-growth forest in this region.[1]

Since the early 1970s the town of Tofino has become home to an increasing number of people who openly espouse a pro-environmental position with respect to how the forests of this region should be used. Once almost solely dependent on logging and fishing, Tofino now boasts that most of its revenue is derived from purely sustainable forms of wilderness recreation tourism such as kayaking, backpacking and whale watching, which are utterly dependent on maintaining the integrity of the Sound's forests, rivers and inlets. In turn, the native bands belonging to the Nuu-chah-nulth Tribal Council, who live on many of the islands outside Tofino, have laid claim to the Clayoquot Sound region and have let it be known that status quo resource extraction will no longer be tolerated.

> **There is a win-win solution. This solution is predicated on the recognition that sustainable communities and economies are subsystems of healthy biophysical systems, and not the other way around.**

In contrast, on the other side of Pacific Rim National Park the majority of the residents of Ucluelet have remained almost solely dependent on the forest industry for their employment and livelihood. Indeed, in the past decade they have witnessed thousands of forestry workers on Vancouver Island being laid off due to pressure on the forest industry to maintain its international competitiveness. This has led to rapid changes in equipment and mechanization procedures resulting in a downsizing of the labor force. And when uncertainty regarding forest policy and access to harvestable timber in Clayoquot Sound is also factored in, tensions have tended to be projected in terms of simplistic arguments of *jobs* versus *preservation*. However, this dichotomy is not new.

People active in environmental issues over the last two decades have witnessed the polarization of debates raging over the protection of wilderness values by preservation of ancient West Coast forests, versus the economic values of logging. In the United States, particularly in the states of Washington and Oregon, this crystallization has been evident in the *owls vs. jobs* phrases used to describe the way the issues are seen. Here the owls are used to represent the environment, and jobs the workers and business. The polarization between the residents of Tofino and Ucluelet may be seen to characterize the rift that exists between environmentalists and those who are stridently anti-environmentalist and claim that environmentalism undermines human and economic well-being. But while this portrait is true to some extent, it fails to take account of the *conservationist* stance held by many proforestry advocates. Consequently, the debate between these towns also reflects a more scholarly debate between supporters of what has been termed the *deep ecology movement* and proponents of *reformist environmentalism*. For some time now, spokespeople from Ucluelet and other forestry-dependent communities have claimed that they are the *real* conservationists—but conservationists who are realistic enough to respect the human benefits that accrue from one of Canada's largest and most economically important industries.

The impression one sometimes gets from these debates is that we must choose between ecologically sound practices and human economic and social welfare needs. In our view, the jobs vs. environment account is a caricature of our situation and options with respect to resolving current conflicts. As long as attention is focused on this narrow account, resolution seems impossible: either we sacrifice the environment for jobs (economic values) in the short term to meet the demands of social justice and human needs, or we sacrifice jobs to save the environment for our long-term interests. This is a no-win situation. However, we believe that there is a win-win solution. This solution is predicated on the recognition that sustainable communities and economies are subsystems of healthy biophysical systems, and not the other way around.

Since the rise of modernity in the 17th century, we have been rapidly converting natural capital to financial capital and changing our ecological systems to meet the imperatives of an ever-expanding consumptive economic system. This has to change. Indeed, for the long-term survival of our own species as well as the many other life-forms with whom we share this planet, we now need to recognize that our economic system is a utterly dependent upon the larger biophysical ecology and that it has to be transformed to meet the imperatives of the latter. In this way we can reach a win-win situation. In this way we can have long-term forestry jobs, healthy communities, and a healthy natural ecosystem. The road into Clayoquot goes in opposite directions—indeed, it symbolically points to the choice between two very different worldviews and sets of values.

In the current conflict over forest preservation and logging we can see that there are definitely two different orientations or approaches at issue. One is the dominant, mainstream, expansionist model of modernism, the other is an emerging ecological paradigm. The *first* is based on an *anthropocentric* model of our relation to nature—humans exist apart from and outside of nature; it accepts a utilitarian value system. In the expansionist paradigm, nature is regarded essentially as a storehouse of resources to be utilized for the meeting of ever-increasing material needs by an ever-increasing human population. Consequently, this position equates growth with the progress of development which, in turn, is regarded as a prerequisite for human happiness and prosperity, claiming that any drop in this growth rate must inevitably result in stagnation, mass unemployment and distress. Those who argue for this position claim that new technological advances can be relied upon to increase global standards of living, harness renewable and more environmentally friendly sources of energy, and increase food production and the availability of other biological products through breakthroughs in biotechnology. In turn, more efficient technologies are seen to be able to solve the problems created by previous technologies, to create substitutes for depleted resources and to replace damaged ecosystems.

On the other hand, the ecological paradigm is based on humans as participants in nature; it accepts an ethic based upon respect for diversity and ecocentric values. The two views in question differ in their sense of values that are intrinsic to nature and to human life. Intrinsic or inherent values are cherished for their own sake. We consider them to be good in themselves; they are ends. Instrumental values are pursued as a means to other things and states that are themselves valued. In the case of valuing the natural world, people holding the intrinsic nature view (the deep ecology movement for example) cherish other beings for their own sake, quite independent of their usefulness or economic value to humans. The instrumentalist nature view (the Shallow Ecology Movement) sees all intrinsic value as vested solely in humans. The result is that the world is valued only as means; its value is as resources to be used for human consumption and enjoyment. The *intrinsic nature* view sees a world rich in inherent values, beings having value in themselves quite independently of human interests. In the *instrumentalist nature* view we have an obligation to manage and control the world to meet human needs and desires. In the *intrinsic nature* view we have an obligation to manage ourselves so as to preserve the beauty and integrity of the planet's ecological processes and functions. *All* beings count; their vital needs must be respected when we design our practices.

Some of the characteristics of this emerging ecological paradigm may be summarized as follows:

- The universe is an interrelated totality, with all of its parts interconnected and interlocked. A corollary to this is the rejection of those dualistic and atomistic categories inherent within the Newtonian mechanistic perspective on which the expansionist paradigm is founded—for example, the epistemological separation of the subjective knower from the objective known, and the radical separation of facts from values.

- Nature is intrinsically valuable; animals, trees or rocks all have worth and value in themselves regardless of what value they may have for human beings. This is essentially an ecocentric and non-anthropocentric perspective and a rejection of the typically quantitative approach to nature with its emphasis on viewing the natural world primarily in economic and utilitarian terms.

- Nature is both a physical and a symbolic forum from which to stand back from modern society. In nature—and especially in the more wild areas—humans are afforded an opportunity to actualize their own inner spiritual, esthetic, and moral sensibilities. Moreover, physical nature—especially wilderness—is a benchmark against which the state of human society may be judged. Consequently, large areas of the natural world should be preserved and protected from human interference.

Throughout the 20th century environmental debates have been polarized in terms of these two dominant perspectives. For example, the same type of polarization that continues to occur over the ancient forests has also been evident in disputes over industrial fishing and agriculture and their ecological viability. The first famous articulation of the polarized views referred to above surfaced in debates between John Muir (naturalist and essayist and founder of the Sierra Club in 1892) and Gifford Pinchot (U.S. Chief Forester who largely determined President Theodore Roosevelt's conservation program) early in this century.[2]

Anticipating the later work of Aldo Leopold, Muir argued for the adoption of an environmental land ethic, but one that would recognize the inherent value of natural entities and their right to pursue their own destiny, to continue to evolve. He believed we should preserve large areas of wilderness so that it can evolve independent of human manipulation—even if no human ever visits such areas. In doing so, he was rejecting a basic tenet of modernism which had come to view nature primarily in utilitarian and economic terms. Moreover, it was to put him increasingly at odds with his contemporary Gifford Pinchot as well as the values that dominated North American society at the turn of the 20th century.

Conservation as championed by Pinchot, on the other hand, was to be an ally of the expansionist paradigm. In many respects, it was for this reason that it had gained a certain legitimacy by 1908 when President Theodore Roosevelt held the first National Conference on Conservation at the White House. And not surprisingly, John Muir was not invited. By 1909 the Canadian government had established its own Commission of Conservation.[3] Indeed, the *wise use* school of Pinchot in the United States and Clifford Sifton in Canada equated conservation with *sustainable exploitation*. For both men, conservation should work against the wastefulness and environmentally disruptive excesses of a developing society, but not against development per se. For land to be protected or *alienated* from resource development and extraction was seen to be politically and economically naive. Indeed, conservationists argued that land must be utilized in the interests of a

Clayoquot Sound, B.C.
Adrian Dorst

growing industrial economy, thereby providing jobs and wealth to the larger society. Ideally, conservation would require that wise *scientific* management procedures be adopted in the utilization of all resources, including forests, soils, waters and wildlife. Moreover, wherever possible, these resources would be harvested in terms of a renewable crop. In this way, Pinchot and others believed that nature's resources could be *used* and *saved* simultaneously and thereby conserved for future human generations.

Pinchot's legacy lives on with those who champion the sustainability of the existing expansionist paradigm. In other words, conservation was to reinforce the dominant industrial expansionist worldview by ideally protecting the ability of the land to provide a limitless supply of resources—hence, *sustainable economic development*. On the other hand, John Muir's position is favored by those proponents of an emerging ecological perspective who believe that we must recognize ecological limits to growth and transform our economies to meet its imperatives—not the other way around. Moreover, it is argued that the products of ecological and evolutionary processes can only be sustained by protecting the integrity of the ecological processes that give rise to them. This necessitates the preservation of large areas of wilderness for the ongoing protection of biodiversity as well as esthetic and spiritual values. In other words, we must ultimately reject the expansionist paradigm and learn to live off the *interest or abundance* of nature while protecting its *biological capital*. Current wise-use strategies consume natural capital and diversity. Hence, the need to go from the current emphasis on models for sustainable economic development to strategies for *developing environmental sustainability*. We would then place our priorities on maintaining biodiversity and ecological processes.

While there is some uncertainty about exact details and specific timetables, people who have knowledge of Earth's ecosystems agree that the large-scale industrial practices, as imposed today upon the biological processes of the planet, are not sustainable. On the other hand, in the modern period most Westerners accept without question modernism's definition of progress, that through science and technology we can have unlimited growth (certainly an unscientific belief), greater and greater wealth, more and more power, more and more speed, and so on. We have partially realized these aims, except for the last several years when the standard of living has not been going up, debt has been increasing, and social problems have multiplied beyond our capacity to find solutions. We tend to look at each of these problems on its own so as to find individual and even individualistic solutions. But the problems, like the debt, have become intractable. Our apparent solutions often create more problems than real solutions. Even as we increase efficiency, cost effectiveness, and competitiveness in forestry (and fishing and farming), and have been cutting greater and greater volumes of timber with fewer workers, at the same time communities based on forestry have had increasingly hard economic times and decreasing employment. The same things have happened in fishing and farming communities. The application of the industrial paradigm of modernism to these resource-based economies has been disastrous, not only for the humans involved, but also for future generations and the ecosystems that produce the needed resources.

Forest ecosystems, for example, produce trees and a great diversity of other organisms and processes beneficial to us. Remove the whole forest by extensive clearcutting and this great productive power is reduced to nearly zero. That area of land will now be recovering for a long time. Recent industrial methods try to turn forests into monocultured agricultural products, and the result of such methods is a dramatic reduction in ecological diversity. This is reflected in the human communities in the reduction from economic diversity to single-industry towns. The methods, scale and economy of industrial forestry lead to depopulation of forest-based communities and to reduced biological, economic and cultural diversity. Ecoforestry maintains and gives rise to greater diversity on many levels. It is based on the recognition that sustainable communities depend on sustainable forest ecosystems.

The expansionist worldview upon which modernism is based reduces all values to a common monetary measure—for example, dollars. If dollars are the only measure widely accepted for evaluating courses of action, then the demands of modern progress (as defined above) will be to use all resources to our maximum ability so as to generate the largest short-term gains. The creation of wealth in this way is often illusory, for it is based not only on increasing public and private debt, but also on increasing social and ecological debts. Even if we took all human interests into account, strove for economic and social justice, and considered the interests and needs of future generations, we would still not be able to resolve our current dilemmas without embracing a larger system of values, a broader, more inclusive understanding of how we participate in local, regional and global ecosystems.

Broader perspectives such as these help us to better understand our whole heritage and the debt we owe to the natural processes that provide us with a rich accumulation of ecological wealth. This accumulation, we can then appreciate, is part of larger sustaining processes that allow abundance to be continually produced. When we look at our problems with a narrower focus, as suggested by the dominant paradigm, we can be led to think that we must sacrifice either jobs or healthy ecosystems. Nothing could be further from the truth; they are interdependent. Thus, if we work within the limits of local ecosystems, but add diversity to our economies, we can produce many levels of value-added activity. The end result will be greater prosperity for all but the few megacorporations that have no interest in preserving local communities or ecosystems.

A solution, then, might be to redefine the wise-use philosophy of Gifford Pinchot. If we consider the needs of future generations of humans over several hundred years, can we not then design practices that take conservation seriously? The crux then will be seen as how to build conservation costs into the system's economics. This approach could buy time. However, in our view it cannot resolve our fundamental problems. We cannot design sustainable practices without a deeper understanding of the relevant values and costs. Any values lost must be figured as costs. In addition, just as a person who is egocentric often fails to perceive community values, so a person who is *anthropocentric* (believes that only humans have inherent value) can have difficulty understanding and perceiving the diversity of ecological values inherent in the forests and Earth. It is not just a matter of short-term versus long-term perspectives, although looking at our situation with a broader temporal perspective certainly helps. It is a matter of a different frame of reference.

The dispute that erupted in the forests of British Columbia in the summer of 1993 over the government/industry decision to clearcut much of the forests of Clayoquot Sound exemplifies the nature of the debate we have been describing. In 1995 the British Columbia government legislated its Forest Practices Code, which promised that forestry would be conducted in an environmentally sound way. To the critics, however, the Forest Practices Code was a band-aid solution that would merely help to prolong the lifespan of a dying industrial forestry status quo. It was still very mainstream, and mainstream thinking is steeped in ideas of sustained yield and cosmetic cuts, for example, those which follow natural contours and boundaries, rather than in understanding whole, natural forest ecosystems with their multitudes of functions, values, beings and processes. Sustaining a steady flow of raw material to be turned into commodities by means of longer rotations and smaller clearcuts could ultimately lead to the same results as the large-scale conversion of diverse natural forests into just a few commercially profitable species and single-age monocultures. This thinking is based on attempting to control and redesign the forest by removing the old forests and replacing them with "superior" desired species which are managed (meaning by the same methods as industrial agriculture, based on machines and external subsidies such as fertilizers, pesticides and petrochemicals).

Our description of the conflicts so far should make it evident that one way to break the impasse would be to change our forest practices so that they are consistent with the ways in which natural forests sustain themselves through diversity, recycling of woody debris, and natural succession and regeneration. If an economy is based on a natural resource and its use, than clearly the elimination of that resource will destroy the economy over time. This has been dramatically shown in the case of much of the Newfoundland fishing industry with the virtual elimination of the northern cod stock.

Considerable clarity in this situation can be gained by considering the conflicting views as representing the clash between the shallow or reform ecology movement and the long-range, deep ecology movement. (With respect to the terminology we have already employed, shallow ecology is very much part of the expansionist perspective and deep ecology is virtually identical to the emerging ecological perspective.) Arne Naess of Norway introduced this terminology in the early 1970s to characterize the two main trends in environmentalism as a worldwide, grassroots movement. It was clear to Naess that people in different cultures argued for an approach to the natural world that took diversity as central. Since the environmental crisis requires fundamental changes in values and attitudes, we cannot go on with business as usual. We must question deeply our fundamental values. People in different cultures have different ultimate philosophies: They could be Buddhists, Christians, or philosophical pantheists, and yet they all share the same Earth. In his travels Naess found that people in quite different places support certain general principles which he articulated as the platform principles of the deep ecology movement.

The platform principles of the deep ecology movement as stated by Naess and Sessions (1985) are:

1. The well-being and flourishing of human and nonhuman life on Earth have value in themselves (synonyms: intrinsic value, inherent value). These values are independent of the usefulness of the nonhuman world for human purposes.

2. Richness and diversity of life-forms contribute to the realizations of these values and are also values in themselves.

3. Humans have no right to reduce this richness and diversity except to satisfy vital human needs.

4. The flourishing of human life and cultures is compatible with a substantial decrease of human population. The flourishing of nonhuman life requires such a decrease.

5. Present human interference with the nonhuman world is excessive, and the situation is rapidly worsening.

6. Policies must therefore be changed. These policies affect basic economic, technological, and ideological structures. The resulting state of affairs will be deeply different from the present.

7. The ideological change is mainly that of appreciating life quality (dwelling in situations of inherent value) rather than adhering to an increasingly higher standard of living. There will be a profound awareness of the difference between big and great.

8. Those who subscribe to the foregoing points have an obligation to directly or indirectly try to implement the necessary changes.

(Quoted from Bill Devall and George Sessions, *Deep Ecology*, Salt Lake City: Gibb Smith, 1985.)

In contrast, the platform principles of the shallow or reform ecology movement are as follows (synthesized by us):

1. Humans and their communities are the only beings that have intrinsic worth.

2. Progress involves applying scientific knowledge to increase technological power so as to satisfy human needs and wants.

3. No developments should be pursued if they seriously damage human interests and the rights of future generations of humans to fulfil themselves.

4. We and our descendants depend upon the resources of the Earth.

5. These resources should be used wisely so that human interests now and in the future are not jeopardized.

6. Pollution and resource waste are in conflict with human well-being and future interests.

7. We should fight pollution and resource depletion.

8. Anyone who agrees with the need to preserve environmental integrity for human benefit should support reforms (higher gas mileage, greater efficiency, etc.) that end environmental degradation and resource abuse.

As the debate has worn on, public perceptions and policies related to forests have also been changing. For an increasing number of people, it has become clear that the mere reform of conventional practices will not preserve the integrity of natural forests in terms of sustaining biodiversity, the ability of forest ecosystems to adapt to new and changing environmental conditions, and protecting the full range of forest values. Consequently, advocates of the ecological paradigm argue that our practices must be redesigned from the ground up so that they recognize the intrinsic value of biological diversity. We cannot develop ecologically sound and responsible practices unless we do take account of and respect both biodiversity and diversity of values—both in natural systems and in the human cultural systems whose whole long-term viability is predicated upon them.

Let us consider, then, how such a redesign might take place. Here is a chart outlining the industrial philosophy of imposing machine structures on nature in contrast to the ecological paradigm:

INDUSTRIAL PHILOSOPHY	ECOLOGICAL PARADIGMS
1. Business as usual	Need new practices
2. Technical fixes for environmental problems	Design approaches that prevent problems
3. Nature as raw material, only instrumental value	Nature is intrinsically valuable
4. Mechanistic models	Whole systems models—community-ordered organic ecosystems
5. Isolated objects, subject-object dualisms	Fields, processes, inter-relationships, interdependent dualities
6. Technical knowledge suffices	Need understanding, wisdom
7. Reductionistic	Wholistic
8. Progress defined economically	Progress defined by all values—moral, spiritual, esthetic, etc.
9. Consumptive lifestyles	New low-impact lifestyles

Next let us consider how this approach applied to agriculture contrasts with the emerging ecoagricultural approach:

INDUSTRIAL AGRICULTURE	ECOAGRICULTURE
1. Capital-intensive	Knowledge and labor-intensive
2. Large-scale monocultures	Small-scale, mixed crops, etc.
3. Simplifies ecosystem	Increases cropland diversity and complexity
4. Imposes management on nature	Lets nature "manage"
5. Uses chemicals, fire, etc.	Uses no biocides and uses fire sparingly
6. Ignores biological communities	Enhances soil communities
7. High input costs	Low input costs

> Advocates of the ecological paradigm argue that our practices must be redesigned from the ground up so that they recognize the intrinsic value of biological diversity.

8. Large agri-business farms	Small, family-sized farms
9. Elimination of rural communities	Regeneration of communities

Finally, let us consider the main contrasts between conventional industrial forestry and ecologically based forestry. Indeed, it may be observed that while the goals of ecologically based forestry are largely in keeping with the principles of a deep ecology approach, at times they overlap with some of the "wise use management" conservation principles of shallow ecology and Gifford Pinchot. In light of current economic and political realities, this should be expected.

Industrial Clearcut Methods
Garth Lenz

INDUSTRIAL FORESTRY

1. Trees are seen as products
2. Short-term production goals
3. Agricultural production model
4. Trees are the only cash crop
5. Trees' survival dependent on humans
6. Chemicals
7. Clearcuts

8. Same age stands of trees
9. Monoculture of single or few species
10. Simplified ecosystem
11. Capital-intensive and corporate-based
12. Redesigning nature
13. Lifespan, 60-100 years
14. Loss of the sacred
15. Older traditions, aboriginal knowledge outdated

ECOFORESTRY

Forests are ecological communities
Long-term sustainability
Forest ecosystem model
Diverse forest products and services
Self-sustaining, self-maintaining, and self-renewing
No chemicals
Harvesting surplus wood and selective removal
All ages of trees
All species of trees

Natural biodiversity and complexity
Labor-intensive and locally based

Accepting nature's design
Lifespan, millennia
Sense of the sacred and mysterious
Older traditions and aboriginal knowledge are sources of wisdom

Methods for attaining these ecoforestry goals are the following:

PRINCIPLES OF ECOFORESTRY:

1. Retention must be the first consideration in any planned removal of trees from a stand. Emphasize what must be left to ensure the protection of such things as rare species, sites of native cultural significance, riparian zones (that is, watercourses, lakeshores, etc.).

2. Leave riparian zones intact. No tree removal should take place in the most sensitive areas. Protect water quality by minimizing alterations to natural drainage patterns.

3. Maintain composition and structures to support fully functioning forests. Important forest structures such as large old trees, snags, and large fallen trees are maintained by letting a minimum of 20 to 30 percent of overstory trees (well distributed spatially and by species) grow old and die in any timber extraction area.

4. Use the lowest impact removal methods possible. Avoid building roads and compacting forest soils as much as possible—all roads should be small-scale, contour, low-grade roads requiring a minimum of blasting.

5. Plan in terms of the needs of the larger watershed, even if owner does not control or own the watershed. A watershed zone plan must designate areas where tree removal is not permitted and those where different levels and types of removal are possible.

6. Prohibit clearcutting as currently practised and utilize ecologically appropriate partial cutting methods that maintain the canopy structure, age distribution, and species mixtures found in healthy natural forests of a particular ecosystem type.

7. Select trees as candidates for removal by considering how abundant and redundant their structures and functions are to the rest of the forest as a whole, leaving potential wildlife trees (to become snags and large woody debris).

8. Allow the forest to regenerate trees through seeds from trees in the logged area. Tree planting will generally not be required because a diverse, fully functioning forest is always maintained, assuring natural regeneration.

9. Maintain ecological succession to protect biological diversity. The process of brush control will be avoided. Over time, all forest phases must occupy every forest site, even on sites managed solely for timber.

10. Prohibit slash burning. Fire is an acceptable tool in landscapes that have a history of naturally occurring fires, but use with caution.

11. Prohibit pesticide use. Disease, insects and shrub/herb vegetation are essential parts of a fully functioning forest.

12. Maintain and restore topsoil quality by leaving sufficient large and small debris.
13. Maintain beauty and other natural esthetic qualities in the visual, sound, and odor landscapes.
14. Always look at the forest as a whole and how each part contributes to the needs and health of the whole in which it resides.
15. Rely as much as possible on local people and markets. Engage in full-cost accounting.
16. Remember that wisdom begins with recognizing our limitations and ignorance. When in doubt, don't![4]

While this form of *ecoforestry* is not yet the norm, there are current indications that there is a trend in this direction. In the wake of the Clayoquot Sound protests and arrests in 1993 the British Columbia government agreed to commission a panel of experts in forest ecology and native cultural concerns to investigate the best way that logging could proceed in Clayoquot Sound. In the spring of 1995 the Scientific Panel for Sustainable Forest Practices in Clayoquot Sound released its final report entitled *Sustainable Ecosystem Management in Clayoquot Sound: Planning and Practices*. To the delight of some and the shock of others, the findings of the panel, if fully implemented, would turn B.C. forest practices on their head. In short, the report, in terms of its values and practices, is not only a scathing critique of industrial forestry, but it is also a major endorsement of ecologically-based forms of forestry. It emphasizes that we must first consider what must be left in the forest to maintain fully functioning forest ecosystems, rather than asking how much we can take out for maximum profit. The Scientific Panel starts with a whole systems view of forest communities:

> The world is interconnected at all levels; attempts to understand it
> entail analyzing its components and considering the whole
> system.... In developing guiding principles, the Panel has tried to
> maintain a wholistic view of forest ecosystems, to recognize
> connections across the landscape, and to draw on both scientific
> knowledge and the *Nuu-chah-nulth* lived experience. Current
> forest management standards will be assessed, and new standards
> developed, in this context. (Report 4, p. 25)

Rejecting the traditional emphasis on purely economic and utilitarian values from the forest, the Panel has advocated the need to protect all forest values and all forestry components—regardless of the value humans may place on them. For example:

> Human activities must respect the land, the sea, and all the life
> and life systems they support. Living organisms have a place in

nature that must be sustained to maintain the health of the system in which they exist. The necessity to maintain natural ecological systems—including the land and sea themselves—supersedes the value that society may place on any individual component of those systems. (Ibid., p. 25)

The Panel has also recognized that the long-term viability of a culture and its economy is utterly dependent on the long-term viability of the ecosystems in which they reside. In other words, the economy must meet the imperatives of the biophysical system, not the other way around:

> Long-term ecological and economic sustainability are essential to long-term harmony. The Panel views harmony as a stable and healthy relationship between people and the ecosystems that support them. Maintaining harmony is the responsibility of each generation to those who follow. Standards guiding land use and resource management should ensure ecological, cultural, and long-term economic sustainability. Current rates of population growth and resource extraction may not be sustainable or permit the desired harmony. (Ibid., p. 25)

The Panel recommended that an ecosystem approach to planning be adopted, one in which "the primary planning objective is to sustain the productivity and natural diversity of the Clayoquot Sound region. The flow of forest products must be determined in a manner consistent with objectives for ecosystem sustainability." (Report 5, p. 153)

The Report rejects traditional clearcut logging in favor of a *variable-retention* silvicultural system that attempts to mimic the characteristics of natural forests. It states:

> The variable-retention system provides for the permanent retention after harvest of various forest structures or habitat elements such as large decadent trees or groups of trees, snags, logs, and downed wood from the original stand that provide habitat for forest biota. (Report 5, p. 83)

In short, the variable-retention technique would:

i. maintain watershed integrity; maintain the stability and productivity of forest soils; maintain waterflows and critical elements of water quality within the range of natural variability and within natural waterways;

ii. maintain biological diversity; create managed forests that retain near-natural levels of biological diversity, structural diversity, and ecological function; maintain viable populations of all indigenous species; sustain the species, populations, and the processes associated with the late-successional forest stands and structures;

iii.   maintain cultural values; protect areas and sites significant to First Nations people;

iv.   maintain scenic, recreational, and tourism values; and

v.   be sustainable—provide for a sustainable flow of products from the managed forests of Clayoquot Sound. (Report 5, p. 151)

The Panel also emphasizes the need to take the cultural and spiritual needs of the native people of Clayoquot Sound into account. It notes that "indigenous people live within the landscape from which they and the rest of society extract resources. Because of their longer, often closer, connections to nature, the cultural and spiritual relationships of First Nations peoples to their environment are different from those of other cultures. Such cultural and spiritual needs must be accommodated in standards governing land use and resource management." (Report 4, p. 25) The panel also specifically recognizes the ecological knowledge of First Nations in Report #3.

Westcoast Vancouver Island old growth rainforest
Duncan Taylor

The systemic approach to the forests of Clayoquot Sound taken by the Clayoquot Sound Scientific Panel emphasizes the close interdependencies that exist among community, cultural, economic, and biophysical sustainability. All too often forest-based communities feel out of control, the decisions for the land being made elsewhere, driven purely by economies of scale. Increasingly, representatives of forest communities have argued for the need to have more control and say over what takes place in their watersheds. This has certainly been the case with regard to the native people of Clayoquot Sound, as well as with respect to the communities of Tofino and Ucluelet. Indeed, there are compelling arguments to be made for increased levels of local control so long as regional and national standards of forest management are maintained.

Current arguments include the following:

i.   Community dependence on exports of a single resource leave the local economy vulnerable to external market variations. Long-term stability requires diversification and investment in the local economy. Such development is best accomplished through local initiatives and planning.

ii.   Outside control of the local resource base often results in surplus revenues being redirected elsewhere. Companies tend to be reluctant to purchase from local suppliers, invest in local manufacturing, or locate head offices and research facilities in the community. Alternatively, it is argued that a community-based forestry would more readily be able to keep revenues within the region.

iii. Small-scale forms of ecoforestry can best protect the wide range of economic and environmental values. For example, community-based enterprises are more apt to be sensitive to the protection of water supplies and wildlife habitat, while providing opportunities for tourist and recreational revenue. It is argued that small-scale forestry may be less wasteful and better able to produce a wider variety of specialized wood products through intensive management. Small-scale is *site-specific*, using a variety of harvesting procedures, and is better suited to the practice of a more environmentally sustainable *wholistic* and ecoforestry-based form of management and technology practices.

iv. Locally controlled resources are responsive to the changing needs, values, and lifestyles of the local population. Control over one's resources gives a greater sense of control over one's life.

North Americans are now at a juncture in their history when they are finally beginning to realize that they are living far beyond their economic and environmental means. We have become wealthy because we have been recklessly converting natural wealth into financial capital, but at a cost which is unsustainable. Like the road into Clayoquot Sound that bifurcates, we have now reached a similar fork in terms of how we live and interact with the larger biophysical world upon which we are dependent. The Clayoquot Sound Scientific Panel's Report points in the direction of an emerging ecological paradigm (or as some would say, "worldview"). It argues for a systemic approach to the management of forest ecosystems and for the recognition that sustainable forestry must take into account the full range of values within a given ecosystem as well as respect the cultural values of those who reside within this ecosystem. The B.C. government has promised to abide by the Panel's recommendations. If it does, it will be the beginning of a radical shift in the way that forestry is conducted in Canada's most economically important forest province. The proverbial horse will have been let out of the barn and forest policies elsewhere in the province will eventually have to come in line with practices that the Panel claims are "not only the best in the province, but the best in the world." (Report 4, p. 8) The gauntlet has been thrown down. Do we have the foresight and the political will to make the transition to ecoforestry—i.e. to ecologically responsible forest use?

> **Like the road into Clayoquot Sound that bifurcates, we have now reached a similar fork in terms of how we live and interact with the larger biophysical world upon which we are dependent.**

In January 1997 the giant forest company MacMillan Bloedel announced that it was going to shut down its operations in Clayoquot Sound for the next year and a half. Workers for the company feared that this was the beginning of a permanent pull-out. A major reason given for the halt in its operations was the need to abide by the strict rulings of the Scientific Panel Report. This, in spite of the fact that the company had received some $9 million from a provincial government fund (Forest Renewal B.C.) to help implement the Panel's recommendations. Critics of the forest industry were quick to note that these recent events merely underscored the argument that conventional forms of large-scale industrial forestry are neither environmentally feasible nor economically profitable under strictly enforced ecological constraints.

PART ONE

Ecoforestry Principles and Practices

Mixed ages, mixed species in natural forest, Bo Martin

1

Critical Elements of Forest Sustainability

Orville Camp

THE PRIMARY GOAL OF ECOCENTRIC FORESTRY (ecoforestry) is to maintain and restore full functioning, natural forest ecosystems in perpetuity, while harvesting forest goods on a sustainable basis. This goal must be grounded in clear ecological criteria that can be monitored so that human activities in forest ecosystems can be assessed and modified as needed. The achievement of this goal is a foundation for sustainable economic and social conditions.

The term "Critical Elements for Sustainability" identifies key components of the ecological processes at work in self-sustaining forest ecosystems. Critical elements for sustainability provide criteria to evaluate whether human activities in forest ecosystems are compatible with long-term sustainability. These criteria will be used for:

A. Evaluating the effects of removing products from a forest ecosystem;
B. Evaluating the effects of human activities such as road building, recreation, etc.;
C. Evaluating "Forest Management Plans" and their "Desired Future Conditions;"
D. Certifying ecoforesters;
E. Certifying forest ecosystems;
F. Certifying goods and products.

PHILOSOPHICAL FOUNDATIONS

There are two contrasting philosophies that underlie how Western humans view forest ecosystems:

1. The mainstream view is an *anthropocentric* philosophy which assumes that humans should manage forests for human benefit alone. This philosophy is based on the belief that humans have a right to dominion and control over nature and its forests. This view underlies conventional forestry, which has

converted natural forests into tree plantations by means of clearcutting and "reforestation." Under this philosophy, foresters write "Forest Management Plans" attempting to describe "current conditions" and the "desired future conditions." The desired future conditions are based on what is best for the industrial economy, not for the forests. This usually results in management of certain favored species of trees to produce timber for sawlogs. This anthropocentric management has historically led to the destruction of fully functioning natural forests and to the extinction of many of their associated species.

Writing the Forest Management Plan and Desired Future Conditions for this type of forestry is a complex and difficult exercise. Foresters are unable to adequately describe existing conditions, and while the imagined future conditions might resemble forests, they are tree plantations. Trees are seen as crops like corn. The forester becomes a tree farmer, and tree plantations simplify the ecosystem and become unsustainable after a few rotations.

The anthropocentric approach to forest management is often seen as the same as legal title to a house. Legal ownership to many forest land managers implies the right to do whatever one wants to "their" forest, including total liquidation. There may be little or no consideration given toward maintaining forest integrity on either the owners' or on adjoining lands. There is even less consideration given to the impact on more distant neighbors, let alone the cumulative adverse impacts on the larger ecosystem and the world.

> **Legal ownership to many forest land managers implies the right to do whatever one wants.**

2. Natural Selection Ecoforestry, an *ecocentric* (full-values) approach, is based on such ecological principles as 'nature knows best how to create and maintain sustainable forests'. Forests are ecosystems where all living things are interconnected and dependent on one another. They are complex communities of living beings. Everything has value. There are no *weeds* or other *undesirable species* in natural forests, except possibly exotics imported by humans. Before removing each tree or any other product, all species and their functions are evaluated for sustainability. Obtaining products from the forest is done in such a way that all species continue to function fully so that nature, not humans, does the managing.

Writing a Forest Management Plan and Desired Future Conditions for natural selection ecoforestry is straightforward. The Forest Management Plan is nature's ecological and evolutionary processes. The selection of trees for removal is evaluated through a natural selection process. We allow nature to set the "desired future conditions." To paraphrase Masanobu Fukuoka, author of *One Straw Revolution*, we practice forestry "...in the image of nature".

Current legal ownership entails both rights and responsibilities, but still allows us to liquidate forests. However, from an ecocentric approach, forest ecosystems belong to all species who live there, including humans. Thus, we have no right to destroy them for our purposes. Ownership means having certain rights to the use of the forest. It does not grant us dominion over the whole forest ecosystem. The legal right to practise ecoforestry brings the responsibility to remove only those products that have been selected for removal through the process of natural selection, provided suitable habitat is retained for all species associated with that particular ecosystem. The three guiding principles of ecoforestry are:

- All forest ecosystem activities shall be based upon addressing forest needs first.
- Only trees selected for removal through the natural selection process are candidates to take from the forest to serve human needs.
- The removal of forest goods and products or other activities must retain the ecological or structural functions of all forest elements.

ECOLOGICAL STRUCTURES & FUNCTIONS

Forest structure

Every forest has various horizontal layers of plants. The five basic ones, from highest to lowest, are the canopy, the understory, the shrub layer, the herb layer and the forest floor. Each of these layers is critical to certain dependent species and each is an essential part of the overall ecosystem. Overall forest ecosystem health and productivity is dependent upon maintaining all layers of the forest.

Forest stand structure is connected to a larger landscape. Maintaining connectivity is vital to many species in the forest. Clearcutting brings forest patches back to beginning seral stages and increases fragmentation and forest edges. This destroys habitat for many species. In the United States we now have far too much forest in beginning seral stages of succession as a result of past industrial forestry activities.

Under ecoforestry practices the following are required:

- Product removal and other activities shall not substantially alter the structural integrity or connectivity of the forest.
- Product removal and other activities shall not cause any known ecological functions to be placed at risk on any given site as a result of those activities.

Climate, soil and water

Climate changes cause soil and water conditions to change. Climate, soil, and water determine what can live in an area. Each layer of the forest structure serves to modify physical influences such as light intensity, light quality, air quality, wind velocity, temperature, water quantity, relative humidity, and evaporation rate, as they filter down through the forest canopy, the understory, the shrub layer, the herb layer, and finally into the soil on the forest floor. At the top, the forest canopy receives the full force of weather. At the bottom, in the soil, light is absent and the temperature and moisture are relatively stable in contrast to higher forest layers. Any substantial change in these conditions, particularly climate, will have major impacts upon the forest ecosystem. Thus,

- Climate, soil and water conditions shall not be altered by human activities to the extent that existing naturally associated species will be unable to thrive.

Canopy dominants

Canopy dominants have major influence on the climate, soil and water conditions below. They strongly influence what plant species will make up the forest structure. The plant species and ages in turn determine the opportunities for animal species. Further, most of the species below the canopy will depend upon the canopy above for their survival. Canopy dominants are thus critically important for sustaining the forest ecosystem health and productivity.

The tallest trees in the canopy of a natural forest add an important structural element to the forest. These canopy dominants have shown their adaptive edge by surviving environmental extremes over a long period of time. They have helped to determine what other species can live in the structures below them. It is crucial, then, that:

- Canopy dominants must be maintained.

Diversity

Animals and plants have evolved together and are dependent on each other. A fully functioning ecosystem will retain the diversity, complexity and richness in each site and across the landscape to allow for this coevolution to proceed.

- Suitable diversity shall be left on each microsite to retain all evolutionary processes and ecological functions.

Ecotones

Ecotones are transition areas where different kinds of native ecosystems join. For example, in nature a tree-dominated forest ecosystem may join a meadow where grass dominates the ecosystem. The trees will moderate the climate in the adjoining meadow and changing soil conditions will make the meadow more suitable for growing trees. Ecotones are the areas where there can be a critical balance between two ecosystems and sometimes only minor changes can lead to one ecosystem replacing the other.

Because ecotones are areas between ecosystems, many more plant species live there than in adjoining ecosystems, where certain species are clearly predominant. More plant species usually mean more animal species, many of which depend upon both ecosystems for their survival. For example, species that forage in openings need cover for hiding in a nearby forest. Ecotones also serve as buffers for species invading one ecosystem from another. Ecotones are among the most sensitive areas.

- Ecotones shall be retained with suitable habitat for all naturally associated species.

Creating artificial forest edges can seriously impact the structural integrity of a forest. It can cause major changes in microclimate and can destroy habitats.

- Artificial edges that destroy the structural integrity of interior forest habitats shall not be created.

The Web of Life

All species are interconnected and dependent upon one another through food chains, pollination, or other symbiotic, parasitic or predacious relationships. Green plants convert the sun's energy into diverse food forms and are called primary producers because they are the basis of the food chains that support all other plant and animal life. Those plants and animals that feed upon primary producers are known as primary consumers. Those that feed upon primary consumers are known as secondary consumers. When any above-ground living being dies it eventually falls to the forest floor. There decomposers feed on and convert them into nutrients for new plant and animal growth. The food cycle is a continuously repeating process.

The more intricate the web of life, the more stable a forest is likely to be. If too many relationships are disrupted (and who knows what is too many) a forest can cease to function fully and it can even die. We see this in clearcuts. Maintaining the whole web of life is critical for forest sustainability.

- The integrity of all species' relationships shall be retained throughout stands.

Nature's Creative Resilience and Flexibility

The evolutionary process in forests is a creative system with resilience and flexibility. Those trees that survive environmental extremes leave more offspring. As age overtakes the most successful individuals, a new species or a more successful variation of the same species may become a canopy dominant. The forest canopy often creates a different environment from the one in which the canopy species grew up. If the environment is quite different, a new species might invade or evolve to replace the old species as the canopy dominant. If the canopy dominant species changes, for example from deciduous to coniferous, a new forest structure may emerge and the whole forest structure will change. If a fire burns up a forest, the canopy dominants and forest structure could revert to an earlier pattern. Nature will rebuild diversity and complexity by natural selection. Natural selection over time produces the optimum species diversity and structural complexity at each site.

- The structure created by natural selection and represented at one extreme by the canopy dominants shall be allowed to evolve naturally.

Genetic Base and Reproduction

Over time those tree species with traits that enable them to survive environmental extremes are the ones most likely to reproduce. These traits develop for a specific site through natural selection. Clearcutting removes these valuable and irreplaceable traits and the productivity of the site will drop substantially. To protect

> The more intricate the web of life, the more stable a forest is likely to be.

and preserve these site-specific genetic traits, only careful selective logging should be practised.

- The accumulative genetic base shall be maintained for all species that have evolved on each site. The genetic base shall be determined by natural selection.

Succession

Ecosystems go through changes in species composition over time. The first plant species to invade a site typically alters the environmental conditions so they are more suitable for other species. This is called succession. The most complex ecosystems (tropical and temperate rainforests) have typically evolved through many stages of succession. This evolution has taken a very long time. When a complex forest, or even only part of one, is removed as with clearcuts, the integrity of the ecosystem is adversely affected. Many species associated with later seral stages are now in danger of extinction, and many others are already extinct as a result of industrial forest management practices. We need to preserve whole forest ecosystems in later seral stages and allow much of the previously destroyed forests to regain their integrity and complexity through natural regeneration.

- No product removal or other forest activities shall be done that will result in the ecosystem as a whole reverting back to beginning seral stages.
- The forest ecosystem shall be kept fully functioning. No harvesting or other activity shall be done that causes species population problems.

Ecological Net Worth

Ecological net worth refers to the total value of all species' functions in a fully healthy forest. The forest as a whole, then, produces a net ecological worth for the larger regional and global ecosystem. Evaluating ecological net worth is one way to gauge whether our activities in a forest are sustainable. Effects on ecological net worth can be evaluated by estimating what it would cost us to replace the functions of species and habitats lost as a result of human activities.

- Ecological net worth shall be maintained in perpetuity.

We have discussed the critical elements of sustainability of natural forest ecosystems. There are many ways that industrial forestry practices ignore these elements and undermine sustainability. Natural selection systems (ecoforestry) based on ecological and evolutionary principles harmonize with these elements necessary for natural forest sustainability. They are in tune with the natural selection and succession patterns. The main elements of sustainability are forest structures, climate (including microclimate), soil, water and air quality, preservation of canopy dominants, maintenance of diversity, protection of ecotones, preservation of genetic base and reproductive habitat, and an overall respect for the great interconnected web of life that natural forest ecosystem communities represent. Our practices must be tailored to the requirements of specific forest ecosystems and forest stands within

Diversify forest use and spend a lot of time on the ground getting to know the forest you work and live in.

a landscape and watershed. Remember that human knowledge is very limited, and err on the side of caution. Diversify forest use and spend a lot of time on the ground getting to know the forest you work and live in. Do an evaluation of ecological net worth, a total-cost accounting that includes the values and contributions the forest ecosystem makes to our whole condition. Finally, humans have lots of ideas, but the forests have the facts. We should let them be our teachers!

Acknowledgments

Thanks to Mike Barnes, Alan Drengson, Doug Patterson and Victoria Stevens for their helpful suggestions.

2

Forest Practices Related to
Forest Ecosystem Productivity

Alan E. Wittbecker

INDUSTRIAL FORESTRY AS A TOOL OF ECONOMICS

THE MYTHS OF THE MUTANT MODERN ECONOMICS have tremendous impacts on how forests are treated. The old analogy of the economy as a machine leads to dangerous assumptions about forests:

- Everything is a resource (and its corollary, everything has a price [and its corollary, everything that does not have a price is worthless]): every forest can be cut to provide wood for human needs. The essence of a resource is that its existence acquires meaning only as it is necessary for human needs and wants. Furthermore, if everything is a resource then everything can be used; the forest, not just the trees, can be used.

- Resources are unlimited: if forests are unlimited then we can keep cutting them (and even if they are not unlimited, by the tenets of modern economics, being a scarce resource makes them even more valuable, because the costs and unused equipment can be written off against other profits). Although many economists admit that forests may not be exactly unlimited, the assumption surfaces again in advertisements about the forest industry where the industry credits itself with planting millions of trees.

- The economy has to keep growing to survive: growth means that the use of the forests will have to keep increasing. If there are not enough old-growth or good timber trees, then all trees will be used for pulp and fibre (for paperboard and fibreboard). If there are not enough trees, then we will have to grow wood in vats. Or we will have to substitute, for example, steel wall studs for wooden ones.

- Any resource can be extended through a substitute: therefore forests are not unique or intrinsically valuable, because they can be replaced with tree plantations, genetically engineered industrial wood cell production or steel or plastic. In economic equations, human-made capital is considered a perfect substitute for natural capital (although interestingly, the equation is never reversed).

- Mass production is most efficient: clearcutting a forest (the incarnation of mass production in forestry) is the most efficient way to extract good wood; high-value native trees are cut without undue expense, while the site is automatically prepared to host a plantation containing only desirable market species, such as Douglas fir. Furthermore, as Roy Keene has pointed out, the planning, fieldwork, and accounting are also simplified. Waste, or the wood not used, is minimized by the process, of course; all noncommercial species are considered a waste of potential growing conditions.

- Obsolescence is necessary for successful growth: obsolete products made from wood are burned, buried in landfills, or stored in concrete hallways, removing them from the cycle of renewal of forests.

- Quality does not matter very much: good materials, good wood from old-growth trees, are not necessary to make high-quality goods. The quality resides in the perception of the consumer, educated by helpful advertising.

- The future is less valuable than the present: forest that may have some value now in a few useful species is worthless beyond a certain time (two years, maybe 20). Modern economics has enshrined this one form of selfish behavior and pretends that it is rational and optimal. Unfortunately, as Constanza and Daly (1991) have pointed out, short-term self-interest is usually inconsistent with the long-term best interests of the individual or society. Economic discounting is not in the best interests of keeping forests complete and healthy.

- Economists can control the economy: by simplifying the forest and raising one species on a tree plantation, economists think that fertilizers and pesticides can control all foreseeable circumstances—changes in and shifts of the system state can be controlled.

These dangerous assumptions are translated into unhealthy and unsustainable practices that also generate problems, from which the forest economy is suffering. Overgrowth is one problem—too many trees are cut because of demands for wood. The complexity of the system and the number of costs increase; this is only a surprise when total-cost accounting is not used. Economic and social instability result from mechanization and the quest for a narrow mechanical efficiency; powerless families are relocated or dislocated as jobs are eliminated by ruthlessly efficient and sophisticated hardware. Forests experience environmental and ecological instability as they are cut; atmospheric and hydrological cycles are simplified and disrupted. Finally, misdirected effort on ill-conceived products, for example, upscale firewood or throw-away chopsticks, wastes precious wood. The present economy cannot adapt to the timescale of the forests or escape its assumptions, so it turns to planning to solve the problems.

PLANNING

Planning in general means deciding on goals to be achieved in specific situations. For central planning (by a state or province or federal government), the goals are usually small and not comprehensive, such as a cutting level or a single

Giant structures in old forests
Bob Herger

species' preservation, and usually end up being a compromise in cost-benefit analysis. For forestry, planning is the "ideal timber goal." This goal is usually stated in terms of consumption, production, growth, or stock, each of which tries to satisfy the needs of the goal that precedes it; for example, attainment of the stocking goal permits attainment of the growth goal.

Most plans address *problems*, such as building roads in forests. Everything else, from employment to pests, is also considered as a problem, and not a direct cultural effect of the implementation of some technology. Most plans seem to be adequate at compiling data about an area, from topographic to climatic. Most plans are also development plans that are comprehensive in the sense of seeking to meet all needs of the public, agriculture, and industry. But they also fall prey to all the assumptions of the industrial culture. They tend to be multipurpose with the aim of providing maximum net benefits through the management of forests and wildlife. Both uses of "multipurpose" and "maximum benefits" are based on misunderstandings, however. Multipurpose in practice means human use, perhaps even just one use: logging; and maximum benefits have proven to be dangerous to long-term sustainability. Modern resource management strives for maximum sustainable yield, based on partial knowledge of species and great ignorance of ecosystems.

Formal development is more concerned with an assembly-line model: simple, isolated, efficient, and easy to maintain. Planning tends to neglect or dismiss the distribution of negative, uncertain, or non-monetary effects. Furthermore, we seem to have no mechanism for developing long-range plans. Certainly, there seems to be no way to deal with long-term, slow catastrophes, such as deforestation. Behind our glass wall of television (life in *vitro*), we become remote from, and indifferent to, the natural systems that support us. We acquire unrealistic images of the world and harmful values and then make bad decisions based upon them. We have not developed qualitative indicators of ecological health or quantitative measures of social health, much less an ecocentric view that would value preserves of nature for themselves. Still, we look to science and agricultural technology to save us.

SCIENCE AND THE AGRICULTURAL MODEL

Since the first agriculture 10,000 years ago, forests have been cut and burned to create fields for food crops. Technological innovation, combined with accelerating population growth, has led to clearing of many forests for agriculture.

In the 1700s, forests came to be studied as ecosystems and then resources. German forestry in the 1800s was relatively wholistic and comprehensive as a science (Toumey 1947). Enderlin extended silviculture from observation to a more scientific foundation. Heyer analysed a site factor in a forest and systematically developed a theory of tolerance (capacity to endure shade). Others, including Mayr, Duesberg, and Dittmar, applied biology, chemistry, and physics to silvicultural theory. Ebermayer recommended establishing forest experiment stations in 1861.

As forests came under management, however, vast plantations replaced the dark woods famous in myth and story, until most of the German forest was managed plantations by the 1930s. Plantations were orderly and neat, with no windfall or "trash" allowed on the ground.

American forestry was founded on this model and has followed it. Forest reserves were set aside starting in 1891 to protect water supplies and to ensure adequate timber. Gifford Pinchot headed the U.S. Forest Service, which was based on the conservation ideas of wise use and sustained yield. Pinchot established his brand of forestry as sustainable, as did Leopold, as do the new foresters. In fact, Pinchot's sustainability was based on the German management concept of sustained yield from the 18th century.

Industrial forestry was quick to take advantage of the scientific understanding of forests and trees, starting in the mid-1800s. By the 1980s, scientific research had resulted in technological applications for growing, genetically "improving," harvesting, and processing woody material on an unprecedented, vast, and unconsidered scale. Industrial companies established tree breeding and fertilization programs, whose goal was usually fast growth. Pine plantations in the southern United States were rated as a success and served as a model for plantations elsewhere; Australia, New Zealand, Chile, and South Africa replaced many of their native forests with exotic pine plantations, using species like Monterey pine. Other countries, such as Brazil, India, Spain, and Madagascar, established plantations with exotic species, such as eucalyptus.

Much research conducted by industry labs, university faculties, or agencies, such as the Western Forests Products Laboratory or the U.S. Forest Products Laboratory, has concentrated on the efficient processing of more kinds and smaller sizes of timber. The technology has been used to improve processing of wood products, using computer-directed sawing patterns, beam lamination, better adhesives, drying schedules, and preservatives, so that less valuable species and smaller size trees can be used.

Forest managers have adapted newer technologies, including biotechnology, computer modelling, remote sensing, and geographical information systems for monitoring, managing, and cutting. Advances in communication technology permit the rapid exchange of data, information, and opinions. Of course, if the data do not fit the paradigm or belief system, then they are ignored.

Sometimes the data are interpreted for anticipated gains. Because young timber grows faster than old timber, the U.S. Forest Service sometimes approves the removal of two acres of old timber for each acre of young timber in a plantation, i.e. ACE, the allowable cut effect. Although that is true of the growth rate, it is not true of total volume. Furthermore, the younger trees in plantations are planned to be part of a short rotation. The 1,000-year-old trees that were cut were not part of a 1,000-year rotation, but part of the inherited capital of the land. For forestry to be meaningfully sustainable, then the rotation length should match the forest being cut.

> **For forestry to be meaningfully sustainable, then the rotation length should match the forest being cut.**

With the plantation system, forestry came to be treated as a special form of agriculture. Agricultural systems are distinctive types of human-modified ecosystems laid out to increase production per unit (hectare or acre), which is done by duplicating the highly productive pioneer stages of succession. In order to be successful, however, and increase food output per unit, agriculture has become industrial: with a large capital outlay for equipment, new technology, from combines to biotechnology, fertilizers, and pesticides, and market supports to hide a few of the real costs, industrial agriculture is very energy-intensive.

Like agriculture, forestry uses soil to produce a crop for the purpose of increasing wealth (or perhaps just revenue). Like agriculture, forestry is renewable (unlike mineral or oil extraction). Like agriculture, forestry is based on knowledge of many fields, including botany, soil science (pedology), and meteorology. Like agriculture, forestry deals with vast areas. Unlike agriculture, forestry deals with wild plants on wild soils. Furthermore, trees are very long-lived, unlike crops of annuals. Unlike agriculture, the crops are not as resilient to being cropped annually. Unlike agriculture, the trees have greater requirements of the forest than grasses do of the grasslands. Trees are directly responsible for soil fertility and tilling.

Beginning in the 1940s, it became evident that the plantation system, with single species even-aged trees, was susceptible to catastrophic change—wind, pollution, insects—in a way that natural forests were not. Some forests began to die as forests. The forestry machine was in trouble. A metaphor for industrial forestry might be a high-powered, gas-engined vehicle somewhat like a snowplow, but with only an accelerator pedal and rearview mirror in the comfortably appointed, fully automated, air-conditioned cabin—no brakes, no steering wheel, no windshield, no reverse, just one forward speed. No wonder it does so much damage. It has no real controls.

TRAGEDY AND EXCESS

The success of agriculture in natural grasslands led to its use as a model for agriculture everywhere and then for a model for all organic resources. Humanity has taken over the habitats and ecosystems of other animals and plants, simplified them, and converted them to the production of protein and other resources. As ecosystems are degraded, deforestation, desertification, and drawdowns are occurring at the scale of an ice age or comet impact, but the result is more meaningful to us than these historical events, since we are dependent on the ecosystems we are changing. We take our rapid population growth as a requirement and depend on nonrenewable resources to support our numbers and lifestyles, ignoring long-term deficits, carrying capacities, and limits. Some of these trends (perhaps we should call them gigatrends because of their age and size) have been noticeable for thousands of years, but nothing has been done to halt them. History records that some civilizations tried to manage their resources and failed. These gigatrends might end in tragedy for humanity.

For the Greeks, the operation of tragedy resulted from success taken to great lengths; that is, where successful behavior in one context is applied to all contexts, with the result that the opposite action occurs from the one desired. Humans in moderate numbers were able to take what was needed from natural ecosystems without interfering with natural processes. Our dominance, once so successful because of our big brains and tool-using hands, has now become self-destructive. With rapid and intense development, ecosystems collapse or stabilize at a simpler state.

Most of the noncultivated land surface of the Earth is being managed; wolves, caribou, salmon, redwoods and irises are managed or else destroyed. Even a modern, balanced exploitation may destroy forests and fisheries. Currently, many resource managers espouse the ideas of equilibrium maintenance and maximum sustainable yield. These ideas are poor guides to sustainable management. By trying to maintain habitats in equilibrium, we often set them up for catastrophic decline, for instance, in fire-climax pine forests, or destroy resident species, e.g., the spotted owl. One possible solution is to relate human use to the natural productivity of ecosystems.

ECOLOGICAL PRODUCTIVITY OF FOREST ECOSYSTEMS

A forest is an energy/matter system. Needham (1941) suggested that living systems are energetic systems competing for materials. From another perspective, they are energy-organizing material systems. Each perspective emphasizes different aspects of the system: a matter-organizing energy system emphasizes novelty; an energy-organizing matter system emphasizes conformation. Transmission of information is more closely linked to organization of matter than energy. Furthermore, suitable energy (appropriately low and usable) is what the systems need, not raw, unconverted sunlight. Neither energy nor matter is ontologically superior to the other; both are dimensions of a STEM (Space/Time/Energy/Mass) field (Wittbecker 1976).

The trees in a forest convert sunlight to sugar. The efficiency of conversion hovers about 1 percent, perhaps barely exceeding it on good sites. Over half of the sugar is converted to energy for respiration to keep the tree alive; over half of what remains in leaves and roots is consumed by insects, fungi, and animals dependent on it (and almost a third of what remains is below ground). Most of the massive productivity of forests is not in stem wood. The productivity depends on many other factors besides the interception of sunlight: climate, moisture, nutrients, predation, cycling, fire and others.

The forest is also an ecosystem. Ecosystems result from the interaction of all living and nonliving factors of the environment (Tansley 1935). These systems are profoundly affected by both random and purposive physical and biological factors. As a result, habitats change and organisms adapt. By modifying their habitats in the process of living, organisms change the characteristics of the system and force further adaptation. More important, organisms are limited in varying degrees by the productivity of the system. Human populations inhabit specific ecosystems and adapt to (and are limited by) the productivity of ecosystems (to what extent remains to be seen).

The structure of a forest is based on material and energetic exchanges. The matter present is biomass (B); the material output is primary productivity (P). Their relation (P/B) is the flow of energy per unit biomass. The total amount of biomass or energy produced by populations of plants (autotrophs) and animals (heterotrophs) through growth and reproduction is the productivity of the system. Primary productivity is the rate at which organic material is created by photosynthesis. Bacterial photosynthesis and chemosynthesis contribute to gross productivity, but much less significantly. Gross primary production (GPP) is the rate of energy storage by photosynthesis (equal to the photosynthetic efficiency) in plants. The maintenance and reproduction of plants is paid for by the energy expenditure of respiration (R). The amount of energy stored as organic matter after respiration is identified as net primary production (NPP), which equals plant growth efficiency. The calculation of NPP is shown by:

$$NPP = GPP\text{-}R$$

To measure net primary productivity, many items must be considered. For example, from a field planted in cereal, samples should be taken regularly to determine losses of old leaves, insects, and nonedible material (weeds). At harvest, plants are dried and weighed. The net productivity equals the sum of stems, leaves, flowers, fruits, roots, and insect loss, minus the initial seed sown. For a forest the measurement is very difficult. The total amount of organic matter, or standing crop, is the biomass.

NPP accumulates through the history of a system as plant biomass expressed as kilocalories per square metre (Kcal/m^2). The kilocalorie is used as a unit of energy flow and production; it is a useful common denominator for these calculations. The problem of confusing production (amounts) with productivity (rates) is avoided here by considering all values per unit area (m^2) over the entire year (m^2/yr). The biomass minus the decomposition in a system is the standing crop biomass of that system.

The energy stored in heterotrophs (consumers such as saprobes [animals that live in organic matter]) is referred to as secondary production (SP) or assimilation. Secondary productivity is defined as the formation of new protoplasm by heterotroph populations. However, the percentage of net primary productivity eaten by animals is not equal to secondary productivity, because only a small fraction becomes organic matter in the animal. Some food ingested is unused; in caterpillars, for instance, this may amount to over 80 percent. Of food that is digested and assimilated, that which is spent on respiration does not become organic matter. The remainder is considered secondary productivity, as growth of the individual or as part of reproduction. Although a mature (nongrowing), non-reproducing animal has zero secondary production, a population of animals usually has measurable secondary production since some individuals are usually growing or reproducing.

Mixed natural conifer forest
Bo Martin

Secondary productivity corresponds to net productivity in plants. Total assimilation in animals (almost impossible) corresponds to gross productivity in plants. Studies in secondary production are difficult; the species must be measured for population density, age distribution, food consumption and utilization, growth, and reproduction; bacterial, fungal and parasitic populations must also be considered.

Community Production

Biomass accumulation is the increase in community organic matter as the difference between the gross primary productivity and the total community respiration. This difference is also the net ecosystem production or the net community production. It is usually less than the net primary production. The storage of energy or organic matter not used by heterotrophs is net community production (NCP). The relationship between productivities (where Ra=autotroph respiration and Rh=heterotroph respiration) is of the order shown by:

$$GPP = NPP + Ra = Ra + Rh + NCP$$

In a balanced ecosystem, NPP equals respiration; in an accumulating system,

NPP usually exceeds respiration by 1-10 percent. Although stable ecosystems tend to produce a maximum GPP, species, biomass, and the production to respiration ratio (P/R) continue to change long after the maximum has been achieved. In fact, as the GPP approaches an asymptote, respiration increases. In a mature community, temperate or tropical rainforests for instance, NCP approaches zero, as adapted heterotrophs become more efficient at using production. In accumulating systems, such as grasslands or young forests, NCP can range from 20-30 percent. A balanced system is integrated and self-perpetuating, where production (the photosynthetic fixture of carbon) is balanced by respiration (the oxidation of carbon). As a system becomes balanced, the pressure of selection of organisms shifts; the capacity to live in crowded circumstances with limited resources is favored. Populations that depend on rapid individual turnover (r-selection) are not as successful as populations of large, long-lived individuals (K-selection). As an ecosystem ages, pressure is put on populations by other populations. Competition and predation become more complex. Pioneer species such as lodgepole pine are replaced by transitional species such as white fir, or by mature species such as cedar or hemlock. The changes are referred to as succession.

Maturity

Succession decreases the flow of energy per unit biomass, according to Ramon Margalef's (1968) concept of maturity. The energy required to maintain an ecosystem is inversely related to complexity. Any ecosystem not subjected to outside disturbance changes in an orderly and directional way: the complexity of structure increases and the energy flow per unit biomass decreases. The physical environment limits the type of change. Homeorhetic (stable flow) mechanisms protect the system from many disruptions. Thus, maturity is self-preserving.

The concept of maturity is important to the understanding of complexity and diversity. Margalef proposes maturity as a quantitative measure of the pattern in which the components of an ecosystem are arranged. The life-form communities and physical elements are related in a definite pattern, which is a real but untouchable property (structure). In general, this structure becomes more complex as time passes, as long as the environment is stable or predictable. The structure acquires a historical character. Maturation, as a function of historical processes, increases the levels of complexity of an ecosystem.

This concept of maturity, as an attribute of a community, is related to structural complexity and organization. Maturity increases with time in an undisturbed community. The species diversity, that is, the information content of a community, also increases with maturity, leading to a more complex spatial structure. Diversity incorporates species richness (how many different kinds are present) as well as a measure of abundance (how many of each, as individuals or biomass). Other aspects of diversity, such as life cycles, are less often considered. The energy in a mature system goes to the maintenance of order and less for the production of new materials.

In general, diversity is higher, and life cycles are more complex; symbiosis between species increases, and nutrients are conserved. More mature systems have a richer structure and a lower productivity per unit biomass; there are more steps in the trophic pyramid, higher efficiency in every relation, less energy loss, and less energy is needed to maintain the system. Complexity and diversity offer advantages for living forms. Complexity allows increases in size, which allows the colonization of harsh environments. Diversity allows more effective behavior through specialization; for example, a specialized organelle may digest less common molecules.

Margalef states that biomass and primary production increase during succession, but the ratio of productivity to total biomass drops. According to Pielou (1974), species diversity decreases and pattern diversity increases during succession. There is also an increase in the proportion of inert matter, and an increase in structures like animal paths and burrows. Odum (1971) has noted trends in ecological succession:

- the community production decreases;
- individual lives are longer and more complex;
- diversity is high and well-organized;
- there is a closed slow exchange rate, where detritus is important;
- symbiosis has developed, and conservation and stability are good; and
- there is a high biomass in a web like food chain.

The increase in diversity is related to a multiplication of niches; this process goes with longer food chains and stricter specialization. Animals on top of food chains and those with more specialized habits show a higher efficiency. This results in a gain in efficiency of energy use in advanced stages of succession. The more mature systems are found in regions of high temperature: tropical rainforests and coral reefs. Stability should be more important than temperature; there are stable and mature communities in the deep ocean, caves, and cold areas.

Natural succession may operate in a similar way to a hologram, in the sense that the subparts of the system can maintain a potentiality for all possible behaviors that could flow from any part of the system. Native Hawaiian biota appear to be rejuvenated by volcanic eruption; they are better equipped to reinvade areas than exotic species. Successions are stopped by fluctuations, by volcanoes or storms, called exploitation by Margalef (1968), adding that the effect of natural exploitation in general is rejuvenating. Whatever accelerates change and energy flow in ecosystems reduces potential maturity. In an exploited system, diversity drops and the ratio of primary production to biomass increases. Mature systems can regress to earlier forms when exploited. Ecosystems are constantly evolving under the influence of physicochemical processes poorly understood and so far more powerful than those that result from human activities. The reality is more complex than just systematic succession and maturity.

> **Ecosystems are constantly evolving under the influence of physicochemical processes poorly understood and so far more powerful than those that result from human activities.**

ECOLOGY TO ECOFORESTRY

Disturbances in a forest are regular but unpredictable events. Many of them kill trees. Mortality is a normal part of the life cycle. Mortality in forests usually occurs from a combination of factors. By trying to prevent one kind of mortality, industrial forestry merely sets up another kind. Ecological forestry accepts a typical percentage of death as the normal condition, necessary for the renewal of the forest. The rate of death per year in an old forest is remarkably consistent at about 1-2 percent, even with windstorms, fires, disease outbreaks, and animal damage. In spite of Boise Cascade's recent advertisement about our public forests ("Let our public forests rot or burn again? What a waste!"), rotting and burning do not produce waste and are an integral part of the cycle of life and death in the forest.

As a forest ages, it thins itself naturally. The number of trees decreases as the stand ages; the remaining trees are typically bigger (and more desirable to timber companies). As the frequency of disturbance increases, the forest becomes adapted to the disturbance. Even pine plantations in the southeastern U.S. that are managed with controlled burns are less damaged by wildfires. However, after long periods without disturbance, a catastrophic disturbance is more likely; where wind and fire are absent, the probability of insect and disease outbreaks increases. Yet, even catastrophic disturbances like hurricanes rarely damage more than 5 percent of a forest. (Forests have not had time to adapt to human disturbance; furthermore, human disturbance can influence up to 100 percent of a forest.) More than being agents of mortality, insects, diseases, and animals are native components of complex food webs in ecosystems that contribute to the selection of certain kinds (including healthy) and ages of trees, which determines the composition of the forest, changing over time. Mammals and birds disseminate seeds. Insects pollinate some trees and overwhelm others (rarely more than one percent of a forest). Diseases remove stressed trees (also probably a low percentage in the order of one percent). Their effect on the long-term health of a forest can only be regarded as positive.

Beavers create wetlands
Bo Martin

The mass production of low-quality pioneer wood in a biological system causes the system to be unbalanced and vulnerable to attack by vectors usually kept in check by natural enemies or limited opportunities. This means that the vectors disease, infestation, etc., must be controlled by biocides or other extreme measures such as cutting. Furthermore, after clearcutting, the site has to be "prepared" for young seedlings selected for rapid growth in a simplified managed environment.

Human intervention into mature systems is usually detrimental. In early successional stages, there may be larger net community production totals, which can be harvested by humans without damage to the system. One reason gross productivity cannot be harvested by humans is that it would destroy the ecosystem; the wealth of the system would not be sustainable.

Forestry can never be sustainable under the assumptions of Newtonian science (where nature has a stable, predictable order), the industrial worldview and the old economics. Besides being based on more appropriate stories, ecoforestry assumes an ecological economics that is based on ecological science with new paradigms. While some scientists as late as the 1980s were trying to find the causes of forest death to preserve the plantation system, other scientists and managers were starting to plan for more natural forests (multiple species, uneven-aged, ground-cover, windfall, etc.).

Foresters are usually only concerned with a small part of the productivity of the forest, that is, the Current Annual Increment (CAI) of trees as a measure of the material added to the tree stems in a year. This change, called "growth," has to be determined by two different measurements, each of which is usually an estimate. The growth is a composite number arrived at by adding the Survivor Growth (trees still alive at the end of the year) to the Ingrowth (new trees reaching marketable size at an arbitrary DBH [diameter at breast height, 4.5 ft. or 1.37 m above ground]) and subtracting the mortality as well as any volume harvested. The amount of growth that can be taken is the "forest yield." Growth is calculated as a volume (cubic metres), because that is how it is estimated; productivity, on the other hand, is calculated as a weight (grams per square metre) or energy (kilocalories), depending on how it is measured.

The net growth, without reference to soundness or defectiveness, is calculated with a simple formula:

$$G = A\text{-}M\text{-}Y\text{+}I = V2\text{-}V1$$

where G is the net increase including ingrowth, A is accretion, V1 is the stand volume at the beginning of the year, V2 is volume at the end of the year, Y is the yield volume, I is ingrowth, and M is the mortality volume.

The "Allowable Annual Cut" (AAC) for a plantation is simply equal to the annual growth, whereas the AAC for old-growth forests is the total timber volume divided by the rotation period of a typical plantation (50-100 years). In 1984, the B.C. Ministry of Forests projected the long-term sustained yield would be about 57 million cubic metres of timber per year. In 1989, the AAC was 72 million cubic metres and 85.2 million cubic metres were cut on public and private forests. By contrast, the "Allowable Sale Quantity" (ASQ) on U.S. Forest Service forests was only 50.6 million cubic metres on an approximately equivalent land base. In 1988-89, 246,876 hectares of B.C. were clearcut, 91% of the cutting that year. Clearcutting is prescribed as the logging method on 90% of the allowable cut in B.C., according to forester Herb Hammond.

The productivity of the forest (NPP) should be the basis for the AAC. Neither the AAC nor the NPP are accurate measures due to the complexity of the subject, the forest, and due to the variance of the annual estimates of production. Because

Human intervention into mature systems is usually detrimental.

any operation with a human dimension has subjective and qualitative elements, we need a wholistic, conceptual plan.

A plan should consider the whole system. Ecological planning considers the health of the system, which is based on intimate knowledge of the system. Direct observation and traditional knowledge yield far more "information" about the societies of plants and animals than autopsies or mathematical models. A comprehensive plan would proceed in stages:

1. Identify the place within its natural boundaries. Most places exist in a uniquely identifiable ecosystem, with recognizable boundaries and a unique history and character.

2. Calculate the optimum amount of wilderness to preserve the natural cycles indefinitely. If the current wild area is less than the calculations, restore the difference and set it aside as a preserve.

3. In the remaining area, zone areas for appropriate use, including conservation and artificial areas, e.g., roads or buildings.

4. Identify the resources needed for human use, including timber and the productivity of the areas. This productivity can be used to calculate rational exploitation through cutting rates.

5. Conduct the harvest in such a way as to minimize damage and maximize value.

> Ecological planning considers the health of the system, which is based on intimate knowledge of the system.

We have to examine the natural and cultural histories of a place as part of our comprehensive plan, which is actually a deductive, synthetic, conceptual model based on data generated from research on: biological productivity, the rates of resource use, cultural valuation, minimum wilderness preservation, air and water quality, genetic minimums, nonrenewable resources, appropriate technological innovation, the importance of cultural frameworks, adventure, research, beauty, uniqueness, and other intangible experiences. A deductive approach is necessary because accurate measurements of productivities in most ecosystems are lacking and exactness in values is misleading. A synthetic approach is necessary to integrate quantitative and qualitative data. In combining qualitative and quantitative measures, it is simpler to set aside the first and then to calculate the second. The model must be conceptual because of the inherent fuzziness of the systems.

ECOFORESTRY BASED ON NET COMMUNITY PRODUCTIVITY

For one simple model, consider the forest as a corporation. After all, politicians and law enforcement officers are impotent to stop the destruction of forest ecosystems. The simplest way to give the forest a voice in its development is to incorporate it (C.J. Hagen 1991) following international law. A corporation is just a legal entity with its own rights, privileges, and liabilities. Although a corporation is independent from its founders, it is a human construct and the forest corporation would need human representation in the human system. (Permanent site foresters would probably act in the best interests of their home.) The forest corporation would not be really different from most corporations. Like other corporations, its primary purpose would be to maintain its own existence and maximize its wealth. It would optimize its values, which would include tree and fungus values, as well as human ones. This strategy would solve the problem of cutting too much of the forest; the forest itself would be untouchable capital. Most of the shares would be treasury shares; anything more than par value would go to capital surplus to be distributed as dividends. The dividends would be the net community productivity (NCP).

The NCP is profit. The NCP of forests of varying maturities varies itself from almost 0 percent to over 10 percent. The most NCP one would expect in an old-growth forest would be 0-2 percent. In a young ponderosa pine forest the percentage may range from 5-10 percent. In early seral stages after some catastrophic change, alder growth may produce 15 percent NCP. Some energy-subsidized pine plantations in Britain exceed 30 percent for a short time.

Humans can take part of the profit, the NCP. For example, in a Ponderosa pine forest of 2,200 hectares, with an NCP of 2,100 kilocalories per square metre per year ($2,200 \times 2,100 \times 10,000 = 4.62 \times 10^{10}$ Kcal per forest), the NCP is equal to 1×10^7 kilograms of dry weight, which is equal to 4.1 million cubic metres of wood (weight of ponderosa pine is 0.41 kilogram per cubic metre).

As long as humans limit their take to the NCP, the forest is truly sustainable. If the human managers take part of the NPP, they compete with other animals in using forest resources. Competition and use are healthy, remember, so that may not be too bad, but the forest may not be sustainable indefinitely unless the human managers replace some of the same functions as the creatures they are competing with. And if they take all of the NPP and most of the GPP, then they interfere with the operation of the ecosystem and that interference is destructive (Wittbecker 1995).

Obviously, we could cut any forest at any rate; we have been doing so. But the rate at which we cut determines what the forest will look like over time. For instance, if we were to cut all forests at a 1 percent rate, then they would all probably develop old-growth after several hundred years, depending on the species, even if they started out as young forests characterized by pioneer species. If we were to cut forests at a rate of 10 percent, the forests would never develop beyond an early stage of maturity. In order to exploit rationally, the cut should never exceed growth, the harvest should never exceed renewal, as it can in industrial forestry.

DIFFERENCES AND RECOMMENDATIONS OF ECOFORESTRY

It is obvious, and will become more so, that the differences between industrial forestry and ecoforestry are fundamental. Ecoforestry cannot be derived from industrial forestry. Industrial forestry is a failing system, a small-scope, once-through, temporary process for transforming forests into deserts by killing the forests (silvicide). Ecoforestry is a maturing stage that bases forestry in a community context and limits the use of the forest to that which the forest can afford to provide and remain healthy. If the metaphor for industrial forestry is a high-powered plow with a rearview mirror and an accelerator, then ecoforestry is a solar-powered device with windows, a brake, steering wheel, reverse gear, and handholds as well as precision cutters.

Somehow, through an ecoforestry approach, we need to become intimate enough with the forest to fit our needs into the production of the forest without interfering with it. Ecoforestry would optimize cutting instead of maximizing it, harvest a percentage of the natural interest instead of the ecological capital, on very long turn-around of 250-750 years instead of 10 to 100-year rotations, and allow self-ordered renewal of the forest instead of rapid planting of selected strains. Ecoforestry encourages diverse forests instead of single-species, even-aged plantations.

Ecoforestry can make several recommendations that would preserve diversity and complexity and avoid numerous extinctions:

- Protect the core of the forest, its soil and water.
- Promote cutting practices that respect the productivity and complexity of many aged forests, leaving large important structures such as snags and logs.
- Work with rotation periods geared to ecological times, such as 200 or 500 years.
- Allow natural processes such as fires, infestations, and regeneration to operate in the forest as much as possible.
- Reduce fragmentation through the design of forested areas, taking into account the genetic diversity of the trees, catastrophic conditions, minimum viable populations, corridors, and edge effects.
- Grant timber leases that are contingent on the maintenance of productivity and diversity of the land.
- Prohibit practices that are destructive such as pesticide applications or clearcutting.

SUMMARY

The forest is a weblike system that produces many things that are useful to human beings. Ecoforestry proposes ecologically responsible practices that permit a diversity of forest uses within its limits of productivity and stability. Limiting the practices to net community productivity or even a percentage of net primary productivity would help save forests, but it would require better planting and restoration of clearcut areas, ecological planning and management of national, corporate, and private forests, and improved use of wood products through reduction and recycling and a re-evaluation of human needs. Ecoforestry will progress with the replacement of the industrial paradigm, an ecological ethic, broadened ecological economics, and the participation of forest workers, students, and managers everywhere.

> Ecoforestry proposes ecologically responsible practices that permit a diversity of forest uses within its limits of productivity and stability.

3

The Battle for Sustainability

Jim Drescher

SUSTAINABILITY IS ON EVERYONE'S MINDS AND LIPS THESE DAYS. But our understanding of, and rhetoric about, it is mostly conceptual, rather than rooted in experience. This is because we continually give away to others the privilege of being foresters and farmers, rather than taking it as our rightful heritage. But we *are* foresters if we care for even one tree, and we *are* farmers if we watch even one carrot grow. As foresters and farmers, we have the very challenging opportunity to begin to implement and demonstrate sustainability on the ground and in the forest, but what are the most effective means? And even if it all goes well, is it possible to turn the tide of destruction that has fallen upon our land?

Our motivation comes from our experience of being in the natural forest, and on the eroding mountainsides, learning about the effects of ecological diversity and simplicity from the inside out. The desire to protect the natural world by working with the land comes naturally to intelligent, gentle, and courageous people (this potentially includes all human beings) who spend enough time alone in the forest. One of the very best instructions I ever received was from my father, when I was very young. He suggested I go to the forest as often as possible; it was OK, occasionally, to go with a friend, or even a dog, but usually I should go alone. This is the pithy instruction of Ecology 101. Sometimes we go to the forest out of fascination; sometimes it is out of the desperation that comes from witnessing the collapse of ecosystems and communities. In any case, as we experience the natural forest, we develop a passion to promote sustainability.

In some ways, having the motivation to protect the land is the easy part. More difficult is how to learn how to implement and how to communicate protection. Of course, the process is not linear; learning, communicating, and implementing grow together organically. As our understanding increases, so does our ability to manifest and teach; as we experience "doing it," our knowledge becomes wisdom and our words become genuine, and so on. There is no logical beginning or end point.

However, here we are talking, so we must begin with language, defining the words that represent our experience. So what is the common language of forest and farm people interested in sustainability?

1. *Ecosystem* is the big word meaning all lifeforms and their nonliving associates, including the whole web of interrelationships among them.

2. *Economy*, in the grandest sense of this smaller word, is the ecology of our made-up world, the human-made whirlpool within the constraints of the total ecosystem. "Constraints" means that if the economy demands more resources than the ecosystem can continue to provide, both ecosystem and economy collapse.

3. It follows that *ecological sustainability* and *economic sustainability* are mutually dependent, in other words the economy depends on a surrounding healthy ecosystem, and the ecosystem depends on a low-impact economy; therefore, sustainability means ecological sustainability *and* economic sustainability.

4. *Sustainability* means stability. There is no such thing as sustainable growth; there never has been in the history of this Earth. In fact, it is physically, as well as philosophically, impossible in a finite world.

5. *Diversity* means both ecological diversity (the variety of life-forms and natural structure) and economic diversity (the variety of human work and products for trade). It has been shown, theoretically and empirically, that diversity promotes stability, and simplicity undermines it. It should go without saying that sustainability is directly dependent on diversity.

The test of how sustainable our activities are is whether they decrease, maintain, or increase diversity. For example, we know that clearcutting is not sustainable because it radically reduces diversity, but it is more difficult to demonstrate the sustainability of the alternatives. It is easy to say small-scale, labor-intensive, diversified practices are better, but the counter argument is that this will reduce efficiency.

Here we have the fundamental problem with industrial forestry and industrial farming, a simple misfortune of definition of the word "efficiency." Industrial forestry, like industrial agriculture, defines efficiency as production per unit of "industrial" cost; in other words, the cost that is accounted for and paid for within the producing industry, without regard for the financial and social costs incurred in the greater human-made whirlpool called the economy, and without regard for the costs incurred outside this whirlpool altogether in the surrounding ecosystem. We could call this kind of efficiency "industrial efficiency." "Economic efficiency" is a slightly bigger definition and takes into account all costs in the human-made whirlpool, but not the costs in the surrounding ecosystem. Economic efficiency only leads to sustainability when there are no net ecosystem costs, i.e. no loss of natural ecological diversity. It can give the illusion of sustainability up to the point at which the surrounding ecosystem costs become too great, causing the collapse of both ecosystem and the dependent economic spin within.

Industrial efficiency always depends on minimizing labor costs. We are told that we should be proud that we are so efficient that only three percent of our population grows the food for us all, that we can harvest ten times as many trees with one-tenth as many workers. In this culture obsessed with efficiency, we are impressed. But to define efficiency in this way is to dangerously undermine any semblance of sustainability. For example, heavy mechanization, which increases industrial efficiency, results in denuded mountainsides, soil compaction and erosion, water pollution, destruction of salmon streams, and general degradation of wildlife habitat. It causes ballooning government deficits and the collapse of rural communities as unemployment soars. Is this the inevitable cost of efficiency? Must we give up our worship of the gods of efficiency if we are to sustain our economy and the natural world? Perhaps not.

The problem is not with our efficiency obsession. It is with our definition of efficiency. If we define the word in the biggest way, then our striving for greater efficiency becomes a positive force. In pre-industrial times, and non-industrial backwaters, efficiency was/is understood as production per unit of resources or production per unit of total cost, including social and ecosystem costs. In other words, maximizing value from each unit of land, or other resources, on a continuing basis, is efficient. Important questions are how we can best care for the land that supports all beings, how much can be made of one tree, and how much food can grow on one square metre of land. To maximize this "natural efficiency" of forestry and farming requires and allows more time, more care, and more people per unit of production. Results include reduced net cost to the ecosystem, smaller government, smaller government deficits, more meaningful employment, and improved possibilities for sustainability of rural communities.

Well, so much for definitions. How do we implement our understanding of diversity and natural efficiency? How can we practise sustainability in our woodlots and farms? The first necessity is to maximize diversity of species, age, structure, genetics, operating methods, and usable/salable products. Generally speaking, practices that increase economic diversity are complementary with increasing biodiversity, and vice versa. Natural foresters Merv Wilkinson and Orville Camp and ecosystem farmers Wendell Berry and Wes Jackson have offered us many useful practicalities about diversity.

If we can grow food *and* fibre, our economic situation will be more stable (less vulnerable to adverse weather, market fluctuations, etc.) than if we concentrate on only one or the other. In the same way, if we have 30 products, for our own use and

Horse logging
Chip Vinai

to sell, sustainability is more likely than if we have only 15. The stabilizing influence of diversity in the ecosystem works the same way. More diverse systems resist fire, windthrow, disease, nutrient deficiencies, and insect population explosions more successfully than simple systems.

The second necessity is to maximize "natural efficiency," or productivity per unit of resource. For foresters and farmers, this means minimizing ecosystem impacts, adding value on site, and exporting from the woodlot farm only those products with high "value to biomass" ratios.

Natural efficiency usually increases as mechanization, scale, and human "needs" decrease, and as labor intensity increases. If a high level of natural efficiency permits us to manage only 40 hectares rather than 160, this will mean more intensive care and an increase in self-sufficiency, which will promote sustainability, not only for our families, but for our communities altogether. The implications for quality of life are obvious.

Clearly, this model of diversification and natural efficiency is the opposite of the popular "free trade" notion, which depends on increasing specialization (simplification) and industrial efficiency, on decreasing labor and increasing mechanization, and on decreasing family, community or regional self-sufficiency. Social and ecosystem costs that are not direct costs of industrial production are ignored by the free trading transnational corporations. In fact, calling international deregulation "free trade" is a little like calling nuclear submarines "marine ecosystem protectors." Unfortunately, the spin seems to be working as the whole world falls into the trap of ecological and economic vulnerability. Who stands to benefit by this?

If we are to counter the trends toward simplification and industrial efficiency, we must broaden and intensify our knowledge and experience, starting with our own home economics. First, we should eat the food that grows on our land, as much as possible, and only sell or barter the surplus to acquire what we can't grow. Second, we should grow and process our own fuelwood, posts, poles, logs, and lumber, again selling or bartering only the surplus to provide for our other needs. If we can make more of the products we need, such as cheese and furniture, both product diversity and natural efficiency will increase. This will promote economic stability in our homes and lower our impact on the surrounding ecosystem.

Furthermore, the more valuable the products we produce, the less land we have to manage. For example, if we sell logs roadside, we may have to work a 160-hectare woodlot to make a living. Having a small bandsaw mill for making lumber may mean we only have to manage 80 hectares. By adding a planer/moulder, the required acreage may come down to 40 hectares. Similarly, smaller grain fields will be required if wheat is sold in the form of bread, and so on. Of course the biggest land-saving strategy is to reduce our own "needs."

One might ask, "Isn't it a lot of hard work to do all these different things on one woodlot farm?" Yes and no. To a certain extent labor is substituted for capital, which means more time working and less time wheeling and dealing, more cost for labor, less for machinery. But also the elements of this diversity can be mutually supporting if each part provides the needs for other parts and uses the natural production and labor that is surplus and available. There are limitless ways to set up your woodlot farm to do this. Grazers can mow orchards and control certain pesky insects in the process; chickens can till gardens and turn compost; ginseng can grow in the natural shade of birch groves, and so on. These "savings" and natural efficiencies have been explored extensively by Bill Mollison, who coined the term "permaculture," for a permanent agriculture that maximizes production while minimizing ecosystem costs.[1]

As much as possible, the biomass in the woodlot farm should be recycled in perpetuity. Only when absolutely necessary should anything be brought into the system from outside, such as food, oil, iron, plastic, etc. Products exported from the land should be as high in value as possible relative to their biomass. In other words, better to sell lumber than logs; better to sell dressed lumber than rough; better to sell furniture than lumber, etc. Every pile of brush, every kilogram of hay or sawdust that stays on the land where it grew is most valuable there. Brush is for wildlife and soil nutrition; hay is feed or mulch; sawdust is bedding for horses, which becomes compost which becomes soil which becomes carrots which become manure which becomes compost and so on. Carroll Wentzell, my predecessor on our farm, said it simply, "If it doesn't come from the farm, you don't need it." The implied corollary was, "If it is on the farm, it belongs here."

An important requisite of maximizing diversity and natural efficiency is finding the right balance between forested land and naked land. Clearings should be small patches surrounded by forest, and the total should be kept to a minimum, because soil is much harder to care for when there is no natural forest to build and protect it. Since the forests have produced the fertility of the soil in the first place, ways must be found to continue to bring the benefits of the forest into the fields. Forest-based compost continues to build "forest" soil on the cleared land. Brush walls are another important method of bringing the protection, nutrients and diversity of the forest into the fields and gardens. Suffice it to say here that the purposes of brush walls include wind protection, heat collection, shade, soil nutrition, water retention, and wildlife habitat. They are made from the tops and branches of trees harvested from the woodlot.

The details are limitless, but if we directly experience the principles of ecosystems and economies, and if we apply what we continually learn to our own homes and woodlot farms, then communication about diversity, efficiency, and sustainability will occur naturally. Our woodlot farms and our lives will become examples of alternatives to the increasingly evident "dead ends" of corporate concentration, industrial efficiency, and "free" trade. But will our small examples be enough to change this world?

> **As much as possible, the biomass in the woodlot farm should be recycled in perpetuity.**

The real enemy of sustainability is aggression toward nature and toward human communities. This enemy cannot be defeated by greater aggression. However, there is a natural, and ultimately human, collection of weapons that can be effective if kept sharp. Without these weapons, which are the natural heritage of every human being, we could not even contemplate subjugating the enemy.

To be human is to be naturally intelligent, gentle and courageous. Wielding the sword of intelligence allows us to cut through confusion to uncover things as they are. Gentleness is the power to care about what happens to all other beings. Courage is the ability to bring to action our intelligence and gentleness. It is the warrior quality, without which even intelligence and compassion cannot change the world's definitions of efficiency.

Weapons, enemy, and warriorship sound pretty aggressive and without intelligence and gentleness they are. Courage alone just compounds the confusion. Courage can be neurotic courage, which is the "courage" to promote one's own trip, or it can be genuine courage, which is the courage to be human. Neurotic courage cannot subjugate the enemy; it only feeds the enemy. It won't further sustainability, but only aggression; the giant transnationals and their client-states cannot be defeated on their own ground of aggression.

Our only advantage in this battle for the trees, soil, water, and for our communities is our humanity, which we share as students, loggers, farmers, executives, fishers, bureaucrats, politicians, and even corporate shareholders; that humanity manifests as intelligence, gentleness and courage. Our challenge is mutual: to encourage each other to wake up to things as they are.

This is a war. It is the ultimate war because it is the war against aggression. But if it is a war to be won, it must be won for all people and all beings. The battleground must be soaked with cheer and humor and kindness; for if it is not, then there will be losers. And if there are losers, the war is not over; aggression toward nature and toward human communities will continue.

Can the war be won? Logic and reason and recent history all point to a negative answer. It is hard to imagine what forces could divert society from its self-destructive path. Even so, some believe there is still magic in this world, magic that feeds on little lives living cheerfully, in accord with human principles and with nature. Each of us has the opportunity to invoke that magic by taking our human place as natural foresters and ecosystem farmers.

> **The real enemy of sustainability is aggression toward nature and toward human communities.**

4

Why is Ecologically Responsible
Forest Use Necessary?

Herb Hammond

THE IDEA OF "SUSTAINABLE DEVELOPMENT" has been based on the illusion that "we can have it all." Sustainable development is an oxymoron, suggesting that we can sustain ecosystem functioning while achieving steady economic growth. In parts of the world where poverty reduces people's capacity to use forests and other ecosystems in ways that protect ecosystem functioning, *some* economic growth for a *limited period* of time may be necessary to avoid intensifying pressures on ecosystems. However, the affluent, consumer-based economy of much of North America and western Europe is not sustainable, because it increases degradation of ecosystems to support the goal of perpetual economic growth.

If we are going to sustain anything, the first priority for human use of ecosystems, including forest ecosystems, must be to protect ecosystem functioning. This priority recognizes that economies are subsets of human cultures, which are subsets of ecosystems. Thus, if human use does not sustain ecosystem functioning, it cannot sustain human cultures or the economies that make up human cultures. Until recently, technologically equipped human beings have been able to temporarily avoid the consequences of ecosystem degradation by moving exploitation of ecosystems from one part of Earth to another part of Earth, and by inventing substitutes for previously "sustainable" resources. However, common sense tells us that this approach cannot be continued indefinitely.

Ecologically responsible forest use protects ecosystem functioning by protecting, maintaining, and restoring (where necessary) the *composition* and *structures* that are the basis of ecosystem functioning. The composition of a forest ecosystem refers to the parts that make up a particular forest area, such as the different species of plants and animals, the type of soil, and the slope gradient of the terrain. The structures of a forest are the arrangements of the parts. Forest structures include large old trees, large snags (standing dead trees), large fallen trees, the arrangement and depth of soil, organic layers, and the pattern of forest ecosystem types across large forest landscapes. Together, the composition and structures of forest ecosystems, from the largest landscape to the smallest soil microbe, are necessary to maintain fully functioning forests. Ecologically responsible forest use applies this principle through time, taking into account natural forest disturbance types, patterns, and frequencies.

In contrast, conventional timber management constantly alters and removes forest composition and structures at both landscape and stand levels. The biological legacies of thousands of years of natural forest development continue to support tree growth after logging in most "second-growth" forests. Therefore, many people think that conventional forestry works. The examples below demonstrate the importance of protecting forest composition and structures to maintain forest functioning.

FOREST LANDSCAPE EXAMPLES

In order to maintain forest landscape functioning, human activities must maintain connectivity. This is achieved by protecting the composition and structures of *riparian ecosystems*, which are the wet forests adjacent to and immediately upslope from creeks, rivers, wetlands, ponds, and lakes. As well, landscape-level plans need to provide for *cross-valley movement corridors*, which furnish travel routes for animals and plants to cross the ridges that separate one riparian ecosystem from another. Cross-valley corridors are not "natural"; before human beings began extensive modifications of forest landscapes, animals moved freely throughout, and occupied all of the landscape. However, with human modification of forests, cross-valley corridors have become a necessary component of forest landscape plans in order to provide protected travel corridors between human use zones.

Successional patterns, the stages of forest growth that follow natural disturbances, are also critical composition and structures of forest landscapes. The proportions of particular successional phases in the landscape (i.e. early successional forest, young forest, mature forest, and late successional or old-growth forest) need to be maintained over a variety of timescales, from years and decades to hundreds and thousands of years, in order to maintain forest ecosystem functioning. Each successional phase, with its characteristic composition and structures, provides vital functions to maintain forest ecosystems, from the smallest patch to the largest landscape, through short and long periods of time. Estimating the portions of a landscape that were occupied by various successional phases includes estimating the frequency, types, and extent of medium- and large-scale natural disturbances. Carrying out such an estimate is important.

For example, the only two nutrient input phases in a forest lifetime occur in the shrub-herb and late successional or old-growth phases. Because the late successional or old-growth phase lasts for the longest time, compared to other successional phases, old-growth tends to play a dominant role in maintaining forest functioning in most forest ecosystems. Old-growth forests provide the highest quality water of any forest

> **If we are going to sustain anything, the first priority for human use of ecosystems, including forest ecosystems, must be to protect ecosystem functioning.**

phase, because their multilayered forest canopies and their large amounts of decaying wood intercept and hold water. The old-growth phase is also the only forest phase that contains certain specialist organisms necessary for landscape- and stand-level forest functioning. For example, late successional forests contain the majority of carnivorous insects that eat the herbivorous insects that feed on trees. Also, certain specialist fungi that protect tree roots and move water and nutrients from the soil into trees are found only in late successional forests.

In contrast to natural forest functioning, conventional timber management proposes to shorten the shrub-herb phase and eliminate the old-growth phase over significant parts of forest landscapes. Following this approach degrades ecosystem functioning in a variety of ways, and will eventually lead to ecological collapse of forest ecosystems. This has already happened elsewhere in the world. For example, forests once surrounded the Mediterranean Sea. As the trees were steadily cut, the land was converted to an arid, inhospitable, treeless desert. In North America, the mouth of the Dunk River estuary on Prince Edward Island, once the site of deepwater shipyards, filled with silt as timber cutting upstream reduced the capacity of the soil to hold water, resulting in flooding and in the washing of forest soil into the sea.

Nevertheless, conventional forestry tends to evaluate its success by how many trees are cut and grown rather than by ensuring that all parts of the forest ecosystem are maintained. Thus, there is an illusion of healthy forests when, in reality, the forests are in serious decline.

STAND-LEVEL EXAMPLES

Trees are only a small portion of the composition and structures needed for a fully functioning forest. Nevertheless, trees, both living and dead, are critical structural members of the forest's framework. We need forests to have trees, and we need trees to have forests. In particular, large old trees, large snags, and large fallen trees have irreplaceable roles in forest functioning, and they provide one of the most important examples of the necessity of protecting stand-level composition and structures if we hope to maintain long-term forest functioning.

Large old trees are literally an ecosystem unto themselves. Some insects and small mammals live out their lifetimes solely within the confines of a single large tree. Large old trees, due to their extensive foliage area, catch large amounts of precipitation, permitting it to drip slowly through the canopy to the forest floor, thereby providing the soil with adequate time to absorb and distribute water. About 30% of the precipitation, be it snow or rain, that falls on the crown of a large old tree evaporates into the atmosphere and moves somewhere else. In a watershed dominated by large old trees, this function prevents the watershed from being overloaded with water and helps to distribute water to other parts of the landscape.

Snags, or standing dead trees, function as homes for cavity-nesting birds that eat insects that eat trees. Thus, maintaining snags throughout a forest stand is a necessary part of keeping agents of change, such as bark beetles, in balance with

> **Conventional forestry tends to evaluate its success by how many trees are cut and grown rather than by ensuring that all parts of the forest ecosystem are maintained.**

other parts of the forest. As snags soften, what was once a home for a woodpecker becomes, with a little expansion, a home for a pine marten.

Fallen trees, particularly large fallen trees, play myriad functions. As snow drifts over a fallen tree, it leaves a void space where the curve of the fallen tree trunk touches the ground. This provides an extremely important winter habitat niche for a number of animals, including mice, voles, and pine marten. As the fallen tree decays, it becomes the foundation for future forest soil. Trees that fall across a steep slope serve as natural dams to hold soil in place. One of the most important structural roles of fallen trees is water storage and filtration. Fully decayed wood holds about 20 times as much water as an equivalent volume of most mineral soils. Thus, fallen trees are Mother Nature's water storage and filtration system. In order to function properly, even a small watershed must contain millions of tons of decaying wood well-distributed throughout the drainage basin.

HUMAN EXAMPLES: THE BENEFITS OF ECOLOGICALLY RESPONSIBLE FOREST USE

These landscape- and stand-level examples, illustrating the functions of some important forest composition and structures, show why practices such as clearcutting and elimination of old-growth forests are incompatible with maintaining fully functioning forests. If the degradation caused by clearcutting and removal of old-growth forests were more evident, people might be more willing to adopt ecologically responsible approaches to timber management. However, because forests operate on such long time frames, and because, for millennia, forests have been building biological legacies through many generations of trees that have lived, died, and become incorporated into the forest soil, human activities that remove composition and structures do not immediately appear to be as damaging as they actually are.

However, as timber managers continue to degrade composition and structures of forests, from landscape to stand levels, damage to forest functioning becomes cumulative. Eventually this approach leads to degraded ecosystems, which provide fewer ecological functions than the fully functioning forests they replace. Because forest degradation occurs relatively slowly, successive generations of human beings inherit degraded forests which they assume to be natural, "healthy" ecosystems. In other words, we don't live long enough to see the results of our mistakes.

Ecologically responsible forest use attempts to avoid loss of forest functioning by maintaining forest composition and structures from the smallest soil bacteria to the landscape patterns of a large forest watershed. We may not understand the functions of particular forest composition and structures; nevertheless, an ecologically responsible approach protects all composition and structures. When parts of the forest are altered during activities such as ecologically responsible timber management or tourism, this alteration is as non-aggressive and respectful of natural processes as possible. Provisions for the replacement of forest composition and structures are built into ecologically responsible plans and activities.

As well as providing for the protection and maintenance of forest functioning, ecologically responsible forest use fosters the development of diverse, sustainable human economies. Because ecologically responsible forest use creates the least modification to forest ecosystem composition and structures, it provides for the largest diversity of compatible forest uses. In other words, by maintaining trees on the sites where we practice timber management and by ensuring that ecologically viable old-growth stands are found in reasonable proportions in each landscape, we provide an environment where the broadest spectrum of uses, from adventure tourism to timber extraction, can coexist. Such a range of activities is not possible where conventional timber management systems, such as clearcuts and tree plantations, are employed.

From a timber standpoint, because ecologically responsible timber management produces steady supplies of mature wood, the long-term economic benefits of an ecologically responsible approach exceed those of conventional timber management practices. Mature wood, long-fibred and strong, is superior for many uses, from structural materials and pulp to furniture and fine cabinets. In comparison, short-fibred, juvenile wood is not as strong and will warp and twist easily.

Mature wood is produced when the cambium layer (the single layer of cells between the wood and the bark) divides around dead branches or no branches. Obviously, increasing amounts of mature wood are produced as a tree gets larger and older. Research indicates that old-growth Douglas fir trees contain about 80% mature wood, while 60-year-old Douglas fir trees contain only 10-20% mature wood. Under ecologically responsible timber management, trees grow for longer cycles, not only to better maintain forest functioning, but also to produce steady supplies of high-value mature wood fibre. In contrast, conventional timber management is based on cutting cycles or rotations that provide primarily low-value juvenile wood. Thus, ecologically responsible timber management maintains supplies of high-quality mature wood fibre similar to that provided by natural old-growth forest ecosystems. This will ensure a healthy timber economy in perpetuity.

5

Ecologically Responsible Restoration and Ecoforestry

Alan Drengson and Victoria Stevens
with input from Maureen Gordon, Doug Patterson,
Sharon Chow and Duncan Taylor

INTRODUCTION: ECOFORESTRY BACKGROUND

THIS DOCUMENT SETS FORTH A RATIONALE AND GUIDELINES for applying ecoforestry for purposes of restoring forestlands removed by clearcutting, and for restoring greater structural diversity to second- and third- growth tree plantations. Ecoforestry can be used as a restoration strategy in areas that have been cleared and are now pastures and fields. These can be restored to natural forests by encouraging natural transition zones (ecotones) adjacent to natural forested areas. The industrial methods applied to agriculture, forestry and fishing have depleted these natural ecosystems and this in turn has decimated our rural communities. One of the major applications of ecoforestry worldwide will be for purposes of restoring full-functioning forest ecosystems. We must revitalize human and natural local rural communities. Ecoforestry is a total system of restoration and sustainable practice that creates the basis for vibrant rural life.

The practice of industrial forestry applies modern industrial agricultural methods to all forestlands, except designated wilderness and other reserves. The latter represent a small percentage of the total forestland area of the world. Industrial forestry simplifies ecosystems, systematically removes natural forests and replaces them with monoculture plantations, or, more recently, with a small number of "desirable" tree species. The even-age, single-species products of industrial forestry are not natural forests. Its large-scale clearcuts are not representative of natural disturbances. Its practices destroy forests and rural communities.

In many places in the world, only small fragments of natural landscapes and habitats remain. Species diversity is in sharp decline, with an increasing rate of species extinction. It is now recognized that human survival over the centuries and millennia requires protecting the remaining diversity, as well as local restoration of biological and other forms of diversity necessary for full-functioning ecosystems. Ecologically responsible use of forests, grasslands, alpine areas, oceans, air and fresh water requires changes from industrial agriculture, forestry, mining and fishing, to practices based on ecological principles, paradigms and ecocentric values.

Ecological paradigms and ecocentric values represent a different way to meet human needs in our relationships with the natural world. (When we refer to nature or natural forests, we mean the total ongoing evolutionary processes in any place, and on Earth as a whole, that have resulted in local and global biodiversity. These processes also produced the human species.) We participate in nature, and our awareness and culture give us responsibility to integrate our actions with our natural surroundings. It is known that many ancient and existing primal cultures exemplify ecological wisdom (ecosophy) specific to their places. This wisdom is gained by dwelling for generations in the same bioregion. Through dwelling we develop a sense of place. This arises in part by learning from natural processes and imitating them as much as possible. In natural systems, complexity and variety of structures promote a diversity of functions and ecosystem development to higher levels of integration. This in turn generates new values and multidimensional possibilities for meaning, which support cultural diversity. A complex ecosystem has a multitude of stories to tell, and many levels of values to be appreciated.

Human knowledge of how ecosystems function is very limited. We will probably never understand all the complexities in a single ecosystem (such as an entire watershed or a human being). These are probably more intricate than we can imagine, especially as we can only imagine what we already understand. We approach our subject, therefore, with humility and the recognition that no set of practices, science or philosophy is ever complete. We must err on the side of caution to minimize our impacts. We do this when we are mature enough to have a sense of Self that transcends the narrow ego identity that strives to be Number One. If we approach our relationship with ourselves, each other and the natural world, with an awareness of our limited knowledge, we are able to expand our sense of self to include the whole world. We can harmonize our interrelationships with it and its myriad beings.

We learn to the extent that we are receptive to the wisdom in our natural endowment and in other beings. Cultural diversity is intricately tied to the diversity of places. It arises from place-specific knowledge and wisdom. Ecoforestry is not a domination approach aiming for power over the natural world. Its practice is self-correcting. It learns from the wisdom of forests and their indigenous dwellers. To dwell in a forest is to become part of its complex ecological functions. Ecoforesters, then, are natives of the land.

Our challenge is to develop cultural and personal values that do not disrupt the integrity of remaining full-functioning natural forests and other ecosystems. We should diversify our economies and practices to the specifics of the places and

Ecoforestry is a total system of restoration and sustainable practice that creates the basis for vibrant rural life.

bioregions in which we dwell. Ecocentric practices must be learned on a global scale if we are to save what remains and restore what has been degraded in natural ecosystems. The Ecoforestry Institutes in both the U.S. and Canada are dedicated to this effort.

RESILIENCE, RESTORATION AND RECOVERY

Young Douglas fir
Bo Martin

Natural systems are far more resilient than most people realize. Those with experience in ecoforestry approaches to natural forests, as well as in ecocentric restoration practises, have seen very positive results. Where ecologically responsible restoration is practiced, the recovery of natural forests and other ecosystems can be astonishingly rapid. The natural world is imbued with living creative power. Nature and its beings are intelligent; they are purposeful in seeking values and accumulation of wisdom. From the complexities of geography and climate, a diversity of biological features evolves. Today we know that natural species and organisms are not unconscious mechanisms, and that matter is energy and process. The dualisms of the modern Western worldview remove humans from the natural world and de-spirit it. Such dichotomies are not tenable. The practice of ecoforestry is a unified spiritual, moral and practical undertaking. It builds sustainable communities and new cultures out of forest-based media of total values. The Restoration Guidelines presented here are part of the Ecoforestry Institute's efforts to summarize and make accessible the new practices, science and philosophies of ecologically responsible relationships with forests. This is a core purpose of the *International Journal of Ecoforestry*, the Ecoforestry Institute Occasional Papers, and the training and certification programs of the Institute.

Given the above, we propose the following guidelines for the practice of ecologically responsible restoration. Because of the sad state of so many forest and other ecosystems, restoration should be a major priority. We do not regard our guidelines, standards and certification criteria as fixed. They are evolving and represent our present understanding. Suggestions are welcome.

ECOFORESTERS' GUIDELINES FOR ECOLOGICALLY RESPONSIBLE RESTORATION

1. In a forest, whether plantation or natural, thinning should be based on increasing or maintaining the complexity of structures.
2. In clearcuts or plantations of second growth, piles and singles of large, rotting woody debris should be created or left.
3. Thickets and brush piles are valuable structures and create habitat for furthering biodiversity. Do not remove them.
4. Uneven spacing, which creates variable-sized openings in an otherwise

closed canopy, will increase structural diversity and specific habitat niches.

5. Boulder piles and other physical structures, such as berms, terraces and windbreaks, increase topographic complexity, which helps restore diversity and aids the transition to full-functioning ecosystems.

6. Restoration should not use toxic sprays such as herbicides, pesticides or fungicides.

7. Where possible, exotic species of plants and animals should be removed.

8. Do not introduce exotic species of plants and animals. Gather seeds for reintroduction from nearby native sources. Unless a forest is completely isolated, the animals will reintroduce themselves when the habitat becomes appropriate and corridors are provided.

9. In fields and open areas, where the aim is restoration of native forest, cease mowing and cultivation.

10. Identify, protect and restore riparian areas.

11. Leave dead and dying plants, trees and animals.

12. Use no artificial fertilizers, but only natural feeds such as native legumes, woody debris, etc.

13. Repair or retire road areas; e.g., stabilize banks and cuts with native plants, such as mixtures of grasses, clovers, etc., by broadcasting large numbers of mixed seeds. Use only natural fibres for nets and similar devices to stabilize soil and banks.

14. Create new wetlands, ponds, etc. using a variety of low-impact means. Restore former wetlands, swamps, etc. by removing or plugging installed drainage systems.

15. Remove fences and other artificial barriers to biological flow and movement of species.

16. Install nestboxes and feed plants for birds and other species, and create microhabitats for small species such as insects, microbes, etc.

17. Use the Bradley Method for restoring brush and removing exotics. (See John Seed's article in Chapter 20 of this book.)

18. Reintroduce native species of plants and animals.

19. Respect and learn from the wisdom of indigenous cultures.

20. Keep heavy machinery use to a minimum. Low-impact technologies are labor intensive, and thus create more work and jobs, have positive benefits for local economies, and increase the prosperity and stability of rural communities.

21. Consider all values in restoration plans and practices. For example, take account of ecocentric values inherent in natural processes and beings; do total-cost accounting and not just narrow cost-benefit analysis; do a multiproduct and service assessment for small- or large-scale restoration projects; do community value assessments, both human and natural; do

diversity assessments stressing ecocentric values.

22. Natural forces, such as water, wind, fire and so on can be used for restoration purposes, as in the maintenance of fire-dependent species.

23. Rely on natural regeneration and minimize intrusions; "learn when doing nothing" is the best strategy.

24. Do research and monitoring of restoration projects.

25. In general, do not use agricultural animals, except as draft animals (use only native seeds in their diet).

26. Avoid, as much as possible, industrial and other agricultural practices when restoring natural areas.

27. Sometimes restoration requires excluding human use and entry for a long time. Reference areas, such as intact natural forests, should be designated, as well as degraded areas in which nothing is done, for purposes of comparison and research.

28. Respect the creative, restorative power and wisdom of natural beings and the Earth.

29. When in doubt, don't! Always seek to discover what you can cease or avoid doing. Restorers should do no harm. Recovery is often a matter of only removing industrial human intrusions.

These guidelines enable us to learn as we go and therefore leave options open. Over time such practices give us a wealth of options.

CERTIFICATION OF RESTORATION PRODUCTS AND SERVICES

Restoration work sometimes yields materials and products that can be used for human purposes. These often have a market value. Facilitating the transition to ecologically responsible practices requires the certification of restoration work and products. There is considerable overlap between ecoforestry as practised in restoration and as practised in existing natural forests. The standards and criteria for responsibility in each instance have much in common. These are educational contributions that help to empower practitioners and consumers to act in ecologically responsible ways.

PROPOSED CERTIFICATION STANDARDS FOR SERVICES AND PRODUCTS FROM ECOLOGICALLY RESPONSIBLE RESTORATION

1. Value-added products and services are given priority.
2. No large-scale clearcuts are done.
3. Petrochemicals are not used in restoration.
4. Heavy equipment use is minimized; low-impact technologies are stressed.
5. Landscape and site values (especially esthetic) are always taken into account.
6. Materials that take a long time to produce, such as wood fibre, are used for

> If we destroy the environment, there will be no jobs, no economy and, eventually, no human life.

durable products with maximum value added.

7. Restoration is carried out using natural processes, encouraging natural regeneration as much as possible.

8. The progress of ecologically responsible restoration should be measured by comparisons to full-functioning, self-maintaining, evolving ecosystems.

9. Restoration efforts should halt environmental degradation and accelerate natural healing processes. Transition and temporary measures are often required.

10. Restoration projects should have strategies for regenerating all natural, indigenous values.

11. Restorers should show respect for ecocentric values and nature in their actions.

Conclusion

The environment is not a special interest, but a human necessity. Environmentalism is not the preoccupation of an elite group. The environment is our home, our context and our place. We are part of it and it is part of us. The destruction of our home-places and of sustainable ecosystems concerns all humans and all other species. If we destroy our contexts, we are doomed. This is not a matter of jobs vs. environment. If we destroy the environment, there will be no jobs, no economy and, eventually, no human life. *Economics must be based on ecocentric values, nonviolence, equity and sustainability.* Mainstream institutions must be changed so that ecological paradigms and values permeate every area of contemporary life.

Ecoforestry Institutes

The Ecoforestry Institutes in the U.S. and Canada are dedicated to research, dialogue and continuous learning. They publicize and teach ecologically responsible forest use and restoration. They work with groups and people who want to work and live in ecologically responsible harmony with natural forests. They are nonpartisan, charitable institutes based on continuous learning and development of ecocentric practices.

The environmental crisis is a profound cultural challenge that requires creative, open-minded learning and action. EFI is a learning organization and believes that a diversity of alternative organizations is necessary if we are to address our serious problems. EFI applauds organizations working for social justice, ecological responsibility, world peace and other noble causes.

The Ecoforestry Institute is dedicated to education that facilitates ecologically responsible forest practices, based on a shift from anthropocentric to ecocentric values. They invite persons who share these values to support their work.

Ecoforestry Institute Mission

The mission of the Ecoforestry Institute is to foster ecologically responsible forest use through education and related programs and services. The Institute has the following specific purposes:

1. To engage in dialogue with interested persons aimed at deeper understanding of ecocentric forestry (ecoforestry);

2. To develop an educational process to facilitate a paradigm shift from industrial forestry to ecoforestry;

3. To educate and train interested persons in the knowledge, techniques and arts of ecoforestry so that they may serve as ecoforestry practitioners, consultants and teachers;

4. To develop and monitor demonstration ecoforests on private and public forestlands where members of the public can see working models of ecologically responsible forestry and fully functioning natural forests from which forest goods are being harvested in a sustainable manner;

5. To develop, in cooperation with others, criteria for ecologically responsible forest uses, and standards for certifying ecoforestry practices, practitioners, materials, products and artifacts;

6. To research and communicate to a wide audience the deepening knowledge of the multitudes of values and functions of natural forest ecosystems, as reflected in "leading edge" work in conservation biology, landscape ecology and related disciplines;

7. To respect and cooperate with indigenous peoples, to learn from them the wisdom of the places where they have dwelled for centuries;

8. To cooperate with other persons, organizations and agencies to develop educational and training programs and services consistent with the Institute's mission.

Those who prepared this document have been associated with the Ecoforestry Institute as advisors, employees or board members.

PART TWO

Maintaining the Ecosystem

Diversity promotes richness, Bo Martin

6

Monitoring for Ecosystem Management

Richard Hart

ECOSYSTEM MANAGEMENT IS A SOCIALLY DEFINED PROCESS whose fundamental limitation is the lack of a collaborative approach with nature. If the bottom line continues to be focused on system outputs, with humans "at the controls," we haven't progressed beyond new terminology for the old paradigm.

We are at a juncture in global living. To protect the environment, it is imperative that we rekindle the respect for and understanding of the ecosystem's natural flows, structures, and cycles, and displace the traditional emphasis on the protection of such individual elements as popular species or natural features. This attitudinal change includes social self-diagnosis, as we are in "the dance" together. Until we pay enough attention to these natural flows, arrangements, and connections to grasp what the ecosystem's needs are and respond to them, we will continue to degrade the collective life of the environment.

As an exercise, I offer the following as an approach for observing and recording a forest ecosystem. This approach is based on the following observations:

- The actual substance of which the forest environment is made consists of patterns, rather than things or individual species.
- The distinction between growing and declining patterns is not arbitrary but can be arrived at objectively.
- If you ask, "Where does the forest environment come from?" you'll find it is generated by a patterning of ecological ebb and flow across a suitable landscape.
- The successful adaptation to a complex forest ecosystem requires an enormous amount of minute local adaptations, which insist that large numbers of species have to be engaged in the process.
- The forest environment is constituted of a large set of events that are objectively definable by specific outcomes.

The consequences of these facts include the practical changes:

- between the Earth and its species;
- between the Earth and the collective ability of species to respond flexibly to situations beyond their normal patterning in the processes of adaptation and repair;
- in the flow of energy through the environment and its biotic community; and
- in the ecosystem's collective patterning of shared needs and governance, which we will define as its health or soundness.

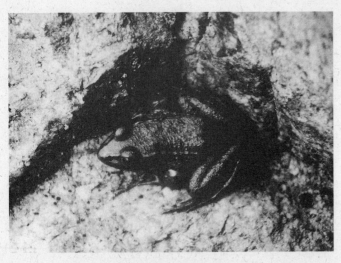

Amphibians are critical indicator species
Jerry Valen Demarco

Taken as a whole, the process of observing patterns in these relationships leads directly to a fundamentally different way of perceiving ecosystem management. We almost have to "start from scratch" with our perception of how species link with one another. We have names for species but we don't have names for their dynamic relationships. We do have labels for bundles of relationships, such as aquatic macro-invertebrates. Yet, as an example, we don't have one for the relationship between caddis fly and dipper. They both have similar needs, but they also have very dissimilar ones when they enter each other's environments. They each follow distinct patterns that overlap to meet their needs and fulfil the function of their relationship. Furthermore, each species possesses bundles of relationships that increase geometrically as they radiate outwardly to involve more species.

Indigenous peoples have names for many of these relationships, usually in verb form. They understand and respect the importance and intelligence of species connectedness. It is obvious that these relationships are fundamental. What is not so obvious is that these relationships are generated by rules. Each species is ultimately a product of the rules inherent in its gene system, and the interaction of those rules creates and sustains its life. The rules that apply at the beginning of a process are relatively simple in comparison to the complexity of the end product. This is accepted as a part of bioscience, but for most people it is not emotionally real. So the idea that there can be a set of rules which ultimately generates the environment is difficult to take. Consequently, the idea of systems of rules actually generating structure is not widely shared.

However, rules actually create the species in an established order during the course of embryonic development. Over the course of many generations adaptation occurs and the original rules are "revised" to fit the needs.

By observing all these processes and patterns, one can begin to generate the kinds of observation pertinent to an ecosystem's well-being. This is where we come in.

Monitoring the connections is important because it brings the inquiry back to the ultimate intent of ecosystem management: the attempt to discover and describe the structural correspondence between a species and its environment. A healthy species not only fits its environment well, but also defines or clarifies the collective life it adapts to. We perceive this clarity to be the richness and wholeness of its structure. An unhealthy or absent species confuses the collective life it interacts with, and we perceive this as static, fragmented or degenerating.

The distinction between wholesome and defective structure is a matter of fact, not value. Other species are there, such as pathogens, to take defective structure back down to its basic components to be reinvested in a structure that works. This is the rule. It is not random, yet it is vulnerable to unnatural disturbances for which its patterning doesn't possess information. The ecosystem proceeds to construct and repair from its patterning, however disrupted or fragmented. It may also take a considerable amount of time to re-establish a community, given that there are habitat and resources sufficient to meet the community's needs. The free functioning of a forest ecosystem, therefore, is the key to its structure, and the source of the wholistic patterning that it possesses.

Grizzly bears , a wide range indicator of healthy ecosystems
U.S. Park Service, Yellowstone

The forest ecosystem is a large-scale pattern of millions of very minute events. The environment requires an enormous amount of minuscule local adaptations between the Earth and its users. The essential intent of ecosystem management is the construction of a fabric of events that weave through the common connecting points for species events within the forest. The ultimate goal is to collect the information that details the establishment and maintenance of "comfort zones": the climate, nutrients and mobility suitable for species viability.

The Pacific Northwest of North America comprises many distinct subregions to which traditional, across-the-forest management does not adequately address or adapt. The patterns that support the diversity in decomposed granitic soils are not of the same configuration as those present in high elevation volcanics or clays. We cannot continue to presume that what is good for one forest is good for another area within the same administrative jurisdiction. We need to pursue a credible path that allows decision-makers to look at the fabric of intelligence gathered within a biome and let that information guide human activity in the forest.

7

The Function of Snags

David Lukas

THE YUBA WATERSHED INSTITUTE near Nevada City, California, is currently approaching its first on-the-ground management decision in partnership with the BLM (Bureau of Land Management) and the TFGNA (Timber Framers Guild of North America). The trial run of this decision-making process is now focusing on one tree in preparation for the more complex task of looking at all the BLM parcels later this spring. But this is no ordinary tree, and in its quiet unassuming manner it reflects the many threads that will underlie future decisions of the YWI and the San Juan Ridge community.

The tree in question is a five-foot diameter Ponderosa pine that towers 205 feet (62.5 m), leaving you slightly short of breath looking up along its massive trunk. It is probably one of the tallest trees on the ridge, but by examining stumps in the surrounding forest you can tell it used to have many more big neighbors. Although it was spared being cut by loggers, this magnificent pine has been recently killed by bugs.

The question, therefore, in its simplest terms, is whether to harvest this large standing dead tree for its high-quality timber or to leave it as an integral component of the essentially old-growth forest that surrounds it. A question like this tends to immediately polarize opinions. It is important to remember that it is not so much the outcome but the process of this decision that is significant. What makes the work of the YWI unique is that it tries to think of the landscape first, followed by developing technologies and management that stem from rootedness in place. The principles of such work arise from what the Norwegian philosopher, Arne Naess, calls a "deep-seated respect, even veneration, for ways and forms of life". This is offered as an alternative to the resource-extraction bias of decisions made by the industrial political hierarchy.

Located in one of the southeasterly-tending ravines of the BLM Lonesome Lake parcel, this tree is part of a band of dense mature forest stretching from the fire access road down to Spring Creek. Measurements taken in the vicinity of this pine revealed that there are about 11 trees per acre (4.5/ha) with a diameter greater than 30 inches (76 cm), which places this stand in an "old-growth" category. The one old-growth component critically lacking, however, is large dead standing trees.

From aerial photos and on-the-ground exploration it appears that this stand occurs within the bounds of the drainage, primarily on the shaded northeast-facing slope. The canopy is composed of Ponderosa pine and Douglas fir, with lesser numbers of incense cedar and sugar pine. Huge old stumps on the slope indicate that Douglas fir used to be a more substantial element but was selectively harvested. A few large black oaks still survive though they are now heavily shaded under the canopy. The understory is a rich mosaic of pine, fir, cedar and oak seedlings completing the stand's diverse representation of size and age classes.

There are some questions we might ask in making a decision on this tree: what do we want at some future time, especially in terms of landscape; how do we accomplish such goals; and what might we see as potential problems? Broader questions are followed by more specific ones: what kind of wildlife might use this large snag; what other roles could it fulfil in this stand; what is its specific economic value if harvested; and how does it contribute to the local economy?

Len Brackett estimates that there are 5,000 board feet in the first 40 feet (12 m) of trunk with a potential value of $4,000. In order to receive top dollar and provide the finest quality lumber for woodworkers the YWI would cut, mill, and season the wood here on the ridge. It would then be offered on the market as a high-quality product at the going rate offered by woodworkers.

The foremost concern of the YWI is the quality of landscape resulting from any and all management decisions, no matter how minor the decision may seem at the time. What is meant by this term "landscape"? For some it evokes scenes of manicured yards and pastoral paintings, for others it may mean endless vistas of harvestable trees, and for others, mountains, valleys, meadows and everything we see in nature. It is perhaps all these things and many more, for landscape suggests the merging of nature and culture across a diverse physical terrain; in a manner of speaking, landscape is an ecology between interdependent human and biotic communities. As the writer Barry Lopez remarks, "One learns a landscape finally not by knowing the name or identity of everything in it, but by perceiving the relationships in it."

This is the task, then: to work on the level of perceiving relationships, to think as members of a broader community rooted in place. Does this particular stand of trees serve as a wildlife corridor between the upland portions of the Lonesome Lake parcel and Spring Creek? Is this big pine a component of that corridor? How long

Snags as habitat
Victoria Stevens

*Snags are essential components
of forest ecosystems*
Bo Martin

will this tree release stored nutrients into the soil through the process of decay? Will animals come and nest in the cavities of its trunk? Will people come and gaze at its enormous size, show their children the decaying giant and explore the growing forest around it? These are some of the landscape questions, questions that look at energy pathways and connections between all members of the community. The answers we come up with will shape and become part of our relationship to the landscape; this big tree stands as one step towards deciding that future. At this time several members of the YWI and TFGNA are working in consultation with BLM and Forest Service biologists to evaluate aspects of this decision. This group will put together the information and present the BLM district manager, Deane Swickard, an outline of alternatives, the rationales for each, and the basis for a decision.

8

Forest Managers Focus on Fungi
as Part of the Big Picture

Maggie Rogers

AT LAST AN EFFORT IS BEING MADE to inventory North American fungi. All over the U.S., and particularly in the West, forest management agencies are looking at their responsibilities in new ways. Some of this will affect all of us who know fungi, for now the forest managers are expected to know more about fungi than ever before.

Why?

If timber can't be the sole support of the agencies, leaders of the U.S. Forest Service and Bureau of Land Management think mushrooms and other forest products can help. Where cutting of forests still goes on, there will be times when saving habitat for rare fungi may halt such activities. The spotted owl hasn't been superseded, but efforts to protect biodiversity are giving the poor bird some respite from its duties as symbol.

U.S. Forest Service research units are busy with a new kind of activity these days. On May 3, 1994, Dr. Randy Molina of the USDA (U.S. Department of Agriculture) Forest Science Laboratory, Oregon State University, Corvallis, introduced the topics for a two-day conference: "Ecosystem Management of Forest Fungi: Some Investigative Methods for Studying Fungi."

Attendees were a mixed lot. Over half were representatives of forest and land agencies; the rest represented national parks, private and commercial businesses, native Americans, mycological societies, and academic research. Even *Sierra Magazine* was represented. That writer looked stunned by the amount of detail he was hearing, and what it might mean.

Here were people apprehensive about the prospect of eventual litigation over timber management practices. People who, for the most part, couldn't tell a *Cortinarius* from an *Agaricus*. (During the course of the conference, it was heartening to hear the number of references to the assistance that amateur mycologists might be able to offer in identification of fungi.)

A pre-registration questionnaire helped conference planners set the agenda. One response was "I am an agency person who has not focused on fungi in the past. Now I need to make management recommendations pertaining to fungi. I hope this conference will serve as a basic biology and management lesson for me."

Alas, not that simple. "How we are currently studying and inventorying" (but not much of "what we can do for you") was just the beginning of an answer for this person's needs. Case scenarios were presented by speakers from Oregon and Washington, and a second-day panel summed up with comments on the session, on current regulations, and on the politics of change.

When attendees asked questions like "Which is the best method for harvesting a particular mushroom and what size and classes of woody debris are important? What are the effects upon a mushroom bed and site productivity, and how can we reduce the impact of harvesting, erosion and compaction?" conference responders too often replied, essentially, "We need to do more research before we can answer."

Members of the Chanterelle Study of the Oregon Mycological Society, having gathered such data for over five years, responded in part to this set of questions, but it was clear that scientists couldn't feel satisfied with one study.

Mushrooms and other fungi in the forest
Victoria Stevens

Much of the concern of agency attendees focused around the "rare, endemic and unstudied fungi" the existence of which could halt timber harvesting. The biodiversity theme surfaced, and focus shifted from how to be trained to how to avoid litigation. Comments ranged from questions like "Are listings of rare, endangered or endemic fungi available? What rules and regulations for management apply?" to brave statements: "The unstudied fungus of today is the forest health indicator of tomorrow."

It was a rich experience to hear these exchanges, to talk with agency people who were trying to do their jobs better, reaching out for answers to questions they hardly knew how to frame. Sharp comments on the reasons for not contracting picking areas for the matsutake harvest, for *not* allowing forest trampling by large groups, could not be ignored. These came, not from agency managers, but from a mushroom group representing pickers who've learned to husband their mushroom areas.

The innocence of some of those asking questions was surprising, until one remembers that most forest management training has been problem-centered. In that world, fungi are seen primarily as pathogens of the forest, rather than symbionts or mycorrhizal companions of trees and plants. The image of the forest as a totally interactive biome is just now becoming real to the managers of our forests. The ideas of forest scientists like Chris Maser (see Issue 21 of *Mushroom: The Journal*, "Ancient Forests, Priceless Treasures"), Mike Amaranthus (Issue 19, "The Fir and the Filament") and Gary Menser (Issue 19, "It's Pronounced My'ko ri'ze") have only recently begun to be accepted by forest managers.

Other questions indicated a need for intensive work sessions in the woods during fruiting seasons, so forest managers could feel comfortable with which fungi grow where, and how to deal with questions of their eventual protection. This presented a role for volunteer teams skilled in identification and teaching.

The session ended with expressions of concern for forest inventory and monitoring methods for organisms as elusive as fungi. From the questionnaire: "Agency personnel have limited identification skills and knowledge of fungi in general. Many are people with little or no previous fungal experience who will be making the decisions about management of the resource. What is the current research? Who is doing it?"

Rotting log and micro habitat
Victoria Stevens

Dr. Jim Trappe presented a lively case scenario of a site where once he'd found a rare fungus, *Gastroboletus umbellus*. He decided to return to verify the site, and found it embedded in a possible timber sale area. Citing current regulations for setting aside an area for inventory, he suggested this process:

1. First look at similar elevations, visit sites, identify the vegetation types, find and map all similar places on large-scale topographic maps. (His site happened to be in mountainous country with ridges and divides.)
2. Withdraw all areas in the habitat (a particular ridge system) from "forest management activities" and add 1/4 mile (0.4 km) buffer strips.
3. At this point, begin the inventory of this fungus *only*, using "systematic wandering," beginning with the preseason, the season, and the postseason. Check habitats and adjacent areas, using expert and volunteer crews. Train them in the basics of orienteering and scouting, then take them to the site. Assign "systematic wandering" areas. Take 4-5 days. Have volunteers mark specimens found, rather than bringing them in; view and photograph *in situ*. Consider what picking the fruiting bodies of rare fungi does to the health of "the colony", then photograph and take voucher specimens.

4. Plan to repeat for Year Two, Year Three, and until some arbitrary date.
5. Finally, decide whether this should become a "mycological preserve" and whether to cage and protect it, and with whom to register the "preserve."

To feel some recognition of the complexity of all this, view his process from three points of view: From that of the forest manager, the timber buyer, and the scientist.

Some of the many forest fungi found in forests
Bo Martin

One of the problems with applying mycological research to these questions has always been the odd and circular combination of (a) the seasonality of the fungi, (b) the lack of available time by professionals for spending longer seasons with a diversity of sites, and (c) the tendency of many mycologists to specialize to the degree that they've looked only for what they needed to see in order to complete their studies.

Another peculiar condition for current studies is that few sites, thanks to the proliferation of logging roads, are isolated enough to be protected against incursion by non-scientists. Once an area is set aside, mapped and data recording begins, the site is public knowledge. Building a trust relationship with the public such as the forest managers in the Chemult Ranger district in Oregon hope to do, is always chancy. All it takes is one picker who can't or won't read the study site signs, and oops, there goes the scientific method.

It's more than mushroom harvesting that's being studied: there's also green tree retention in tree cutting plans, adequate streamside buffering zones, and preferred canopy opening size for continued forest health, all of which have implications for fungi. There is a need, for instance, for studies of younger forest stands and of the effects of compaction by humans, machines and erosion, particularly on drier lands such as those on southern and eastern slopes. It requires a different kind of scientist, one whose personal philosophy can accommodate changing ideas about the inclusion of fungi as an integral part of the forest, one who is flexible and a problem solver rather than a "too focused" research mycologist.

When asked to compare the amount of research available that wasn't solely silvicultural, timber-driven or fibre-cellulose driven, Dr. Mike Amaranthus replied wryly, "Right now we have the equivalent of a 12-inch bat, and we need tools to hit a home run."

Dr. Mike Castellano, Forest Science Laboratory, Oregon State University, scheduled a July 6-7, 1994 invitational meeting designed to create working definitions (read "legally defensible" definitions) for fungal inventory and protection activities. This brought together a stellar group of 40 professional and amateur mycologists and agency representatives from the U.S. and Canada. Field mycologists, taxonomists, herbarium curators, ecologists, forest pathologists and a "devil's advocate" legal specialist traded ideas.

The legal specialist said that current definitions of which fungi are rare weren't dependable, and that fungus identifiers should use a more scientific analysis and rating system if their identifications are going to hold up in court and delay timber sales.

An April 1994 massive three-part document, acronymically known as The ROD (the *Record of Decision Standards and Guidelines* of the U.S. Forest Service and Bureau of Land Management Planning Documents Within the Range of the Northern Spotted Owl) served as a jumping-off point. It contains a listing of over 200 fungi designated by a mycological team. These were based on, in the words of Jim Trappe and Mike Castellano, "A four-tiered rating system":

1. Species thought to be rare.
2. Polypores that land managers could survey for perennial fruiting.
3. Approximately 200 general fungi that are not rare but still need management (usually protection of some habitat).
4. Fungi not "at risk," but not well enough known for the USFS to "manage."

New acronyms flew furiously: ROD (*Record of Decision*), FEMAT (Forest Ecosystem Management Assessment Team, led by Dr. Jack Ward Thomas), *DRAFT* and *FINAL SEIS* (*Supplemental Environmental Impact Statement*), Alternative 9 (of Clinton's Forest Plan, *Final SEIS*), NBS (National Biological Survey), and the five major federal laws that apply to federal land management: NEPA (National Environmental Policy Act), ESA (Endangered Species Act), NFMA (National Forest Management Act), FPLMA (Federal Land Policy and Management Act), and the O&C Act (Oregon and California Lands Act).

By the end of this meeting, the group had reviewed pertinent details of what went on at the May meeting, had agreed to give their working definitions to a committee for polishing and review by participants, and agreed that the owl has been superseded.

The symbol now is the National Biological Survey and Inventory. Tougher to visualize, difficult to shoot. But easier to put in the same frame with "biodiversity" when it's time to talk habitat preservation.

What did these meetings mean for mushroomers?

That USFS and/or park employees who at one time knew nothing about identifying fungal species are now exquisitely aware of their responsibility for fungi, and are also painfully aware that those fungi are tough to identify. (*Consider this if they overreact when mushroomers want to pick without permits.*)

That forest research staff are working diligently to promote fungi as an integral element in the National Biological Inventory, which at first ignored both macro- and microfungi. *Thank them for their efforts.*

That some forest science research units will be designing and developing training conferences and workshops in surveying, identifying and inventorying techniques. *Be there*.

- That forest scientists see a stronger role for volunteers in assisting in field surveys, attending training conferences, and serving on advisory groups on public policy or other roles relating to forest management compliance with new laws and regulations. *Serve in these roles*.
- That there is still many a slip 'twixt the field survey recording sheets, the data, and the creation of a national biological inventory and any positive changes in conservation of fungal habitat, particularly of forest and range areas. This is not just a West Coast activity. Though there may be a model developing in the West, it may well be applied elsewhere. *Keep an eye on what happens*.

And we will, too.

9

The Ecological Role of Coarse Woody Debris

Victoria Stevens

GIVEN OUR INCOMPLETE KNOWLEDGE OF SPECIES and their interactions in ecosystems, biodiversity is more likely to be sustained if managed forests retain the structures of those forests created by the activities of natural disturbance agents such as fire, wind, insects, and disease. There is wide realization that the reserve system is not adequate for the preservation of species and the ecological functions that link them. Effective management must take place both inside and outside of reserves (see Walker 1994). This paper describes what is known about the contribution to ecosystems of one of the structures at risk in intensely managed forests—large pieces of dead, down wood.

A natural forest can be viewed as having two important phases—the building phase (during which available elements are assembled into structures we know as plants and animals), and the deconstruction phase (during which these structures are disassembled into pieces available for rebuilding). We call these the living and decaying parts of the whole life and death cycle; however, both the living and decaying processes involve living organisms. One of the roles of the growing organisms is to build structure, while one of the roles of the decay organisms is to break down structure. Both phases are essential to the ecological processes that have evolved in forests. These processes include the life cycles of vertebrates and invertebrates, fungi and bacteria, and the strategies used by plant structures to accumulate nutrients. All living organisms in forests have finite lifespans after which they become part of the decaying portion of the ecosystem. Soft-bodied organisms and small plant structures generally decay rapidly and provide a quick turnover of nutrients, an addition to the forest floor, and/or a meal for forest wildlife. Large woody material contains very significant stores of carbon and energy and is the foundation of an important forest food web. This large material usually decays more slowly and therefore provides a more steady input of energy and nutrients and longer lasting structures. For example, approximately half of the time that a mature Douglas fir tree is in an ecosystem, it is dead wood. This paper describes the ecological role of the larger, down pieces of wood in the forest. These pieces are referred to as coarse woody debris (CWD).

DEFINITION

Coarse woody debris is defined here as: Sound and rotting logs and stumps, and coarse roots in all stages of decay, that provide habitat for plants, animals and insects and a source of nutrients for soil structure and development. Material generally greater than 7.5 cm (3") in diameter.

In some contexts, it is useful to include standing dead trees in the definition. These wildlife trees or snags are treated elsewhere in this book (Chapter 7).

ECOLOGICAL ROLES

The importance of coarse woody debris in forests has been partially documented although much remains to be discovered. What is known of its function is divided into four interrelated roles:
- its role in the productivity of forest trees;
- its role in providing habitat and structure to maintain biological diversity;
- its role in the geomorphology of streams and slopes; and
- its role in long-term carbon storage.

The importance of each of these roles to an ecosystem varies according to the kinds of natural disturbances common to the area, and the temperature and moisture regime. The following discussion is general and outlines the important roles that could be played by CWD.

Role in Forest Productivity

To a greater or lesser degree depending on the moisture and temperature regimes of an ecosystem, CWD may:
- add a significant amount of organic matter to the soil;
- retain moisture through dry periods, providing a refuge for mycorrhizal roots (fungus-tree root symbionts) and associated soil organisms;
- provide a site for asymbiotic or associative nitrogen-fixing bacteria,
- represent a capital pool of nutrients for the ecosystem;
- provide a site for the regeneration of conifers; and
- contribute to soil acidification and podzolization.

Accumulation of organic matter

All size classes of decaying pieces of wood contribute to the long-term accumulation of organic matter because the lignin and humus of well-decayed wood are high in carbon constituents (Maser et al. 1988). In the dry inland forests of the U.S. Pacific Northwest, woody material is the most important organic material added to forest soils during a stand rotation (Harvey et al. 1981). It improves the moisture-carrying capacity and structure of the soil. To protect the productive potential of a forest soil, a continuous supply of organic materials must be maintained. In the words of Harvey et al. (1981): "Without an adequate soil base, the potential for a good tree crop simply does not exist."

Mycorrhizal root tip associations

Mycorrhizal activity has been found to be essential to the healthy growth of conifers. This activity is a moisture-dependent phenomenon (Harvey et al. 1983). Both diameter and state of decay affect the ability of down wood to hold moisture. In the Pacific Northwest, the moisture content of a decaying Douglas fir tree bole increased as the decay class increased until at about decay class IV (out of five decay classes) the moisture content in summer was 250% of the dry weight (Maser et al. 1988). All size classes of decaying wood act as a moisture store and provide refugia for mycorrhizal fungi during dry periods; however, the larger pieces can hold more water and are therefore more effective at holding moisture and acting as refugia through long dry spells. When moisture returns to a site, it is a much faster process to reinvade the organic layer of soil with mycorrhizal root tips, when refugia are scattered throughout the forest floor. Wood is only moderately supplied with nutrients, but usually occurs in large enough volumes to be a significant source of moisture (Harvey et al. 1986).

Advanced stages of decay in large woody debris
Victoria Stevens

Nitrogen fixation

Dry forests tend to be nitrogen limited (Harvey et al. 1987). There are four natural sources of nitrogen.

1. precipitation that gets nitrogen from electrical discharge (lightning), dust, pollen and air pollutants;
2. symbiotic nitrogen fixation by nodulated plants with symbiotic associations with nitrogen-fixing bacteria (e.g. red alder, *Sheperdia canadensis*, some lichens);
3. nonsymbiotic nitrogen fixation by free-living nitrogen-fixing bacteria that occur in soil and plant residues; and
4. associative nitrogen (N) fixation.

Symbiotic nitrogen fixation is the most efficient, putting many times more nitrogen into the system than any other means (Harvey et al. 1987), but in some interior forests there are few nodulated species, especially after many years of fire suppression. These ecosystems rely primarily on nonsymbiotic sources of nitrogen.

On the coast of the Pacific Northwest, the primary nodulated species (red alder) can only grow in early stages of succession, and thereafter the ecosystem may benefit from nonsymbiotic nitrogen in decaying wood. Although itself low in nitrogen, by hosting the bacteria responsible for nonsymbiotic nitrogen fixation, CWD is a significant contributor of nitrogen in some ecosystems. Harmon et al. (1986) summarized the available studies and found that in a range of forest ecosystems with CWD biomass ranging from 50-113 Mg CWD/ha (Mg = megagrams; 1 Mg=1 million grams or 1,000 Kg), there was a range of asymbiotic nitrogen fixation of 0.3-1.4 kg/ha/year.

Nutrient pool

CWD can also contribute to nutrient storage. This includes the nutrients accumulated in the woody bole during tree growth and the nutrients added from litterfall and throughfall (rain falling through the forest canopy) being intercepted by a down log rather than falling on the forest floor. If the nutrients are added faster than they are leached out by rain, the result is positive nutrient storage. As the wood decays, the nutrients are added to the available pool. Mechanisms for removing the nutrients from CWD and adding them to the available pool vary. Harmon et al. (1994) found that during early stages of decomposition, mushrooms growing on decaying logs increased the concentrations of nitrogen, potassium and phosphorus 38, 115, and 136 times respectively over the concentrations found in the logs. When these mushrooms fall off the logs and decay, they are returning nutrients from the downed wood into the available nutrient pool. Arthropods digest the complex organic molecules in down wood with the help of micro-organisms in their digestive systems, and return the nutrients to the forest in their frass (droppings). Thus, CWD can be a reliable and steady source of nutrients over 100 years. When coarse woody debris is added to the ecosystem at regular intervals and is well distributed, it represents a long-term source of nutrients.

Regeneration

In some wet ecosystems, the tree seedlings with the best chance of success are those that germinate on large pieces of woody debris (Harmon et al. 1986). The understory is so thick in these ecosystems that no light is available to seedlings on the forest floor. The decaying woody boles provide a platform for successful germination and growth.

In some wet riparian forests in the montane spruce zone in British Columbia, researchers found that germination only occurred on the hummocks of very decayed wood (Gyug 1996). Other sites in these forests are too wet to allow germination.

The root mats of fallen trees and the spaces within a matrix of fallen trees can provide refugia from ungulates for some favored shrub species. Schreiner et al. (1996) found that on the valley bottoms of the Sitka spruce - western hemlock forests in Olympic National Park, these refugia were the only places where some shrub species could flower and set seed. Outside of the refugia, the browsing pressure was too high.

> Without an adequate soil base, the potential for a good tree crop simply does not exist.

Soil biology

Forests grow in soil. The health of the soil is reflected in the health of the forest. Soil health is a result of the myriad biological interactions that are a part of the forest ecosystem we call soil. This includes soil arthropods, fungi, bacteria, animal waste and among other things, decaying wood. There are many more species and interactions than we currently know of, but the strategy for assembling available nutrients into parts of a forest ecosystem are all present in natural forests. These pieces and processes may differ between ecosystems, depending on both biotic and abiotic components available. Removing large portions of decaying wood may alter the components of a forest that are part of the place-specific evolutionary history that has resulted in processes and interactions essential for maintaining that forest.

Role in Providing Habitat (Maintenance of Biodiversity)

There is no doubt that coarse woody debris plays an important part in creating habitat for many species of plants and animals. What is known of the ecological value of CWD to wildlife and plants has been summarized in many places (Caza 1993, Harmon et al. 1986, Maser et al. 1988). Down wood provides:

(in terrestrial systems)
- sites for nests, dens and burrows;
- primary energy source for a complex food web;
- hiding cover for predators and protective cover for their prey;
- moist microsites (for amphibians, insects, plants and ectomycorrhizal fungi);
- travel ways across streams, across the forest floor and beneath the snow;
- refugia during disturbance.

(in aquatic systems)
- structure to slow stream flow and create pools;
- places for food to accumulate; and
- cover from temperature extremes and predators.

The following are some examples of CWD use by a variety of species types.

Small Mammals

Coarse woody debris provides a structural link with the previous stand in some ecosystems and as such provides continuity of habitat for some species (Hansen et al. 1991). Carey and Johnson (1995) reported that along with understory vegetation, CWD is the most important habitat factor for small mammals. Healthy small mammal populations help maintain the ecological processes of which they are an integral part (e.g., the dispersal of seeds and of mycorrhizal fungi spores, the maintenance of healthy predator populations, and the control of potentially harmful invertebrate populations).

Arthropods

Arthropods are one of the most diverse groups of animals and one of the least

> **The health of the soil is reflected in the health of the forest.**

understood. Many forms associated with old forests are flightless (Lattin and Moldenke 1990). Flightlessness is one result of habitat stability. For these species, the need to recolonize new habitats because of frequent disturbance has been eliminated. The practice of clearcut logging and slash burning is a disturbance that is not part of the evolutionary history of these insects. In a site in the western Cascades of Oregon, where 90% of the total soil arthropods were destroyed by clearcutting and burning, many species were able to survive within and under decayed logs (coarse woody debris) (Moldenke and Lattin 1990).

Forest floor, Douglas fir ecosystem
Victoria Stevens

Downed logs are also an important colonizing substrate for ants. These ants are an ecologically significant member of the forest community, acting as agents of wood decay, as a prey species for pileated woodpeckers, and as predators of spruce budworm. In a recent study by Torgersen and Bull (1995), approximately one-third of the downed wood log sections contained budworm-foraging ants. This translated to 92 colonies of budworm-foraging ants per hectare in a mixed conifer stand in northeastern Oregon.

Soil micro-arthropods are largely unidentified, but groups of them associated with CWD have been shown to increase the availability and suitability of organic particles for decomposer communities (Norton 1990 in Nadel 1995) and contribute to nutrient cycling and soil formation, (Behan-Pelletier 1993 in Nadel 1995, Setälä and Marshall 1994).

The variability in size, species and the environmental setting of coarse woody debris contributes to the diversity of decay organisms. In addition to the more obvious differences related to size and species, each piece is in a different stage in the decay cycle. It can take more than 1,000 years for the complete decay of large individuals of some tree species in some ecosystems (Daniels et al. In prep.). The stages of decay create varied habitats over time that are used by a variety of arthropods. The earliest invaders inoculate their tunnels with fungi, bacteria, phoretic mites, nematodes and protozoans (Parsons et al. 1991). Later, beetles that feed on sapwood and heartwood tunnel deeper into the log, opening access for other arthropods and micro-organisms. These processes involve hundreds or possibly thousands of species and are a critical link in the carbon and nutrient cycles in the forest.

Nonvascular Plants and Fungi

Many species of nonvascular plants and fungi are associated with CWD. The diversity of these species is related to the diversity of hosts, including a variety of decay stages, and has been linked to forest health (Amaranthus et al. 1994, Crites and Dale 1995). Variability in piece size contributes to this diversity. Some bryophytes and fungi are restricted to very large pieces (Soderstrom 1988, 1989).

In Finnish and Swedish forests naturally occurring fungi are missing where there is a history of clean logging and a lack of CWD. Forest decline in Europe has shown a relationship to decreased ectomycorrhizal fungal diversity (Arnolds 1991 in Amaranthus et al. 1994). Although it is not clear whether the forest decline is a result of decreased fungal diversity or if the two are correlated for some other reason, healthy forests typically have a highly diverse ectomycorrhizal flora (Amaranthus et al. 1994). These fungi have a diversity of habitats and physiological characteristics, which makes each unique in its requirements and contributions to the ecosystem. Diversity may prove important to the response of forests to rapid human-caused changes.

> This diversity equips both trees and forests to functionally adapt to changes in season, habitats, assaults by pollution, or climate change, and may be linked to the ability of Douglas fir to grow well over decades and centuries (Amaranthus et al. 1994, pp. 2158-2159).

At the landscape level, difficulties associated with the maintenance of some nonvascular species that inhabit CWD are similar to those of other species. Spore dispersal is often limited in area, and particularly with lichens the probability of colonization is greatly reduced when habitat patches are too widely dispersed.

Summary

The maintenance of the natural diversity of species across the landscape and the ecological processes of which they are a part will require a realization on the part of forest managers that CWD provides food, shelter, protection, cover, substrate or climate amelioration for many species. Protected areas alone will not prevent extinctions in the next 50 years (Sinclair et al. 1995). Areas of habitat renewal are also critical. Habitat renewal is faster if old forest legacies are left on a site. One of these legacies is coarse woody debris.

Role in Geomorphology

The physical properties of large pieces of wood are important to soil and stream geomorphology. Coarse woody debris contributes to:
- slope stability;
- surface soil stability, prevention of erosion and control of storm surface runoff;
- large woody debris loads in streams.

Particularly where there is a significant slope, CWD may play a role in soil stabilization, controlling the flow of water, soil and litter across the surface of the ground. Material in any decay class, lying across the slope, will reduce soil movement downslope. Larger pieces collect more material on their upslope side, creating a substrate for invertebrate and small mammal burrowing (Maser et al. 1988). Many

Habitat renewal is faster if old forest legacies are left on a site. One of these legacies is coarse woody debris.

studies have documented the important role of CWD in the geomorphology of stream ecosystems (see Gregory and Ashkenas 1990).

Role in Long-term Carbon Storage

Next to fossil fuel burning, the most critical factor in the increase of CO_2 in the atmosphere is the reduction in carbon storage (Harmon et al. 1990). The conversion of old-growth forest to young forest increases the CO_2 released despite the greater uptake of carbon in the young forest because of the reduced storage capacity of the young forest. In some Douglas fir and western hemlock ecosystems, the detrital components (coarse woody debris + soil organic matter) of the forest store 25-30% of the total carbon in the forest (Harmon et al. 1990). Carbon storage is more important in ecosystems with infrequent catastrophic disturbance regimes. The frequent fires and lower productivity of dry and boreal forests keep their carbon storage capacities lower than coastal ecosystems on a per area basis.

Long-term carbon storage is affected by the removal of material from the forest only if after removal the carbon is released more quickly than in the decay cycle. Carbon is slowly released by CWD as it decays in the forest. For large decay-resistant pieces, this can take several hundred to more than a thousand years. Wood that is removed from the forest is made into pulp or lumber. Pulp is often a short-term use and therefore cannot be considered carbon storage. If the pulp-derived products go to landfills, they can be stored for a very long time. Recycling paper products can also extend the storage time of pulp-derived products. Under current practices, lumber-grade wood removed from the forest is depleted of carbon in 50 to 100 years (Figure 1).

Figure 1

Carbon retention curves for three forest product categories and for forest products discarded in landfills.

(from Kurz et al. 1992, p. 33)

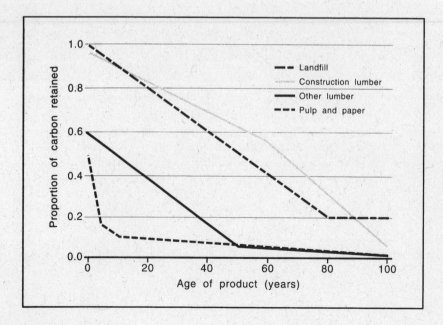

LIFE HISTORY OF COARSE WOODY DEBRIS IN FORESTS

This section describes the fundamental input and decay processes involved in coarse woody debris dynamics. To assist in understanding these processes, a brief outline of the physical and chemical properties of wood and how they change through decomposition is included. This leads to the obvious role played by wildlife tree management in the management of CWD.

Physical and Chemical Properties of Wood (from S. Taylor, pers. comm.)

- Wood is composed principally of organic polymers: primarily cellulose (40-50%), hemicellulose (20-35%) and lignin (15-35%); secondary components include tannins, oils, and resins.
- Wood has a relatively low mineral nutrient content compared to leaf (needle) litter except for calcium.
- Most animals can't break down the complex organic molecules in plant litter. Some animals such as termites have protozoa in their gut that can break down wood.
- Fungi are the primary decomposers of wood as they can produce cellulase and lignase.

Input of CWD (modified from Harmon et al. 1986)

CWD comes from large branches, treetops and whole trees that fall to the forest floor. The following agents are responsible either alone or in concert:

- wind — Both strong winds and more chronic small-scale disturbances cause tree damage (broken branches and tops) and stem breakage. This varies with soil depth and moisture content, geographic location, location in a stand, aspect, and tree species. Often wind is the final agent causing a wildlife tree to fall to the ground and become CWD. The original damage to the tree could have been any of the agents below or a combination of them.
- fire — Fire creates CWD directly or by making trees more susceptible to wind, disease, or insect damage.
- insects — Insects can cause tree death directly or weaken a tree, contributing to its death and eventual fall to the forest floor.
- disease — Tree diseases are usually caused by fungi, but parasitic vascular plants and abiotic diseases (e.g. acid rain) are also contributors to tree death.
- suppression and competition — During the course of stand development, stand density is reduced by competition, or self-thinning. Trees that exhibit slow growth are susceptible to insects and disease. These trees are typically small in diameter and remain standing until blown down by wind.
- slope failure — Trees may fall due to landslides or erosion of surrounding soil by streams. This is often the cause of input of large organic debris into streams.

- senescence — Old age may contribute to the susceptibility of a tree to insects, disease and/or wind.

These influences on CWD input vary enormously in time and space.

Decay of CWD (from Harmon et al. 1986)

Decay occurs in many ways. The following have been identified:

- leaching — Leaching (water percolating through the log) dissolves soluble materials. It is less important in early decay classes as most of the material in these classes is not soluble. As the decay process proceeds, decomposers change the polymers into soluble material and leaching becomes more important. In addition, as fragmentation begins in later decay classes, the importance of leaching increases as the surface to volume ratio increases.
- fragmentation — Fragmentation is the breaking up of CWD into smaller particles. This occurs as insects chew the wood; as vertebrates forage for insects in decaying wood; when partially or fully decayed snags fall; when decayed wood is disturbed by falling plants, wind, rain; or other physical disturbances. It is a significant source of decayed wood in forest soils. Little and Ohmann (1988) found that the forest floor in Douglas fir/western hemlock forests was 5-70% decayed wood, Keenan et al. (1993) reported that in the forests of northern Vancouver Island, 60% of the forest floor mass was decaying wood (including fragmented and coarse woody debris).
- transport — Transport occurs when material is transported out of an ecosystem by falling down a hill or being carried away in a stream. This varies in importance to an ecosystem depending on the steepness of the slope and the proximity to a stream.
- collapse and settling — As a tree decays, the internal structure becomes weak and settling occurs. This usually increases the contact of a log with the ground. At the soil-log interface there is likely increased moisture retention and access for microbes, invertebrates and vertebrates.
- seasoning — Seasoning refers to a series of changes including a decrease in moisture, shrinkage and the formation of cracks that increase access to microbes. Initially it can harden the outside of a log and reduce its susceptibility to fragmentation and interior moisture losses.
- respiration — Respiration by organisms in down wood reduces CWD mass by converting the carbon in the dead wood to CO_2.
- biological transformation — Biological transformations are the metabolic transformation of woody material, e.g. to invertebrates or fungi. This process begins in the first few years the logs are down. In an ongoing, 200-year experiment in Oregon, Harmon et al. (1994) found that mushrooms growing on down wood after one year on the ground were many times higher in nutrient content than the original concentration in the log. This

bioconcentration removes the nutrients from the logs and adds it to the available nutrients in the ecosystem.

Relationship of size to decay rate

Decay rate is very fast for fine materials. Other factors being equal, decay rate decreases rapidly with increasing size until the piece is about 20 cm (7.9") in diameter. At this size, the decay rate decreases at a much slower rate (M. Harmon pers. comm.). The rates at which these processes occur are variable between ecosystems and between species, depending on temperature, moisture and stand history.

Comparison of CWD input and decay patterns in two natural disturbance regimes

Ecosystems with rare stand-initiating events (250- to 350-year mean fire return interval)

These ecosystems have the most infrequent stand-level disturbance events in North America. In some areas the frequency is so low that a forest can be completely replaced when single to multitree gaps are created by trees falling before a stand-level disturbance occurs (Lertzman et al. 1996). These forests are characterized by large volumes of CWD of large size with the highest input rates in North America (Caza 1993). Some large pieces can be part of the ecosystem for more than 1,200 years (Daniels et al. In prep.).

Coarse woody debris
Victoria Stevens

Most measurable canopy or tree attributes of a stand (tree height, canopy cover) begin with low values after a stand-initiating disturbance, but CWD begins at its highest value after such an event. Over the next several decades the CWD decays while the trees grow, but there is little input of CWD (Harmon 1993). Gradually, the forest reaches a steady state (decay rate = input rate), where it remains until the next major disturbance.

Gaps are created when trees die or fall. This results in input of CWD to the system immediately or after some delay. In a study on the west coast of Vancouver Island, canopy gaps were created by three mechanisms—stem snapping (42.6%), standing dead trees (33%) and uprooting (24.6%) (Lertzman et al. 1996). Stem snapping and uprooting add CWD to the system immediately (67% of the tree mortality). The remaining 33% of the trees go through a wildlife tree (snag) stage before falling, in some state of decay, to the forest floor.

Input rates vary widely during the life of a stand. Generally, the stand begins with a large input of CWD and then the input rate drops to near zero for many decades. As the trees grow and suppression and competition begin to cause some tree mortality, the input rate increases. The larger diameter trees of older stands add more to the volume upon falling than the smaller trees of younger stands. Input rates have been reported from 2.4 - 7 m³/ha/year (6.6-19 y³/acre/year) in old-growth ecosystems in Oregon and Washington (*Pseudotsuga menziesii and Pseudotsuga menziesii - Tsuga heterophylla*). Unfortunately, the sampling periods, which ranged from 2 - 36 years, are not long enough to give a true picture of total input over a stand's history. However, it is a snapshot of the input during the period of time during which it is assumed that the total CWD (input + decay) is in stasis.

Flying squirrel, fungi and coarse woody debris are interdependent
Jerry Valen DeMarco

Much of the research on decay rates has been conducted in the ecosystems on the west side of the Cascade Mountains of Oregon and Washington. Decay rates are variable for different decay processes (e.g. fragmentation, transformation, respiration), for different parts of a log (e.g. bark, sapwood, heartwood), for different site conditions (e.g. temperature and moisture) and for different species. Temperature has a dramatic effect on decay rates. In a study in Sweden, birch logs decomposed 2-4 times faster in southern Sweden than in northern Sweden where it is colder (Tamminen 1979 in Samuelsson et al. 1994). Keenan et al. (1993) hypothesize that the cool temperatures on northern Vancouver Island cause slow decay rates, which contribute to the high level of woody debris in those forests.

Ecosystems with frequent stand-maintaining fires (surface fire return interval 4 - 50 years)

In the absence of human fire suppression activities, the CWD in this natural disturbance regime is kept low by frequent fires which may leave the canopy intact. The low intensity of these surface fires would leave large pieces of CWD in the early decay stages. Later stages (4 and 5) would burn readily. The result is lower volumes of soil wood, little fine material and few large pieces of CWD. Occasional canopy fires would result in small pulses of input at irregular intervals.

Link Between Wildlife Tree Management and CWD Management

Management for CWD needs to go beyond simply considering the volume of CWD. During the life of a natural stand, there is CWD input so that a mix of decay classes is present in a stand, and the CWD volume rarely, if ever, drops to zero. Input is often caused by a previously damaged tree (a wildlife tree) falling in the wind. Integrating wildlife tree needs with those for CWD creates a more dynamic system with CWD input during the course of a forest stand's history. The two extreme examples of CWD input and decay described in the natural disturbance regimes above demonstrate the importance of the ecosystem approach inherent in ecoforestry for managing green tree retention, wildlife tree retention and CWD retention to mimic the patterns found in the appropriate natural disturbance type.

CONCLUSIONS

Trees that are removed from the forest cannot fulfil their role in the decay cycle; however, between the extreme cases of clearcutting followed by burning, and no removal, there is an infinite array of scenarios that leave differing levels of wood in the forest. Natural levels are not possible if material is removed from a forest for human use; however, the more that managed forests resemble the forests that were established from natural disturbances, the greater the probability that all native species and ecological processes will be maintained. Natural levels themselves are extremely variable and will therefore allow for variability in recommendations and variability through time.

10

Water and Connectivity

Herb Hammond

CONNECTIVITY

HUMAN BEINGS HAVE A HEART, LUNGS, A BRAIN. A forest has trees, water, and bacteria. However, without elaborate and unpredictable connections between all parts, there is neither a human being nor a forest. Forests cannot be assembled or disassembled like a Lego set. The connectivity or wholism of living organisms, of living forest systems, cannot be described through the linear scientific method. However, as Forman points out, connectivity is responsible for functioning natural systems: "An ecosystem not only provides objects that affect neighboring ecosystems, but in a real sense is moulded and controlled by the accumulation of objects arriving from the surroundings" (Forman 1987).

Connectivity is one of the foundations of a forest landscape. Landscape connections may be viewed as conduits or channels between various parts of the forest. Conduits are critical spots for biological flows. Diverse patches of habitat (i.e. landscape "compartments") are required, but they are only valuable if they are adequately connected.

Healthy natural landscapes are connected by *riparian zones* (wet forest areas that include the streams, rivers, lakes, wetlands). Riparian zones are arranged in a branching network that extends throughout the landscape, and contain varied, repeating patterns of plant and animal habitat. Because of their wet, diverse nature, riparian zones frequently survive large natural disturbances such as fire and wind.

Riparian zone corridors provide migration routes for large and small animals. Large ungulates such as moose and elk use these corridors as migration routes between seasonable ranges (Harris 1984; Thomas 1979). Plant species also migrate across the landscape via riparian corridors. Mammals and birds are instrumental in moving many plant seeds, and some are carried by water. Thus, plant dispersal routes for many species also tend to follow riparian corridors.

Treed forest "corridors" join riparian zones up and down slopes from valley to valley, riparian zone to riparian zone. These forest corridors provide a means for many animals and plants to move back and forth between riparian zones and other habitat patches.

Groundwater, another forest connector, transports nutrients and energy within forest patches and throughout the forest landscape. These ecosystem flows are concentrated and cycled in riparian forests, where they nourish the greatest and most diverse populations of flora and fauna in most forest ecosystems. Eventually the water, nutrients, and energy are released from the riparian forest into watercourses, which disperse them throughout the landscape.

To function and sustain themselves, forest landscapes must retain these natural biological flow patterns at all levels of organization. This is becoming more critical as events such as global climate change, air and water pollution, and the ever increasing human population put additional pressure on forests and all ecosystems. Blocked or significantly altered water, nutrient, and energy flows can lead to forest ecosystem impoverishment, just as blocked arteries can lead to human system failure. Blocked forest connections also have deleterious effects on both animal and plant populations. Retaining corridors for species to migrate may be necessary to avoid large-scale extinctions (Hunter 1988) and is required for forest health and function (Forman 1987).

Amphibians connect water and shore
Jerry Valen DeMarco

The forest landscape functions on many levels, from millimetres of soil, patches of rocks, and stands of trees to whole watersheds. At any point the forest landscape is a web of forest types shaped by variable disturbances over time. Intricate interactions are necessary to sustain the fungi and the ferns, the bacteria and the beasts, the water and the air, the soil and the forest. As humans, our narrow field of vision and our short time perspective make it difficult to appreciate and understand a whole forest stand, much less a whole forest landscape.

People are challenged to understand, to be able to relate to the time and space of forest landscapes. Forests operate on cycles of 200 years to 2,000 years. If we are lucky, our lives may last 100 years. If our governments are lucky, they last four years. Our corporate institutions function on one-year profit and loss statements. We are one-tenth the height of a short tree. More than 40 people would have to stand on each other's shoulders to reach the top of a moderately tall Sitka spruce tree. The person at the top would only be able to see more tree tops, not whole forests. A moderate-sized watershed (e.g. 500 hectares or 1,235 acres) would require months for two people to explore, to map, and to begin to understand the relationships within this landscape.

Our hopes for survival and the survival of forests are inextricably linked with our ability to appreciate and accommodate the vast differences in scale between people and forest landscapes. We are the only organism who ever wanted to dramatically change the forest landscape, and the changes we have made now threaten the survival of the forest itself. It is time to find our place with the landscape network...to think like the forest.

Water is the Connector

Water is life. All living organisms are made up of more than 75% water (King 1961). Clean, clear water cycling through the environment is necessary for the survival of not only forest ecosystems but also the global ecosystem.

Water connects all aspects of a forest. Water from snow melt or rain seeps into the soil and moves through it, or runs along the soil surface until it joins an exposed water table such as a creek. The creek in turn joins other creeks, winding through lakes, streams, and ever larger rivers until the water reaches the ocean.

Plants use water from the atmosphere and soil for cooling, for photosynthesis, and for other growth processes. Water bears the minerals and nutrients from the soil, needed by plants (and animals) to function. Through its leaves, a plant pumps out a significant portion of the water it uses. This water vapor cools the environment and eventually finds its way back into the soil through precipitation. By eating plants, animals acquire the benefits of water used in photosynthesis. Water is also directly consumed by animals from both water bodies and the soil. What is in the water is everything.

A forest acts as a sponge and filter that slowly releases pure water through the soil, into the creeks, and into the atmosphere. Roots from plants (particularly trees), large decaying fallen trees, and soil-organic material hold water for slow, steady release throughout the year. During a storm, millions of litres of water fall on a forest from a great height. The forest absorbs this energy and releases it, one drop at a time. The forest canopy slows the force of water to maintain order and balance. In places where forests have been removed, this buffering effect is lost, and the energy of the falling water is released immediately during a storm. Large-scale landslides and floods are often the result.

Large or small valleys that are collection basins for water are called watersheds. Each watershed is technically composed of an infinite number of smaller watersheds. Each gully, no matter how small, is a watershed. The whole world is one large watershed.

All water required by the people of Canada for home, agricultural, and industrial use is supplied by forested watersheds, either directly through streams, rivers, and reservoirs, or indirectly through groundwater which originates in today's forests or

Forests cannot be assembled or disassembled like a Lego set.

forests of long ago. Humans depend upon maintaining the quality, quantity, and timing of flow (availability throughout the year) of water from watersheds. Protecting our water supplies is in large part done through protecting forests. The highest quality water comes from forests; the older the forest, the better the water (Franklin 1990).

Because water is the connector, we must always consider the downstream effects of all events in a watershed or a forest. The water in small streams or small watersheds may contain no fish. However, the habitat and health of fish in larger rivers or larger watersheds depends upon the health of the small streams that flow into the larger river system. Events occurring on an upper slope in a watershed will affect lower slopes, groundwater movement, and surface water movement connected to that slope. Disruptions in a forested watershed are not isolated, compartmentalized events. They have far-reaching effects, which stretch along the path followed by the water from that forest to the ocean.

Water was here before forests. Water is everywhere within a forest. May it always be fit to drink.

A SPIRITUAL SOURCE

Water in all its forms in the forest
Bo Martin

Anyone who has ever walked in a forest, particularly an old forest, senses a calm and inner peace transmitted by the forest web, an atmosphere not found in human-created environments.

Dr. Wangari Maathai, an African scientist, offers important insight into our current relationship with trees, with forests: "If we lived a life that valued and protected trees, it would be life that also valued and protected us, and gave us great joy. A way of life that kills trees, our present way of life, kills us too, body and soul" (Vittachi 1989).

People who live in forests often prefer this "home" for inexplicable reasons. People who visit forests want to stay there. People who may never visit forests are glad natural old forests exist and feel a personal need for forests.

A Gallup poll published August 31, 1987, shortly after the creation of the national park reserve in South Moresby, B.C., found that 95% of all Canadians favor government expenditures to preserve wilderness areas. This result indicates the priority that people, many of whom may never visit an old-growth forest, place on the protection of our forest heritage. I believe this priority reflects our spiritual bond to forests.

11

Driftwood and How Forestry Affects the Ocean

Chris Maser and James R. Sedell

WE BOTH GREW UP IN OREGON and over the years spent considerable time at the ocean. As boys we remembered the huge piles of driftwood along the beaches, piles that seemed to grow with each winter storm. In fact, one of the challenges of even getting to the sandy shores of the Pacific was having to climb over the jumbled mountains of driftwood. There was so much wood, ranging from small branches to boards to whole trees, that we could build shelters from the wind that easily held fifteen or more people. Enormous piles of driftwood were simply part of the beach, a part we took as much for granted in our growing up as clean air.

Then we were grown and, suddenly, the driftwood mountains were gone. Where'd they go? What happened to them? When did they disappear and why? How could the mountains of driftwood we so clearly remember have vanished without our noticing?

Driftwood, wood carried by water from the forest to the sea, is a critically important source of habitat and food for the marine ecosystem, including the deep-sea floor. But even on its seaward journey, driftwood is habitat and a source of food for a multitude of plants and animals, both aquatic and terrestrial. In addition, some driftwood controls stream velocities, stabilizes stream banks, makes waterfalls and pools, and creates and protects fish spawning areas. Other driftwood protects vegetation's encroachment on floodplains and allows forests to expand. In short, driftwood is a vital contribution in sustaining the health of streams, rivers, estuaries, and oceans, not just in the Pacific Northwest, but worldwide.

Nature's processes through which wood disappears from streams and rivers have positive effects on the ecosystem. Human activities, on the other hand, such as cleaning wood out of streams, logging, and firewood cutting have had negative effects over the last several decades. And yet the consequences of our decisions and actions are both little understood and far-reaching.

Streams historically replenished annual supplies of driftwood to the lower portions of river basins and out into the sea where it washed up on beaches. But the banks of lower rivers and estuaries—the riparian corridor—probably were the common source of large driftwood in the bays.

Substantial amounts of driftwood must have been transported to the sea at the time when most riparian zones were dominated by such large coniferous trees as Douglas firs, western red cedar, and Sitka spruce, and such deciduous trees as black cottonwood, big-leaf maple, Oregon ash, and red alder. Hundreds of millions of board feet of logs and driftwood have entered Puget Sound and Georgia Strait from the rivers draining the Cascade Mountains of Washington and the coastal mountains of British Columbia. They were joined by large numbers of "escapees" from log rafts. Over ten billion board feet of logs are annually stored or travel in the estuaries and the lower segments of rivers in the Pacific Northwest. A one percent escape rate would allow over a hundred million board feet of driftwood to enter the ocean from this source alone.

One can estimate conservatively that in days past as much as two billion board feet of wood per year was transported to the sea. Two billion board feet per year is a small amount when prorated across the entire North Pacific. Large driftwood, an important ecological component of Pacific Northwest streams and rivers, interfered with human objectives, however, and was summarily removed. In fact, people throughout North America have systematically cleaned driftwood from streams and rivers for over 150 years.

From the 1800s to around 1915, streams and small rivers were cleaned of driftwood so that logs could be floated from the forests to the mills. Many streams had several "splash dams" built on them to temporarily augment the flow of water in order to float logs to mills. The net effect of channel clearance and splash damming was to remove large quantities of driftwood from medium and large streams, a significant change from the conditions that formerly existed.

Over the last hundred years, millions of drifted trees and other driftwood have been cleared out of streams and rivers to facilitate navigation and reduce flooding. To this end, streams and rivers have been channelized and dammed and marshes have been drained. In addition, most streambanks have been so altered through logging that they now have dramatically smaller and younger trees of different species than in times past.

Most big western red cedars and Douglas firs have been logged along Cascade Mountain streams and along coastal streams greater than third-order. On private land, more than 70 percent of the coniferous trees greater than 14 inches (36 cm) in diameter at breast height have been logged within a hundred feet of fish-bearing streams.

Driftwood on saltwater beach
Victoria Stevens

Before the great ecological value of driftwood was known, West Coast fishery managers believed that driftwood in streams restricted fish passage, supplied material for driftwood jams, and caused channels to scour during floods. Indeed, during times of flooding such fears might have seemed to be well-founded, but we know now that results of stream cleaning have been ecologically disastrous.

It's now apparent that neither we nor the generations of the future can afford the effects of the loss of driftwood that connects the forest to the sea and the sea to the forest. The loss of driftwood means the destabilization of streams, rivers, estuaries, complexes of sand dunes, beaches, and sand spits, as well as food chains in the oceans of the world, and sooner or later it will mean the loss of such jobs and unique cultural ways of life as commercial fishing because such fish as tuna and salmon both benefit from driftwood during various stages of their life cycles.

Nevertheless, we're still preventing driftwood from even beginning its journey to the ocean by removing as much wood as possible from the forests as a product for human consumption, lest it remain as an "economic waste." Then, by damming rivers, we're preventing what little driftwood even begins its journey from completing it. We've thus severed the connection of the forest to the sea.

Even today, county sheriffs, port commissions, and recreational boaters still routinely clear driftwood from rivers for safety and for personal convenience. As a result, most Pacific Northwest streams and rivers bear little resemblance to their ancestral conditions when they flowed freely through pristine forests carrying their gift of driftwood to the sea.

Consequently, the supply of driftwood for food on the bottom of the sea off the coast of North America is both dwindling and becoming more erratic. For the first time in the evolutionary history of deep-sea animals, the availability of food has become unpredictable.

And if the coastal mangrove forests continue to be destroyed through deforestation, the last direct link of the forest with the sea will be severed. Then the deep-sea wood-dependent species of the world will shrink in both numbers and areas they inhabit and some will become extinct. What does it mean to an ocean's health for its species to become extinct either from an area or from life itself?

Today, we're substituting for driftwood in the ocean and on beaches such non-wooden human garbage as: metal, glass, rubber, plastic, oil, bilge, chemical effluents, medical and household wastes, and raw human sewage, none of which can replace nature's gift of driftwood.

We're thus facing grave, uncomfortable uncertainties through our decisions concerning such renewable resources as driftwood, because we're giving economics and technology higher priority than we're according scientific understanding and spirituality. If we want healthy oceans from which to reap social benefits, we must incorporate a renewable supply of driftwood, including whole trees, into our land-use planning, especially forestry.

> **Neither we nor the generations of the future can afford the effects of the loss of driftwood that connects the forest to the sea and the sea to the forest.**

12

Fire in Our Future

James Agee

THE BOOK *FIRE ECOLOGY IN PACIFIC NORTHWEST FORESTS* has scientifically documented the historic role of fire in Pacific Northwest forests. This chapter places that information in the real world, a world of conflicting values, a playing field on which the scientist has no inherent advantage. Forest fires will occur in the wildlands of our West, from human and natural origin. Fire origin or presence is less relevant than whether that presence helps achieve ecosystem goals. The progression of knowledge about forests and fire has provided some advantages that were not available in the past. More than 50 years ago, the rudimentary science of fire allowed eminent ecologist Frederic Clements (1935, p. 344) to state: "Under primitive conditions, the great [vegetation] climaxes of the globe must have remained essentially intact, since fires from natural causes must have been both relatively infrequent and localized."

Our knowledge has expanded, but so has the complexity of society and the decisions society attempts to make. Knowing more about fire does not directly lead us to a strategy for management; in fact, it makes management strategies more complex. We know that a variety of fire regimes existed on the pre-European landscapes of the Pacific Northwest, and we know in general terms how we have changed species composition and structure by our management practices. Consensus on fire management, however, requires the incorporation of human values, and most past fire management policies have been derived from the view of fire only as a threat, rather than from a broader perspective of values evident in today's society.

We also know that institutions tend to focus on short-term operational objectives, because such actions are easily visualized and achievable. The best example is our attempt in the 20th century to minimize the area burned by wildfire. Because of the threat that fire posed to forest management in the early 20th century, all land management institutions sought to erase it from the landscape. Ecological roles of fire were ignored, and criteria for economic efficiency were rarely applied.

The short-term result was successful: the enemy was fire, and we conquered it...we thought. Our institutions became so effective at presenting fire as the enemy that they exacerbated the problem they were attempting to solve.

The area burned by wildfire in the West since the 1920s continuously declined into the 1960s. Yet a disturbing U-shaped trend is evident in these data and similar data from Canada (Flannigan and Van Wagner 1991). A simple projection into the future from these data suggests an increasing wildfire problem. Such projections may also be too simplistic without a clear understanding of the possible reasons for recent increases and what might be done to avert a continued problem.

One possible reason for recent increases in area burned in the western United States is that natural fire programs since about 1970 have allowed some fires to grow as "management fires" which, under old policies, would have been suppressed when small. As weather conditions change, these management fires occasionally become too large or too intense to remain in "prescription." When they are reclassified as wildfires, the total area burned is added to the wildfire statistics. Without the natural fire policy, the area increase in recent years might not be so significant, but the increases would still be there (and they are present in the Canadian statistics, too). Only the peaks of the area burned in recent years would be trimmed.

A second possible explanation for the shape of the curve might be long-term climate shifts: drought in the 1920s and 1930s associated with big fire years, cooler weather in the 1940s and 1950s, and some unusual strings of drought years in recent decades associated again with big fires. Climate has not been established as the cause of recent increases in burned area, although it is likely the primary cause of the second-order year-to-year blips. A third reason, linked with fire severity as well as fire size, is the buildup of fuel hazards we have fostered through fire exclusion policies. Without fire acting as an agent of decomposition, litter has built up, tree density has increased, and fuel continuity, both vertically and horizontally, is greater than historically. Fires that occur in such fuels are more intense and more difficult to control, even as fire control technology improves. This effect is most pronounced in fire regimes of low to moderate severity, where increased fire area is now burned primarily by high-severity fires. The more successful we are at fire control, the worse the problem becomes: a seemingly insoluble problem if we do not look beyond the short-term objectives.

The lesson learned by renewable natural resources managers is to repeatedly check short-term objectives against long-term goals, continually framing and reframing the objectives in terms of the goals. For example, minimizing area burned is best interpreted as a short-term objective leading to a goal, rather than as a goal in itself, as it was in the past. Wildland management strategies are constrained by the fact that natural resources management is an experiment; natural systems cannot be tuned like an automobile. A natural resources manager dealing with fire must contend with additional uncertainty about the characteristics of fire (Will it stay

> Our institutions became so effective at presenting fire as the enemy that they exacerbated the problem they were attempting to solve.

within certain bounds? Will its intensity change with shifts in weather?) as well as uncertainty about how the ecosystem will react. This uncertainty is higher than with any other silvicultural option available to the manager. This is a major reason why in the past fire was not more widely applied as a management tool.

A MANAGEMENT FRAMEWORK

The *adaptive management* and *ecosystem management* approaches have considerable value in dealing with an uncertain biological world in a rapidly changing social context. Too often, however, they are viewed as goal-oriented systems rather than process-oriented means of achieving goals. Adaptive management is a system by which experimental techniques can be applied to approach elusive and often changing goals (Walters 1986). Ecosystem management is a framework within which adaptive management can function (Agee and Johnson 1988). Both are value-neutral, so they deal not with setting goals but with achieving them. In contrast, the USDA (United States Department of Agriculture) Forest Service's recent embrace of "ecosystem management" is primarily goal-oriented, and although perhaps quite appropriate, is used in a different context than it is in this essay.

The ecosystem, simply put, is any part of the universe around which a line is drawn, with the line being a "permeable membrane" through which many things pass: people, animals, plant seeds, and so forth. Ecosystems are temporally variable, suggesting that the form of a problem and its solution may be different in the future than today. Ecosystems are spatially variable, suggesting that the nature of the problem and its solution will vary across the landscape at any point in time. Ecosystems include people, so an ecosystem management approach incorporates socioeconomic values as a component (but these values do not necessarily have priority over the biocentric values). Different ecosystem components have different boundaries, implying a set of overlapping and interacting systems to challenge the land manager. The permeable membrane concept implies that few problems or solutions will be self-contained within a political boundary.

Implications for resources management flow from these basic properties (Holling 1978, Agee and Johnson 1988). The first is that ecosystems are constantly changing. Even apparently stable fire regimes, such as those in Ponderosa pine forests, were maintained by a cyclic repetition of low-severity fire. The second is that cause and effect may be spatially heterogeneous: smoke from a forest fire may not be a problem in a stand directly upwind from the fire, but it may be a significant nuisance in a town 10 km downwind. A third implication is that ecosystems may exhibit several levels of stable behavior. An ecological progression over time may not be capable of reversal; although this has been documented mainly for alien plant invasions, it may also be true of past ecosystem states that we define as desirable. For example, once fuels have built up around shallow-rooted, old-growth Ponderosa pine, can even low-intensity fire be used to restore natural fuel loads and still keep the pines alive? A fourth implication is that although there are organized connections between parts, not everything is connected to everything else. We should not be paralyzed by complexity, but we must not ignore it, either.

Ecosystem management involves regulating internal ecosystem structure and function, plus inputs and outputs, to achieve socially desirable conditions (Agee and Johnson 1988). It is a process of understanding ecosystem components (including people) and interactions. It neither defines the desirable conditions nor constrains actions to achieve those conditions. Similarly, adaptive management is an iterative approach to managing uncertainty in both biological and social components of the ecosystem (Walters 1986). A successful approach to resources management requires a four-stage strategy (Agee and Johnson 1988):

1. Have well-defined goals.
2. Define the ecosystem boundaries for primary components.
3. Adopt a management strategy to achieve these goals.
4. Monitor the effectiveness of the management strategies.

The iterative nature of this approach implies that either management strategies or goals may change over time. Both flexibility and accountability must be maintained in the process, so that continually shifting goals do not result in a lack of responsibility or accountability for actions.

In the remainder of this chapter I apply these concepts to several land management challenges in which fire will play an important role. These include park and wilderness management; New Forestry; preservation of the northern spotted owl; forest health in the eastern Cascades; and global warming.

PARK AND WILDERNESS MANAGEMENT

National park and wilderness managers face dual mandates: preservation of nature and the enjoyment/experience of these resources by present and future generations of people. I assume that present and future generations of people will be served well by efforts to "preserve nature." Much of my book *Fire Ecology* describes the interaction of fire in natural ecosystems; if we know how disturbance once interacted with these systems, is the maintenance of that process of disturbance sufficient? In the case of many other types of disturbances, the answer is simple because we are powerless. We did not have to suspend the "let it blow" policy after the Everglades hurricane of 1992. We do not suspend the "let it grind" policy of glaciers, or the "let it erupt" policy for Kilauea or Mount St. Helens. But the human relationship with fire is unique: we can and do control, within limits, a "let it burn" policy. Furthermore, we have an ethical responsibility to do so when in society's interest, and this is rarely true for most other natural disturbances that have catastrophic potential.

Our nature preserves, as thrilling and wonderful as they are, are not truly natural systems any more, unconstrained by the bounds of society. Few of these systems are large enough that fire can run free in the forest; the 1988 Yellowstone fires, in the largest nature preserve in the lower 48 states, provide ample evidence of this. Both the flames and their smoke may affect adjacent or distant communities. Further, the "natural" system may have had a significant component of native American ignitions; are these considered natural? Without such ignitions, the structure of the system may be different than with them. This is a social decision, but its resolution has a significant impact on nature. Moreover, there are multiple objectives beyond the scale of the individual park or wilderness, for example, air quality (particularly regional haze) and endangered species legislation. These may place constraints either on ecosystem outputs or on ecosystem states (such as old growth) in the presence of fire.

Fire is in some respects like a spirit in a bottle, but we do not always know whether it is a genie or a demon. It always promises excitement and may result in great fascination and satisfaction; it may also cause death and horror, to humans as well as to other animals and plants (Maclean 1992). We can choose, at least to some degree, the role fire plays as a natural disturbance factor in wildlands, yet how can we choose to control a factor of nature? Stephen Pyne's (1989b) article, "The Summer We Let Wildfire Loose" captures this paradox: We cannot evade the human imprint in parks and wilderness.

Under what conditions may we let the spirit out of the bottle? We must first define our ecosystem goals, outlined by legislation for parks and wilderness, for air quality, for endangered species, and for historic preservation, among other goals. Some of these conflict with one another: the [U.S.] Wilderness Act demands that natural forces be allowed to act "untrammeled" by humans, yet that may be in direct conflict with other types of legislation. Many of the conflicts can be resolved by applying spatial and temporal limits to fire: avoiding historic structures, or not burning during severe atmospheric inversions, conditions that do not universally apply across space and time. Such constraints may, however, result in severe hits to fire as a natural process.

Even with nature as a sole constraint, we cannot agree on appropriate fire management goals (Agee and Huff 1986). Significant controversy has arisen over whether fire should be reintroduced as a *process* or to achieve objectives defined in terms of *structure* for park and wilderness ecosystems (Bonnicksen 1985, Bancroft et al. 1985). Are we mainly interested in re-creating the natural fire regime, or do we want the vegetation and other structural ecosystem components that a natural fire regime should have produced?

Process-related goals are often most applicable to high severity fire regimes, particularly those that have not been significantly affected by fire exclusion policies. In large reserves with little edge effect, reintroduction of most naturally occurring fires may be sufficient to achieve the objective. Where large edge effects occur—for example, the absence of natural fires moving into the reserve from outside as they did

> **Fire is in some respects like a spirit in a bottle, but we do not always know whether it is a genie or a demon.**

historically—prescribed fires might be substituted in a process-oriented framework.

Structure can be defined in terms of individual stand architecture or at the large scale of the patches that make up a landscape. Structural goals have been recommended most often in low-severity fire regimes with small patch sizes, where individual trees or groups of trees may be selectively affected by burning. For example, a prescribed fire might be applied to remove all the white fir trees below 10 m (33 ft.) height in a mixed-conifer forest while preserving the larger sugar pine and Ponderosa pine trees. Even in high severity fire regimes, structural goals may be formulated, such as maintaining a certain mix of patches of varying sizes and ages throughout a watershed by limiting natural fire spread or igniting prescribed fire.

National policy for natural fires has become more conservative since 1988. Managers must now certify on a daily basis that they have the ability to control any fire in their reserve, or suppression action must be initiated. The result of this policy will be longer fire-return intervals with a trend toward later successional stages. Our choice is to accept this eventually "unnatural" landscape mosaic or to produce one that might be closer to natural, either by introducing fire ourselves or by creating fuel-limited zones around areas in which natural fires will be allowed to burn under prescription. This should increase the window of "ability to control" and increase the confidence of managers to allow more natural ignitions to burn. In park and wilderness fire management, we are faced with Hobson's choice, since none of the alternatives are truly natural.

This realization in fact frees us from the dilemma of defining *natural*. We know that today's landscapes are different from those of distant millennia, and we know that a variety of future natural landscape configurations is possible, although some may be more desirable than others (Christensen et al. 1989, Sprugel 1991). Human intervention and manipulation will be necessary to preserve the natural processes, and knowledge of natural fire regimes will help in the definition of acceptable envelopes of natural ecological conditions in the park and wilderness areas of the West.

NEW FORESTRY

New Forestry is an attempt to incorporate ecological values with commodity (timber) production. Such an approach offers an alternative to what has become a traditional emphasis on timber production on public lands, particularly those managed by the USDA Forest Service. The principles and practices (Hopwood 1991) and the scientific basis (Franklin 1992) of New Forestry suggest that much of the rationale has evolved from experiences in the western Cascades area of Washington and Oregon. These forests have high-severity fire regimes, grading to moderate severity on drier landscapes of this subregion. Application of New Forestry principles to other areas should be done by adapting these principles as necessary rather than by adopting them wholesale.

The scientific basis for New Forestry rests on the examination of natural forests and streams as ecosystems (Franklin 1992). An underlying assumption is that the suite of natural forests we inherited had many of the biodiversity characteristics we wish to maintain in the future: viable populations of animals, or the structural diversity of forests. Maintaining biological diversity may depend on maintaining a mosaic of patches of different successional stages and making the transition between them less abrupt.

Older forest as described in much New Forestry literature is usually the most structurally diverse, with large live trees, large snags, large downed logs, and a multilayered understory. These features are characteristic of the natural old-growth forests of the *Tsuga heterophylla* zone and perhaps some of the *Abies amabilis* zone, but certainly not of Ponderosa pine or many mixed-conifer forests, because those natural old-growth forests developed with much more frequent and low-severity fire. These drier forests had more open understories, fewer down logs, and possibly fewer snags.

The concept of biological legacies—living and dead organic materials that are carried over into new stands after disturbance—may be relevant to biodiversity. Sometimes, however, this paradigm conflicts with what we know about natural

Controlled burn
B.C. Forest Service,
Photo Archives

forests. For example, Franklin (1992) notes that most natural disturbances, whether wind or fire, leave behind a significant component of green trees as well as a legacy of snags and logs. Franklin's intent is to suggest that by maintaining structural complexity during a harvest operation, desirable postlogging structural complexity may be restored in a much shorter period of time (80 years) than if the forest is left to recover after clearcutting. Yet natural fire has not always left a significant component of green trees on the landscape in the *Tsuga heterophylla* or *Abies amabilis* zones. Where it has left significant overstory in drier forests, logs on the forest floor may have been consumed on a regular basis. Nature, therefore, may not be the best guide. Rather, the identification or maintenance of desirable structures to achieve ecosystem objectives is preferable. This may mean, in a New Forestry concept, that significant green trees should be left in a natural fire regime where postfire green trees were historically rare or absent. It may mean that downed logs should be preserved where once they were less abundant.

The "natural forest" paradigm around which much of New Forestry is implicitly organized is less a meaningful guide than a definitive identification of desirable ecosystem character, whether or not it is natural. Understanding the natural system is essential to managing it. But using the patterns of the past, even when correctly interpreted, as a narrow guide to the future is far too constraining. We must *adapt* mimics of natural pattern if we are to be successful in the future. New Forestry has much to offer if it is more than natural forestry.

The northern spotted owl (*Strix occidentalis caurina*), one of the best-known owls in the world, was listed as a "threatened" species under the Endangered Species Act in June 1990. The primary threat to the owl is the fragmentation of its habitat in forests of Washington, Oregon, and northern California. It typically uses old-growth forests and other forests with similar characteristics for nesting, breeding, and rearing young. As of late 1992, a draft recovery plan for the northern spotted owl was in circulation, proposing 196 designated conservation areas (DCAs) over 3 million ha (7,412,898 acres) of federal forestland in the region. The DCAs include currently suitable owl habitat plus younger forest that may mature into suitable habitat. Each DCA is intended to provide habitat for at least 20 owl pairs. Federal lands between DCAs (called matrix lands) will be managed under a 50-11-40 rule (50 percent of the landscape must be covered by forest averaging 11 inches [28 cm] dbh with 40 percent average cover).

The plan is designed to provide suitable habitat so that viable populations of owls will persist into the future. Good habitat appears to be associated with older forest that has large live trees, standing snags, downed logs, and multilayered canopies. But the act of breaking up the landscape into a series of adjacent DCA polygons from Washington into northern California makes the implicit assumption that this habitat will remain stable over time. That is, it assumes that owl habitat will be created from young stands within DCAs and maintained in old stands. This requires effective forest protection strategies, which begin with a clear understanding of natural disturbance regimes.

Forest protection strategies for protection of spotted owl habitat were discussed by Agee and Edmonds (1992), and much of the following discussion is summarized from that report, an appendix to the spotted owl recovery plan. They divided the range of the owl into three large subregions: West Cascades, Klamath, and East Cascades, based primarily on characteristics of historical disturbance regimes. Based on these regimes, they rated the risk of common disturbance agents in each subregion.

The West Cascades subregion has the highest probability of a successful fire suppression strategy for DCAs. This subregion receives more precipitation than the other two, and mature to old-growth forests have relatively low potential for surface fire behavior. There is a chance of a large fire complex due to unusual lightning storm/east wind events, but the probability of such an event is low and it is likely to be beyond management control if it occurs. Global climate change, if it creates more lightning or increases fire behavior potential, may alter predicted fire disturbance patterns. An aggressive fire suppression policy is recommended for DCAs of the West

Cascades subregion. This may conflict with park and wilderness management objectives in the subregion, which otherwise might allow some natural fires to burn in old-growth forest.

In the East Cascades and Klamath subregions, fire exclusion has helped create a broader landscape pattern of multiple-canopied stands with thick understories, thought to be suitable for northern spotted owl habitat. It appears that at the same time that clearcutting and fragmentation have reduced owl habitat in these areas, a policy of fire exclusion has helped to increase owl habitat in protected areas. Whether on balance owl habitat has increased or decreased in any local area due to these offsetting factors has not been determined and is irrelevant to future management; what is important is how the existing or potential habitat can be protected into the future. These same two subregions have the highest potential for habitat loss through wildfire. The primary forest protection strategy employed in the recovery plan is to increase the number of DCAs in those areas and provide for the protection of territorial single owls outside DCAs. Given the uniform nature of the problem, this is as effective as adding more dominoes to a closely packed line; it is likely that all will eventually fall unless some are managed under a different strategy. A longer term adaptive management strategy for fire potential will be needed to conserve owl habitat.

Recent experience with large, uncontrolled fire events in the Klamath subregion is likely to continue if a total fire protection strategy is attempted across the whole of this subregion. Such a strategy might be successful in the coastal or high elevation portions of the subregion—the *Sequoia sempervirens* coastal belt, and the *Abies concolor* and *Abies magnifica* zones—but not across the widespread mixed-evergreen and mixed-conifer forests. Through effective fire exclusion, the moderate-severity fire regimes of the past have been replaced with high-severity fire regimes. When fire historically occurred, owl habitat may have been damaged for a decade or two and destroyed for longer times only in limited areas. The wildfires of today, burning in higher fuel loads and more uniform multilayered canopies, have resulted in an increased proportion of stand replacement fire, which will destroy owl habitat. Some sort of fuel management program is recommended to increase landscape diversity relative to fire, so that the potential for catastrophic fire is reduced. Some of the fuel reduction could be integrated with timber removal, but such removal must be planned to achieve owl habitat objectives, with commodity production as a result, rather than an objective.

The East Cascades subregion is at most risk from catastrophic fire effects because of its lower species diversity as compared to the Klamath subregion and the generally frequent fire-return intervals documented in this area. Additionally, forest health problems verge on an epidemic, which increases wildfire potential while at the same time reducing owl habitat. As in the Klamath subregion, fire regimes have been shifted from low-moderate severity to moderate-high severity as a result of effective fire exclusion.

> **Forest health problems verge on an epidemic, which increases wildfire potential while at the same time reducing owl habitat.**

Two types of fuel management strategies are proposed for the Klamath and East Cascades subregions: underburning and fuel breaks. Each addresses different objectives. Understory burning reduces dead fuel loads and vertical fuel continuity within a treatment area. Although this reduces catastrophic fire potential for some time, the elimination of a multilayered understory may result in suboptimum owl habitat at that site, so it should not be done over wide areas of any DCA in the same decade. Where evergreen hardwoods make up the understory, as in the Klamath subregion, regeneration of understory canopy will occur more rapidly than where the understory is composed of conifers (more typical of the East Cascades subregion). Fuel breaks are designed to compartmentalize units by creating a zone of reduced fuel between them, which allows safe access for fire suppression forces during wildfires. Fuel breaks may also allow better containment possibilities for wildfires within given compartments. They are normally installed on ridges and can be visually pleasing if well designed.

> **Paradoxically, owl habitat may have to be reduced to save it.**

Paradoxically, owl habitat may have to be reduced to save it: a cyclic fuel maintenance program will help to protect large areas from stand replacement fire events. The strategies employed will have to be developed for individual DCAs. The efficacy of these treatments, however, has not been well established. The mix of prescribed burning and fuel breaks will have to be experimentally applied to landscapes and monitored over time, with the more successful treatments being applied more widely. This is an example of adaptive management at its best. Replicated treatments will be necessary to account for variability in landscapes and the sensitivity of surrounding communities to forest fire smoke.

FOREST HEALTH IN THE EASTERN CASCADES

The choices to be made in fire management associated with spotted owl protection are in one sense easier than those made in fire management for forest health. There is a single primary objective in owl management: maintaining viable populations of owls through maintenance of habitat. The forest health issue is complicated by the vagueness of the term "forest health" as well as the number of competing interests for the outputs of the forests east of the Cascades. In its simplest form, a healthy forest is one that is capable of maintaining desirable character or condition (visually attractive, and relatively resistant to insects, disease, and fire) while sustaining desirable outputs (recreation, timber, wildlife). Forest health is a global concern, but regionally the focus has been on the drier forests of eastern Oregon and Washington because of the obvious forest decline seen there. Insect populations seem to remain at high levels; disease pockets, once localized, are expanding in scope; and fires that once spread lightly across forest floors are now stand replacement events.

A recent analysis of east side forest health (Gast et al. 1991) concluded that fire played an important role in the evolution of natural ecosystems, and that it is an important option in managing for long-term productivity of the forest. Two major constraints to implementing this option are intermingled: private ownership and smoke. Larger blocks of uniform public ownership will be easier to manage, as fire will be safer and easier to apply in situations where public/private property boundaries do not fragment the landscape.

The most significant constraint is smoke. Although frequent maintenance burns may produce little smoke, initial restoration burns will consume biomass that has accumulated for many decades. Restoration burns will kill smaller live trees, which will add dead fuels to the ground over time. These sites will have to be underburned when moist, and combustion will be relatively inefficient, producing more smoke per ton of fuel consumed. A rough idea of the magnitude of potential consumption, at least for the first round of restoration burns, can be estimated by evaluating the Ponderosa pine and mixed-conifer types in eastern Washington. Prescribed fire-return intervals determine the proportion of the landscape to be treated each year over the first cycle. Tonnage is estimated from restoration burns in similar forest types, and the addition of "activity fuels" from ongoing harvest is added at the 1987-91 level (DNR 1992), a time of decline in tonnage due primarily to air quality concerns. The total consumption is about three and a half times the 1977-91 average, or eight and a half times the 1987-91 average.

After the first 15 years, when a second round of burning in Ponderosa pine sites would start, tonnages would only slightly decline, because additions to the dead fuel category from the first burn would be consumed by the second. Measuring the total impact of such a program requires adding effects on wildfire area and fuel consumption. During the first cycle of burning, little immediate positive impact on area burned by wildfire would result, but results might begin to show after the first 10-15 years. These figures are very rough but are presented as a means of gaining perspective on the magnitude of the problem. They suggest that if air quality constraints remain high, forest health concerns will have to be prioritized.

Forest health and public health are to some extent mutually exclusive objectives under current fuel and regulatory conditions. We will have to pick our highest priority sites on which to reintroduce fire and expand treatment on lower priority sites only to the limits of social acceptance. Using the example already given, if we were to treat only 25 percent of the landscape in these forest types, we would be close to the tonnage of the 1977-91 period. Recognizing that the natural role of fire cannot be reapplied across the landscape, even if biologically sound, is a biological adjustment to the forest health solution. Putting up with more prescribed fire smoke, in part possibly offset in the long run by less wildfire smoke, is one of the social adjustments to be made.

Timber salvage operations may be an important part of the process of restoring forest health. Partial cuts that remove the shade-tolerant trees will produce wood, though of smaller diameter, and will remove coarse fuel from the sites. Medium and fine fuels (branches and leaves) will be left onsite and will cause increases in those categories of fuel. A key to success is to leave the more fire-tolerant, and generally larger, species—such as western larch and Ponderosa pine—whenever possible. Adapting or constructing lumber mills to use the smaller true fir and to some extent Douglas fir will be another social adjustment to forest health solutions, but it will require a social contract to supply such materials in predictable quantities.

The transition to ecosystem management in eastside forests requires complex adjustments in traditional institutions: the Forest Service, the forest industry, conservation organizations, and the communities of the region. Everybody wants a solution, but the solutions are not cost-free. Current problems of forest decline are not future scenarios; they are here, at least in some areas like the Blue Mountains. Business as usual is costly to everyone, so there is a good chance that adaptive management approaches can be adopted. Fire will be a central theme in any such approach.

GLOBAL CLIMATE CHANGE

The forests of the Pacific Northwest will be subject to significant environmental change if current predictions about global warming are accurate (Franklin et al. 1991). Greenhouse gases, including carbon dioxide and methane, which trap outgoing radiation from the Earth, have been increasing because of agricultural activities and fossil fuel consumption. Mature forests are better buffered against such change than regenerating forests, because the environment is more critical for seedlings than for mature trees. Mature trees will alter growth and morphology patterns as a first response to environmental change; seedlings will often die.

Significant forest change will occur after a forest has been disturbed by logging or by a natural disturbance factor, such as fire, when new seedlings must cope with a changed climate. An interesting feedback mechanism in this process of global change is that fires will also add carbon dioxide to the atmosphere, so that if global warming accelerates fire activity, fires could also accelerate the warming process. Most ecological predictions assume that global warming will result in an increase in fire as a disturbance factor. This may be a simplified assumption. My intent here is not to disprove this assumption but to show the complexity of making such an assumption.

For both Pacific Northwest and Rocky Mountain forests, changes in future climate have been projected, although climate and ecological reconstructions at a regional level appear speculative: if climate scenario A occurs, the forests are projected to change in one way, while if scenario B occurs, the forest should change in a different way. For the Rocky Mountains, one of the scenarios is a warmer, drier climate, either with or without greater efficiency of plant water use (due to higher CO_2 levels; Leverenz and Lev 1987). Under this scenario, fires are projected to increase in frequency and severity (Romme and Turner 1991), but no evidence to support this conjecture is provided. In the Pacific Northwest, temperature changes up to 5°C are projected to result in significant alterations in the distribution of forest

Forest health and public health are to some extent mutually exclusive objectives

types of the region. Plant communities will probably not move as intact units across the landscape, as the authors recognize. They note that some species will be capable of faster migration than others, but the large magnitude of potential change is there. Increased frequency of fire is claimed to be certain, and increases in intensity are stated as probable (Franklin et al. 1991). The apparent rationale for these statements is that as environments now found to the south "move" north with global warming, so will at least portions of the associated fire regimes. The increase in intensity is assumed to be due to increased fuel loads of stressed forests with higher dead tree components. The major assumptions in common between these projections are that the controlling factor for fire activity is moisture and that this is fairly represented by potential evapotranspiration. In fact, there are several controlling factors, and not all are correlated with moisture.

The seasonal distribution of moisture is important in such predictions but existing models cannot project seasonal precipitation with any certainty. Lower annual precipitation but an increased proportion in the dry season may result in no net change or even less fire activity. The fire cycle model generates fire activity in the western Cascades based on seasonal moisture, lightning activity, and presence of easterly wind. Offsetting changes in the latter two factors could negate any increase in fire activity due to drier summers. Two new runs of the fire cycle model were made, both assuming a 25 percent decrease in summer precipitation, with the first assuming no change in thunderstorm or east wind activity and the second assuming a 25 percent decrease in both factors. Other factors remaining constant, a decrease in summer precipitation significantly increases the occurrence of fires across the region from 40 percent to 90 percent. However, if other factors associated with fires decrease, the net change ranges from a 10 percent decrease to a 20 percent increase. Until we have a better mechanism to project changes in synoptic weather associated with global warming, reasonably justified projections about fire activity are not possible.

Recent projections of the effects of global climate change on Canadian forest fire activity have concluded that increased temperature due to a doubling of carbon dioxide is most likely to drive changes in fire activity (Flannigan and Van Wagner 1991). Precipitation is less important in projections of increased fire activity in Canada because it was projected to increase for many Canadian stations, and due to lack of data, sequences of dry periods were assumed to mimic those of the past. Increasing temperature affects the drying phase of the "moisture codes" of the Canadian Forest Fire Weather Index in two ways. First, assuming a constant dew point, relative humidity and equilibrium moisture content decline and, in the Canadian system, the rate at which fuel dries after a rain increases. Second, assuming little change in relative humidity (that is, dew point increases along with temperature), a fire danger index called "seasonal severity rating" is projected to increase 46 percent across Canada with a possible similar increase in area burned.

> **The forests of the Pacific Northwest will be subject to significant environmental change if current predictions about global warming are accurate.**

Cranbrook, British Columbia, the most westerly station, has a 30 percent projected increase.

We have only a rudimentary understanding of the interactions between climate change and fire activity. Although it is tempting to envision a global warming scenario with larger, more intense wildfires across the region, there is little evidence to suggest that the inferno is inevitable. We need to focus research on more precise climate scenarios, including those affecting fire ignitions, before we can draw realistic inferences about fire.

A tantalizing precursor to conclusions about global changes and fire activity in the Pacific Northwest is the seeming historical relation between large, intense fires and global cooling episodes. In the past millennium there have been three major sunspot minima: the Wolf, Sporer, and Maunder. During such times, the energy output of the sun is slightly less. Midlatitude glaciers have advanced during such times, and these are considered periods of global cooling. Superimposition of large fire events of the past results in a surprising correspondence between sunspot minima and large, intense fires. Whether this is a cause-effect association is unknown, but it may represent a change in the frequency of long- and short-term drought, thunderstorm occurrence, or the frequency of east winds across the Pacific Northwest. This adds another cautionary note to simple assumptions about global warming and fire.

13

The Worth of a Birch

George Matz

Birch are the cornucopia of the boreal forest, furnishing the forest with an abundance of benefits that help sustain a variety of fauna and flora. The boreal forest would not be the same ecologically, economically or spiritually without the bounty and beauty of birch.

Birch provide a diversity of benefits throughout their lifespan and beyond, starting with a tiny seed. It is fortunate that birch yield an abundance of seeds since the future of an individual seed is not good. Many are culled and few are chosen to complete the growth cycle and become a mature tree. But the birch seed that we will follow is so destined.

This tree begins as a tiny spring flower nestled in the catkin of an old birch, high on a hillside overlooking the Tanana River in interior Alaska. The old tree is one of the few birch still left on the southeast slope of the hill that is now mostly covered with a canopy of white spruce. As spring turns to summer, the flower becomes a seed, a tiny nutlet with two wings.

Then, on a hot July afternoon, a lightning bolt comes crashing down from billowing cumulus clouds, igniting a tinder-dry black spruce on the north side of the hill. A wildfire starts, quickly spreads, skips over the ridge and torches several acres of white spruce near the old birch, but leaves it untouched.

On a breezy day in late fall, our seed twirls down from the dangling catkin where it is embedded and lands in a snowy opening where the fire reduced the majestic white spruce to sticks of charcoal and the mossy ground-cover to bare soil. This is an ideal place for a birch seed to settle. Ash from the burnt vegetation will increase the pH of the soil and provide essential nutrients needed by the seed when it germinates. Also, the thick loess soil deposits on the hillside are well drained and free of permafrost. But most of all, now that the ground will not be shaded by spruce, the birch will have good exposure to the radiant energy of the sun.

Spring comes with a frenzy. The temporary void of vegetation created by last

---

ABOUT BETULA

Birch trees (genus *Betula*) are not exclusive to the boreal forest, but it is these vast conifer/hardwood forests which circumscribe the cold northern latitudes of the world that are most closely associated with birch.

Of the 40-some species of birch that exist in North America, Europe and Asia, only three species are found in Alaska. Two of these species (dwarf arctic birch and resin birch) are stunted shrubs that grow in muskeg, tundra or alpine slopes where few, if any, trees are able to obtain the nutrients necessary for growth. The other species (paper birch) is a medium-sized tree found in the northern forests of North America from Newfoundland to Alaska.

Paper birch has several geographical varieties. According to *Alaska Trees and Shrubs* by Leslie Viereck and Elbert Little, three varieties found in Alaska's spruce-hardwood forests are: Alaska paper birch common to the forests of the Interior and Southcentral, Kenai birch found mostly in the Cook Inlet region, and Western paper birch which extends into some of the large river valleys of the Southeast that have headwaters in the Yukon or British Columbia. Where ranges overlap, these varieties will hybridize. In fact, even dwarf and resin birch will hybridize with paper birch.

---

summer's fire quickly fills in with fireweed, horsetail, bluejoint grass and other pioneer species, establishing the first successional stage (moss-herb) after the fire. Our birch seed, now a seedling, has to compete for survival along with a million other birch seeds for every acre of burn. The competition for sunlight and nutrients is severe, and most seedlings fade away.

A few years later, our favorite birch seedling has grown into a sapling. This second successional stage (tall shrub-sapling) is reached about the same time that the local population of snowshoe hares begins to recover from its crash just previous to the fire. The sweet inner bark of deciduous saplings is a favorite source of food for the snowshoe hare. The expanding population of hares nibbles away at the birch saplings that cover this part of the hillside. Again, many trees do not survive. Those that do are given some relief when the population of lynx, a major predator of snowshoe hares, also begins to rebound a year or two later.

The sapling we are following also survives the onslaught of numerous moose that now inhabit the area. During winter, moose persevere by browsing on the twigs of the willow and birch that prospered immediately after the fire. Heavily browsed trees may have their growth stunted, reducing their ability to compete with other saplings.

Moose prefer munching on the tops of birch saplings because the outer bark on these fast-growing branches has fewer lenticels than branches near the bottom. Lenticels are little, white, scab-like objects that contain distasteful chemicals, defending the tree against herbivores. The faster a birch sapling grows, the sooner its top will be out of reach from the stretching neck of a moose. But a heavy, wet snow can be a real setback to a young, limber, fast-growing birch. Bowed by the weight of the snow, the top branches of the tree can now be easily reached by moose. When tugging on these already burdened branches, moose will sometimes snap a sapling in two, disfiguring its growth if it does survive.

Birch saplings are more than fodder for herbivores. In earlier times, indigenous dwellers of the boreal forest considered birch saplings an essential material for winter transportation. Clarence Alexander, a Gwich'in from Fort Yukon, says that the strength and flexibility of birch made excellent frames for snowshoes, which gave Athabascan hunters the mobility they needed to hunt and trap during the winter. Birch was also used for making bows and sleds, two other implements essential to the hunter. Since not every stand of birch is identical, a good hunter would need to know not only where to find animals to hunt or trap, but where to find the best trees for making tools and weapons.

THREE DECADES LATER

It is now about 30 years after the fire, and the third successional stage (dense tree) begins. An even-aged stand of birch, all having germinated immediately after the fire, is now the dominant tree on this patch of hillside.

If you stood on the other side of the river, you could witness the beauty of birch. The ever-white streaks of birch trunks add contrast to the spreading evergreen boughs of white spruce spared by the fire. The crown of the birch grove adds a flare of color that changes with the season. Its leaves burst into a vibrant green in the spring, age to a darker green in the summer and then turn radiant gold in the fall. Even in the winter, birch adds color to the forest, its brown buds becoming redder with the approach of spring.

The leafy crown of the birch tree also adds to the ecological patterns of the forest. The closed canopy of the birch stand shades the forest floor, hindering the growth of herbs, shrubs and even its own seedlings. But the shade is not as limiting to the white spruce seedlings slowly growing beneath the birch that will eventually dominate the hillside. It will be nearly a century, however, before the white spruce will succeed birch as the dominant species.

In addition to shade, the crown produces seed and litter. The birch we are observing nears its most productive age for seed-bearing at 40 to 70 years. Although the amount of seed production varies from year to year, each summer our tree

Young birch forest
Bo Martin

produces about 15 pounds [6.8 kg] dry weight of catkins that contain about 9 million seeds.

Both the catkins and seeds provide an important source of food for birds. Ruffed grouse feed on the catkins. Birch disperse their seed in the fall and winter when redpolls, chickadees and other resident songbirds need an abundance of food to survive the cold weather. A stand of birch in interior Alaska can have an annual seedfall of 72,800 seeds per square metre [1.2 sq. yards]. By contrast, seed production by the next most prolific tree, white spruce, is only about 4,000 seeds per square metre.

Besides seeds, the birch canopy litters the forest floor with leaves. When shed in the fall, the litter smothers moss growth that would insulate the cool soil, encouraging permafrost. The litterfall from a stand of birch will typically weigh from 1.8 tons to 3.6 tons per acre [0.73 to 1.46 tons/ha], more than any other tree in the boreal forest. The decomposition of this litter adds nutrients such as calcium, magnesium and phosphorus to the soil. These nutrients will be utilized by the slower growing white spruce. Once again, our birch serves as a provider for another species, even its successor.

Other forest life thrives on the birch itself. Hungry porcupines will girdle the bark off the trunks and branches of birch. Beavers, from the slough next to the wide bend in the river, will waddle up the slope to take the juicy birch, branch by branch, to the water below.

COMMERCIAL HARVEST

Forty-five years after the fire, the fourth successional stage emerges. The birch stand is now considered a hardwood forest. Our favorite tree is nearly 60 feet [18.3 m] tall and 10 inches [25.4 cm] in diameter at breast height.

It is during this successional stage that hardwoods like birch have their greatest commercial value. Steve Clautice of the Alaska Division of Forestry in Fairbanks says that about half the commercial timber volume of the Interior consists of hardwoods. "Birch is the most significant hardwood tree," he says. "Birch makes up about two-thirds of the hardwood volume, and aspen about a third."

Commercial value can be obtained from living trees. Entrepreneurs in the Anchorage and Fairbanks area have turned an old practice into an innovative, energy-saving process and a new Alaskan product: birch syrup. This process uses reverse-osmosis, rather than heat, to remove 80 percent of the water from the birch sap.

Every spring for the past few years, Jeff Weltzin, founder of the Original Alaska Birch Syrup Co., has been tapping about 10,000 birch trees on 720 acres [291 ha] in the hills above Fairbanks. He says "The tree has to be at least 40 years old to produce enough sap. Those 60 to 80 years old seem to produce the most sap."

A mature birch tree will produce about a gallon of sap per day. Peak flow conditions will last 10 to 14 days. This will boil down to two or three eight-ounce bottles of tangy syrup that currently sell for $8.50 [U.S.] apiece. Birch can be tapped year after year, making it a good example of sustainable forest use.

Live birch also provides bark. Athabascans used birch bark to make canoes and baskets for everyday use. They still make plenty of birch baskets, which are now sold as native handicraft, larger ones selling for over $100 [U.S.].

In Alaska, the most common use of harvested birch is firewood. Considered the best firewood in the Interior, birch yields about 18.2 million BTUs for every cord of dry wood. Steve Clautice estimates that the annual current demand for firewood in the Tanana Valley area alone is about 15,000 cords, half being birch.

Bob Zackel in Fairbanks contends that firewood is not the best use of prime birch. Owner of Alaska Birch Works, Bob prefers to use birch for manufacturing tongue-and-groove panelling. Instead of getting $100 a cord for firewood, Bob says, "I can get $1,200 to $1,400 for an equivalent amount of birch."

An important point Bob makes is that not every large birch is usable. He prefers trees that are 40 to 60 years old, with a diameter of 10 to 14 inches [25-36 cm]. Bob says, "about 60 to 75 percent of a tree this age will be sawable. With trees that are over 75 years old, only about 20 to 40 percent will be sawable. As birch trees get older, they develop heart rot, which weakens the wood and gives it a reddish color, eventually making it unsuitable for commercial purposes other than firewood."

John Manthei, owner of Custom Woodworking in Fairbanks, makes quality birch furniture and cabinets. He advises that "birch has to be used with discretion." Although its grain has sensuous curves, too much of it can create a confusing pattern for some people. Nevertheless, John believes, "there is good potential for utilizing Interior birch, providing it is cut selectively because of the low percentage of high-quality trees typical of the Interior forest." This means low volumes of harvest, which favor operations that are able to get more value-added from a tree.

A birch in winter
George Matz

Another user of prime birch trees is the Great Alaska Bowl Co. in Fairbanks. Using a 22-step process, the company makes wooden bowls out of blocks of wood. Marti Steury, company president, says they can make up to 54 sets of bowls (four bowls per set) from a 32-foot log [9.75 m] with a 14-inch [36 cm] diameter. A complete set sells for $129. Marti estimates that the economic value added to a log this size will be at least $4,000, which doesn't include turning rejects into byproducts such as bird feeders, or the value added by several artists who use the bowls as their media.

Birch has a wide range of economic value to Alaskans. Looking at the options that exist with one large tree having few defects, making birch syrup will yield about $20 worth of product per year. This is nearly as much as if the birch were harvested and sold as firewood, which would bring in about $25 (it takes at least four large birch trees to make a cord of wood). If this tree were made into panelling, however, it would be worth about $300 or more. But the biggest money-maker is birch bowls, which have a value greater than $4,000 a tree.

TODAY'S DILEMMA

It is now 1993, 60 years after the fire. Our birch tree is facing a new dilemma. Although it has been a survivor in the natural world, its fate may be decided by an alien process. The Alaska Department of Natural Resources, Division of Forestry, which now manages the land where our birch tree resides, has included this area in its "Five-Year Forest Operations Schedule" for the Tanana Valley. Released in June 1993, this draft plan initially proposed large-scale logging on 80,000 acres [32,376 ha] of boreal forest, starting in 1994 and lasting 10 to 20 years.

Like the forest itself, however, forest management seems to go through periods of change. The intensive management that was favored just a few years ago by foresters seems to be transforming into what is now called "ecosystem management," where value is given to all species, not just those having the greatest commercial value.

And just as a species survives by adapting to the conditions it is faced with, so does an agency. Partially because of strong public opposition to the five-year plan, the Division of Forestry announced in October 1993 that any large-scale logging in the Tanana Valley will be delayed until 1997. Meanwhile, they plan a more thorough inventory of forest resources.

If left to contend with just the forces of nature, our birch tree will continue to grow for a few more decades. Growth will then yield to decay and spires of white spruce will soon dominate the hillside. Heart rot will afflict the old birch, creating good opportunities for woodpeckers to drill out nesting cavities. An unusually strong wind will eventually sweep through the forest and the weakened tree will topple.

Even then, it will still provide. The birch's rotting trunk lying on the ground releases nutrients for plants and creates habitat for a diverse array of small animals.

Whatever evolves in the next few years will not only determine the fate of our birch tree, but the future of Alaska's boreal forest. Will large-scale clearcutting on many of the hills around Fairbanks leave bare flanks for the next few decades? Or will most of the boreal forest remain intact and continue to provide a diversity of ecological, economic and esthetic benefits?

14

The Effect of Nature-Oriented Forestry
on Forest Genetics

Lutz Faehser

FORESTS ONCE COVERED NEARLY ONE-HALF of the Earth's mainland surface; humans have now reduced that proportion to one-fifth. Most of the surviving forests are still undergoing changes caused by human interference and valuable tree species such as Brazil wood are already extinct. Economic interests dictate the terms of existence and as a result, many of the commercially uninteresting genera of trees have been supplanted by species of high commercial interest, such as eucalyptus, gmelina, acacia, shorea, pinus, and picea.

Apart from the denudation of the forest—20 million hectares per year in the tropics alone—"modern" commercial forests are witnessing a rapid depletion of the originally luxurious, rich genetic information. This genetic erosion is dangerous to the very survival of the forests in the long run, as it is simultaneously an erosion of their innate capacity to adapt to changing ecological conditions. In view of galloping ecological changes due to radioactivity, pollutants, the greenhouse effect, the ozone hole, etc., our forests are more than ever in need of the widest gene pool to survive.

At the same time, the Earth's five to six billion people want to live in good health, dignity and comfort. Wood is a renewable resource, has multiple uses and is easily recyclable. Its production, however, can no longer be allowed to threaten the existence of our forests. Forest management must strictly follow the rules of nature to satisfy economy as well as ecology.

In the last few decades, Central Europe has taken initiatives toward ecological forestry, in view of the devastation of its natural forests 300 years ago. If this pro-nature attitude to forestry would replace predominantly prevalent anti-nature systems of plantation, monocultures, clear-felling [clearcutting], use of pesticides and gene technology, the genetics of forests would improve, along with their chance for survival.

The Influence of Silviculture on Genetics

Silviculture systems have very specific aims for cultivating forests. The most prevalent system the world over is clear-felling with monocultures and replantation. The ecological, social, esthetic and economic deficiencies of this nature-alien technique are becoming increasingly clear. Some foresters are seeking alternatives.

The *clear-felling system* in Europe is as old as modern forestry itself, that is, 300 years old. It was first introduced to calculate and control the surface or the usable wood-mass. The aim was to cut only as much wood as would grow in a certain area, which is the principle of sustainability.

The *technical measures* of clear-felling are:
- clear-felling on a fairly large area;
- reforestation by planting or sowing;
- periodic cleaning and thinning;
- use of chemicals (fertilizer, pesticides) and machines (forwarders, processors); and
- final harvesting (clear-felling) at the end of a rotation period.

The *forest structure* that is subject to clear-felling is marked by the following characteristics:
- The tree-canopies form a closed, horizontal layer (monolayer) and the trees are even-aged (Figure 1);
- Only one species (monoculture) or at best a small number of species are represented. They are often fast-growing exotic species;
- The ground vegetation is deficient, whether it be due to lack of light or due to degradation of soil fertility.

The typical *dynamics* resulting from these characteristics are:
- Trees shoot up high with rapid growth in the early years;
- Intraspecific competition allows for only two reaction-patterns: to remain in full sunlight or die in the dark under the canopy;
- The fast growth of the trunk, the high canopy and a disproportionate relation of the height of the tree to the diameter of the trunk result in low physiological vitality and a high mechanical instability. In Germany, almost 50% of the trees in clear-felling systems must be harvested well before the normal end of their lifespan;
- Trees that have died due to disease, storm or snow are replaced by planted trees;
- Chemical or physical forest protection impede natural immunity against diseases. In addition, disease-producers or insects widen their spectrum of influence, aided by their resistance to pesticides;
- Clear-felling is done when trees are biologically immature. The average rotation period in Europe is roughly one-fifth of the biologically possible

age, down to one-fiftieth in the tropics. For example, eucalyptus trees are harvested after seven years, although they can live for 350 years.

GENETIC CONDITIONS IN THE CLEAR-FELLING SYSTEM

The clear-felling system leads to the following genetic conditions:

- Natural genetic information has disappeared or has been severely reduced, making place for gene imports;
- The gene imports are in most of the cases not adapted to the specific site; they are phenotypically or genotypically selected products with a restricted gene pool. The criteria for selection or breeding are maximum performance in terms of the volume of growth, shape of the trunk, and resistance to disease and insects;
- Through intraspecific competition and selective processes like cleaning and thinning, only those trees that exhibit a rapid growth in early stages and are extremely needy of light are given preference;
- The yield of seeds is achieved just a few times during the life of a tree, as the trees are harvested soon after or even before their full sexual maturity;
- The generative reproduction at a site is not part of the program. The age-old processes of evolution and genetic adaptation to the site have been lost, and thousands of years of evolution are required to catch up.

All other elements and relations that make up the ecosystem forest are also destroyed physically and genetically in the clear-felling system. Human beings, animals, and plants that were a part of the ecosystem have lost much of their grounding. Thus, an infinitely complex and incredibly optimized natural world has been sacrificed in favor of narrow quantitative models by wood producers. Today we know that these quantitative models are wrong. They have brought short-term profits to a few at the cost of all.

> **The principle of nature-oriented forestry is to minimize human interference as much as possible.**

Figure 1
The basic structure of industrial model forestry.

THE NATURE-ORIENTED SYSTEM

For centuries in Central Europe, a nature-oriented system was intensively practised in small woodlands. Farmers harvested from time to time a few thick trees needed for building and repairing their houses. And decades spanned the time between these harvests. This method was "discovered" and recommended by forestry science about 100 years ago. The recommendation met with little enthusiasm initially, but following the worldwide fiascos and catastrophic consequences of anti-nature methods of forestry, an interest in this alternative has been revived. In the former West Germany, nature-oriented forestry has been "prescribed" for all state-owned forests in the last few years.

The principle of nature-oriented forestry is to minimize human interference as much as possible and not to counter forest dynamics.

The *technical measures* consist mainly in selective harvesting of single trees, which are either sick, badly shaped or have reached a relatively large diameter for the end-product. The age of the tree does not play a role. Thus the continuity of the forest is guaranteed through natural rejuvenation.

Forests maintained by the nature-oriented system have the following *structure*:
- trees are uneven in age and are of many species (Figure 2);
- old and young trees are mixed together horizontally and vertically in a confined space;
- enough light allows for natural regeneration beneath old single trees.

Figure 2
The more diversified structure characteristic of a natural forest.

The *following dynamics* result from this forest structure:
- Old trees randomly tower over young ones, develop full seed production and guarantee natural regeneration;
- Diverse conditions of light, nutrients and water guide the quality and quantity of natural regeneration;
- Diversity allows for intra- as well as interspecific competition, successional stages continue for a number of centuries: pioneering, youthfulness, physical optimum, aging and decay. These phases are spatially distributed throughout the forests in irregular mosaics.

	Clear-felling System	Nature-oriented System
STRUCTURE	• even-aged, monolayer	• uneven-aged polymorphous
	• monoculture	• mixed stands
	• often exotic species	• mostly indigenous species
	• none/little ground vegetation	• abundant ground vegetation/regeneration
DYNAMICS	• fast growth in youth	• growth in relation to changing stimuli until advanced age
	• selection of light-demanding species	• selection of shade-tolerant species
	• intraspecific competition	• intra- and interspecific competition
	• low physiological vitality and high mechanical instability	• physiological and mechanical stability
	• clear-felling early in the lifespan of trees	• selective cutting of single trees at advanced age
	• regeneration through planting/sowing	• natural regeneration
GENETICS	• imported gene pool	• naturally-influenced gene pool
	• low adaptation to sites	• evolutionary adaptation to sites
	• artificial selection and breeding of plants	• natural selection
	• none/little seed production	• abundant seed production
	• no genetic continuity after rotation period	• eternal genetic continuity through natural regeneration

Figure 3
Structure, dynamics and genetic situation in the clear-felling system and the nature-oriented system.

Genetic Conditions in the Nature-Oriented System

The genetic situation of heterogeneous, uneven-aged, mixed forests greatly differs from that of homogeneous monocultures (Figure 3):

- The original genetic information is still intact;
- The natural selection process is unsettled by production-oriented interference;
- Generative reproduction is preserved as an essential bridge between generations and as the most intensive phase of evolution;
- The harvest of individual trunks constantly produces new conditions, giving rise to new genetic partnerships. Thus, debilitating inbreeding by repeated self-pollination and pollination by the same neighboring trees is minimized;
- A few healthy old trees stand guard over younger ones, having seed potential for long periods of time;
- Natural regeneration allows 20 times more plants to grow per unit of space than artificial planting.[1] Natural selection favors the capacity of young trees to grow for the long term and tolerate shade, while growing straight toward the light and building up resistance against disease;
- Ever-changing site qualities and a corresponding selection process guarantee a great diversity of the gene pool;
- All the forest species group into subpopulations which evolve (in terms of mutation, selection, isolation and migration, etc.) at the same time. Thus, the optimum biological strategy for adaptation is reached.

Of course, in a system of forest use, not all the demands of ecology and protection are met. It is imperative therefore that portions of commercial forests are kept exclusively as genetic reserves (10-20% of the area) and linked in a network. Dead wood (approximately 10-20% of the wood volume) should remain as "biological gold" for the innumerable animal and plant species; a few trees must not be harvested, but allowed to decay naturally.

Summary

Forest management is fast developing as a survival strategy due to overpopulation, climatic changes, pollution and poisoning of the soil, water, air and the denudation of the last primeval forests. A nature-oriented management of forests promotes the development of an optimum level of genetic information. If such forestry can support the special needs of local populations, demonstrated since 1972 in India (Malhotra 1989), there is more hope for our future.

PART THREE

Ecoforestry—Past & Current Examples

Selection logging with horses, Chip Vinai

15

A New Vision for Forest Ecosystems:
An Interview with Herb Hammond

Mitch Friedman

"YES, HUMANS ARE A PART OF NATURE, but you will never see a fungus driving a feller-buncher." So said Herb Hammond at a debate over forest use in British Columbia. In the landscape of B.C. forestry and environmental politics, Herb is a true maverick. Despite efforts by the Association of B.C. Professional Foresters to discipline him and efforts by the timber industry to silence him for his controversial stands, Herb is leading the way in Canada to sustainable forest use, community empowerment, and a network of protected areas based on ecological principles. [Editor's note: He and his associates are working in close cooperation with the Ecoforestry Institute to set up pilot certification and training programs in British Columbia.]

Herb holds a Master's degree in Forest Ecology and Silviculture and has 20 years experience as an industrial forester, researcher, teacher, and consultant. His firm, SILVA Ecosystem Consultants, and the SILVA Forest Foundation have served and informed indigenous peoples and communities. He is the author of the book, *Seeing the Forest Among the Trees.*

Mitch Friedman: Describe your current work.

Herb Hammond: The majority of our work continues to be with indigenous people, rural communities, and grassroots environmental groups. Although specific objectives vary widely, much of our work focuses on critiquing conventional timber management plans and preparing alternative wholistic forest use plans. Both start with a landscape ecology analysis, and include stand ecology analysis and wholistic cost-benefit analysis (total-cost accounting). Thus we help communities understand both the ecology and practical economies of conventional timber management in contrast to sustainable, wholistic forest use. Once we have provided them with our critiques and alternative plans, we also help the communities empower themselves to reassume control of local forests through community forest boards that operate by consensus and provide a seat for all interests.

We can develop new ways of thinking about and relating to the forest that ensure that it will continue to sustain us.

One of our most exciting projects is to incorporate our landscape ecology analysis, which results in developing protected landscape networks by drainage basin, and our system of wholistic forest use zoning into a computer GIS program. As we refine our analysis procedure, we will provide the software and training in its use to indigenous people, rural communities, and environmental groups.

Mitch Friedman: What are the larger applications of your work?

Herb Hammond: All forest planning must begin by applying the principles of landscape ecology. If we are to protect biological diversity—which is the only way that we can maintain fully functioning ecosystems and, therefore, sustainable societies—we must put in place systems of planning and using the forest landscape maintain natural landscape patterns. In other words, establishing parks and wilderness areas alone is insufficient. If the riparian ecosystems, cross-valley corridors, sensitive sites (e.g. thin soils, steep slopes, and wetlands) and old-growth areas that connect parks and wilderness areas are not managed as protected landscape networks, we will eventually lose even the biodiversity that we thought was protected in the parks and wilderness.

I believe that applying our systems of landscape analysis, protected landscape networks, and wholistic forest use zoning would provide a sound framework for developing provincial land-use plans. These land-use plans would result in protecting about 25% to 30% of the land base from consumptive human use. This is an absolute requirement if we are to talk about sustaining anything.

This approach does not mean a poorer economy or fewer jobs. Indeed, because of the need for better planning, more labor-intensive/forest-sensitive practices, and value-added manufacturing, protected landscape networks and wholistic forest use zones will mean more diverse, stable employment than is currently generated by the increasingly mechanized logging and milling industries. Another economic point to emphasize is meaningful employment, rather than short-term jobs. Restoring thousands of hectares of degraded forests in British Columbia and using remaining natural forests in ways that maintain fully-functioning forests requires skilled, dedicated people capable of solving problems with finesse rather than with larger machines.

I believe that wholistic forest use offers a blueprint, from landscapes to individual stands, across British Columbia, indeed, throughout the world. I'm not suggesting that we have all the answers. All I am saying is that we have followed Mother Nature's lead and if others are willing to join us in enriching this idea, I am certain that we can develop new ways of thinking about and relating to the forest that ensure that it will continue to sustain us.

Mitch Friedman: Are there opportunities through CORE (Commission on Resources and the Environment), the Protected Areas Strategy, or other processes to incorporate wholistic forestry into provincial forest management, or is something else needed?

Herb Hammond: Unfortunately, I think these government processes suffer from two common and likely incurable ailments:

a) They are human-centered, not ecosystem-centered. As such, they look at the forest as a pie to divide up among various competing human interests, rather than as an interconnected, interdependent web within which various human interests must carefully fit.

b) They are political processes designed and implemented in a linear manner from the top down. As a result, CORE and the Protected Areas Strategy do not understand either the depth of the ecological crisis or the complexity of rural politics.

What is needed is community-directed processes operating within the requirements of ecological responsibility and balanced use. This could be implemented simply by enshrining the principles of wholistic forest use in legislation as minimum requirements for forest use across the province, and then devolving power to community forest boards.

Mitch Friedman: What obstacles exist to the widespread application of wholistic forest use?

Herb Hammond: Implementation of wholistic forest use means a loss of industry power and lower profits (note, I did not say no profits). Thus, the timber industry has spent millions of dollars in high-profile public information campaigns such as the B.C. Forest Alliance, to attempt to discredit wholistic forest use and other alternatives. I don't think it will work, because in the end ecosystem-based approaches have truth on their side.

Also, the government sees their political fortunes more closely tied to the timber industry than to the forest and the people. Thus, just as with the timber industry, the provincial government sees wholistic forest use as a threat to maintaining power and control over people.

Mitch Friedman: Are scientific principles being effectively utilized by the B.C. ministries and environmental groups to protect biodiversity and other environmental values?

Herb Hammond: While some people are becoming aware of landscape ecology, nobody in the mainstream is effectively applying this science. Within government and industry, even for those who are aware of landscape ecology, there is a reticence to apply this profound science because it will mean protecting more in the order of 25% to 30% of the B.C. land base rather than the political compromise of 12%. Environmentalists have attached their fortunes to protecting this 12% of B.C., distributed among representative (whatever that means) ecosystems.

Mitch Friedman: What differences exist between B.C. and the Northwest U.S. in terms of environmental goals and strategies?

Herb Hammond: In many respects, I think that the goals that we all have in our hearts as environmentalists are very similar. We recognize that forests sustain us; we do not sustain the forests. However, I think that differences in political structures, legislation, and the length of time we have been involved in this struggle result in some significant differences between us.

People in the Northwest U.S. have been at it a little longer only because the crisis occurred sooner than for those of us in British Columbia. Thus, it seems to me that a good portion of environmentalists in the Northwest U.S. have moved beyond the "campaign" approach designed to raise awareness and educate the public about the nature of the environmental crisis in the forest. While not universally true, it seems that they have moved into the stage of trying to articulate the solutions ecologically, economically, and socially.

16

Working Models of Ecoforestry:
From Theory to Practice

Mike Barnes and Twila Jacobsen

ONE OF THE MISSIONS OF THE ECOFORESTRY INSTITUTES in the U.S. and Canada is to demonstrate a range of forestry practices that are ecologically responsible in seeking to protect, maintain and restore fully functioning forests, while harvesting forest goods from some portions of the landscape to meet vital human needs.

THE MOUNTAIN GROVE CENTER ECOFORESTRY DEMONSTRATION FOREST

The Ecoforestry Institute's home and headquarters is located on the 420 acre [170 ha] forest of the Mountain Grove Center (MGC) in southern Oregon. Both organizations share a common mission to practise, demonstrate and educate people about ecologically responsible forest use. The Mountain Grove Center is nestled within the 2,400 acre [971 ha] Woodford Creek Watershed.

Other neighbors in the watershed include the Bureau of Land Management (BLM), which manages 1,154 acres [467 ha], and the remaining approximately 800 acres [324 ha] is owned by a half-dozen private timber companies. In the fall of 1995, amid concerns about BLM's planned timber sale on McCollum Ridge with its many 350 to 500-year-old Douglas fir trees, the Ecoforestry Institute (EI) and the Mountain Grove Center (MGC) contacted Diane Chung, District Manager of the Glendale Area Resource District of the BLM, and asked the BLM to join us in a watershed partnership to demonstrate an ecosystem-based forest use strategy across the Woodford Creek watershed.

THE WOODFORD CREEK WATERSHED PARTNERSHIP

The BLM agreed to cooperate with EI and MGC in the formation of the Woodford Creek Watershed Partnership (WCWP) with the following objectives: (1) to develop an ecosystem-based forest strategy for the Woodford Creek watershed; (2) to establish a framework for cooperative implementation of a model forest to demonstrate to the public an approach to ecosystem-based forest use at a watershed level; and (3) to develop a long-term joint stewardship arrangement for the ongoing caretaking and restoration of the Woodford Creek watershed (Draft "Woodford Creek Watershed Cooperative Agreement"). We also contacted the other timber companies in the watershed to seek their participation.

LANDSCAPE ANALYSIS AND DESIGN FOR THE WOODFORD CREEK WATERSHED

To accomplish the objective of developing an ecosystem-based forest strategy, the partnership decided to conduct a landscape analysis and design. BLM agreed to fund Dean Apostol, a landscape architect and member of the EI's faculty, to conduct a three-day landscape analysis and design workshop. The landscape design workshop, held January 16-19, 1996, was attended by Diane Chung and 10 members of her staff. Another 10 representatives of the MGC board and community and EI board and consultants attended, including: Steve Radcliff, MGC board president; Phil Gremaud, forester, Rogue Institute of Ecology and Economy; Dennis Martinez, restorationist; David Parker, MGC director, former MGC forest manager and representative of the Umpqua Watershed environmental organization (Roseberg); Richard Hart, research director of the Headwaters environmental organization (Ashland); and Juan Mendoza, Oregon Reforestation Cooperative and EI director.

The accomplishments of this landscape design workshop went far beyond our expectations. All parties agreed to practise forestry in the Woodford Creek watershed based on a long-term landscape design, which includes some of the following characteristics:

1. To restore the pine/oak savannah ecosystem type that occupies portions of the S/SW slopes in the watershed. Due to the absence of fire for at least the last 80 years this ecosystem type has increasingly been shaded out by Douglas and grand fir. The landscape plan calls for restoring this ecosystem type by thinning some of the understory fir, removing fire ladders, using controlled burns, and then replanting with native grass seeds. First, however, the partnership will conduct a survey to identify remnant native grasses and propagate the seeds so that we will have native grass seed ready to sow soon after the controlled burns.

2. To protect most of the remaining remnant old-growth stands and trees left in the watershed, and to replace this forest structure along riparian areas, both annual and ephemeral, and on the steepest slopes. MGC also plans to manage its forest as a multispecies, multi-aged forest with old-growth characteristics across the 420 acres [170 ha] of the valley floor.

3. A range of timber cutting patterns, i.e., selective logging and patch cuts, will be used on MGC and BLM lands, which will seek to protect, maintain and restore the structures, composition and functions of a fully functioning forest across the watershed. It is assumed that the private timber companies will likely practise plantation forestry, using clearcutting or sheltered cuts

on 50 to 60-year rotations.

FOREST ASSESSMENT AND INVENTORY OF THE WOODFORD CREEK WATERSHED

In order to ground the landscape design in knowledge of which trees, plants and animals actually live and grow in the watershed, the partnership agreed to next conduct a forest assessment and inventory of both MGC and BLM lands. The objective of the forest assessment and inventory is to provide us with baseline data prior to any future management activities in the watershed.

This work on BLM land was done through a contract with the Rogue Institute's "Jobs in the Woods" program. Three workers from the Rogue Institute and three of us associated with Mountain Grove conducted the assessment on BLM land for three weeks in July 1996. BLM was pleased with the results of the data collected and put up additional funding to complete the assessment, which was conducted in October. The assessment on MGC lands was completed in November.

ECOSYSTEM RESTORATION SURVEY AND STRATEGY

MGC decided to conduct a native plant survey on MGC lands. We hired Dennis Martinez, a restorationist and member of the EI faculty, to do this work. This survey was expanded into an ecosystem restoration survey and strategy, based on plant community associations. This information will assist us in restoring plants and ecosystem types, i.e. pine/oak savannah.

AN ECOSYSTEM-BASED FOREST USE STRATEGY

Together the landscape design, the assessment and inventory data, and the restoration survey and strategy will be integrated into the ecosystem-based forest use strategy for the Woodford Creek watershed. We also want to use the draft "Standards for the Certification of Ecologically Responsible Forest Use," currently being developed by the Pacific Certification Council (PCC), as a guide in the development of our watershed plan. At the same time, we want to use our process in developing an ecosystem-based forest use strategy for the Woodford Creek watershed to guide the development of the PCC's final "Standards for the Certification of Ecologically Responsible Forest Use."

Following scientific review, we expect to begin implementation of the ecosystem-based forest use strategy for the Woodford Creek watershed in the spring of 1997.

EI'S EDUCATION AND TRAINING PROGRAMS

Increasingly, the work we are doing in the Woodford Creek watershed will be the basis of EI's education and training programs.

ECOFORESTRY DEMONSTRATION FOREST

The partnership plans to develop a public demonstration forest. Since Mountain

Grove and the Woodford Creek watershed are adjacent to Interstate highway I-5, it is easily accessible for visitors. MGC recently constructed a new entrance road, directly facing on to I-5. We plan to construct a parking area, a kiosk with a carved watershed model, trails, and interpretive signs. Visitors will be able to take a walk in a forest where they can see a demonstration of forestry practices that seek "...to protect, maintain and restore a fully functioning forest ecosystem on a watershed scale." As the old adage says: "seeing is believing."

Both Ecoforestry Institutes have developed a network of foresters, forest workers and forestland owners who are practising ecologically responsible forestry. There are a number of other forests that demonstrate ecologically responsible forest use.

17

Respecting the Forest

Ruth Loomis

I WAS TOLD OF A CLEARCUT VALLEY by Merv Wilkinson, a "citizen" forester who has tended his forest for 50 years. "A prime example of stupidity," he said of the clearcut. "And it could have been logged with respect for the life that lived there. It could have been sustained by selective logging with respect for life in the future...the grandchildren of the eagle and the grandchildren of the trees. Our generation has no right to remove that future. We are doing it as fast as the buck can be put in the bank. Stupidity...." And I thought of this man who truly feels the symbiotic relationship between humans, forest and earth.

I drove the back road to the valley, viewing the results of current forestry practices. It was a scene of scarring and ripping into the earth, creating wounds that fester. Water flushed down hillsides carrying to the sea the basics of survival: topsoil. The scars were glazed with jutting rock formations. It will be hundreds of years before a seedling can grab a roothold and precariously survive in this desert zone created by human activity. Replanting had been tried, but failed. Merv was right. I thought of his word "stupidity" as I drove through a moonscape of stump shadows where a forest once stood. I was thankful for citizen ecoforester Merv Wilkinson who has shown hundreds of people who have visited his forest, Wildwood, a wholesome and respectful way to log.

Merv lives in and with his 136 acre [55 ha] forest at Yellowpoint, Vancouver Island, B.C., Canada. He removes forest products by cutting in five-year cycles. He has done so for 50 years and is now in the middle of his 10th cut. His forest will have the same volume of board feet after this cut as was cruised in 1945—1,500,000 b.f.— yet he has removed 1,672,000 b.f.!! Merv has removed more from his forest than was there originally. "I work with nature," he says. "I never cut more than is grown annually."

Stand with him under the 1,800-year-old seed tree in his forest and listen to the birds and the wind. The spicy smell of earth as your feet press on fallen needles awakens a sense of peace. Being in Merv's forest feels whole and connected, never fragmented. This is not the experience in a forest logged by industrial forest "farm" methods.

Merv Wilkinson is well known for his respectful forestry, a method of selective sustainable removal of products from a forest while maintaining its integrity. "There is too much we *don't* know. We need to respect that. Everything here is a unique ecological community, some understood, some not, but one thing for certain, I can't improve upon nature's arrangement!"

Merv has basic fundamentals for a healthy and productive forest. He knows the annual tree growth (approximately 2% per year) and the species value according to the land and terrain. He thins for light and growth to encourage a proper canopy. He knows that seedlings in his climate zone need about 50% light on the forest floor. It is important to encourage proper soil conditions by leaving debris for building humus, and to plan roads carefully avoiding erosion and unnecessary impact. He is expert in directional falling of trees to avoid damage and provide an easy pull for the skidder. Merv proudly points to immature trees that could have been totally destroyed in the removal of others if he had not been able to control the falling direction. "Those are part of the future forest. No need to replant in Wildwood. Reseeding occurs naturally and if there are too many, I may find I have some thinning at Christmas time!"

Merv's forest is a place of beauty and peace. He is content. The deer, eagles, wood ducks and pileated woodpeckers hunt and browse through Wildwood observing this man as he observes them. He points to a tiny hummingbird nest hidden in soft fir branches. "Even though I have fourteen habitat trees for the critters, I try not to cut in the spring when the birds are nesting."

At Wildwood, Merv's work is respectful work, an example of harmony with nature while managing a forest.

> **Merv has removed more from his forest than was there originally.**

18

Sustainable Forestry at the Crossroads:
Hard Lessons For the World

Monika Jäggi and L. Anders Sandberg

In 1994, THE SWISS MINISTRY OF NATURAL RESOURCES announced the possibility of a substantially increased allowable cut for the national forest industry. This increase, it was claimed, met the recently formulated principle of sustainability as defined by the 1992 United Nations Conference on Environment and Development (UNCED) (Bundesamt et al. 1994). The announcement rested on a long history of sustainable forest use and provides, we argue here, a window of analysis on the problems and prospects of forest sustainability generally. We provide a historical account of Swiss forestry, the prospects of its success, and some preliminary comparisons between the Swiss and Canadian experiences, the latter being the place of our current research. We here point to the different traditions of forestry in the two countries, yet argue that there are parallels between the Swiss forestry model and some of the forest management schemes pursued or advocated by North America's First Nations.

Sustainability (*Nachhaltigkeit*) has constituted the key principle of Swiss forestry for approximately a hundred years. Up to the Second World War, sustainability was used to describe sustained yield (*nachhaltige Holznutzung*), a term used in commercial forestry to describe a situation where the annual forest harvest equals the annual forest growth. After the Second World War, the concept changed to include multiple use. In the 1990s, provisions for sustainability in a new forest law encompassed a concern for forest ecosystems and an equal consideration for both the quantity *and* quality of the forest.

Based on the history of Swiss forest management, we address the following questions: How has the meaning of forest sustainability changed in Switzerland? What are some of the past and present conditions that form the foundation for building forest sustainability? We further explore tensions between sustainable forestry as aspired to in the Swiss model and the pressures to stay competitive in an international market, where exploitive and intensive industrial forestry is dominant. What are the lessons for change in both Switzerland and Canada?

FROM EXPLOITIVE TO MULTIPLE USE FORESTRY

The temperate forest covers 29 percent of Switzerland and it is one of the nation's most important renewable resources (Bundesamt für Umwelt 1992, p. 34). Approximately 80 percent of the 1.2 million hectares of forest is productive (Bundesamt für Statistik 1993, p.112). The forest is also of major socioeconomic benefit, a recreational and cultural resource, and an important factor in stabilizing soils and a fragile topography.

Before 600 AD, forests were an open access good in Middle Europe. Farmers cleared the land with axes and fire, but ecological damage was not extensive because clearings were limited. The forest was composed mainly of oak trees in the lowlands, and beech, silver fir and spruce in the mountains. Around 600 AD, much of the forest became the property of the church and landed gentry, who promoted extensive forest clearings, viewing trees as obstacles to the advancement of civilization (WWF 1984).

Most clearings of the lowlands for agriculture and settlement ended in the 13th century. By that time, some of the negative effects of deforestation were felt. Native fauna, such as the aurochs (*Bos primigenius*), were extinct. The moose had withdrawn to the largely untouched forests of Northern and Eastern Europe. Forest cutting moved to the mountain flanks, which caused avalanches, falling stones and landslides in the valleys below, severely damaging valley communities. In a few mountain valleys, people began to view the forest as a means of protection from landslides and avalanches. Beginning in the early 14th century, the forests above those communities were protected by a local measure (Schutzbrief). In most other areas of Switzerland, however, exploitive forest practices continued.

During the late Middle Ages, the exploitation of the Swiss forest intensified due to the steady growth of settlements. Initially, firewood was the primary need. Many other of life's necessities were also made of wood, such as houses, tools, plows and domestic and industrial fuel. Wood shortages soon followed. At the beginning of the 19th century, demand for wood increased further as a consequence of industrialization. Increasing amounts of wood were needed to construct railways and to extract lead and zinc from ore. Substitute energy sources, such as coal, were scarce. In response, fast-growing exotic tree species, frequently spruce, were planted as monocultures in clearcut areas of the lowlands. These forests were mainly seen as wood reserves.

In the first Swiss Federal Constitution (Bundesverfassung) of 1848, the responsibility of forestry matters remained with the cantons. Lowland cantons had already then passed forestry legislation. In the mountain cantons, however, where the forest exploitation had just started in earnest, forest legislation was lacking, apart

> **Sustainability has constituted the key principle of Swiss forestry for approximately a hundred years.**

from the few Schutzbriefe. This had dire consequences. Natural disasters became more frequent, especially in the lowlands, where floods occurred, destroying fields, roads, houses and endangering lives. In order to prevent further damage, the first national forest law was issued in 1876. This law was initially applied to the clearcutting of the mountain forests but was extended to all forests in 1902. An immediate cutting freeze was established for the remaining forest fragments and the principle of sustained yield was introduced. The consequences of this law can still be seen today. In the lowlands a mosaic pattern of forests among cultivated lands contains the same volume of wood as in 1902 when the law was first applied. However, although it was one of the most progressive forest laws in Europe in regulating the quantity of harvest, it failed to protect the quality of the forests. Diverse forests in the lowlands were still transformed into spruce monocultures. Only in the mountains did foresters recognize the need to replant locally adapted seedlings for strong and stable mountain forests capable of protecting settlements.

The significance of the forest as a place for recreation became obvious after the Second World War. Industrialization brought increased material wealth, and the lowlands became more urbanized and densely populated. The perception of forests thus gradually changed from being resource producers to having multiple use functions, such as protection of the landscape and recreation (Bundesamt für Umwelt 1992, p. 35). The meaning of sustainable (used in the sense of sustained yield only) changed, too. To guarantee the newly recognized functions, the protection of the forests as an ecosystem became an important issue, leading to a new forest law in 1992. The law, which received extensive input from environmental groups, focuses on long-term planning, selection logging, strict monitoring of the annual allowable cut, and reforestation with naturally adapted tree species. The law bans planted monocultures and the use of pesticides and fertilizers (Schweizerisches Bundesgesetz 1992, p. 6). The goal of the law is also to allow continued logging while preserving the forest as an ecosystem, maintaining biodiversity, preventing the shrinking of forested areas and ensuring forests as places for multiple use. Many of these provisions were already included in the law of 1902, such as selection logging and a controlled annual allowable cut, but multiple use was only a recommendation. Today, the Swiss forest legislation is considered one of the most progressive of its kind in Europe; *the government officially recognizes the economic and ecological advantages of a newly defined sustainability*.

Today, the Swiss forest legislation is considered one of the most progressive of its kind in Europe.

SUSTAINABLE FORESTRY IN SWITZERLAND

No international consensus exists today on the definition of forest sustainability (Sullivan 1994). Swiss forest sustainability is built on some of the principles that the 1992 United Nations Conference on Environment and Development agreed were vital, though the conference only led to an agreement called "The Non-Legally Binding Authoritative Statement of Principles for a Global Consensus on the

Management, Conservation and Sustainable Development of all Types of Forests" (Forestry Canada 1993). In the following, we describe sustainable forestry as stated in the 1992 Swiss legislation and as applied to Baselland, the canton that is at the forefront of the implementation of the new forest legislation. According to convention, the cantons take approximately 10 years to fully implement new legislation.

Swiss forest sustainability rests on a highly decentralized pattern of forest ownership. In 1993, 320,000 hectares [790,709 acres] or 27 percent of the national forest was privately owned in small parcels. Most of the rest, approximately 880,000 hectares [2,174,450 acres] or 73 percent of the national forest, was owned publicly by approximately 3,900 Swiss municipalities—a sharp contrast to Canada, where most of the forest is owned by the 10 provinces. The Swiss forest is managed on the basis of local public participation, employing local knowledge and meeting a diversity of local needs (Burnand et al. 1991, p. 16-29). Land-use decisions are made on the basis of multiple use, meeting local needs, and applying local knowledge provided by the members of a municipality, local environmental organizations and professional foresters. Communication between different interest groups is considered important. For example, it is not unusual for a government forester to be a member of a local environmental group. Decisions are further based on the characteristics of the forest. Non-timber aspects such as esthetic values of a landscape are given the same priority in the planning and decision-making process as timber aspects.

Different laws at the federal, cantonal and municipal level provide the framework for decisions about forest use. The broad objectives for the cantons are defined in the new federal forest law of 1992, but every canton defines its own specific objectives (Schweizerisches Bundesgesetz 1992, p. 6). Municipal Forestry Commissions then set objectives and priority functions in consultation with the cantonal Department of Forestry and Land Management. These objectives are represented in the municipal land-use plan of each municipality in the canton. Within the municipal land-use plan the forest is divided into zones with different degrees of protection. Within these zones the forest can be logged more or less intensively, depending on its priority function. The cantonal forester, the Department of Land Management and the Municipal Forestry Commission decide collectively, while physically in the forest, which areas should be logged and then record their decision in the local forest management plan. Decisions about priority functions are based on several questions: Is the function of a forest to protect a village more important than harvesting wood for a nearby industry? Should a forest area be set aside for recreational/tourism use? How extensive should harvesting be? Should priority be given to preservation? Decisions on forest use are further based on local forest site (*Standortskarte*) and local forest inventory maps. The forest site map supplies information on forest and site characteristics (e.g. diversity, soil, potential damage as a result of too much recreational use). The forest inventory map describes

> **Swiss forest sustainability rests on a highly decentralized pattern of forest ownership.**

the age, species composition and density of the trees. Prior to final decisions, priorities can be discussed in public and modified by input from environmental groups and citizens as indicated above. Such a decentralized ownership and decision-making pattern makes small-scale community forestry possible, where decisions are made by the municipalities and not shareholders of multinational corporations. This is what makes Swiss forestry more personalized, where forests and people remain in continuous contact (Raphael 1994).

Monitoring the annual wood production on public land is an additional measure to guarantee multiple use forestry and is made possible through a system of intricate measurements at the municipal, cantonal and federal levels. The most important is the annual allowable cut (*Hiebsatz*). It specifies the amount of wood for each forest user that can be cut per year without depleting the overall wood volume. The *Hiebsatz* determines the short-term use of forests. It has been set by the government every 15 years since 1880 for public wood production in forest management plans at the municipal level (Burnand 1991, p. 27). It can be modified by the forester or the municipality to set an appropriate site-specific annual cut level as described in the land-use decision-making process. The *Hiebsatz* also applies to private forests if the forest covers more than 25 hectares [62 a].[2] In such forests, the local forest management plan is worked out with the private owner and the cantonal and municipal authorities. The Department of Forestry at the cantonal level monitors the *Hiebsatz* through annual wood statistics which date back to 1885. The statistics take into account the *Hiebsatz* of each canton to control possible over- or underuse of the forests. The Swiss forest inventory, introduced in the 1980s, is an additional instrument (Köhl 1995).

Selective cutting in Switzerland
Monika Jaggi and
Anders Sandberg

The preservation of forest diversity is another important component of the new Swiss forest law. In order to maintain a forest in different age classes and species, it is important to preserve strong, durable and locally adapted trees. No exotic species can be planted (Schweizerisches 1992). Forests are reforested with locally adapted seedlings with special attention given to mountainous areas. Reforestation in the mountains takes place with seedlings grown in mountain nurseries. Seedlings grown in the lowlands, even if of the same species as those in the mountains, do not have the genetic composition to withstand the harsh climate and the soil conditions of the mountains. In 1992, six million seedlings were planted in Switzerland. Generally, their survival rate is close to 100 percent because of their local adaptability, and the intensive care taken in young and medium-age growth stands (up to 60 years).

Today Swiss forests grow under natural conditions. Though forests are thinned for firewood, no pesticides or fertilizers are applied. Recently, natural rather than artificial regeneration has been promoted, which is not only cheaper but maintains the gene pool of local trees. Swiss environmental groups have supported the position that forests should be allowed to grow back naturally. Their ultimate goal is to convince the forest authorities not to log or build access roads in certain forests to preserve biodiversity. They demand that 10 percent of all forests should be protected, with representative areas of each characteristic type of forest in the country. With most of the Swiss forest being second growth and used commercially, only small fragments of forests, mostly in remote areas of the Alps, are protected today.

Selection logging, the removal of select trees individually or in small groups, is an irrevocable part of Swiss sustainable forestry. It takes place from November to April and is considered necessary to ensure multiple use. Low-impact methods are applied for wood removal, such as using small machines that require only small logging roads and minimize soil compaction and soil erosion. Clearcutting is allowed only under special circumstances identified by the cantonal Forestry Department, such as when converting monocultural plantations in the lowlands to diverse forests. However, the clearcut area cannot be larger than one hectare. Selection logging in Switzerland is labor-intensive, especially in the mountainous areas. The most intensively logged forests are therefore in the more accessible lowlands. Horses are rarely used in logging, though farmers may use them for thinning operations.

Outstanding socioeconomic benefits result from selection logging. One benefit lies in the education of forest workers, forest wardens, foresters and forest engineers (Forstwart 1991, p. 1). Selection logging requires more attention than clearcutting. Therefore educating people who perform the actual logging is an important part of forest management. Forestry education stresses working with machines and focuses on aspects of safety, which benefits both the worker and the forest. Raphael (1994, p. 292) describes the system as follows: "The foresters and forest workers are dealing with individual trees on limited forest land, not with large, anonymous tracts of timber. There is no financial reward for liquidating resources; indeed, the professional standards are based on how well regeneration can be accomplished. The forest is seen as a complete entity that grows timber, nourishes wildlife, stabilizes hillsides, provides water, and serves recreational needs. The forester is a caretaker—but not the owner—of this entity. He is a 'ranger' in the old-fashioned sense: a keeper of woods, a steward of the land. As a public servant and an elected official, he is charged with the task of maintaining a healthy, balanced, and productive forest."

Apart from educational benefits, selection logging guarantees a continuous wood supply and year-round long-term jobs. Approximately 120,000 direct and indirect jobs are provided by the forest industry sector. Of these, about 40,000 are

Selection logging is an irrevocable part of Swiss sustainable forestry.

provided by the public forest sector (Forstwart 1991, p. 4). An example is the 3,900 municipally-owned *Werkhöfe*, machine parks of forest harvesting equipment and manufacturing workshops for wood products. Local workers take care of the municipality's forests. In the summer, they perform reforestation, forest thinning, machine care and job training. During the logging season, additional part-time jobs are available for people outside the municipality. Not included in the above mentioned 40,000 jobs are the farmers who represent more than 40 percent of the private forest owners. They log part-time during the winter when labor, machines and tractors, which are used in summer for farming, are employed in the woods. Due to the low extra costs, many farmers manage to make a profit or to break even, even during recessions (Bundesamt für Statistik 1994). More jobs are provided through processing. Wood is mostly processed within a distance of about 50 kilometres from the site of harvest. A web of small-scale logging operations feeds local sawmills, which then provide the raw product for various carpentry shops. Most of the profit and jobs in the processing sector remain in the local or regional area of the forest, even if logging takes place in a remote area. This provides long-term jobs and a steady income for rural people in areas with few local employment opportunities.

In the processing industry, an apprenticeship system is in place to pass on skills. Switzerland's processing industry is based on high quality work that can require years of education. Approximately 80,000 people are employed in about 7,000 privately-owned secondary-wood processing establishments, which manufacture lumber, pulp and paper, particleboard, plywood, furniture and construction material. Another example of sustainable forest management is the pulp mill Cellulose Fabrik Attisholz AG. The mill was built in 1881 and continued, up until very recently, to be supplied with local pulpwood grown on a sustained yield basis.

Maintaining biodiversity through sustainable forest management minimizes the risk of job loss in the forest industry. Forest diversity is also the best guarantee for success in future markets of wood products.

FORESTS AGAINST WHITE DEATH—THE MEANING OF *SCHUTZBRIEFE*

Approximately 20 percent of the Swiss population lives in mountainous areas, thanks to the *Bannwälder*. Without these protective forests, no villages, no tourist resorts, no mountain economy could exist in the remote regions of Switzerland.

The *Bannwälder* grow high up on the mountain flanks and protect the villages below from avalanches and falling stones. One-third of the Swiss forest is highland protective forest. Pine trees constitute 70-90 percent of these forests. Today's protective forests are mostly the result of reforestation of clearcut areas or natural regeneration.

The value of the *Bannwälder* was recognized only in a few places during the Middle Ages. The so-called *Schutzbrief* legislation, prohibiting cutting and cattle ranging in the forest, was implemented in Muothathal in 1339, Altdorf in 1387, and

> **Local workers take care of the municipality's forests.**

L'Etivan in 1575. Today the need for healthy *Bannwälder* is recognized in the Swiss forest law of 1992. *Bannwälder* are less expensive than artificial avalanche constructions, and are necessary if avalanches are likely above the *Bannwald* or after a *Bannwald* is destroyed (WWF 1984).

SUSTAINABLE FORESTRY UNDER PRESSURE

The Swiss forestry model seeks to maintain a balance between ecology, economy and culture. Small-scale community forestry, local wood manufacturing and local decision-making are claimed to be as important as financial profits. Yet the Swiss forestry model is pressured by the globalization of forest production and the presence in the world market of cheap wood fibre and forest products. Judging from a global economic perspective, Swiss forestry is too costly, too labor-intensive and its products are too expensive. In spite of government subsidies, public forest production has operated at a deficit for several years (Bundesamt für Statistik 1993, p. 50). Swiss forestry cannot compete with forest industries located in more favorable geographic areas where exploitive and intensive forest management practices often prevail. Negative ecological and economic consequences have resulted.

Given that it is too expensive to harvest the commercial forest potential, there is a growing imbalance in favor of older over younger forest growth. One of the main characteristics of sustainable forestry—the balance between older and younger growth—is thereby threatened. This is particularly the case in the mountain regions where only 25 percent of the forest is logged. This represents a particular problem because, according to current thinking in forestry circles, older and dying forests are not considered to be able to protect mountain settlements. The situation is exacerbated by the impact of acid rain. Eighteen percent of the Swiss forest is now damaged but the government, unlike many other European governments, does not acknowledge acid rain as a damaging agent (Hasler 1994). The economic consequences of costly forestry are equally dire. Production costs of Swiss forest products are extremely high when using standard economic criteria. The price of one cubic metre [53 cu. ft.] of coniferous wood (*Nadelholz*) is 120 SFr. compared to 60 SFr. in Sweden (Jordi 1996). This is why the forest industry is opposed to the efforts of the Forest Stewardship Council to introduce certification standards to the industry: industry spokespeople estimate that it would add another 10 SFr. to the price of a cubic metre of coniferous wood (Jordi 1996). The high price of local wood has led to increased wood imports (Bundesamt für Statistik 1993, p. 50, 57-59). In 1993, only 4.3 out of a possible 7 million cubic metres of harvestable wood was cut, while total domestic wood consumption was 6.5 million cubic metres. The imported 2.2 million cubic metres came mostly from European countries. Approximately 543,000 tonnes of pulp were also imported, approximately 11 percent coming from Canada, the second largest supplier to Switzerland (Jahresstatistik 1993, p. 11,12,611).

> The Swiss forestry model seeks to maintain a balance between ecology, economy and culture.

There are at least three options open to the Swiss forest sector in responding to the pressures of the global forest products market. One is to adapt to international trends and promote the rationalization and restructuring of the forest industry. This might mean consolidation of forest lands, the introduction, where possible, of intensive mechanized forestry and economies of scale in wood processing, and expansion of branch operations abroad. There are some indications that this is currently the favored path. The sawmilling industry is being restructured into fewer, larger units (Gubler 1994). The Cellulose AG Attisholz now operates a pulp mill in Chile, where production costs are cheaper (Brugger et al. 1994). To meet these industrial trends, there is also a policy of enlarging the districts supervised by foresters. In the lowlands, this will mean an increase in size of forest districts from 100-200 to 500-600 hectares [247-494 a to 1,236-1,483 a] and cutbacks in the employment of foresters. The rationalization and restructuring of the Swiss forest industry, however, can only be a limited and short-term solution. To apply industrial rationalization criteria through the introduction of mechanized forestry, for example, is almost impossible. Forest workers cannot easily be replaced by machines because of a difficult topography, mixed forests in different stages of growth, selection logging and intensive recreational forest use.

A second option might involve the abandonment of forestry for industrial use, leaving the forests as preserves, for protection, as bioreserves, or for tourists and recreationalists, leaving the Swiss wood processing industries to import their wood supplies. This option requires a rethinking of the current position that only a 'working forest' is capable of protecting sensitive landscape features. Recent evidence suggests that even the 'natural' forest can fulfil the same function (CH-Forschung 1996). While the preservationist option might meet with approval by local environmentalists, it may intensify unsustainable forestry from the regions where Switzerland draws its supply (Sedjo 1993).

A third option to the globalization of the forest industry, and a more critical stand, would be to protect domestic forestry. There are several measures that can be taken. One would include some type of protection for Swiss forest production, going against the grain of the GATT (General Agreement on Tariffs and Trade) and the general liberalization of trade, but possibly facilitated by Switzerland's political neutrality (standing outside the European Community, for example) and justified by the lack of sustainable forestry in most other countries. In a global market, the lowest common denominator of sustainable forestry determines economic efficiency and market share. The adoption of the concept of full-cost accounting would change this situation, suggesting that "when social and environmental costs are factored into the cost of wood products, corporate industrial forest products are considerably more costly than products that come from ecoforestry [sustainable forestry] sites, which seek to protect environmental and community sustainability" (Patterson 1994). This would respond to the 1992 UNCED forest principles of establishing international criteria for the conservation, management and sustainable development of forests and the encouragement of a fair international trade in forest products. This initiative would welcome, rather than oppose, the efforts of the Forest Stewardship Council to introduce certification standards to industry.

As long as the Swiss forest model is exposed to wood imports from unsustainably managed forest regions, and as long as the Swiss, along with wood consumers worldwide, are unwilling to pay the true value of local forest products, the Swiss will contribute to the decline of sustainable forestry and support the process of forest and landscape destruction elsewhere.

LESSONS FOR CANADA AND FROM CANADA'S FIRST NATIONS

Prior to 1900, the Swiss forests were cut indiscriminately with often disastrous and tragic consequences. Mountain villages were buried under landslides and lowland villages were flooded. In response, Swiss forest policy changed to halt deforestation by recognizing formally that the national forest has multiple functions.

The early Swiss concept of forestry still appears common in Canada though shifting environmental values might propel change for the future. However, geographical and political reasons in Canada have prevented the implementation of the principle of sustainable forestry. A vast hinterland with rich natural resources, including untouched old-growth forests, has promoted exploitive use. But resource abundance does not tell the full story. Canada's heritage as a staple producer for metropolitan markets is still felt (Nelles 1974). Provincial governments work closely with distant transnational corporations in the quest for revenue and jobs (Marchak 1995; Pratt and Urquhart 1994; Western Canada Wilderness Committee 1993). Forestry as a science rationalizes the clearcutting of old-growth forests in spite of the serious problems with regeneration. Forest management is clearly based on the interests and science of large international corporate interests (Richardson et al. 1993).

Yarding logs in Swiss forests
Monika Jaggi and
Anders Sandberg

The problems of corporate forestry are well documented. Corporate forestry eliminates jobs through mechanization, and clearcutting provides merely logs and crude lumber products for export (M'Gonigle and Parfitt 1994). Such processes do not provide as many jobs as selection cutting and value added industries. In 1992, 289,000 direct and 440,000 indirect jobs were provided by Canada's 12,600 forest establishments (Forestry Canada 1993, p. 94). In Switzerland, approximately 40,000 direct jobs and 80,000 indirect jobs were provided by 15,700 forest establishments (Forstwart 1991, WWF 1984). These numbers include the municipal *Werkhöfe* and private establishments. Only 1.2 million hectares [3 million a] of productive forest covers Switzerland, whereas the Canadian productive forest covers over 240 million hectares [593 million a] (Dunster 1990). The Canadian forest sector thus provides 3 jobs per 1,000 hectares [1.2 jobs/1,000 a] of productive forest lands, whereas the Swiss counterpart provides 83 jobs per 1,000 hectares [34 jobs/1,000 a].

Current Canadian forest practices have led to frequent ecological and socioeconomic conflicts within and outside Canada. One area of conflict arises from forest harvesting on lands used by Canada's First Nations. Today, First Nations not only take frequent action against such practices, but they have also begun to launch claims for the right to control land and resources (Wagner 1991). Most such claims have a legal basis, as aboriginal rights are recognized in the Canadian Constitution, though their exact meaning remains to be worked out in the courts and at the negotiating tables. Once settled, there will be considerable redistribution of resource management authority. First Nations management schemes, which may share power and responsibility with existing government structures (called co-management), is one strategy to increase First Nation involvement (Berkes et al. 1991). Such management arrangements may involve First Nations exclusively or combine state and aboriginal management systems. State management systems based on 'scientific' data, private property rights, and the law may have to be replaced by (or balanced with) local management systems based on local custom, tradition, knowledge and social sanctions (Berkes et al. 1991). Common property rights might apply, too, where forest lands are vested in communities rather than individuals. Running small-scale community forestry in a co-management arrangement could mean protecting the resource base through local control and the creation of local industries (Ontario Round Table 1992, p. 32-36). Though few First Nations' forest management schemes have been implemented and assessed, some examples, such as the Dokis near Georgian Bay in Ontario, the Kluskus in British Columbia, and the Menominee in Wisconsin, point to the potential for success in the past and present (Angus 1990; Berkes et al. 1991; Flader 1983; Jimmie 1991; Nesper and Pecore 1993).

First Nations' concepts of forest lands bear some resemblance to what Niesslein calls social binding, a concept rooted in Germanic law that allows society to impose restrictions on the ability of private forest owners to dispose of their land (Niesslein 1984). This is also what Netting has described in the Swiss mountain village of Törbel where extensive land resources, such as forests, pastures and water, were owned and managed on a communal basis well into the modern era (Netting 1981). The recognition and revival of such historical notions could well benefit sustainable forestry. In Swiss forest management, power sharing between local resource users and the government is in some respects built on these concepts. As local management and co-management of resources might become a key principle of sustainability in Canada, the Swiss forestry model could be something to learn from.

Enough forests remain to allow for a change in forest management in Canada.

> **The Canadian forest sector thus provides 3 jobs per 1,000 hectares whereas the Swiss counterpart provides 83 jobs per 1,000 hectares.**

So far, however, power saws have worked more effectively than political mills. The future will tell whether local challenges will overcome the global pressures that now threaten forest sustainability everywhere. The Swiss forestry model and Canada's First Nations provide lessons on the prospects and constraints of viable future alternatives.

19

A Forest for Scotland

Donald McPhillimy

THE VISION

A FOREST POLICY FOR SCOTLAND should have, at its center, the vision of a country with many more trees. All communities, from the hearts of our towns and cities to the distant villages and crofts, need more trees, woods and forests. But these needs will not be met by present-day government policies. A fundamentally new understanding of the relationship between trees and people is needed if forestry is to meet public aspirations.

A forest is more than its tree species. The natural forest that developed over most of Scotland after the last ice age was a dynamic ecosystem, supporting a wide range of plant and animal life. It waxed and waned over the centuries influenced both by climatic change and human activity. Much of this activity was, however, inspired by short-term objectives and failed to appreciate that forests needed longer term care.

Forest policy must be linked to a better appreciation of ecological processes. Scotland needs its future forest resource to be managed in a sustainable way, building on the forest capital, not frittering it away. Consideration of soil, water, biodiversity and energy use must be an integral part of the policy-making process.

A new forest policy for Scotland must include many more trees in the places where people live and work; it must include the creation of woods and forests managed for a wide variety of products and public uses; it must include a massive expansion of the natural forest remnants that Scotland is so fortunate to have inherited from earlier times. A new policy must develop from a fundamental reappraisal of how we use the land and how local communities are able to influence the evolution of their forest resource.

A narrow perspective for forest policy in Scotland must be avoided. Global concerns encompassing climatic change, the use of fossil fuels and the destruction of tropical and temperate rainforests cannot be ignored. They are part of the vision that

Scotland needs for its future forests.

CRITIQUE OF CURRENT FOREST POLICY

British forest policy is a continuing program of afforestation which governments have justified by appealing to a succession of different objectives: strategic reserve of timber, return on investment, reduction of imports, locking up of carbon dioxide and, most recently, providing "many diverse benefits." The program has appeared to justify the objectives rather than being justified by them. The planting target of 33,000 hectares [81,542 a] per year is arbitrary and meaningless in the absence of a meaningful forest policy.

LAND-USE INTEGRATION

Despite repeated statements concerning the integration of land-use objectives by the government, numerous instances point to complete failure. Nature conservation and forestry objectives are put directly at odds with each other in many cases such as Glen Dye. Government agencies for agriculture, nature conservation and the countryside all have statutory powers to support forestry activities and yet no policy exists, either to integrate them or to optimize the allocation of public money.

SOCIAL OBJECTIVES

Rural communities have increasingly become disenfranchised from the land-use decision-making process due in part to the prevailing political attitudes to landownership. Upland farmers in particular have not found a way of remaining on the land and establishing a forest enterprise. The only option in the face of declining incomes has been to sell the land for forestry with grave consequences for the social infrastructure of many rural areas.

Employment in the forest is increasingly in the form of contract labor working from a distant base and only injecting a portion of wages into the local economy. Processing industries are increasingly owned by foreign companies and limited wealth creation takes place in the locality of the forest. The forests produce a limited array of products for consumption in markets outside the locality. The forest itself is often owned by absentee owners.

LAND OWNERSHIP

As J.K. Galbraith put it so well, "personal interest always wears the disguise of public purpose." This public purpose has been articulated effectively by the landowning lobby and, indeed, many public benefits flow from some of the best forestry in the country in private hands. The key failure has been to control the degree of public benefit arising from the public support given to private owners for minimal return, either to the public or to local communities.

ECONOMIC BENEFITS

Government analyses have shown that forestry has consistently failed to attain conventional national targets. Continuing afforestation has been justified by altering targets and by citing national social and environmental benefits. These "nontimber" benefits, however, frequently did not exist or were negative; i.e. they constituted net costs. Forests should be designed and managed to provide substantial public goods in the form of environmental and social benefits. Economic assessment methods and our entire definition of economics need to be widened and altered to take account of this.

SILVICULTURE

Some of the best silviculture practised in Scotland today takes place on family-owned estates where generations of skilled foresters have been free to practice their art with the long-term vision required for environmentally sound forestry. Some of the worst is to be found on exposed sites in the uplands where Sitka spruce plantations have seen no management since they were planted, and where no thinning takes place. Clear-fell and replant with Sitka spruce is the silvicultural system that dominates Scottish forestry.

RESEARCH AND EDUCATION

Forestry research has tended to concentrate on technical issues relating to timber production and the mitigation of the worst environmental impacts of modern forestry practice. A completely new research agenda is required to address such fundamental issues as sustainable forestry, carbon budgeting, multipurpose forestry, watershed management, forest ecosystem design and integrated land-use systems.

Forestry and conservation education should be key elements of the school curriculum.

NATURAL FORESTS

Scotland now has less than 2% of its natural forest cover left. The condition of the remaining resource today is perilous. A major government commitment is required to restore the natural forest of Scotland.

RED DEER

Existing legislation, currently under review, has proved inadequate and the voluntary arrangements that exist in the form of Deer Management Groups have not measured up to the task of reducing the population sufficiently to restore woodland and other damaged ecosystems.

THE FORESTRY COMMISSION

The FC has had an unenviable task, which it has tackled with dedication and patience, given the constraints and direction it has had to work with. It has not

> **Some of the best silviculture practised in Scotland today takes place on family-owned estates.**

taken a sufficiently independent view, being caught in the impossible position of being responsible for regulation, advice to government, implementation of government policy, research and forest establishment and management. It has been responsible for some of the most unimaginative and damaging afforestation in Scotland and has built up for itself a major credibility problem.

THE FOREST INDUSTRY

The forestry industry has been almost universally concerned with but one aspect of forestry, a byproduct of forests: timber. Indeed the private owner's organization is called Timber Growers U.K. A change of name and a change of attitude is required.

THE INTERNATIONAL CONTEXT

In 1987, the U.K. consumed 49 million cubic metres [1,730,000,000 cu. ft.] of timber of which 11% was home produced. In 1988, the import bill for timber was £6.6 billion. Such figures have been used repeatedly to argue for further expansion of forestry in Scotland. Much more fundamental issues need to be faced before it can be used as a *prima facie* argument. Is the U.K. "entitled" to make such demands on the global forest resource? Is it a reliance that is based on a sustainably managed resource?

FUNDAMENTAL PRINCIPLES

The fundamental principle on which this forest policy discussion paper is based is sustainability. A natural forest is self-sustaining. Managed forest must be capable of producing timber and other forest products without eroding the capital base: the soil, the water regime, the species diversity, the biomass and the esthetic qualities of the forest.

Fundamental principles of a policy for the forest of Scotland that should underpin its formulation are *ecological* and *socioeconomic* sustainability.

ECOLOGICAL SUSTAINABILITY

The majority of issues fall into 4 subdivisions:
- The soil complex
- Water
- Biodiversity
- Energy

The soil complex

Soil is the most fundamental and precious natural resource. Brown earths will support a wide range of tree species. Gleys, which form 40% of the uplands, have increased since deforestation. Deep peats form 15% of upland soils. Afforestation can lead to problems of irreversible shrinkage and net production of carbon dioxide from deep peat soils. Conifers and other species such as Calluna tend to increase the podzolization of podzols whereas broadleaves and other species such as bracken and

Agrostis-Festuca grasses tend to stabilize or reverse these processes. Modern plantation forestry uses high inputs to fit the soil to a very small range of species without trying to work with natural soil processes. This is unsustainable.

Water

Loss of water through interception and evaporation, higher flood peaks, lower drought levels, erosion, sedimentation, leaching of fertilizers, transference of airborne pollutants, and effects on energy inputs are some of the effects of plantation forestry. Forests can play an important and beneficial role in the water cycle. The key is to build in the beneficial elements and eliminate the negative ones.

Biodiversity

A rich mosaic of ecosystems, species and genes is part of the principle of holding the Earth's resources in trust for future generations. Diversity is also linked to adaptability to changing circumstances and to stability. Diversification of species and structure reduces the risk of catastrophic damage from pests, wind or fire. Experience of the benefits of a more natural and diverse silviculture has been gained in many places. For example, the conversion of natural forests to plantations in Germany in the 19th century gave rise to reduced productivity. A return to a more ecologically sensitive silviculture in the 20th century improved productivity. This parallels the "new forestry" emerging in the northwest of North America. British plantation forestry, despite advances in landscaping and the treatment of edges, is building up future problems through overdependence on one simple ecosystem and a lack of biodiversity.

This practice is not sustainable.

Energy

Very little research has been carried out on energy use in forestry. We should be locating forests and designing forest management and timber processing systems that will function efficiently in a future world where less energy may be available. Closely tied in with the issue of energy use is the question of the carbon cycle and concerns over global warming as a result of carbon dioxide emissions.

SOCIOECONOMIC SUSTAINABILITY

This has two components:
- People
- Economics

People

Forests and their management are also about people. Existing land-use policies have failed rural Scotland. Scottish rural communities are fragile and, whilst some establishment and harvesting jobs are gratefully accepted, decisions such as moving to no-thin regimes are made at a distance by the Forestry Commission or absentee owners, and these can start a downward spiral of depopulation. It is desirable also

> **A sustainable forest requires a sustainable workforce.**

that foresters of all levels, and the communities in which they live, should have pride in their forests. This requires a greater degree of local control or ownership and greater local processing of forest produce so that the wealth generated by the forest will circulate through the local economy and bring it to life. If local jobs and local processing were at the forefront of forest design, a different forest might ensue. A sustainable forest requires a sustainable workforce; that is, one with a greater stake in the forest than at present.

But forests are not purely local affairs. The public at large should have a say in the forests they largely pay for and may wish to walk in. Will they be full of wildlife or purely timber producers? Will they have the characteristics of the natural forest or will they be tree factories? Will they give access to the open hills or block them off? Esthetic, spiritual and recreational values will be optimized in the forest of Scotland.

The Scottish Highlands
Duncan Taylor

Economics

Forest economics should be concerned with providing mechanisms to ensure that society derives maximum benefit from the environmental, productive and esthetic outputs of forests. The forest of Scotland will, therefore, need to be subjected to a greatly modified and extended kind of economic thinking than what currently pertains. Full account will need to be taken of externalities; discounting will need to be modified or abandoned; the rights and preferences of local communities, future generations and other land users will need to be accounted for. It may also be necessary to look at measures other than money to assess the economics of forest operations (e.g. energy). The creation of wealth far from the forest by companies and forest owners who fail to invest in the local economy should be discouraged.

In conclusion, the forest of Scotland needs to be based on fundamental principles of ecological and socioeconomic sustainability. These principles are not options. They are all necessary and any system that fails to meet them will ultimately fail.

FOREST LOCATION

Sustainable, diverse forest should be the dominant vegetation over most of the natural forest zone of Scotland, as it is in our neighbor to the east—Norway. The justification for vast agricultural and sporting landscapes is diminishing today. A new balance is required. Each alternative land-use—agriculture, conservation, recreation, industry, housing and infrastructure—will have a place within the forest, each will be accorded its allocation of resources (including land), and integrated with the whole.

FOREST DESIGN

What will the ideal forest of the future look like? It will be located around and between other land uses as defined by optimum land use. Its design will be based on the fundamental principles discussed earlier in the paper. The forest will take time and sensitive management to evolve, both out of the existing forest resource and from new effort.

There will be an establishment/pioneer phase when substantial amounts of nonrenewable resources will be required to overcome some of the existing environmental problems. After this a steady-state phase will gradually develop. This forest will be sustainable and form a renewable resource. It will range from the first Betula nana at the tree line on Ben Nevis to the last rowan planted down by the docks of Stranraer and Wick. It will be multipurpose, with widely varied species, and a structure related to soils, climate and management objectives. It will be diverse and full of wildlife.

The design of this forest is considered in three parts:
1. The Natural Forest
2. The Extensive Forest
3. The Intensive Forest

The Natural Forest

The Natural Forest would represent a woodland type almost completely lacking in the present landscape. After establishment, minimum intervention would allow this zone to become as close as possible in structure and species composition to Scotland's natural forest. Within this zone would be much of Scotland's wild and remote country.

The Extensive Forest

The Extensive Forest would be very much the largest zone. A forest diverse in structure and species composition, it would provide significant amounts of timber and be integrated with agricultural activities, settlements, and recreational facilities. It would provide a valuable resource base for local communities and would be largely owned and managed for maximum benefit to the local economy. True multiple use would be practiced with recreation, wildlife conservation, timber production and agriculture all playing a part in the management of the forest.

The Intensive Forest

The Intensive Forest would represent forest closest to the plantations of today but significantly modified in respect of species composition, management systems, ownership and use. This forest zone would be concentrated on better land, closer to population and industrial centers and have good access.

Overall

Overall it is expected that a much greater value of timber will be harvested than at present. The degree of intensity is a measure not only of human effort and management, but also of resource inputs, accessibility, scale and ecological diversity and stability. The character of the forest will change as it approaches other land uses so that one blends into and is enhanced by the other.

A clear vision and a sound but flexible policy are required to guide forestry in Scotland into and through the next century. This will be the period when the environmental issues that are central to forestry will finally make themselves felt, not only here but in a global context.

20

The Bradley Method of Bush Regeneration

John Seed

A METHOD HAS BEEN DEVELOPED IN AUSTRALIA for regenerating native bush. It is named the Bradley Method after the two sisters, now deceased, who devised it.

Should it be our wish to bring back the native vegetation that once covered a particular piece of Earth, they found that no heroic tree planting measures are called for. Rather, this humble technique requires us only to remove all foreign influences while causing the minimum possible disturbance to whatever native vegetation still exists.

Thus, the first step may be to fence off the area we have chosen to keep cows or goats at bay. It may also be necessary to take steps to prevent fire from invading the land. We must then be able to identify all species of plants that we encounter, both the exotics and those native to the area. We need to recognize them not only in their mature form but also when their seedlings first poke out of the ground. Then the method is simple: remove the exotics without treading on the natives. Encouraged in this way, the native species begin to come back, growing stronger in each ensuing season.

There is only one other rule: start from the strength. It may be that in the area we wish to heal there are deep scars, erosion gullies perhaps, that break our heart, and it is our wish to immediately tend to these. In order to succeed, however, we must resist this temptation and start from the strongest expression of native vegetation in our management area.

If our area is an inner-city park that has been lawn for a century, our beginnings may be from a tiny patch that the mower couldn't reach and where a few native weeds flourish. If there is a forgotten corner where a few pioneer tree seedlings have emerged, we start from there. Carefully stepping backwards, removing exotics as we go, we invite the bush to follow. It is painstaking work. Each year, the process accelerates as the native intelligence of the place emerges and the life force quickens.

More and more species emerge as the conditions necessary for their growth are re-created. As one species of pioneer completes its work in, say, repairing the soil with shade and leaf mulch, it becomes scarcer and is succeeded by the next. The microclimate slowly changes and, one day, after perhaps seven years of this patient, rewarding service, we may find to our astonishment, a seedling emerging of a climax species that has not been seen here in the city for 100 years. Was the seed dropped by a bird that alighted in the branches of a pioneer now reaching 100 feet above? Is it possible that the seed lay dormant in the ground since it was first cleared, waiting for this moment when conditions were again suitable for its return? We will never know.

And when the accelerating advance of the native bush finally reaches that erosion gully, it now has the vigor and the necessary species to be able to recolonize and integrate it and slowly bring it back into harmony.

Human is not the hero, proudly planting thousands of trees, reclaiming the desert, healing the Earth. Rather we are humble in the face of the superhuman intelligence of nature, and *invite* the original nature of the place to return.

There is something very spiritual about the Bradley Method. Encoded within it is a deep trust in the native intelligence of the Earth; she *knows* what is meant to grow in this place and she also knows, unerringly, the particular stages of succession that will best take us from whatever kind of degradation exists at present back to climax.

In my travels, I have encountered systems akin to the Bradley Method in several different countries. I found one example as I travelled around India in 1987 lecturing on rainforest conservation and the deep ecology movement. In Bhopal I visited one of the most enlightened foresters I have ever met. His name was Chaturdevi and he was professor of the new school of forestry that had been established in that city just a few years before. His school had been granted a large area of ground, a couple of thousand acres as I recall, and the first thing he had done, before the first brick was laid for the school buildings, was to fence the land. It was at that time a desolate thorny desert denuded by goats and recurrent fires set by the goatherders to encourage succulent new growth. Chaturdevi hired armed guards to keep the goats at bay and watch for fires. The first task he set his students was to inventory the vegetation that grew there. In the beginning, they discovered stunted remnants of a few tree species that had managed to survive the former regime—just a few sticks here and there whose leaves had been chewed back as soon as they emerged.

By the time that I saw the land some four years later, more than 80 species had reemerged, as I recall, and in many places the vegetation was pumping, accelerating back towards its climax status. The armed guards were still there.

In many other places, from Russia to the United States, I have found, to my surprise, understandings akin to the Bradley Method emerging independently and unbeknownst to each other. Perhaps it should come as no surprise. Perhaps this phenomenon is *itself* a manifestation of the Bradley Method, only working here on

> Human is not the hero, rather we are humble in the face of the superhuman intelligence of nature.

the level of the human psyche, rather than the biology of a landscape. Surely the human psyche is itself a product of the landscape; we ourselves grow from the soil, are made of soil. In this case, the most appropriate metaphors for understanding psyche are biological ones. Techniques that facilitate the return of native vegetation may also help us understand how wild common sense can return to the denuded mind. The spontaneous emergence of the "Bradley Method" in different places around the world can then be seen as an expression of the return of a trust in nature after centuries and millennia of human arrogance.

What I first learned of by the name "Bradley Method," then, may be one stage in the succession of the return of native wisdom and humility to the clearcut modern mind, when the exotic influences of *anthropocentrism* are removed. By anthropocentrism I mean the ubiquitous modern idea that the human is the center of everything and that order comes into the world only through human control and ingenuity. The rejection of anthropocentrism has sometimes been termed "deep ecology."

One of the understandings of deep ecology is that the sense shared by most modern humans of being isolated, alienated and separate from nature is illusory. In fact, we are Earthlings, we *belong* here. We have evolved on this planet for 4,000 million years of organic life and are made of Earth. Our soul too, our psyche, is Earth-born, emerging from the exquisite biology of this planet, continuous with it. The ubiquitous illusion of separation springs from the false ideas of human "otherness" and superiority that thousands of years of Judeo-Christian and other traditions have created within us.

As we root out these pernicious false ideas of our own grandeur and importance, we "fall in love outwards" (Jeffers) and the truth spontaneously emerges of who we *really* are: "plain members of the biota" (Leopold). As the exotic influence of the dominant paradigm recedes, we realize (with Commoner) that "nature knows best" and our native intelligence pops spontaneously from the ground of our being.

When we see the Bradley Method as being equally applicable in the reawakening of native human intelligence as in the re-emergence of a biological ecosystem, several corollaries suggest themselves. First, we don't need to plant new ideas in each other's minds. If we can root out the alien ideas, the ecological insight springs forth spontaneously. We need to know ourselves, to create an inventory of our mind, to learn to recognize the ideas, feelings, habits, blockages that prevent us from experiencing our unity with nature. Which parts of us are harmonious with our larger system? How can we compassionately root out destructive habits and conditioned ideas without unnecessary disturbance and self-hatred?

Secondly, start with the strength; there's nothing wrong with preaching to the choir. In fact it is more important to strengthen the experience of deep ecology among those who already love nature and work for the Earth, than to waste our energy trying to convince the CEO of the EXXON erosion gully about the importance of a biocentric ethic. Strengthening ecological empathy and insights within the conservation community will make it ever stronger and more capable of making inroads into corporate culture, the Vatican and other bastions of anthropocentrism.

21

Special Forest Products: Past, Present and Future

James Freed

THE USE OF NONTIMBER PRODUCTS FROM THE FOREST is not new. All of the present-day commercial products were used by native people and early European settlers. Their uses of forest plants helped them sustain everyday life. They used every part of the plant and every plant within the forest.

Some uses they made of these plants are similar to what we use them for today:

- Bear grass, sweet grass, cedar roots, spruce roots, cedar bark, yew, horsetail fern, willow, rush, cattail, birch bark, vine maple, big-leaf maple, cherry bark and nettles were all used in making woven products, which ranged from baskets to clothing. The baskets were used for cooking, storage and carrying. The best baskets were tightly woven and used personally or for gifts. The more loosely woven baskets were used as trade items with other tribes and early European settlers.
- Yew, cedar, bigleaf maple, white pine, willow, oak, ocean spray and dogwood were all used to make cooking implements, tools, and weapons.
- Yarrow, coltsfoot, fungi, algae, moss, lichen, cow parsnip, salal, rose, salmonberry, nettle, cattail, hemlock tree, red cedar, ferns, and yew were all used as medicines by the Northwest native people.
- The roots, bulbs, tubers, stems, leaves, buds, cones and berries of most forest plants were all critical to the daily nutritional needs of the people who lived off the land. Many plants were used for adding flavor to bland foods.

Plants from the forest and ranges played a more important role in the lives of natives than animals did. Unfortunately, the knowledge of how to identify and use these plants has been lost to most native people. The main reason is the plant world was not a male concern; it was the domain of women. Men took care of hunting, housing and defence, while women took care of the nutritional and medical needs of the family. One Chehalis woman told me that both plant and animal worlds were equally important. The man caught the salmon and the woman made it a complete meal. The salmon was good by itself, but a perfect meal was produced when the salmon was stuffed with herbs, roots and berries.

Many native people feel that before we can save the forest, we must learn about all the other things that can be produced from the forest aside from lumber and paper. We must become forest managers, not timber managers. Some of the early timber managers were very observant people. They constantly looked for ways to increase their income from the lands they logged. They also looked for ways to provide income for the months and years when timber was not in demand.

EARLY U.S. MARKETS

The first formal company to market specialty forest products from the Pacific Northwest was the Kirk Company in Puyallup, Washington. In 1939, Kirk marketed evergreen huckleberry, salal and sword fern. Realizing that these plants kept their leaves when picked, they marketed them to local retail florists and then to wholesale florists in California and Illinois. By the 1950s, the demand for floral greenery was so big that it became a major industry in Puget Sound and western Washington. Most major companies were located near Puget Sound because the best salal and evergreen huckleberry were found near salt water.

The industry quickly expanded to other greenery. Cedar boughs, white pine tips, Douglas fir limbs, Oregon grape, holly, red-tipped huckleberry and juniper were harvested and marketed from September to May, when the plants were tender during the growing season. Increased demand during the 1950s and 1960s forced some floral companies to add refrigerated storage. This enabled them to maintain the quality of the greens and sell them during the summer months. However, the cost of operating these storage units was quite high and forced many companies out of business.

To meet the demands for floral greens, many of the wholesale houses set up a network of small buying houses all over western Washington and the northern coastal range of Oregon. This enabled the wholesalers to concentrate smaller loads from the individual pickers into larger truck-size loads that could be moved to processing plants. This system is still in place today, although there are only nine large wholesale buyers providing the greenery market for Washington, Oregon and British Columbia.

The pickers of evergreen plants were always on the lookout for other cash opportunities. They started stripping cascara bark in the 1930s to supply the natural laxative markets. An average 2.5 pounds [1.1 kg] of laxative per year per person was consumed in the U.S.; with such a high demand, many cascara trees were stripped. Foxglove was also picked for the digitalis market for heart medication. These markets diminished in the late 1970s when synthetic laxatives and digitalis were developed. The loss of this market caused the pickers to look for more products. In the 1950s, they started picking cones for the nursery seed markets to supply the demand for new forest seedlings to replant clearcut lands. They realized that empty cones would make

> **The plant world was not a male concern; it was the domain of women.**

great additions to the Christmas greenery markets. Many millions of cones were harvested directly from the forest floor to meet the demands of the wreath and crafts industries.

The demand by specialty stores for fresh nuts, mushrooms, berries and herbs has always been high. Many logging families supplemented their income by picking berries and mushrooms and selling them to restaurants, small grocery stores and home canneries. When there was no commercial market for these products, they were often used by the pickers to improve their diets.

The wild edible markets have come and gone many times over the last 50 years. Some fluctuation was caused by changing eating habits, but most was caused by the ups and downs of the timber industry. When there was timber to be cut and marketed, the loggers cut timber and forgot about special forest products. The demand for wild berries is on the increase again for jams, jellies, juices, fruit leathers, liquors and wines. I have been asked to locate wild huckleberries for a few fresh baked pies as well as for a Northwest jelly producer.

THE INDUSTRY TODAY

While the industry has experienced constant change since its start, rapid change has occurred only in the last 10 years. Shorter timber rotations have removed large tracts of land from production. Products and companies have come and gone and new laws have been enacted and enforced. Conflicts between user groups are on the rise. New forestry practices required new management plans. The demand for new products from the forest coupled with an increased demand for higher quality, older product lines have caused forest-land managers, pickers, buyers, law enforcers and wholesalers to shake their heads.

And yet more changes have occurred: intense timber management programs were implemented as large tracts of lands were set aside to protect wildlife and water quality. Land managers have had to use environmentally friendly methods to increase their total income. The problem was that no one knew how to manage or assess the value of special forest products because they had been viewed as weeds—weeds that were in competition with the real crop: timber. Millions of dollars had been spent to figure out how to kill all the plants interfering with the production of wood fibre for lumber and paper products. Now methods to maximize profits by marketing and managing "weeds" were needed without the information necessary to make wise decisions.

The harvesting and sale of bear grass has become one of the fastest growing products of the floral and crafts greenery industry. It is used for dried flower arrangements. The beauty of the bear grass plant is its stiff stem, which when dry provides a perfect supplement to other dried flower arrangements. Absorbing natural dyes evenly makes it very valuable to the crafts industry. However, there are complications. Some feel that bear grass is not being harvested sustainably. Native people need it for their ceremonies and crafts. Others feel that its harvest competes with wildlife needs. Some managers are trying to kill it to plant trees, although it stabilizes the soil. Other managers want high harvest fees that some harvesters cannot afford. Commercial harvesters want exclusive permits to bear grass areas. Low start-up costs permit large numbers of migrant workers to enter the forest. Some harvesters are willing to defend their areas with guns, and others are simply harvesting without permits.

How we deal with all these concerns for bear grass will show us how to deal with other special forest products. Presently in the Northwest, we are looking at each product individually in terms of regulations, but hopefully a method for evaluating, protecting and regulating the harvest will be devised for all products.

Mushrooms offer an even greater potential and liability than they did five years ago. As lands for the production of mushrooms are depleted around the world, the demand on Pacific Northwest mushroom lands has become greater. New markets in all Pacific Rim countries have identified over 400 species of fungi with a potential commercial value. New markets in the U.S. have begun to view the wild mushroom as an important product for the upscale buyer. The North America Free Trade Agreement is enabling new buyers from Canada and Mexico to look to the Pacific Northwest for meeting ever-increasing demands for fresh and canned mushrooms.

With this increased demand comes a need to have a consistent labor supply. In the late 1980s, wholesale buyers began hiring contract labor teams. These teams were often staffed by Mexicans and immigrants from Southeast Asia. They worked hard, asked few questions, took payment in cash and produced large, consistent quantities. Some of those early contract laborers have started their own companies to supply many special forest products.

A major problem with such companies and their contracted help is their lack of invested interest in the forests they harvest from, being concerned primarily with making quick profits. As well, their harvesting techniques may be doing long-term damage to the forests, but we have little way of knowing, because reliable research on mushroom production does not exist.

A side problem with the use of migrant labor is the upset of local people, who feel they have a right to pick where they have picked for years without permits. In Mason County, Washington, public meetings were held at which over 250 people voiced their concerns on lost rights. They often did not have any legal rights to harvest but had been permitted to do so by landowners; in some cases, the landowners were not aware that valuable crops were being harvested from their lands.

Consequently, land managers now require permits to harvest mushrooms and other specialty forest products. Almost all large timber companies and the U.S. Forest Service require permits for commercial harvesting of specialty forest products. The need for permits especially affects part-time pickers who do not have the risk capital to pay for permits if adequate supplies of mushrooms are not available. In

Mushrooms offer an even greater potential and liability than they did five years ago.

addition, there are efforts in Washington to charge out-of-state pickers a surcharge for picking permits. New laws are being drafted at this time that will increase the penalties for possession of mushrooms or specialty forest products without a signed permit from the landowner. Other laws are being proposed to require all buyers of specialty products to keep complete records of every purchase.

The last notable change occurring in the last five years is the increased demand for knowledge. Until I included special forest products in my curriculum at Washington State University, I did not see much interest in forest management. I now conduct classes on plant identification and management for real estate brokers, planners, home owner associations, the U.S. Forest Service, timber companies, small woodlot owners and managers, economic development organizations, and environmental groups. The size of plants, the time it takes to replace a harvested plant, and cash flow are all concerns of the participants. Small woodlot owners feel positive about protecting the environment and maintaining a constant cash flow by extending forest rotations. They do not need big equipment or large acres to be successful, and can often create products from their homes.

WORKING TOGETHER IN COMMUNITIES

The future of this industry demands that it be flexible to adapt to the ever-changing needs of society. Flexibility has made it possible for existing special forest product companies to be in business after 50 years. As long as unrealistic expectations are not placed on it, this industry will continue to grow and thrive. But it will not offer replacement for lost timber jobs, nor will it be a replacement for timber management. Instead, a strong specialty forest product industry will help future land managers maximize their forest resources. In some cases, this industry will enable land managers to meet the needs for wildlife management and still remain profitable. I envision this industry providing a supplemental cash flow to timber industries that will enable them to grow timber on longer rotations.

The timber land managers of today will become the natural resource land managers of the future. They will have the skills necessary to manage all plants to maximum potential in an integrated community of plants. They will know how each of the plants supports and is supported by its plant community.

In the future, we will examine how special forest products help in community— not just economic—development. For too long have the U.S. Forest Service, government officials and industry made the decisions and told community members what they wanted. To make a developing industry a stable one, we must listen closely to all members of the industry, not just the ones in power now.

I have presented over 50 workshops in the past five years to people looking for ways to use existing resources to strengthen their communities. Successful special forest product companies can be run out of garages or old barns. This is a labor-intensive industry that benefits from people working together. Even large special forest product companies are now realizing they need staff to supply small

> **A strong specialty forest product industry will help future land managers maximize their forest resources.**

cooperatives and communities with raw materials. The more forward-looking timber companies and special forest product wholesalers realize that they can increase their markets by working with cooperatives.

In the last five years, newly formed cooperatives have come to manage timber lands, making wreaths for large companies, harvesting, sorting and boxing floral greens, and harvesting and drying medicinal plants. It does not take much effort to start to organize a cooperative and give real power to the members, who often enjoy having a say in their futures for the first time in their lives.

New specialty markets are developing around the world and foreign buyers have shown much interest in special forest products from Washington. In 1993, I participated in the Washington Agriculture Showcase and showed some of the products from Washington forests. I was overwhelmed by the interest in these products from Mexico, China, Taiwan, Japan, Korea, Germany, France, and the Philippines. The Chinese buyers, for example, wanted names of people who could supply them with herbal plants and mushrooms immediately.

The diverse ethnic markets of the U.S. are very valuable to special forest product producers. The largest population of Koreans outside Korea is located in Tacoma, Washington. Yet most of the stores serving this population import their products from Japan. Why must a Tacoma company buy mushrooms grown in Washington and Oregon from Japan? The reason is that we have few small packing companies with the ability to label products in the various languages necessary to access the market. In the near future, cooperatives will form that establish certified kitchens to place any label on any size of container to meet the special needs of consumers.

Such new small food processing cooperatives would increase the value of mushrooms. They would also remove some of the strain on lands producing mushrooms. Fewer mushrooms are needed for a retail market than a wholesale market to obtain the same cash flow. Mushrooms purchased for $5 a pound from the picker are often sold for $5 an ounce to restaurants.

SUPPORT IS NEEDED

There is uncertainty regarding the involvement of native people in the development of this industry. Because of the spiritual and cultural importance of these plants to native people, they will have a major say in how far and fast this industry grows. If their needs and knowledge are incorporated in all forest management plans, the plans would have the support and strength that the courts would never give them. If native needs and knowledge are sought by all members of the industry, the demand for special forest products would increase worldwide.

I see a coming together of natives and others to develop a system in which knowledge is shared when there is a commitment by everyone to protect the forests that support the plants. The special forest product industry might be the first industry in which native people have the special knowledge and insight necessary to help it grow strong. I also see native people developing industries based on their knowledge and usage of plants to enable their communities to make better use of their natural resources. The special tax breaks for tribal industries would enable them to become active leaders in cooperatives that could include their neighbors as well.

We need strong financial support to gather native knowledge now. We must listen to native people who have lived on these lands for thousands of years. We must learn how they made their crops sustainable. We cannot afford to wait 15 or 20 years for scientific research to show us how to manage these crops. We need new product and market development, not just economic analysis of what is happening now. We need to organize a marketing strategy that promotes all the products from the Pacific Northwest, not just the products that big companies can afford to promote.

We need strong support for all public land managers to integrate special forest product management into all forest management plans. We need as much research money for learning how to manage these crops to increase forest health as we have spent on trying to eliminate "weeds." We need public agencies and large timber companies to work with universities to develop training programs to strengthen communities to make their own decisions. The special forest product industry cannot thrive under the heavy hand of big business or big government. Permits, rules and regulations must be streamlined to make it possible for people to take advantage of time-sensitive crops. Public land managers and timber companies must evaluate all methods of compensation from users of their lands. Trading cultural practices for products may be better over the long term than charging fees for harvesting.

The development of a Pacific Northwest special forest products institute would support the sharing of information and the coordination of financial resources for research and promotion of Pacific Northwest specialty natural resource products. The institute could sponsor educational programs, industry promotional events, videos, and tape cassettes for all managers, buyers, harvesters, public officials, law enforcers, educators, environmentalists, students, tribes, companies and individuals who have an interest in using special forest products to improve their lives or their communities.

The future is in the hands of the people in this industry. I was once told by a Catholic bishop that you should not wait for God or the government to solve your problems or provide opportunities for you. If you wait for the government, you will be very disappointed with the results. The federal government has bigger fish to worry about than helping you or your community survive.

The following quotes may help those planning a future with the special forest product industry:

- "An empowered person is one who has taken responsibility for his or her own survival." *Unknown*
- "You cannot solve the problem with the same level of thinking that created the problem." *A.E. Einstein*
- "The mind, once expanded to the new dimensions of a larger idea, never

> **The special forest product industry might be the first industry in which native people have the special knowledge and insight necessary to help it grow strong.**

returns to its smaller size." *Oliver W. Holmes*

This industry will be strong in the future because many people have seen a little piece of the action for themselves and have taken the steps necessary to gain the skill and knowledge to make it happen.

To obtain a guide for organizing a special forest product cooperative, contact the author at 1835 Black Lake Blvd. SW, Olympia, WA 98512-5623.

22

"The Earth's Blanket:"
Traditional Aboriginal Attitudes Towards Nature

Nancy J. Turner

"...Flowers, plants and grass, especially the latter are the covering or blanket of the earth. If too much plucked or ruthlessly destroyed earth sorry and weeps[.] It rains or is angry and makes rain, fog and bad weather" (James Telt, ethnographer, unpublished notes on Nlaka'pamx, or Thompson, plant knowledge, ca. 1900, cited from Turner et al. 1990, p. 54).

Understanding and living sustainably within a particular environment has been a matter of survival for the aboriginal peoples of Canada, as it has for indigenous peoples the world over. A definition of "*indigenous people*," as "...a cultural group in an ecological area that developed a successful subsistence base from the natural resources available in that area" (Kuhnlein and Turner 1991, p. 2) reflects the close relationship aboriginal people have had with their environment, a relationship that embodies dependence, familiarity, awe, respect, and kinship. This chapter focuses on aboriginal peoples of Western Canada, but the concepts expressed are widespread in aboriginal teachings.

Despite, or perhaps because of, their detailed knowledge of the natural world, aboriginal peoples have regarded many aspects of nature as "powerful," or magical. There is a spiritual side of nature, addressed in traditional ceremonies, prayers and "stories," going far beyond its modern role solely as a "resource" to be exploited by people in their quest for survival and the acquisition of wealth. The philosophy expressed in the introductory quotation, reflecting the power and persona of nature, and the necessity to use it carefully and not abuse it, was widely taught to aboriginal children and young adults by their elders.

"Never waste anything." Everything has a purpose, people were taught, even those things frequently regarded as useless by most people today. The sinew from a whale's back made the strongest kind of rope for the Nuu-chah-nulth people of the

West Coast of Vancouver Island; fine powder from sharpening giant mussel shells for chisels was used by the Ditidaht of Vancouver Island as a lubricant for the skin when people spun nettle fibre into string on their bare legs; salmonheads were used all along the Pacific Coast to make a rich, delicious and highly nutritious soup; the eyeballs of a bison were used for glue by the Blackfoot of Alberta; the ribs of a deer were softened, split into slivers and used for awls by the Secwepeme, or Shuswap, and other peoples. The bark of trees, generally removed and discarded in modern sawmilling, was used traditionally as a source of fibre, basket materials, medicine and even food (Turner and Hebda 1990, Gottesfled 1992).

Old growth forest
Sierra Club of Western Canada

Red alder (*Alnus rubra*) is a plant species that epitomizes the contrasting attitudes people have towards nature. It is a tree of western North America, regarded by industrial foresters of the Pacific coastal region as a noxious weed that competes with commercial "fiber" species such as Douglas fir (*Pseudotsuga menziessi*). Alder is variously sprayed with herbicides, such as Round-up, girdled with special circular saws to kill it, or removed by cutting. Among Northwestern aboriginal peoples, however, it was, and still is, highly valued. In some mythical traditions, alder was formerly a woman with red skin, transformed to her present state long ago as a gift for other humans. Its soft, even-grained wood is ideal and it is also an ideal fuel for smoking fish and meat for carving bowls, masks, and rattles. Its bark, which turns bright orange or red with exposure to air, was a major source of dye. It was used for coloring fishnets to make them invisible to fish, and for red cedar bark (*Thuja plicata*) used in clothing, mats and ceremonial neck rings, providing a contrasting hue with the natural brown.

The cambium and inner bark tissues of red alder were eaten in spring by the Saanich and other Coast Salish peoples of Vancouver Island. Alder bark is also the source of important medicines, used by aboriginal peoples for treating a variety of ailments from tuberculosis and internal hemorrhaging to skin infections. Preliminary screening for antibiotic properties at the Department of Botany of the University of British Columbia showed it to be effective against a wide range of bacterial pathogens. One need only look at the story of western yew (*Taxus brevifolia*) (see McAllister and Haber 1991) to find an example of a tree hitherto regarded as "useless" whose commercial value has sky-rocketed following the discovery of a promising anticancer compound, taxol, in its bark. Red alder may well become another "yew story." Aboriginal people have known, used and valued both of these species for centuries.

"The Earth's Blanket:" Traditional Aboriginal Attitudes Towards Nature

Among the Kwakwaka'wakw (Kwakwala-speaking people, formerly Kwakiutl) of coastal British Columbia, everything used was honored with a prayer, acknowledging its healing or nurturing role and its power to help. The following prayer, recorded by ethnographer Franz Boas (translated from Kwakwala), is addressed by a medicine gatherer to an alder tree along a river bank. The man wishes to use the alder's bark to treat his wife, who is spitting blood [from tuberculosis]:

> I have come to ask you to take mercy, Supernatural-Power-of-the-River-Bank, that you may, please, make well with your healing power my poor wife who is spitting blood. Go on, please, pity me for I am troubled and, please, make her well, you, Healing-Woman, ...and, please, stop up the source of blood, you Causing-to-Heal- Woman, and, please, heal up the cause of trouble of my poor wife, please, you, great Supernatural One... (Boas 1930, p. 237-238).

Four pieces of the bark were carefully removed, taken home, and administered with additional prayers to the "Healing-Woman" alder. All medicine harvested must be used; if it is thrown away or wasted, the person could suffer hardship in some way, because of the disrespect shown. The practices of careful harvesting and use of such materials allowed for their continued utilization over many generations—in other words, sustainability.

What does all this mean for protection of biodiversity? Aboriginal peoples need to use their environment, and the other living things in their ecosystems, for survival, as all of us do. However, the attitude of respect, gratitude and honor, and the spiritual relationship humans have had with nature in traditional cultures is important in determining how they used their environment. Religious attitudes in traditional societies may be metaphorical guidelines for sustainable living. Prayers, stories and ceremonies abound in the aboriginal societies of Canada and elsewhere that teach people the principles of sustainability. Take only what you need, and do not waste what you take. *Harvest with care. Honor and appreciate everything you get and everything around you. Share with others; do not hoard. Observe carefully for signs of scarcity or overuse, and if you find them, change your use patterns. Remember, nature can affect your life, for good or for bad, depending on how you treat it.*

If society at large were to uphold these principles, and follow them, doubtless we would all be more successful at living sustainably and preserving the other life-forms of the planet.

Nothing in nature is wasted
Bo Martin

23

The Fire Practices of Aboriginal North Americans

Stephen J. Pyne

IT IS OFTEN ASSUMED THAT AMERICAN INDIANS were incapable of greatly modifying their environment and that they would not have been much interested in doing so even if they had had the capability. In fact, they possessed both the tool and the will to use it. That tool was fire.

It is hard now to recapture the degree to which Indian economies were dependent on fire. In its domesticated forms, fire was used for cooking, light, and heat. It made possible ceramics and metallurgy. Its smoke was used for communication. It felled trees and shaped canoes. It was applied to the cultivation and harvest of natural grasses and forbs such as the sunflower, of berries such as the blueberry, and of nuts such as the acorn and mesquite bean. Broadcast burning along the coastal gulf plains and in the Alaskan interior drove off mosquitoes and flies; the human control of mosquitoes may have been responsible for the destruction of more Alaskan forest than any other cause. Fire was sometimes used to kill off broad expanses of forest, which might then be harvested for firewood. Broadcast fire could be used more circumspectly to produce such delicacies as the caramelized confection that resulted from burning sugar pine cones on the ground. Of course, fire could also be handled carelessly: parties of warriors and hunters rarely extinguished campfires and signal fires since they burned on someone else's land. It was common practice, for example, to set fire to a downed tree for a campfire and then leave it where it might continue to burn for days.

Fire was used ceremonially as a part of actual or ritual cleansing or as sheer spectacle. Lewis and Clark reported an evening's entertainment by tribes in the Rockies that consisted of torching off fir trees, which then exploded in the night like Roman candles. The Apaches were said to burn off miles of mountain landscape in the belief that the conflagration would bring rain. Fire was a practical purifier, too. Oregon Indians used smoke to harvest pandora moths, which infested pine forests; the moths would drop from the trees to the ground where the Indians could gather them up as food. California Indians used smoke to drive off the mistletoe that invaded mesquite and oak.

Broadcast fire sometimes served as a means of economic extortion, and it was commonly employed for military objectives, both as a tactical weapon and as a strategic scorched-earth policy. The Cree and Assiniboine attempted to drive off early Hudson's Bay Company posts on the Plains by burning, but the traders took protective measures and the tribes resorted to a more complicated scheme. By firing wide stretches of prairie in the fall, they hoped to drive off the buffalo and then reap a handsome profit as middlemen when the company was forced to approach them for pemmican. But the forest ranged too far, the buffalo were driven deep to the south, some villages were overrun, and the Indian speculators found themselves indebted to the company for supplies to tide them over during the winter. In the 1880s tribes in the Dakotas attempted a similar strategy against the incursion of cattle ranches, eventually burning out strips for hundreds of miles along the routes of cattle drives and forcing ranch hands into roles as firefighters.

Even more widespread was the use of broadcast fire to clear the surrounding woods of underbrush and thus prevent the unseen approach of a hostile force. The desire to open up fields around villages, trails, and hunting sites was an almost universal reason given by Indians setting this type of fire.

Fire was essential to those Indian agricultures not dependent on irrigation. Where yield was light, the natural fertility could be maintained almost indefinitely by setting fires to recycle the unused debris. Where yield was high, as in maize culture, additional fertilizer had to be added or new lands cleared and burned. In either case, the absence of chemical fertilizer or manure from domestic livestock often made fire the only practical mechanism for replacing nutrient losses in the soil. What might appear to be a random firing and gathering of products often represented the semi-domestication of both plants and wildlife. The cycle of fire varied according to the crop and the intensity of yield: cereal grasses were fired annually; basket grasses and nuts, every three years; brush, perhaps every seven to 10 years; large timber, for formal swidden agriculture, on a cycle of 15 to 30 years or even longer. Broadcast fire also rid the fields of vermin and disease.

Of all Indian uses for fire, the most widespread was probably the most ancient: fire for hunting. At night torches spotlighted deer and drew fish close enough to canoes to be speared. Smoke flushed bees from their hives, raccoons out of their dens, and bears out of their caves. Recognizing that new grass sprouting on a freshly burned site would attract grazers by its superior palatability, Indians placed snare traps on small burned plots—in effect, baiting the trap with field grass. The Apaches used smoke to lure deer driven mad by flies and mosquitoes. Fire hunting—the strategy of surrounding or driving the principal grazers of a region with fire—was universal. In the East it was used for deer; in the Everglades, for alligators; on the prairies, for buffalo; along the tules of the Colorado River, for rabbits and wood rats; in Utah and

> **Fire was essential to those Indian agricultures not dependent on irrigation.**

the Cordilleras, for deer and antelope; in the Great Basin, for grasshoppers; in California and the Southwest, for rabbits; in Alaska, for muskrats and moose...

In the early 19th century Thomas Jefferson speculated that fire hunting was "the most probable cause of the origin and extension of the vast prairies in the western country."

Such prairies were extensive and by no means limited to the western country. Apart from the general opening up of wooded areas that resulted from broadcast fire and clearings, special "deserts," or "barrens" (as early Europeans referred to them), were maintained for the harvesting of wildlife. The Indians had little use for closed forests, whose main attraction was as a potential source of fertilizer for swidden agriculture. In the absence of domesticated livestock, meat had to come from hunting, and through fire Indians maintained the reserves they required, the grassland or forest-grass ecotone that proved so productive of game. In this way fire hunting was not only a tactic of harvesting but also one that sustained and expanded the habitat on which it depended.

It is likely that these fire practices and the environments they shaped were expanding at the time of European discovery. The dominant vegetation type in America at that time may well have been grassland or open forest savanna. The role of fire in sustaining these landscapes is incontestable; when broadcast burning was suppressed as a result of European settlement, the land spontaneously reverted to forest. Rather than a climatic change, the general encroachment of grassland into forest from the Holocene to the advent of European settlement may have reflected the penetration of nomadic hunting cultures enlarging the range of their prey. The buffalo, for example, crossed the Mississippi from the west about AD 1000. By the 16th century the buffalo entered the south; by the 17th, its range extended into Pennsylvania and Massachusetts. This expansion could have been accomplished only through a change in habitat, partly due to climate but largely a result of the application of anthropogenic fire.

Indians understood the precepts of fire prevention, too. Debris was cleared from around villages; cooking fires were situated carefully; campsites on long grass were avoided or the grass was first burned; and when necessary, fires were fought... Most tribes lived in fire-filled environments, often of their own making; ignorance of fire-control methods or indifference to basic precautionary practices would have been disastrous. The evidence suggests that early European colonists were generally ignorant of wildland fire and of methods to control it, just as European foresters in the 19th century were ignorant of prescribed burning as a silvicultural technique. It was from the Indian, into whose fire environment they moved, that the European immigrants learned basic survival skills.

It would be a mistake to generalize too broadly about the fire practices of particular tribes. Fire practices were to some extent circumscribed by environmental constraints. And, since tribes underwent migrations, experienced internal evolutions, and were forcibly dislocated, their relationship to the land was constantly changing. Nor is there any evidence to suggest that the tribes lived in some perpetual ecological harmony with one another or with their environment, upset only by European intervention. The ruins of ancient civilizations—the mound builders in the Ohio Valley, the Anasazi of Mesa Verde and Chaco Canyon, and the Hohokam of the Southwest—testify to the existence of impressive cultures that vanished long before Europeans arrived.

The resulting mosaic of anthropogenic fire regimes is as complex as the historical geography of the cultures themselves. But even if Indian practices had been uniform in intent, which they were not, or homogeneous in technique, which was not possible, the fire seasons of the different regions of the United States did not coincide, and the fire regimes were intrinsically distinct. The prospect of scorched earth across the continent as a result of Indian burning in the autumn, for example, was impossible. Fire was predominately local, although the multiplication of local effects could produce surprisingly extensive cumulative results. The modification of the American continent by fire at the hands of Indians was the result of repeated, controlled surface burns on a cycle of one to three years, broken by occasional holocausts from escape fires and periodic conflagrations during times of drought. Even under ideal circumstances, accidents occurred; signal fires escaped and campfires spread, with the result that valuable range was untimely scorched, villages were threatened, and buffalo were driven away. Burned corpses on the prairie were far from rare.

So extensive were the cumulative effects of these modifications that the general consequence of the Indian occupation of the New World may have been to replace forested land with grassland or savanna or, where the forest persisted, to open it up and free it from underbrush. Most of the impenetrable woods encountered by explorers were in bogs or swamps from which fire was excluded; naturally drained landscape was burned nearly everywhere. Conversely, almost wherever the European went, forests followed. The Great American Forest may be more a product of settlement than a victim of it.

Through the use of fire, both confined and broadcast, Indian tribes created an environment favorable to their existence. It was an existence and a fire regime often well suited, at least for a transitional period, to the frontier culture that superseded them, as well. The forest species most likely to survive the Indians' fire regime, pine and oak, were precisely those most valuable for logging. Grassland corridors such as the Shenandoah Valley were maintained by fire and provided major thoroughfares for the dispersal of settlers. The lush wildlife that provided subsistence for early

Controlled burn of understory
B.C. Forest Service
Photo Archives

vanguards of frontiersmen depended on a habitat created and sustained by the Indian pattern of broadcast fire; as settlement progressed, converting "deserts" into farms and forests, the abundant game vanished.

The habitat that supported so rich a natural population of grazers and browsers was ideally suited for the domestic stock introduced by Europeans and upon which their agrarian economy was so heavily dependent. In the same way that herders of domesticated stock occupied the openings previously maintained for the harvest of wild game, immigrant farmers moved into the former fields of the aboriginal people, fields cleared and fertilized with fire. The early agriculture of the American colonists resembled nothing so much as the shifting agriculture of the Indian, although it was pursued at an accelerated rate. From Indian examples the colonists also learned fire hunting and the techniques for controlling and surviving fires so common in the high fire regimes they suddenly occupied. Just as European and American exploration of the continent was advanced by having native guides, so settlement advanced thanks, in good measure, to the preparation of Indian hunters, harvesters, and farmers.

24

Man of the Woods

Cheri Burda

WHILE NO STRANGER TO INDUSTRIAL FORESTRY, Bob Woods has evolved in harmony with the woods he manages. The photo album he keeps in his truck displays snapshots of an earlier time, with clearcuts and his logging camp in the foreground. These are juxtaposed with more recent photos of innovative machines and healthy stands of intact forest.

After years of witnessing and participating in the clearcutting of second-growth forests around Campbell River and his hometown of Courtenay, on northern Vancouver Island, B.C., Bob started his own business in selection logging in 1976. His company, Enviro-Harvesting Inc., evolved with the belief that forests must be nurtured and watersheds protected. He envisioned harvesting the forest carefully and perpetually, nurturing an unhealthy, sunlight-starved plantation into a dynamic forest with diverse species and ages. By drafting models for selectively logging second-growth stands, Bob created logging equipment from modified farm tractors so that old logging roads would not need upgrading. Essentially, he designed machinery to work with the terrain, not against it.

Based on the amount of plantations in his forest district requiring attention, Bob predicted that selective thinning would emerge into a predominant silvicultural practice. He landed a commercial thinning job with the Forest Service in 1979, but such contracts with the Forest Service have not been plentiful. Enviro-Harvesting Inc. was ready to change how forestry was practised, but the forest industry was not ready to change. Nor was it ready for Bob. "Many people have said that Bob was 20 years ahead of his time," explains his wife, Maizie. "Bob never cared about making money. He had his beliefs and stuck to them."

THE "SHORT LOG" SYSTEM

Bob developed the "short log" system of logging, aimed at maximizing value from second growth while minimizing impact to the stand and the soil. Short logs are trees bucked in the forest to 13 1/2 feet [4.1 m], after they are felled and before they are yarded. About half the length of regular commercial logs, short logs are ecologically and economically advantageous for many reasons.

Logs are graded according to a number of features, including size. Regardless of the diameter at the butt end, if the log tapers to less than 8 inches [20 cm] in diameter, it is graded for pulp. By bucking the trees into two short logs, the larger half can be graded as a sawlog. "It comes down to greater utilization, better quality," Bob explains. "We must recover more value from our forests."

Short logs require a smaller space for swinging when they are yarded, resulting in minimal or no damage to standing trees. Bob's mini-highlead system, a drum and winch apparatus built onto the roof of his excavator, yards the logs easily and precisely, negotiating standing trees and avoiding bumps and crashes. Small logs also require smaller, less harmful equipment: Bob's excavator puts 3 pounds per square inch [20.7 kPa] of pressure on the trail. The short log system requires no skidders that drag logs out of the forest, carving up the trail and disturbing the soil.

Long logs require bigger loaders accommodated by bigger roads. With short logs, Bob can employ a light trail system instead of building roads. The most significant feature of Bob's trail system is the care and effort invested in protecting the trail itself from soil damage. Bob utilizes all the limbs and needles from felled trees, placing them meticulously on the trail to create a thick layer of protection. Instead of using conventional methods to level coarse terrain, such as digging or ballasting—laying crushed rock to form a road bed, Bob builds up the dips and gullies with woody debris.

The same trail system is used for each selective cut, and the first logging is minimal, which is followed by an assessment of the ecological impact. The impact determines the following selective cuts. "You have to know the forest to understand how one cut will affect the other trees, the hydrology and the entire stand," explains Bob.

A FOREST SERVICE CONTRACT TESTS BOB'S TECHNIQUES

Enviro-Harvesting Inc. is a small untenured company that seldom enjoys a secure timber supply. Bob has had to rely on private land and woodlot owners who contract his services, and is currently bidding for small jobs under the Small Business Forest Enterprise Program. Recently however, Enviro-Harvesting was awarded a small timber sale in the Campbell River Forest District, designated as an experimental job for the Forest Service. Bill Hughes, Forest District Commercial Thinning Coordinator, admitted that the Forest Service chose the toughest possible terrain for Bob to demonstrate his trail building and logging methods. "The site represented all the potential problems: heavy slash, sensitive soil, and steep hills," Hughes stated. Consequently, Bob's trails curved intricately to avoid difficult grades, sensitive areas, rocky ground and marked trees selected to remain standing.

Bob developed the "short log" system of logging, aimed at maximizing value from second growth while minimizing impact to the stand and the soil.

Bob had to work in thigh-deep debris left behind by a juvenile spacing operation 10 years earlier that left all the felled trees to rot. He made use of the debris, laying it on the trail for protection and to level the ground. (Interestingly, Bob bucks and sells logs smaller than many of the ones abandoned by this spacing operation.) The result was zero compaction. I stuck my hand deep into the fibrous mass but could feel only needles and twigs. The soil far beneath was undisturbed. Hughes visited Bob regularly to inspect his work, digging holes every 30 metres. In 7 years of inspecting timber sales, Hughes described Bob's work as "the lightest on the land" he had ever seen.

Bob's prudence and attention to detail revealed itself in the cautious methods he used to protect streams and creeks. We crossed a couple of small bridges constructed to prevent the equipment from affecting the water system in any way. Bob carefully fashioned a log bridge over a trickling creek no more than a foot in width. After the last cut, he will remove the logs and take them to market, and use the excavator to remove any remaining debris.

Milling on site
Chip Vinai

The trail cover of woody debris also acts as a filter for rainwater, preventing any runoff or soil erosion. Bob pointed to a swamp down the hill that is protected from any damage due to road construction by conventional methods, which significantly impact soil and watersheds, causing erosion and sedimentation. "We must end clearcutting to protect the watersheds," said Bob. "It's not just overfishing we have to worry about—it's bad logging."

The Forest Service job allowed Bob to perform his magic on the forest, but it did not permit him to select the trees. The Forest Service did the selecting, removing 40% of the stand's volume. Bob is concerned that too much volume was removed on the first cut and fears that the next cut will be a clearcut, as Hughes indicated would likely be the case. Conventional forest management employs selective logging—actually commercial thinning—as a silvicultural method to allow superior trees to grow in an improved environment; minimum soil damage is important only because it helps to maximize the growth and volume of the thinned plantation.

It seemed absurd that Bob's time and care may mean nothing in 30 years after a clearcut. I asked Bob if there was a chance that this particular stand could be ecologically harvested in perpetuity. He looked at me and said, "That's your job to bring about such alternatives," referring to the Ecoforestry Institute and other organizations working for change. It was never more clear to me that the environmental movement has the potential to protect not only forest ecosystems and biodiversity, but also forestsworkers who depend on the survival of the forest.

PRIVATE WOODLOT MANAGEMENT

We drove for an hour to one of Bob's favorite sites (and mine), Father Charles Brant's property near Courtenay. Bob logged an initial cut there in early 1994, removing only 15% of the forest's volume. I visited Father Brant's forest over a year ago, just as Bob was completing his work. The forest had impressed me then with its healthy canopy, diversity and wildlife. I remember watching a woodpecker on a snag, and chasing clumsily with my camera after a deer.

Now, a year later, the forest was even more magnificent. The forest floor was green and lush. Seedlings thrived in sunlight streaming through new canopy openings, yet were sheltered by strong parent trees. We stood knee-deep in vegetation now carpeting the trail. Returning to visit this woodlot was uplifting for both of us.

We then drove to a nearby private woodlot, owned by forester Al Hopwood. The young stand needed a tremendous amount of ongoing attention. The forest floor was like a dark desert, with juvenile trees crowding one another. Unlike the Forest Service site, the small trees spaced by Al and Bob were not discarded to rot; many will be utilized. The future goal is to remove the optimum number of trees, use the logs, and leave enough organic material to provide nutrients. Although the work ahead seemed insurmountable, Bob delighted in the possibilities: "This is a perfect opportunity to demonstrate how to properly manage a forest every step of the way."

Not surprisingly, the edge of Al's woodlot suffered blowdown from an adjacent clearcut, a private woodlot owned by a big corporation. Bob commented on the effect on the local watershed: "The filter system is gone, and there won't be anything to work with for another 40 years. Al's place, on the other hand, could keep a family going for years to come."

EMPLOYING THE COMMUNITY

Bob believes that labor-intensive management of second growth not only nurtures our forests back to health, but also employs communities. His employees enjoy and appreciate working with him. "I'm happy to be working in my community," said Randy Brower, a former contract faller for a number of clearcutting companies. "The money goes back into the community and the people living in the community are employed."

Bob involves his crew at every level. They learn and perform every job, from precision falling and yarding, soil and stream protection, to bidding on contracts. Their work is interesting and challenging. "I've learned more with Bob in six months than I did in 15 years of logging—important things like soil compaction, scarring damage and how to protect the environment," claimed Charlie Parkinson. "We could employ the Comox Valley, perhaps all of B.C., with the amount of second

> **Bob believes that labor-intensive management of second growth not only nurtures our forests back to health, but also employs communities.**

growth we have, if we logged it properly."

Neil Blackburn, who has been with Bob the longest, emphasized the importance of small-scale forestry: "The registered professional foresters for the big companies criticize Bob's type of operation, claiming it cannot supply enough lumber for the world. I say, let's take care of our own island first."

As Bob's crew reiterated, Enviro-Harvesting is "new," and the logging industry does not like "new." "The whole industry has to change," insisted Wayne Beckwith, who trucks Bob's logs to the local mill. "Existing equipment is too big. It breaks everything. Regular logging trucks, for example, are much too big for short logs. We need new equipment, new trained workers, new road systems. This new way of logging could keep people working all year long on timber that would have otherwise been broken, wasted."

Whether or not enviro-harvesting is adopted by the forest industry, it is certain that Bob will continue to develop innovative methods and equipment. "He's been doing this all of his life," joked Maizie, "waking up in the middle of the night to write down ideas or draw a machine." Hughes explained, "Bob is not a regular logger; he's an inventor." And people are beginning to notice and appreciate his work. The same loggers who told Bob that his ideas would never work are now purchasing equipment originally designed by Bob. Bob and his crew are becoming accustomed to frequent visitors, from school groups and film crews to timber giants MacMillan Bloedel and Interfor. Thankfully, Bob Woods' years of dedication finally have resulted in awareness, an important step towards change.

PART FOUR

Forestry for the Future — Community, Bioregionalism and Certification

Complex layers of structure in natural forest, Bo Martin

25

What's Behind a Certified Label

Herb Hammond

IF BEING "GREEN" IS THE SPIN for business and government in the late 20th century, being "certified" will be the requirement for successful marketing as we enter the 21st century. Certification will be desired, if not required, for everything from government plans and structural lumber to rocking chairs and preserves from forest berries. Should we all feel good about this? Are forest certification programs the catalyst for a new era of ecological restoration and sustainability? Well, that depends upon what is behind the certified label.

A little history is in order here. Certified labeling is not new. For many years private firms like the Canadian Standards Association and Underwriters Laboratories in the U.S. have been guaranteeing that if we buy a toaster or other appliances with their certified label, among other things, they will not electrocute us when we turn them on. More recently various associations and programs, like California Certified Organic and the British Columbia Organic Farmers Association have provided labelling assurances that various foods have been grown and processed in ways that ensure their organic purity. What is interesting about both of these examples is that certification and their labels are concerned with human health and safety. Producers would lose their markets and certifiers would lose their credibility quickly if people received an electric shock from a certified toaster or got sick from eating certified organic food. Certification of appliances and food is not without controversy and scams, but the fact remains that certification to protect human health and safety is a business taken very seriously by consumers.

Does the same incentive apply to certifying forest products? Maybe for the ones that we eat, like mushrooms, berries and medicinal plants. However, we don't eat 2 x 4s and rocking chairs. In most areas, the volumes of these latter types of forest products far outstrip the volumes of the forest products that we eat. There is a growing trend by governments, timber industries, and for-profit certifiers to certify as "sustainable" a wide range of forest practices to both gain access to and confuse the marketplace. Some certifiers are willing to put their label on wood products from clearcuts, from forest areas managed with pesticides, and/or from tree plantations. If the consumer is not aware of what is permitted under a particular label, they may be purchasing a "sustainable" product certified to sustain short-term monetary profits, not certified to protect forest functioning at all scales through time. This situation is

made more creditable and confusing because a group of "captured scientists" (owned by the industrial power structure) is willing to support clearcut forestry as an ecologically sustainable system.

The way out of this dilemma is to insist upon third-party, ecosystem-based certification of forest products. The organizations carrying out this type of certification are not-for-profit certifiers that only recover their costs from certifications, and may offer certification services subsidized by donations or grants from charitable foundations. Ecosystem-based certifiers find their roots in forest activism and in the environmental movement—the source of forest certification.

There would not be forest certification programs without the creativity of forest activists who recognized that timber cutting and timber management practices could be affected by the marketplace through the certification of forest products, particularly wood products. Until major pulp and lumber contracts were cancelled, the timber industry smugly ignored the fledgling certification efforts of forest activists. However, that has all changed with a growing market insistence that wood products come from sustainable sources.

Enter the timber-industry-driven American Pulp and Lumber Association and the Canadian Standards Associations certification programs. The timber industry is poised to begin

A stand in the landscape
Bo Martin

certifying itself. Would you trust a chemical company that certifies that tomatoes sprayed with their products are harmless to your health and contain the same level of nutrition as organically grown tomatoes? Of course not. Then, if you care about the forest that sustains us, you will not accept industrial certification of wood products.

How do you pick the right label? How do you find out what is behind the label? Ask questions:

- Is the certification rooted in ecosystem-based standards that place first priority on protecting and maintaining fully functioning forests at all scales through time?
- Is the certification carried out by a third party not associated in any way with the producer, marketer, wholesaler, or retailer of the forest product in question?

- Has the chain of custody been clearly monitored and certified by the certifying organization?
- Is the certifier and the certifying organization not-for-profit?

The history of environmental activism is full of attempts by industry to co-opt creative ideas promising to help protect Earth. Ecologically based certification of forest products is the newest target for co-option by the timber industry. Whether the timber industry is successful or not depends on our abilities to ask clear, pointed questions and our will to support the principled positions that underlie ecosystem-based forest use. Remember, certification of forest products is meaningless unless we are certain that certification ensures that the integrity of forests has been put first.

26

What is Certification?

Herb Hammond and Susan Hammond

CERTIFICATION OF WOOD PRODUCTS IS AN IDEA that originated in the environmental movement, with support from concerned consumers and forest workers. As envisioned by the environmental sector:

Certification is a way to ensure, via the marketplace, that logging and timber management activities protect the integrity of forests at all scales during and after logging.

This is not to suggest that the solution to local and global forest crises is to replace today's consumption of nonsustainably produced wood with the same level of certified wood. In North America, 30% of landfill is composed of house parts, much of it wood. Much of this wood could be recovered and reused, rather than discarded. Therefore, in addition to protecting forests:

Certification is a way to reduce consumption of wood by encouraging recycling and insuring efficient, nonwasteful uses of wood.

A few environmentally aware architectural firms have already developed ways to assemble wooden houses that are easy to take apart, thereby reducing waste. In some areas, economically viable recycled wood programs already exist. On the whole, however, large-scale recycling programs are expensive to set up.

Ironically, compared to the cost of establishing a recycling program, it is still relatively cheap to cut trees because the market value of trees is based on their value as lumber. If we valued trees for their real worth, including their value in storing carbon, and in protecting biodiversity, air and water quality, wilderness values and wildlife habitat, we would reap a triple benefit: we would discourage logging; we would increase the amount of wood that is recycled; and we would generate sufficient revenue to support wood recycling and protect ecosystem integrity. This is a tall order, but certification is clearly one logical step toward this scenario:

Certification is a means of acknowledging the actual costs of consumptive uses of the forest.

Certification, still in its early days, is encountering many of the same problems as organic food certification and production. Initially, certified organically grown food was hard to find and was expensive. Due to steady market demands, however, the availability of organic food has improved, while prices have steadily dropped. Similar market demands will influence distribution of certified wood because:

Certification is a way of satisfying consumers that the wood they purchase has been logged and produced in ways that protect ecosystem functioning and provide for community stability.

The organic food market is a good example of consumer response to the failure of government efforts to protect the health of both people and agricultural land. In virtually any sector, attempts at government regulation are always plagued by inadequate budgets and changing political climates, *while certification is a creative solution to the challenge of ecosystem protection. Certification shifts the motivation for responsible action from government regulation to market pressure, and rewards those producers who demonstrate ecological, social, and economic responsibility.*

Wood certification is still a very new idea. Several initiatives are underway, but the idea is by no means widespread. Of the various certification proposals being developed in the environmental sector, most have in common certain basic principles:

- fully functioning ecosystems must be maintained both during and after timber cutting
- ecosystem functioning must be protected at all times (both short- and long-term) and at all scales (stand level and landscape level)
- forest-based communities must have fair and legal access to and benefit from the forest close to them.

Every ecosystem-based certification system is founded on a set of criteria that timber cutters and wood suppliers must fulfil in order for the wood they sell to earn the designation "certified." These criteria are specified in long-range ecosystem-based management plans. Some important criteria include:

- maintenance and/or restoration of ecosystem biodiversity
- maintenance and/or restoration of natural regeneration of native species
- protection of water, riparian zones, shallow soils, cross-valley corridors, old growth, and other ecologically sensitive zones
- prohibition of the use of pesticides
- prohibition of slash burning
- restoration of damage to the ecosystem from previous activities such as road-building, logging, or tourism
- protection of indigenous peoples' rights, land, and culture
- protection, enhancement, and diversification of local economies
- community control over forest activities, with fair distribution of any benefits realized from those activities
- decreased consumption, minimal waste, and maximum recycling at all

stages, starting from ecosystem-based planning and continuing to "point of purchase"

- close monitoring of "chain of custody" to ensure that the certifiable wood products are accurately tracked from forest to log yard to mill to distributor to consumer outlet.

In response to certification activities in the environmental sector, certification initiatives are now also being developed in the industrial sector, presented to the public as a method of self-monitoring. On closer inspection, however, industrial certification plans tend to amount to a marketing tool to sell wood. Some of the descriptions of industrial certification programs sound attractive and even similar to environmental sector initiatives.

However, there are major differences between the two:

- Industrial certification standards tend to reflect short-term, profit-driven priorities, such as management activities that manipulate forest ecosystems to produce commercially desirable species on commercially advantageous timetables.
- Industrial certification may give distinct advantages to large corporations that already hold forest tenures and have the financial resources to design and promote new marketing strategies.
- Industrial certification standards may be skewed toward preserving the status quo. For example, standards may emphasize maintaining or stabilizing "historical" patterns of employment, land tenure, and distribution of benefits from resource extraction.
- Industrial certification standards and criteria may be based on scientific principles that are industrially biased, or that result from industrially funded research efforts, rather than from third-party standards and independent research.
- Industrial chain of custody procedures may not be available to public scrutiny. In some cases, a chain of custody may not exist and industrial certification will simply allow companies to claim that a certain percentage of their products meets the industry's certification criteria.

Several indicators will enable consumers to differentiate certification initiatives designed to protect forest integrity from initiatives designed to secure industry profits. Current environmental certification initiatives emphasize:

- diverse community control of forest land
- reduced consumption levels of wood products
- an ecosystem-based approach to timber management
- certification evaluations carried out by independent, nonprofit, third-party agencies
- a direct and positive link between forestworkers, forest-based communities,

> **Industrial certification plans tend to amount to a marketing tool to sell wood.**

wood-users, and environmental activists.

In contrast, industrial certification initiatives are likely to emphasize:
- industrial control of forest land
- continued or increased consumption of wood products
- a timber-based approach to timber management
- certification evaluations carried out by industry-approved, industry-operated, or industry-funded agencies
- the role of industry as the "expert" and the concurrent isolation of non-industrial sectors (forestworkers, forest-based communities, wood-users, and environmental activists) from one another.

27

The Pacific Certification Council

Walter Smith

THE PACIFIC CERTIFICATION COUNCIL (PCC) is a group of five community-based nonprofit organizations that formed a partnership in 1993 to develop certification of wood products. While PCC members represent diverse ecosystems and communities, they have united to promote ecologically-responsible forest management and forest product certification for the Pacific Northwest bioregion—from northern California through British Columbia. PCC members are: Ecoforestry Institute (EI), Glendale, Oregon; Ecoforestry Institute Society (EIS), Victoria, B.C.; Institute for Sustainable Forestry (ISF), Redway, California; Rogue Institute for Ecology and Economy (RIEE), Ashland, Oregon; and SILVA Forest Foundation (SFF), Slocan Park, British Columbia.

At the founding meeting, PCC members confirmed the need to work together to make certification viable and credible by ensuring that each certifier meets criteria and standards applicable throughout the bioregion. The PCC adopted an amended version of the Ten Elements of Sustainability developed by the Institute for Sustainable Forestry.

PCC members are also members of a network of national and international certification organizations. The Canada-United States Association of the Smart Wood Network (CUSA) is a bi-national network of local/regional certification organizations. CUSA members can use the internationally-recognized Smart Wood certification label. All of the PCC members are founding members of the Forest Stewardship Council (FSC), an international organization based in Oaxaca, Mexico. The FSC was set up to accredit bioregionally based certification groups according to broad ecological, social and forestry standards.

The primary goal of the PCC is to promote sustainable forest management and to provide long-term, forest-related economic opportunities for local communities. Much of the current debate over forest management options has been narrowly framed by the issues of land preservation versus continued resource depletion. By contrast, the PCC is promoting forest management certification as a mechanism to provide landowners incentives for practising ecologically responsible forestry.

The certification program has several components:

- forest management and timber harvesting standards that describe such things as how many and what species of trees must be left after harvesting, the density and configuration of the forest road system, wildlife and stream protection measures;
- a systematic and documentable certification procedure, starting with a required long-term management plan that is reviewed by evaluators who are resource professionals; following the plan, several on-the-ground inspections take place before, during and after harvest to ensure that the forestland owner has complied with the standards;
- a licensing program for tracking certified products through sequential changes of ownership, for example from landowner to miller, wholesaler, retailer, and artisan.

The second goal of the PCC is to create a marketing program. Forestlands managed according to the Ten Elements of Sustainability are recognized through the certification of forest products harvested from that land. A unique market advantage will be created for producers and manufacturers of forest products carrying a certification label. As consumer demand causes the ecological forest products market to expand, more landowners will be encouraged to participate in the certification program. A consumer-driven market will compensate operators for the higher costs of sensitive harvesting, and will provide an incentive for owners to manage their forests in ways that benefit their local communities both environmentally and economically.

Education is the third goal of the PCC. Both producers and consumers of forest products need information regarding the sustainability of our forests and the importance of an alternative to current forest management options. An important function of the certification program will be to provide foresters, evaluators, and landowners with information and training in certification.

The PCC has distributed consumer education materials, via publications like the *International Journal of Ecoforestry*, media presentations, conferences, etc., and networked with trade associations, landowner groups and land trusts. Certified forest products in the marketplace will educate the consumer about the differences in forest management practices. Consumers will then more clearly understand the costs and benefits of sustainable forestry, as well as how their purchases can influence forest management decisions. Information on where to purchase certified products will also be provided.

The certification process is actually quite simple, and PCC members will take care of the paperwork. While each U.S. state and Canadian province has differing government regulations for forestry operations, the certification process will include

> **A unique market advantage will be created for producers and manufacturers of forest products carrying a certification label.**

the following steps:

FORESTRY OPERATIONS

1. The landowner/resource manager completes an application form and sends it to a PCC organization and/or contacts a PCC member for a pre-certification site visit. The landowner will be given the certification criteria. After the site visit, PCC member staff will inform the landowner about their potential for becoming a candidate for certification.

2. If the landowner/resource manager wants to pursue certification, the certifier and the landowner negotiate the cost of evaluation and monitoring services. A contract and licensing agreement is made that allows for the specified use of the certification label and describes the conditions required to remain certified.

3. The landowner/resource manager submits a long-term management plan to the certifier. The plan is reviewed for compatibility with the certification standards.

4. An evaluation team of resource professionals makes a preharvest evaluation. A draft evaluation report with recommendations/conditions is written by the evaluation team and submitted to the landowner/resource manager and professional reviewers for comment. A final report is then submitted to the certifier for final approval.

5. Upon passing the initial evaluation, certification is granted. To remain certified, monitoring visits are required during harvest and postharvest. An annual monitoring visit is also required to remain certified, regardless of actual harvesting activities. A written report of findings follows each inspection.

6. The landowner/resource manager must also inform the certifier about where the logs are being sold and/or manufactured. The certifier must be able to track the wood from the forest to the consumer to provide credibility to the market claim.

CHAIN OF CUSTODY

1. All businesses in the forest product distribution chain that take ownership of a certified product must be licensed to use the certification label. A contract is developed between the manufacturer/merchant and the certifier that allows for the tracking of the wood through the chain of custody.

2. Businesses must keep certified material separated from that which is noncertified. This includes logs, lumber, or finished products. Certified material must be clearly identified as certified by labelling the product to eliminate confusion for consumers or personnel handling the products.

3. An inventory system for identifying certified products, purchases, sales and transfers must be developed. Purchase receipts and sales invoices must

identify certified products.

4. Businesses must agree to annual and random audits. All information is kept confidential.

TEN ELEMENTS OF SUSTAINABILITY

1. Forest practices will protect, maintain and/or restore fully functioning ecosystems at all scales in both the short and long terms.

2. Forest practices will maintain and/or restore surface and groundwater quality, quantity, and timing of flow, including aquatic and riparian habitat.

3. Forest practices will maintain and/or restore natural processes of soil fertility, productivity and stability.

4. Forest practices will maintain and/or restore a natural balance and diversity of native species of the area, including flora, fauna, fungi and microbes, for purposes of the long-term health of ecosystems.

5. Forest practices will encourage a natural regeneration of native species to protect valuable native gene pools.

6. Forest practices will not include the use of artificial chemical fertilizers or synthetic chemical pesticides.

7. Forest practitioners will address the need for local employment and community stability and will respect workers' rights, including occupational safety, fair compensation and the right of workers to bargain collectively. We will support and encourage development of worker-owned and -operated organizations.

8. Sites of archeological, cultural and historical significance will be protected and will receive special consideration.

9. Forest practices executed under a certified Forest Management Plan will be of the appropriate size, scale, time frame and technology for the parcel, and adopt the appropriate monitoring program, not only to avoid negative cumulative impacts, but also to promote beneficial cumulative effects on the forest.

10. Ancient forests will be subject to a moratorium on commercial logging, during which time research will be conducted on the ramifications of management in these areas.

28

Standards for Ecologically Responsible Forest Use

Herb Hammond

PROTECTING AND MAINTAINING HEALTHY, SUSTAINABLE SOCIETIES, including economies, requires the protection, maintenance, and restoration, where necessary, of fully functioning ecosystems. Maintaining fully functioning ecosystems requires recognizing some important principles that are well-grounded in ecological science:

1. From microbe to globe, Earth is a whole system interconnected and interdependent.
2. Earth functions to sustain the whole in a complex adaptive system that is dynamic, yet (in human time frames) stable.
3. All ecosystem structures have functions. If we lose the structure, we lose the functions.
4. People are part of Earth. What we do to Earth, we do to ourselves.
5. Human plans must encompass landscape ecosystem time frames of centuries, not short-term development timetables of one to five years.

Our plans and activities in all the landscapes that make up Earth must honor and embody these five principles. The SILVA Forest Foundation's standards for ecologically responsible forest use, be it timber management or ecotourism, are based upon these five principles.

Forests are extremely important landscapes within which to apply ecosystem-based principles. The forests of Earth regulate climate; store, filter, and purify water; purify air; and are made up of more plants, animals, and micro-organisms than any other terrestrial ecosystem. What occurs in Earth's forests directly and indirectly impacts all other terrestrial and aquatic ecosystems at all scales.

Ecologically responsible forest use applies to a variety of human activities in the forest, from timber extraction and public recreation to adventure tourism and ranching. The SILVA Forest Foundation's general standards for timber management are described below. Eventually, the SILVA Forest Foundation hopes to have programs that certify a variety of forest uses as "ecologically responsible." However, due to the extensive influence that timber management has on the forest around the world, we have decided to concentrate our present certification efforts on timber.

This document establishes the framework for the SILVA Forest Foundation's certification program for ecologically responsible timber management. Three handbooks are currently being developed:

HANDBOOK 1: *The Process of Wood Certification* outlines the procedures and the technical variables included in assessing a timber operation for certification. This document will be of use to certifiers, timber managers, and operators.

HANDBOOK 2: *Technical Standards for Wood Certification* describes detailed standards for ecologically responsible timber management for a number of forest ecosystem types, and gives suggestions for safe, practical ways to meet these standards during timber management operations. This document will be of use to certifiers, timber managers, and operators. In other words, Handbook 1 explains the variables that will be measured in the certification process, while Handbook 2 defines specific criteria that must be met for each variable in order to achieve certification.

HANDBOOK 3: *Forest Protection Through Certification of Wood* along with a general discussion of ecologically responsible forest use, provides a nontechnical summary of Handbooks 1 and 2. This document provides general public education for those interested in forestry and wood products, and will serve as a good introduction for potential certifiers, timber managers, and operators.

GENERAL STANDARDS FOR ECOLOGICALLY RESPONSIBLE TIMBER MANAGEMENT

The primary standard for ecologically responsible timber management is: All plans and activities must protect, maintain, and restore (where necessary) a fully functioning forest ecosystem at all temporal and spatial scales. Forest composition, structures, and functioning must be maintained, from the largest landscape to the smallest forest community, in both short and long terms.

Two important forest ecosystem concepts are encompassed within this general standard for ecological responsibility: forest landscapes and forest stands.

The forest landscape is the large-scale view of a forest. A forest landscape is a mosaic of interconnected, interdependent stands or patches that are repeated in a pattern across the larger landscape. This pattern has both spatial and temporal components. Ecologically responsible forest use requires that all planning and activities begin at the regional/landscape levels. When planning for human use, landscape-level decisions are made for watersheds of small (less than 5,000 hectares [12,354 a]) to moderate size (5,000 to 50,000 hectares [12,354 to 123,548 a]). In regional planning processes, forest landscape-level considerations are expanded to watersheds that encompass hundreds of thousands of hectares.

> **What occurs in Earth's forests directly and indirectly impacts all other terrestrial and aquatic ecosystems at all scales.**

In current planning for many activities, particularly timber management, many people tend to focus on small forest parcels. This is a result of our limited spatial view, short timeframes, and cultural conditioning. Ecologically responsible forest use requires that all planning and activities start at the landscape level. The character and condition of the forest landscape dictate what is ecologically possible at the stand level.

Forest stands refer to the ecosystem scale where a relatively homogeneous forest unit can be identified. The composition, structure, and ecological functions within a stand are similar enough that an ecologically responsible forest use prescription can be applied uniformly within the stand, without encountering changes in ecological parameters that may produce unexpected or undesirable results.

In the past, "stands" have largely been defined by narrow timber characteristics driven by short-term economic variables. However, to maintain fully functioning forests at the landscape and stand levels, stands must be defined by ecosystem factors necessary to maintain fully functioning systems. The stand size and scale are determined, not by rigid or desired human management criteria, but by ecosystem parameters related to natural disturbance patterns and movement patterns (i.e. energy, nutrients, water, and animals).

Human scales are closest to forest scales at the stand level. Thus, the stand level is the scale where visible human modification occurs. However, ecologically responsible forest users must always remember that what occurs at the stand or visible scale impacts a variety of other scales, from the large landscapes to the microscopic.

LANDSCAPE-LEVEL STANDARDS

Landscape planning and standards operate at the broad scale. Because all forest stands are part of a related landscape, forest use planning must start at the landscape level in order to maintain landscape health and functioning. Landscape characteristics (the natural spatial and temporal landscape pattern) and condition (changes to the landscape as a result of human modification) will influence what can be done at the stand level. Required landscape level standards for ecologically responsible forest use include:

A. Define a protected landscape network. Components include:
  1. riparian ecosystems (includes riparian zone and riparian zone of influence)
  2. representative stands or ecosystem types, old-growth forests particularly important
  3. ecologically sensitive areas
  4. cross-valley corridors

(Note: Large protected reserves (50,000 hectares [123,548 a] and larger) are part of a protected landscape network for large landscapes. This component must be added where landscapes more than 300,000 hectares [741,290 a] are planned.)

B. Establish ecologically responsible forest use zones that include:
 1. cultural use
 2. ecologically sensitive
 3. fish and wildlife
 4. recreation/tourism/wilderness
 5. ecologically responsible timber extraction
C. Develop restoration plan(s) as required.

STAND-LEVEL STANDARDS

Human plans for modification generally focus on the visible stand level, but also have effects on both the stand level at invisible or microscopic scales and on landscape levels. Required stand-level standards for ecologically responsible forest use include:

A. Protect and maintain composition and structures to support fully functioning forests at all scales:
 1. Existing large snags and fallen trees will be protected. In the case of snags, this may mean leaving groups of large living trees in order to avoid potential safety hazards to loggers.
 2. In order to ensure an ongoing supply of old trees, snags, and fallen trees, an ecologically appropriate minimum number of large overstory trees (well distributed spatially and by species) will always be present on the site and will be permitted to grow old and die.
 3. Reaching the minimum number of large overstory trees shall generally occur in four or more cuts spaced relatively equally over 100 to 200 years.
 4. Young trees that regenerate following partial cuts will be designated as eventual replacements for large trees to ensure that the minimum standards for overstory composition and structure remain in perpetuity.
B. Use ecological tree growing periods—for example, 150 to 250+ years.
C. Prohibit clearcutting as currently practised. Timber extraction methods shall mimic natural disturbances both spatially and temporally. These methods shall utilize ecologically appropriate partial cutting methods that maintain the canopy structure, age distribution, and species mixtures found in healthy, natural forests in a particular ecosystem type.
D. Prohibit slash burning.
E. Maintain/restore fire where necessary for ecosystem functioning.
F. Allow the forest to regenerate trees through seeds from trees in and adjacent to the logged area. Tree planting will generally not be required because a diverse, fully functioning forest is always maintained.
G. Maintain ecological succession to protect biological diversity. The practice of "brush" control will be avoided.
H. Prohibit pesticide use.

I. Minimize soil degradation by:
1. minimizing road impacts (including skid roads) by minimizing width, disruption to drainage, and frequency
2. avoiding use of roads (including skid roads) wherever possible
3. minimizing all construction associated with logging activities
J. Protect water by:
1. protecting riparian ecosystems
2. minimizing impacts on drainage patterns
3. prohibiting activities in erosion-prone areas
4. minimizing sources of sediment input into streams
5. deactivating old roads (including skid roads) to re-establish dispersed water movement patterns.

RESTORATION STANDARDS

As with other forms of ecologically responsible stewardship the process of restoration involves solving problems with finesse and ingenuity, rather than with force. Soft approaches that protect all the parts of the ecosystem must replace aggressive approaches that label some parts as valuable and other parts as worthless or harmful. Careful restoration includes four important principles:

1. Restore the forest at the stand level while making sure that these activities rebuild landscape connections.
2. Mimic historical ecological processes.
3. Restore whole watersheds/large landscapes.
4. Treat the causes of degradation, not just the symptoms.

Note: Restoration plans and activities shall be carried out with local people, ideally with those who inhabit the forest.

People experienced in agricultural restoration have found that degrading land use activities have often been designed by specialists and accomplished by powerful technologies, such as large machines and pesticides. In contrast, effective restoration requires all kinds of people with all kinds of skills. People with shovels will be as important as people with machines. Restoration must be more than a swift afterthought or hopeful solution to a single problem, no matter how commendable the impulse.

Some of the important activities that might comprise an adequate restoration program include:

A. restoration of soil health, including:
1. breaking up compacted soil surfaces
2. introducing vegetation to stabilize soil, build soil nutrient levels, and restore water holding capacity
B. establishment of natural drainage patterns
C. encouragement of natural diversity by reseeding (instead of replanting)

> **Restoration plans and activities shall be carried out with local people, ideally with those who inhabit the forest.**

         naturally occurring herb, shrub, and tree species

D.   planting trees and shrubs where required for stabilization and diversification of a degraded forest community

E.   carefully reintroducing animal and micro-organism species

F.   restoration of riparian zones by re-establishing streamside vegetation

G.   stabilizing stream banks and diversifying stream channels by reintroducing large logs (until natural large fallen trees are available)

H.   careful reintroduction of natural and human-induced fire by limiting the practice of fire suppression to specified areas (near human dwellings and in wholistic timber management zones)

SOCIAL STANDARDS

Timber management must be socially responsible as well as ecologically responsible. The SILVA Forest Foundation's general standards for socially responsible timber management are:

1.   Timber management shall take place only after securing the informed consent of the indigenous people whose forest is being considered for management.

2.   The needs and culture of indigenous people shall be fully protected during and following timber management operations.

3.   Indigenous people, where they so desire, shall take a lead role in timber management planning operations.

4.   Participation by local communities in decision-making and in the equitable distribution of benefits to the local community will be promoted.

5.   Timber management shall maximize employment of local workers and promote community stability.

6.   Workers' rights, including occupational safety, fair compensation, and the rights of workers to collectively bargain will be respected.

7.   The development of worker-owned and -operated organizations will be supported.

CONCLUSION

Ecologically responsible forest use begins from the humble understanding that the forest is an interconnected web that focuses on sustaining the whole, not on the production of any one part or commodity. All of the standards summarized in this paper, including protecting and maintaining composition, structure, and functioning; respecting biological limits; and limiting the scale of our activities, apply to every kind of human use, whether we are building a wilderness lodge, grazing cattle, or cutting timber. Ecologically responsible practices accept the control of natural processes—nature is at the wheel—and mimic the subtlety, diversity, and unpredictability of natural changes, while using the forest carefully in a variety of ways. Ecologically responsible forest use focuses on what to leave fully functioning forests—not on what to take.

Comments on these draft standards are welcome. Please send to Herb Hammond, SILVA Forest Foundation, P.O. Box 9, Slocan Park, B.C. V0G 2E0.

29

The Bioregional Basis for Certification:
Why Cascadia?

David Simpson

THE FACTS ARE BEGINNING TO SUPPORT A LONGSTANDING SUSPICION: small-scale, community-based forestry can become a cornerstone for restoring not only North American forests, but community and culture as well. And it is most likely the only way forestry and the forest products industry will become truly sustainable.

Sustainable forestry throughout Cascadia is developing through the commitment of people—environmentalists, forest workers, natural scientists, restorationists and others—who share in common a land with natural integrity. There are many social and political distinctions between the regions of Cascadia, but the similarities are as important as the differences. Cascadia includes parts of five United States (i.e., California, Oregon and Washington, and the Columbia River basin of Idaho and Montana), much of British Columbia, and most of coastal southeast Alaska.

Cascadia, where the great rainforests of the Pacific Northwest reign supreme! Where the majestic Sitka spruce, Douglas fir, hemlock, redwood, cedar, pines, oaks, yew, alder, maples, and many others have thrived beside the Pacific basin, where great storms brew in the Gulf of Alaska, where torrential rains, potent winds, and vast tectonic and volcanic forces periodically shake cities to their core and burst mountains. Cascadia, the land of the salmon, settled on a shifting ocean edge where we have built massive, fragile cities dwarfed by giant mountains. Cascadia is our home ground, our territory, the greatest forestland in the world. It is ours to wean back from global economic forces and growing cultural indistinction into which it is being drawn, as everywhere around the world.

DECENTRALIZATION: NOT WHY, BUT HOW

Clearly, we are approaching a moment in history when dramatic changes in the way we are governed, or govern ourselves, are taking place globally. Decentralization of government is happening all around us. The question is, how can decentralization be done in a responsible fashion? In the U.S., the loudest voices for decentralization of government power present their cause under the generic term "privatization." Essentially, they are demanding the selling of properties and services to the private sector. Rationales for such actions are perceived inefficiencies of government management and provision of services, or the need to reduce the federal deficit. Usually, such arguments are couched in free-market ideology, which is a flaw in privatization.

CASCADIA

Map of Cascadia
David McCloskey,
Cascadia Institute.

Privatization means that when the chips are down, the sale of assets or functions goes to the highest bidder, who is rarely the community of people to be affected most by the sale. Large commercial interests are given more opportunities to gain increasing control of local economies and cultures, which do not benefit. Low-paying jobs might be the best result from corporate deals, which result in losses of stability, quality of life and community spirit. Trading control by remote governments to control by remote corporations is hardly a great deal.

Localization is another means of decentralization that may be more effective and empowering. While privatization is a tool of free-market economics, a means of control by those who can afford acquisitions, localization is democratic control of local resources and services by those who have commitment to place and community: the residents. Admittedly, there are probably untested waters about how localization can succeed. However, one key to success is creating standards and guidelines: you write into the deal about how, given the best knowledge available, the store ought to be run.

In a study of Italian politics,[1] political scientist Robert Putnam discovered that some communities were more capable or ready for self-regulation than others; the distinguishing characteristic was accumulation of social capital, a term developed by Putnam. Social capital is the strength that communities build through long-term commitment to working, recreating, and celebrating together. Shared love of place is both a term of social capital and a product of it. Perhaps we need to develop a way to evaluate how communities become ready for self-regulation. Once such a determination is made, then government can step back.

Localization is a process, not a surrender, by which management of local resources and services is returned to residents committed to places as they meet standards that guarantee a level of overall responsibility to the whole of society and the planet. Such standards must not bind communities to picayune details of management, but rather serve as guidelines that guarantee a general level of ecological and social responsiveness. There are also no formulas for standards. Each community must be allowed to develop guidelines based on the distinctive realities of its place. The needs of both the forest and the people must be considered. People-based, localized forestry, practiced under guidelines that guarantee ecological and social responsibility, is a better economic deal than control of forest lands by governmental and corporate powers. Certainly it is a better deal for communities. Consumers, too, will be the winners.

The Significance of Bioregionalism

How does bioregionalism affect localization? Bioregionalism means that places on the planet differ from one another. There are real distinctions in terms of natural history, weather, geology, topography, botany and biology that together determine the character of a place. In some places still, and in most places prehistorically, human culture was moulded by these distinctions. Native cultures were built on experience within, and observation of, place. With the advent of industrial-technological society, some of us were granted the illusion of freedom from many elements of place.

Environmentalism has shown us that much of this freedom is illusory. Fossil fuels are finite and their unfettered use is destructive to natural systems. Many, if not most, of our technologies trap us in a sea of proliferating pollutants and nonrecyclable wastes. Vast inequities produced by arbitrary shifts and exploitative relationships in a technologically driven economy threaten to drown civil society. Given all this, it becomes clear that we have to reorient ourselves to the realities of where we live.

Bioregionalism is a movement to reorient culture to better fit the places of which it is a part, as cultures have done for centuries. It is readaptation and reinhabitation. There are no clear routes, no codes, maps or checkpoints. It is as much an instinct as an effort, a predisposition based on the physical world and our natural limitations, such as how far a person can walk in a day or how much wood is needed for winter.

In terms of economy and governance, localization does not mean a return to isolation, provincialism or separation. It means a return to focus on community as the essential building block of society, and a unification of communities tied to each other by virtue of natural realities, shared interests and values and a market interdependence that guarantees economic and cultural exchange. By virtue of common ecosystems within continents or ocean basins, whole regions are united. One of these is Cascadia.

Why bioregionalism? Why Cascadia? Our commitment to place within a larger region in common can inspire our sense of majesty and respect for Cascadia. Once

West Coast mixed native rainforest
Bo Martin

we leap to an identity with place and region, other elements will fall into perspective. Once we become responsible citizens of a region, rural and urban, our respect for the land unites and motivates us. The Pacific Certification Council is built on its Cascadian identity and a commitment to the forests that sustain us.

Winter alpine forest
Bo Martin

30

Certifying Ecologically Responsible
Forest Use and Restoration:
Future Direction for the Ecoforestry Movement

Mike Barnes and Twila Jacobsen

THE PUBLICATION OF THIS ECOFORESTRY ANTHOLOGY is an important stage in the process of the ecoforestry movement becoming conscious of itself, not only as a body of theory and practice, but also as an emerging global network of people who care for and about forests and who seek to create sustainable lifestyles and communities. In addition to the Ecoforestry Institutes in Oregon and B.C., ecoforestry centers and projects have organized independently in Nova Scotia, Papua New Guinea, Russia and elsewhere.

This anthology comes at a critical time in the development of forest products certification programs. We have an historic opportunity to participate in and affect two processes that are currently underway: first, to complete the Pacific Certification Council's (PCC) "Standards for the Certification of Ecologically Responsible Forest Use" for the Cascadia bioregion, and secondly, to develop FSC (Forest Stewardship Council) regional standards for the accreditation of certifying organizations for both the Pacific Coast/U.S. and B.C.

This anthology contains a number of essays from the special issue of the *International Journal of Ecoforestry* (IJE) on "Certification in Cascadia" (Winter 1996) where the Pacific Certification Council put forward its bioregional vision of certification. One important accomplishment of the PCC during 1996 was the completion of draft "Standards for the Certification of Ecologically Responsible Forest Use and Restoration," written by Herb Hammond of the SILVA Forest Foundation. These standards seek to incorporate earlier certification standards developed by the other member organizations in the PCC, including those of the Ecoforestry Institute. [See "Ecologically Responsible Restoration and Ecoforestry," Alan Drengson and Victoria Stevens, Chapter 5 in this book.]

The Ecoforestry Institutes have collaborated with other NGOs to build a unified certification organization with the capabilities and funds necessary to make certification work. However, this collaborative work has been challenging—sometimes because of our own failings and sometimes because of real differences in values and understandings. Collaboration requires each organization to be true to its mission and yet, recognizing the limitations of our knowledge in the face of complex ecosystem dynamics, we need to approach collaborative efforts with humility, flexibility and a spirit of cooperation. We do not know the answers; we must continuously test and revise our ecological theories in the crucible of practice. *A commitment to ecoforestry is a dedication to lifelong learning.*

AN ECOCENTRIC APPROACH TO FOREST USE AND RESTORATION

From the perspective of the Ecoforestry Institutes, certification is a market strategy to link forest goods and products that come from forests where an ecocentric approach to forest use and restoration is practised with environmentally conscious consumers willing to purchase these goods and products, even at a premium price. An ecocentric approach to forest use and restoration is characterized by an understanding that forests are complex, living communities that sustain us. We don't sustain them. The goal of an ecocentric approach to forest use and restoration is to mimic the processes and patterns of forests in order to learn to augment their natural abundance—so that we can live from the increase! This is what we mean by "sustainability." We are challenged to use our human intelligence and creativity to protect, maintain and restore forests as fully functioning systems, while harvesting a range of forest products in the process. We must not kill the goose which lays the golden eggs!

However, there are significant differences in the definitions and range of practices that are considered "sustainable" by different certification organizations, even among NGO (nongovernment organization) certifiers. Some certify that forest management plans consider and lead towards improvements in the environmental impacts of industrial forestry, even though forests are still perceived and treated mechanistically as dead resources, rather than living systems. Others certify that forest practices are "sustainable" primarily in terms of "sustained yield," where the volume of timber to be harvested is limited to the net annual growth, even though the focus is still primarily on sustaining timber, rather than sustaining forest ecosystems.

"Ecologically responsible forest use and restoration" moves beyond an anthropocentric perspective of forests and seeks to certify that "whole forests" are being protected, maintained and restored, while forest goods and products are being harvested from appropriate areas, even as forest goods are harvested. "Ecologically responsible forest use and restoration" needs to be practised and certified at both the landscape and stand levels in order to protect biodiversity and to understand natural disturbance patterns necessary to design forest use and restoration plans.

With the future of the PCC in development, the future of the "Standards for the Certification of Ecologically Responsible Forest Use and Restoration" are also in progress. The member organizations of the Pacific Certification Council have yet to reach agreements on a number of critical issues: (1) standards for certification to be used in the Cascadia bioregion, and (2) terminology to be used.

1. Draft "Standards for the Certification of Ecologically Responsible Forest Use"

The Pacific Certification Council is currently conducting outreach to key stakeholders about these draft standards. This dialogue among the members of the PCC and with other stakeholders has raised many important questions, such as the following:

- Should certification require landscape-level design and planning to protect biodiversity?
- How will landscape-level analysis and design be paid for?
- How do natural disturbance regimes shape forest ecosystems?
- How can natural disturbances be used as models to design timber cutting patterns?
- How much old-growth needs to be protected and recruited?
- How much inventory data is necessary for ecological planning and monitoring?
- Is clearcutting ever ecologically responsible?
- What size and distribution of patch cuts are necessary for regeneration of native species?
- What are we restoring a forest ecosystem back to?
- How much timber can be cut from a stand at any one time and still maintain a fully functioning forest?
- Which is being certified: "well managed" forests or "ecologically responsible forest use?"

2. Terminology

The lack of agreements on terminology remains a stumbling block. Without such clarity, it is difficult to know what we mean—much less what we are certifying. Our choices about what terminology to use can directly reflect differences in understanding of ecological realities and of practices considered certifiable as "sustainable," or they can be strategic differences about how best to communicate with different constituencies.

The Ecoforestry Institutes consider it critical to use ecological language to make clear that we are speaking of certifying *an ecocentric approach to forest use and restoration* that recognizes forests as living ecosystems. We prefer to certify using the language currently proposed in the PCC's draft "Standards for the Certification of Ecologically Responsible Forest Use."

> Adopting ecological language is an opportunity to replace the mechanistic language of industrial forestry that speaks of forests as dead resources.

- The term "ecologically responsible" is an ethical statement of caring for a forest in the best ways that we know how, based both on ecological science and indigenous knowledge of people who live in place. It is always a matter of judgment whether our interventions into forests and other ecosystems are "responsible." Certification is about values and ethics, as well as about practices, products and markets.

- Likewise, we prefer the term "*forest use*," because it is inclusive of forestry and yet includes a wide range of other uses. It is critical that an ecosystem approach to forests be based on a recognition of the wide range of values that forests contain, i.e., clean water, wildlife habitat, "special forest products," and recreation.

- We prefer not to certify forests as "well managed," because of the ambiguity of the meaning of "management." From an ecocentric perspective, forests are more complex than we can understand, much less manage. Yet it is critical that we manage human intervention in forests. However, even based on this meaning of the word, management needs to be designed to work with nature's processes and patterns. Accordingly, we would agree to use the terminology of certifying "well managed" forests, if there is clarity in the definition of what we mean by "management."

In the spirit of cooperation and collaboration, we would agree to use the terminology of "sustainable forestry" to certify forestry practices and to describe forest products in the marketplace if "sustainable" is defined in ecocentric terms and translates into ecocentric practices.

The NGO certification movement has a significant opportunity to adopt an ecological language that will enable us to communicate clearly among ourselves, ecological scientists and philosophers, environmental organizations, as well as with the ecologically conscious consumers who will purchase our goods and products. Adopting ecological language is an opportunity to replace the mechanistic language of industrial forestry that speaks of forests as dead resources, with a language that describes a living reality of which we are a part, not separate. Chet Bowers, a director of the U.S. Ecoforestry Institute and a professor of Education at Portland State University, explains the importance of ecological language:

> Each distinctive cultural mode and ideology is rooted in the way the language system of a culture (spoken, written, kinesthetic, musical, architectural, etc.) encodes and reproduces in the present the patterns handed down from the past. Put simply, as members of a culture learn to think and communicate with the language system that sustains the "reality" of the group, they in turn reproduce the patterns—even as they struggle to modify patterns regarded as especially outmoded. The use of the cultural language system thus involves individuals quite literally being thought (that is, the language thinks us as we think within the language) and re-enacted

by the living patterns that have their roots in the past.... Our vocabularies should enable us to think and communicate about the complexities of living as members of cultural and biotic communities.[1]

Our ability to speak in an ecological language allows us, as NGO-sector certification organizations, to communicate effectively among ourselves, as well as with ecologically conscious consumers who will purchase our brand of certified "ecoforest products." Can certification succeed as a strategy to shift towards ecological forestry practices if it defines itself with "...the very same (language and) cultural orientations that have contributed to destroying the environment in the name of 'progress'?"[2]

PROPOSALS FOR FUTURE DIRECTIONS

1. As we look ahead, the Ecoforestry Institutes will continue to be active members of the PCC and work to develop standards, funding and the infrastructure necessary for a certification program to certify forest goods and products from forests where an ecocentric approach to forest use and restoration is practiced. The draft "Standards for the Certification of Ecologically Responsible Forest Use" provide the foundation for what will likely be the best ecosystem-based standards for the practice and certification of "sustainable forestry" yet written.

   We support the continuation of the PCC, or another bioregional certification organization, to serve as the "keeper of the standards," to represent the bioregion with the FSC, and to develop the infrastructure for sustainable forest product loops between practitioners and consumers as part of the development of larger watershed and bioregional economies.

2. In the meantime, the Institutes will continue to move ahead at our respective paces to develop a certification program that will support goods and products from the practitioners of ecoforestry. We recognize that we are involved in a long-term shift and that the ecoforestry movement is still in the process of defining the theory, practices and standards of an ecocentric approach to forest use and restoration (ecoforestry).

   The Ecoforestry Institute (EI) in Oregon is planning to conduct its first certification of the forest use plan and the "Fire Hazard Reduction and Pine/Oak Savannah Restoration" logging at the Mountain Grove Center. The 400 acre forest also serves as an ecoforestry demonstration and teaching

Old hardwoods in river delta
Bo Martin

forest. This first certification will allow us to ground-test the PCC's draft standards. EI's certification team will consist of Dr. Dave Perry, Professor of Ecosystem Science at Oregon State University, and representatives of other members of the PCC and Smartwood.

3. The Ecoforestry Institute/U.S. plans to continue discussions with Smartwood about which certification standards and terminology they will use in the Cascadia bioregion. We will also continue to discuss with them designing and providing education and training programs for certification evaluators.

4. The Ecoforestry Institutes will continue to participate in the Forest Stewardship Council (FSC), particularly in the current processes to develop regional standards for the accreditation of certification organizations both in the Pacific Coast of the U.S. and in B.C.

CONCLUSION

Based on such agreements on standards and terminology, the Institutes will work cooperatively with a larger NGO certification organization or network, like Smartwood. The Institutes could then focus more of their efforts on other aspects of their mission: education and training in the practice of "Ecologically Responsible Forest Use and Restoration"; working with forestland owners to develop forest use and restoration plans; establishing other demonstration forests where "ecologically responsible forest use and restoration" is practised; and building cooperatives and networks of forestland owners and ecoforestry practitioners.

We believe this anthology will stimulate further growth of an ecoforestry movement that practises and supports an ecocentric approach to forest use and restoration in watersheds across our bioregions and around the Earth.

31

An Ecoforestry Land Stewardship Trust Model

Tyhson Banighen

THERE IS A BASIC PARADOX INHERENT IN THE PRIVATE OWNERSHIP of forest resources: If you own the forest, you can exploit it for short-term profit; if you don't own the forest, why should you care enough about the forest's future to wisely manage it in the long term? (Raphael 1981, p. 235).

A land stewardship trust with an ecoforestry management plan to steward the forest can deal with this paradox. Forest stewardship is making land-use decisions that nurture the health of the natural environment while fulfilling the goals of those stewarding the land's resources. The Land Stewardship Trust (LST) model is a legal agreement ensuring that the owners, harvesters or managers of the forest or collectively the stewards cannot exploit the forest resources such that the forest ecosystem is damaged. At the same time, the agreement provides incentives for the steward to act in self-interest while simultaneously acting in the best interests of the forest.

THE NEED FOR A LAND ETHIC

Aldo Leopold, a professional forester and founder of the Wilderness Society, wrote in 1949:

> There is as yet no ethic dealing with man's relationship to land and the animals and plants which grow upon it.... The land-relation is still strictly economic, entailing privileges, but no obligations.... Obligations have no meaning without conscience, and the problem we face is the extension of the social consciousness from people to land. All ethics so far evolved rest upon a single premise: that the individual is a member of a community of interdependent parts.... The land ethic simply enlarges the boundaries of the community to include soils, waters, plants, and animals, or collectively: the land. (Leopold 1966, p. 239)

It has been over 40 years since Leopold wrote those words. Now the need for a land ethic with obligations is even greater, as we realize there are limits to progress based on our utilitarian ethic of unlimited growth.

TURTLE ISLAND EARTH STEWARDS

Turtle Island Earth Stewards (TIES) is a nonprofit charitable society incorporated in Canada in 1975. One of TIES' objectives as a society is "to research, develop and teach stewardship of the land and its resources within an ecological context." TIES acts as a Community Land Trust (CLT) for the Shuswap-North Okanagan region and has general designation with the Province of British Columbia to enter into conservation covenants.

THE IMPLEMENTATION OF A LAND ETHIC

To establish a land ethic with obligations, TIES developed the Land Stewardship Trust (LST) model and accompanying legal documents.

Using an LST, TIES can assist landowners, ranchers, private woodlot owners, municipalities, regional districts, other groups or individuals to place their lands or forests in trust while using conservancy and stewardship principles to protect and manage land. The necessary legal documents were completed in 1996. Conservation covenants protect the long-term ecological integrity of the land or forest while at the same time allowing an ecoforestry plan to be entered into as a condition of forest stewardship. The same documents can be adapted to protect and manage agricultural lands or protect the cultural beliefs of the Doukhobor people who believe only God can own the land, or assist indigenous tribes to hold lands as common property in trust for their people.

The documents deal with the paradox between the long-term need for preservation of the forest ecosystem with the short-term need for resource extraction. The legal documents include conservation covenants registered against the title of the land to protect the long-term viability of the ecosystem, while the Stewardship Agreement, which in the case of forest management is an ecoforestry plan, clearly spells out the parameters for harvesting, all of which can provide the necessary conditions for wood certification.

WHAT IS A LAND STEWARDSHIP TRUST?

An LST is an ecosystem approach to land-use planning using land conservancy and land stewardship principles. Depending on the needs of the landowner and the conservation priorities of a local community land trust, an LST agreement can integrate elements from other land trust models into one comprehensive trust agreement. The various land trust models are as follows:

Conservation Land Trusts. A conservation land trust creates nature preserves that protect unique and special ecosystems. The Nature Conservancy of Canada, the Nature Trust of B.C. and the Ecological Reserves Branch of B.C. specialize in this kind of trust activity to protect endangered species of plant and animal communities. An LST can set aside ecologically sensitive areas such as riparian zones, lake foreshores, wildlife corridors or ecological reserves as part of a comprehensive ecosystem-based land-use plan for a property or a number of properties in a watershed.

Affordable Housing Land Trusts (AHLT). The affordable housing land trust is a private, nonprofit corporation created to acquire and hold land for the benefit of a community and to provide secure, affordable access to land and housing for community residents. In particular, AHLTs attempt to meet the needs of residents least served by the prevailing market. AHLTs prohibit speculation and absentee ownership of land and housing, promote ecologically sound land-use practices, and preserve the long-term affordability of housing (ICE 1988). Similarly an LST can be structured to provide access to land for those who could not otherwise afford to buy the land, and the implementation of ecologically sound land-use practices is a necessary condition for residency on trusted lands. An LST agreement can also incorporate a housing component or establish use rights for stewards to live on and/or derive a livelihood from the land held in trust.

Agricultural Land Trusts. An agricultural land trust uses land conservancy techniques, such as conservation covenant and estate planning devices, to maintain the farmland virtually in its present natural condition and to prevent the decline of agriculture and the family farm. Similarly, agricultural lands in an LST can be stewarded according to a set of clearly defined, ecologically sound principles, such as an Organic Farm Certification process being a condition of ongoing stewardship.

Forest Land Trusts. Forest Land Trusts can be structured in various ways. An agreement can be reached with one landowner, a group of farmers (or landowners) or a woodlot owners' group to donate the "development rights" of their forested land to a land trust and receive a tax credit for doing so. A landowner or a group can form a partnership and pool the value of their trees in a long-range ecoforestry program managed by the partnership and/or the land trust. Such a plan can increase the value of the trees several fold and brings an additional income to farmers and landowners (ICE 1980).

An LST Agreement can incorporate any of the above concepts. The key is to protect the ecological integrity of property, such as the forest ecosystem, in perpetuity by using conservation covenants registered against the title of the land. In addition, an ecoforestry management plan is registered with the covenants as a Forest Stewardship Plan for a 5-year, 25-year period or for as long as the owner wants the plan to be in effect. The owner can also determine how the plan can or cannot be changed over time and by whom. Future stewards, if the land is sold, must abide by the ecoforestry management plan for the duration of the plan. The agreement can also be structured so the landowner's descendants can have the right of first refusal to manage the property as long as they abide by the plan and the conservation

> **The key is to protect the ecological integrity of property, such as the forest ecosystem, in perpetuity.**

covenants. This means a management plan can be in place from generation to generation so that various ecoforestry approaches can be monitored over time to document the various successes and failures.

TIES as a CLT has the responsibility to monitor the trust agreement on behalf of this and future generations. We usually involve volunteers who live in the area to monitor the agreement. These volunteers would work with a registered ecoforester to do periodic onsite walk-throughs. If the covenants or management plan are violated, the land trust is notified and, in turn, the landowner. After due process, if the situation is not rectified by the landowner, then TIES would cancel the stewardship agreement. TIES' responsibility in this case would be to find new stewards who were willing to manage the forest according to the agreed-upon plan.

In addition to incorporating aspects of the other land trust models, as mentioned, an LST can be designed to include some or all of the following purposes:

- To ensure that an ecosystem approach to land-use planning incorporates the values of ecosystem preservation as well as land stewardship as a land ethic with obligations.
- To ensure the long-term health of the ecosystem by establishing ecosystem health indicators that are monitored at watershed or community level.
- To ensure that stewardship rights to the use of land and resources are dependent on complying with a land ethic with obligations.
- To establish a baseline inventory of the property to be placed in trust to determine which ecologically sensitive areas need to be protected and which can be wisely managed.
- To ensure that use-rights to land and its resources are monitored against a baseline of site-specific data that could include scientific data as a means to protect the long-term health of the ecosystem.
- To ensure that the legal agreement supports mutually nurturing long-term relationships between people and land so that the stewards can realize their own personal dreams, while at the same time fostering a thriving natural environment.
- To provide community control of land and its resources as the basis for community-based and ecologically sound sustainable development.

APPLYING THE LST MODEL TO LINNAEA FARM

Linnaea Farm, a 311-acre farm on Cortes Island, B.C., is a good example of how an LST model uniquely blends concepts from the other land trust models.

The conservation land trust aspect of Linnaea includes two ecological reserves: one a high bluff, and the other forest lands bordering Gunflint Lake, which is a designated volunteer bird sanctuary.

The CLT aspect allows the members of the community of Linnaea, as stewards, access to land they could not afford to buy.

A yet-to-be-negotiated LST agreement would ensure long-term occupancy of the land by the stewards dependent on the wise stewardship of the agricultural and forest lands. State-of-the-art conservation covenants would be registered against the title of the land, and the health of the ecosystem monitored over time to ensure the long-term protection of the heart of the farm and its surrounding ecosystem.

At present, TIES as the land trust is negotiating an LST agreement with the present stewards of Linnaea Farm. The agreement will include both an agricultural and a forest management plan based on sound stewardship principles as conditions of residency.

THE WHYS, HOWS AND ADVANTAGES OF PLACING LANDS IN TRUST

Lands can be placed in trust in either of two ways. The land or forest can be protected by not allowing the land to be bought and sold, as in the Linnaea Farm case. In this way the land is placed in fee simple trust (i.e. owned by a land trust, in this case TIES). This agreement and others can be structured in such a way that the land ceases to be a commodity that can be bought and sold for speculative gain, nor encumbered or used in any way except as outlined in the trust agreement. In this way the value of the land drops and then stabilizes because it can no longer be sold for development purposes.

Using this method the landowner essentially trades short-term speculative gains for long-term private and social benefits. These benefits are derived from land conservancy and/or the wise stewardship of resources in perpetuity. If lands or forests are bequeathed or the land or money to buy land is donated to a CLT like TIES then the donation qualifies as a tax-deductible gift. If the present owner is willing to sell the land to the CLT at less than the market price, assuming the CLT has money to buy the land, then the difference between the appraised value and the selling price less the capital gains tax is tax deductible.

High value-added products
Cheri Burda

If the owner does not want to give up ownership rights, because he or she may need to borrow against the title or sell the land in the future, then conservation covenants can be placed on the land or the development rights sold, donated, or bequeathed to a community land trust in order to protect the ecological integrity of the land, or to implement wise stewardship practices. The main issue is not who owns land and resources, but how the land and its resources are managed ecologically and in a sustainable manner for present and future generations.

If the conservation covenant is donated to the CLT then the appraised value of the covenant is considered a charitable gift. The land taxes will also be lowered by the portion of the property placed in trust.

Another financial incentive in British Columbia is that Forest Renewal will pay for bank stabilization and riparian restoration work on private property if the landowner agrees to a conservation covenant registered against the title to protect the work undertaken.

ADVANTAGES OF USING THE LST MODEL

While LSTs provide for local community control over the "ownership rights" to lands and resources by placing them in public trust, the real advantage for the community is to be able to ensure that the "use-rights" to lands and resources are conditional on their wise use. The important issue, then, is how to implement and monitor a stewardship ethic with obligations at the community level, whether the lands are owned privately, cooperatively, or by the Crown.

For example, both Crown land and lands in trust are held as "commons" for the common good of society. A commons is an economic resource like forest lands that are subject to individual use but not to individual possession.

The essential difference is that Crown lands such as the forest of British Columbia can suffer resource depletion or degradation—an eventuality characterized by Hardin (1968) as the tragedy of the commons: ownership by all managed by a distant government can be as indifferent in consequence as no ownership at all. In contrast, lands in an LST are managed locally and are used according to an underlying ethic of responsibility.

THE LST MODEL AND ECOLOGICALLY SUSTAINABLE DEVELOPMENT

The goal of a land stewardship ethic is to protect a sustainable ecologic system as the necessary underpinning for both sustainable social systems and sustainable economic systems, whether at the community, bioregional, provincial, national, international or global level.

Sustainability requires decisions to be made in three areas: biologic, economic, social. For *biologic systems* the goal of sustainable development is: maintenance of genetic diversity, resilience, and biological productivity through the recognition of ecological thresholds and the need to merge human activities with natural replenishment cycles. For *economic systems* the goals are: satisfying basic needs, achievement of equity, and increasing useful goods and services. For *social systems* the goals are: maintenance of cultural diversity, provision for participation and self-determination, social justice, and institutional adaptability (Barbier 1987, p. 101-102).

The World Commission on Environment and Development's 1987 report, *Our Common Future*, defines sustainable development as "development that meets the needs of the present without compromising the ability of future generations to meet their own needs" (WCED 1987, p. 43).

All development, whether sustainable or not, is dependent on a sustainable ecological system as the necessary underpinning for a sustainable socioeconomic system; if nonexistent, there will be an inevitable socio-environmental systems crash. While the LST model is designed to protect ecological sustainability and to manage lands and resources held in public trust, the same stewardship principles could be applied, if there were sufficient political will, to manage Crown lands, or for that matter, the global commons.

Once the sustainability of the ecological system is protected, then the LST model can be used to operationalize sustainable socioeconomic development at the community level by using the principles of Community Economic Development (CED).

THE LST MODEL AND COMMUNITY ECONOMIC DEVELOPMENT

Local ownership and control is the best for both LSTs and Community Economic Development (CED). The Social Planning and Research Council of British Columbia states:

> Community Economic Development is concerned with fostering the social, economic and environmental well-being of communities and regions through initiatives, taken by citizens in collaboration with their governments, community agencies and other public and private organizations, that strengthen local decision-making and self-reliance, cooperative endeavors and broad participation in community affairs (Claque 1986, p. 6).

According to this definition, CED is sustainable development by and for a local community, and an LST is a technique for implementing CED.

For example, when private forest lands are placed into an LST, communities can practise self-governance through forest stewardship that provides for both sustainable CED, and environmentally sound, integrated forest management. Forests managed in trust incorporate the following CED principles, to name a few: local ownership and control of enterprise, local permanent employment creation, worker/employee participation, equality, cooperation, interdependence of economic, social, and environmental factors, and opportunities for all citizens to participate fully as contributors and consumers.

HOW A COMMUNITY LAND TRUST ACQUIRES LANDS AND FORESTS TO BE PLACED IN TRUST

There are a number of ways in which lands and forests can be acquired by a CLT from landowners: by outright purchase, by donation, or by bequests of lands in fee simple or conservation covenants. To understand conservation covenants, or purchasing development rights, think of owning land as holding a bundle of rights. A landowner can sell or give away the whole bundle, or just one or two of these rights, e.g., the right to manage the timber on the land. To give up certain rights, while retaining most of them, the landowner deeds a conservation covenant which may apply to the entire parcel or a portion of it. Exactly what the landowner gives up, and what he or she gets in return, is spelled out in terms of each conservation covenant's legal document. By granting conservation covenants or development rights to the forest, landowners can be ensured that their forests will be protected and/or wisely stewarded in perpetuity without giving up their ownership rights. Conservation covenants can also be tailored to the specific ecological concerns of each landowner.

A community can also use the same principles to obtain the development rights to land and its resources in order to protect the ecological and scenic integrity of the community and its surrounding environs.

WHY USE THE LST MODEL TO MANAGE LAND AND RESOURCES?

An LST ensures that the use-rights to lands and resources are held in public trust and are conditional on the application of a land stewardship ethic, which both protects the ecological integrity of the land and its resources, and allows stewards to derive income from them.

STEWARDSHIP OF THE FOREST

The LST model applied to lands with forests can provide for the preservation and conservation of old-growth forests, as well as the wise use of forest resources—not just for economic gain but for recreation, education, or spiritual nourishment.

HOW DOES AN LST MANAGE THE FOREST?

A certified ecoforester familiar with the principles of wholistic forestry would assist the owner to establish an ecoforestry management plan that, in turn, is approved by the CLT. The legal agreement ensures that the plan, as well as the conservation covenants, is a condition of residency on the land and/or harvesting of the forest.

The ecoforestry plan would be site-specific as to geography, soil type, tree species, rate of growth, etc., and would be designed to ensure the long-term viability of the forest ecosystem. Forest harvesters would submit five-year forest-management plans to the owner and/or to a community land trust like TIES. Each harvester would outline how they intend to steward the forest in compliance with the ecological conditions placed on the forest lands in trust.

If a forest harvester is a third party then the harvest plan, has to be acceptable to both the owner and the CLT and be in accordance with the ecoforestry management plan. The CLT's function with the assistance of a certified ecoforester is to ensure the forest management plan will guarantee a healthy forest in perpetuity. The owner's responsibility is to manage the forest according to the conservation covenants and the ecoforestry management plan. The harvester's responsibility is to remove the wood without violating the agreement. Working together, the landowner, harvester and CLT can maintain a healthy forest.

How to Create a CLT to Manage Forest Lands

TIES helps establish independent local Community Land Trusts, or a local group can become a chapter of TIES. There are many creative ways in which lands and resources can be placed in trust to be protected or wisely stewarded—the possibilities are only limited by our collective creativity within existing provincial and federal laws.

Why Use the LST Model to Manage Forest Lands?

Using the LST model to manage forested lands has a number of economic, social and political advantages. Economic advantages include: decreased land taxes, economy of scale, government funding, river bank restoration and riparian restoration funds, and long-term planning, as well as being a technique to apply CED or sustainable development at the local level. Other reasons are political in nature, such as community control of resources and being able to set an example to government. Finally, some are social, such as collective ownership of resources or providing right livelihood in the community.

Decreased Taxes

Timber on residentially zoned lands can be costly to the landowners, as Lasqueti Island residents discovered when they received their 1989-90 tax assessments. The B.C. Assessment Authority added timber values to their previous property values. As a result, the land values jumped significantly if the majority of trees on their land were greater than 13 inches in diameter, the minimum size mills accept as merchantable timber (Rusland 1989). However, if these timber stands were placed in trust or under conservation covenants, the lands could be reclassified as forest lands. According to a Port Alberni assessment authority, "forest land isn't assessed until the timber is cut" (Rusland 1989).

Economy of Scale

All the timber on private lands can be stewarded by a CLT under one management and harvesting plan. To increase the economy of scale the land stewardship trust can also apply to manage timber on Crown land under a woodlot licence. If sufficient timber is managed by a CLT, about 2,000 acres [809 ha], then the economy of scale permits hiring a part- or full-time resident forester to manage the forested lands.

Funding Availability

Individual landowners usually do not have sufficient lands in forests to qualify for funding from the Canadian Forestry Service under the Private Forest Lands Program, whereas a CLT as trustees of the collective forest lands could qualify.

Forest lands under the jurisdiction of municipal or regional governments can obtain funding from the Ministry of Forestry as part of their Community Forestry Program. There may be ways in which a CLT can collaborate with local governments or in the future, qualify for these funds.

LONG-TERM PLANNING

A CLT using the LST documents provides the secure long-term land tenure necessary for wholistic forestry based on all-age management, selective logging and a sustained-yield cut, which in turn ensures a permanent forest cover for wildlife and recreational use.

Long-term generational planning creates a balance between short-term and long-term profits, and allows for a steady forest income—profits that stay within the local community—replacing the boom-and-bust cycles common to communities that rely on clearcut logging practices.

RIGHT LIVELIHOOD

Forests in trust provide secure long-term work, a right livelihood that promotes a form of living that also enlarges the spirit. Trees planted today become a community forest for tomorrow.

COMMUNITY CONTROL

When private forest lands are placed in public trust or protected by conservation easements, the community begins to gain control over a local resource. Presently there are no controls over how forests are managed or harvested on private land. Usually, developers and logging companies simply clearcut and subdivide.

COMMUNITY PLANNING

A considerable amount of community planning is necessary to place forest lands in trust. In the process local citizens will develop a deeper personal relationship with the forest as a complete ecosystem that not only grows timber, but nourishes wildlife, stabilizes hillsides, provides water, and serves the recreational needs of humans.

SETTING AN EXAMPLE FOR GOVERNMENT AND INDUSTRY

By placing forests in trust, a strong message is sent to government and the forest industry that the public sector can manage forests in perpetuity, not only ecologically, but economically for the benefit of the whole community. As long as the lease agreement is upheld, then the integrity of the forest ecosystem, as well as the forest company's use-rights, are protected in perpetuity.

If citizens want to change the way forestry is done in B.C., then a good way to start is by creating a local CLT as a demonstration forest project that can show citizens, forest companies, and government that there are viable alternatives to clearcutting. In the process, the community will become familiar with the long-term economics of wholistic forestry, and be able to present a strong case to the forest

Forests in trust provide secure long-term work, a right livelihood that promotes a form of living that also enlarges the spirit.

industry and the government of B.C. that stewardship obligations monitored by local citizens are a prudent way to manage all of B.C.'s forests.

CONCLUSION

Land Stewardship Trust documents are a set of legal tools that can be used by a community in many creative ways to implement sustainable development plans at the community level. The implications of managing forests in trust are economic, social and ecological and could include the following:

- New jobs through diversification;
- Increased productive use of the forest by pooling small tracts of forestland to be managed collectively;
- Tax incentives for landowners;
- Strengthened local economy by increasing revenue to landowners and the community;
- New possibilities for value-added forest products;
- Resource profits that are dependent on the wise stewardship of the ecosystem;
- Establishment of community economic development in the forestry sector by and for local residents—for this generation and for future generations;
- Creation of conservation zones or ecological reserves to include old-growth forests, wildlife preserves, wildlife corridors, watershed buffer zones, etc.;
- Protection of the integrity of ecosystems or watersheds;
- Maintenance of a community's ecological integrity through the conservation of wildlife habitats and/or wilderness;
- Protection of agricultural lands for agricultural purposes;
- Provision of access to land for low income people, that they cannot otherwise afford to buy, in order to establish cooperative or community ventures;
- Provision for appropriate development by keeping the ecological impact of the development to a minimum.

Ecologically sustainable development at the community level cannot happen overnight. Leopold stated:

> We shall never achieve harmony with land, any more than we shall achieve justice or liberty for people. In these higher aspirations the important thing is not to achieve, but to strive....

Managing a forest according to the concepts of an LST is one way a community can strive towards a land ethic. As Leopold says, "for a durable scale of values—we need an environmental ethic that can endure from generation to generation, not only to deepen our relationship to the land and forests, but to each other, the planet and to all of life."

32

The Economics of Ecoforestry

Jim Drescher

ONE DEFINITION OF ECOFORESTRY is "ecosystem-centered economic forestry." It involves the extraction from the forest of biological material to be used by humans. "Ecosystem-centered" means that maintaining, or restoring, the full complement of ecological diversity (including species, age, genetics, and structure) and the full function of the natural forest is prerequisite to any harvesting activity. "Economic" means that the material benefits from the harvest are greater than the long-term costs of extraction, including all social and environmental costs.

When I was first challenged to take this concept from the theoretical to the practical, in other words, to set up a working example of ecoforestry for the Maritimes, I hoped that we could demonstrate that "doing it right" doesn't cost more than clearcutting or high-grading. It turns out not to be as simple as I had hoped. A large part of the site we chose for the experiment had been a working ecoforestry woodlot for 150 years. We are continuing the established practices on those parts of the land and have begun various restoration techniques in areas of the forest where the natural diversity and function had been severely reduced.

Our phase of the experiment began only in 1990, so it is far too early to comment on long-term results of the restoration work. However, logging is ongoing in many areas and the costs of doing ecoforestry in this way are becoming better understood. Although detailed cost breakdowns are always site-specific, it is clear that the direct ecoforestry harvesting costs, on forestland where restoration has begun only recently, are as much as twice the cost of clearcutting or high-grading that same land. However, when one includes in the formula the changes in value of the land on which the harvesting is done, and on the land adjacent and downstream, ecoforestry, even in restoration situations, is far less expensive than conventional methods. On the other hand, in areas that are already all-aged, species diverse, and structurally complex, ecoforestry harvesting costs, when the logs are milled on site, are not greater than "industrial" costs on equivalent land.

Pulp companies, industrial sawmills, and logging contractors only consider the short-term costs that they *must* pay, the so-called internalized costs. They have done their homework, and they know it is more profitable to clearcut. The community, present and future, will pick up all the spinoff costs, which include a decrease in land values, soil erosion, stream siltation, damage to public roads and bridges, disruption of surface-water flow cycles, species extinction, damage to fish stocks, reduction of recreational values, and loss of local employment. Until the clearcutters are assessed and charged for *all* the costs of their harvesting, they will continue to clearcut; our society is subsidizing them to do so, in large part on public land.

But what about the small private woodlot owner, who must bear some of the long-term, as well as immediate, cost of harvesting? In this case the decision whether to practise ecoforestry will be based on how well the landowner understands the long-term economic accounting. First let's look at the simple part. Stumpage value is what a logging contractor will pay a landowner for the right to remove trees from the forest. "Stumpage" will vary depending on the tree species and size, terrain, accessibility, and proximity to markets. "Forestland Value" is what an ecoforester will pay a landowner to transfer title to the land. It also will vary depending on the same criteria as for stumpage. In this part of the Acadian Forest Region, the Forestland Value of very good woodland, before logging, is approximately twice the stumpage value. After logging, the cutover land is worth $100-$300 per hectare [$247-$741/a].

For example, if I own a 40-hectare woodlot with a stumpage value of $50,000, it may have a Forestland Value of $100,000. If I want to liquidate the value from that woodlot I could sell the stumpage to a clearcutter or high-grader and get $50,000. I would be left with a "cutover" piece of land worth somewhere between $4,000 and $12,000. So by clearcutting the woodlot, I would have lost $38,000 to $46,000 in value. Clearly, "liquidation logging" is quick money and financial foolishness.

Why would the ecoforester pay approximately twice the stumpage value for woodland? Because that is its economic value as a long-term growing site. He or she will be able to harvest material from that woodlot year after year in perpetuity. Why wouldn't the ecoforester pay the same price, less the stumpage value of the trees that were removed, after the site had been logged? Because its long-term economic value will have been seriously reduced due to the reduction of ecological diversity on the site. It will not support a heavy, healthy forest again for hundreds or thousands of years.[1] Most of the economic value as forestland will have been destroyed.

Beyond this immediate accounting there is the long-term accounting, which is to the credit or debit of society as a whole, not directly to the landowner alone. It may be a bit of a reach for a small private landowner to take these factors into account in making decisions about his or her woodlot, but more and more people are beginning to tune into this larger world. This is where the differences between ecoforestry and industrial forestry really become dramatic.

Long-term economic viability is what is popularly called "sustainability." The foundation of sustainability is ecological diversity, which includes species and age diversity, genetic variability, and structural patchiness. The logic for this has been detailed elsewhere,[2] but the main point is that industrial forestry, in the course of harvesting trees, severely reduces the ecological diversity on the site. This, in turn, delays the possibility for long-term sustainability on that site by hundreds of years.

It also has repercussions beyond that particular piece of land, because "we're all downstream." In other words, the effects of forestry practices are not limited to the site of harvesting. Accelerated surface water runoff from clearcut land worsens the flushing effect, swelling streams and rivers immediately after rains, or in the spring when the snow melts, and leaving those watercourses low or dry in July and August. In addition to the cost of soil erosion, this damages fish stocks, particularly salmon which need more steady flows to provide for their spawning journeys upstream. The warmer water, which also results from clearcutting, carries less oxygen, vitally needed by salmon, trout, and other aquatic life.[3]

When roads and bridges are washed out by the swollen streams draining clearcuts, who pays to repair the damage? Not those responsible for the clearcutting, but the taxpayers. When jobs in the community are lost because the forests have been clearcut and have therefore stopped producing timber, who pays the financial and psychological costs? Not the landowner or the contractor or the sawmill or pulp company, but society as a whole. When its diverse forests are clearcut, the joy and pride of local people in "their place" is reduced. Visitors no longer stop to admire the beauty of nature, but hurry on to the next "rest" stop. As we must learn, when nature is degraded, the well-being of the whole society is diminished.

The most dangerous long-term effect of clearcutting is reduction in ecological diversity and the concomitant reduction in the opportunities for healthy economic diversity. When diversity is reduced, the stability of the ecosystem and the economic viability of the community are put at risk. In short, clearcutting and high-grading mean lost value for the landowner, whether that be "the Crown" (all of us) or an individual. In addition, it means damage to the natural environment and loss of employment for the local community.

Let's look at a real-life example. In 1994, an 80-hectare woodlot on the east side of Wentzell Lake in Nova Scotia was clearcut. The towering hemlock, spruce, pine, maple, birch, ash and oak had provided shelter for countless species of plants and animals, and a steady supply of cool water for the LaHave River for thousands of years, and enjoyment for the local community for the past 150 years. In addition, the land had yielded a steady supply of valuable lumber to the area and a regular income for the landowner. It had employed local people on a regular basis doing woodswork and sawing lumber. The woodlot's last steward died in 1992, leaving the woodlot to his heir, who was persuaded by a timber broker and contractor to clearcut the forest. The timber broker said, "It will be good for the forest to clean up all those old trees,

> The foundation of sustainability is ecological diversity, which includes species and age diversity, genetic variability, and structural patchiness.

and you will get a lot of money." The inheritor of his uncle's wealth was convinced, and the liquidation began. It continued until almost all the vegetation was gone. The rains came and the topsoil flowed down the hillside, exposing the rocks and subsoil. The small stream that drained the area still runs heavy with silt after each rain, and then dries up a few days later. The public road, under which the small stream had flowed for years, washed out after the first big storm. The Department of Transportation sent backhoes, loaders, and trucks to repair the road and dig a new channel for the wild water—straight into the lake. The walking and riding trails so enjoyed by the community are just memories. The sun bakes the barren hillside and the winds sweep across, sucking out the moisture from the remaining plants and soil. This woodlot will provide no more employment for this, or any, community for a thousand years. The landowner, who got the money from the sale of the stumpage, lost well over $100,000 in value—flushed down the drain like the rain. He was abused: by the timber broker; by the choppers; by the heavy machinery; by the government; by the forestry schools; and by his own ignorance. And all of us downstream are abused also, but laying blame doesn't restore the forest.

What alternatives does ecoforestry present? In offering a different way of harvesting that protects ecological diversity, it strengthens the foundation of forest stability and community economic sustainability. It tends to increase the economic value of woodland and reduce the costs of public works, unemployment, and the degradation of public confidence.

But what about the specific costs and benefits of setting up a woodlot as an "ecoforestry woodlot"?

We could go back to the example of a 40-hectare [99 a] woodlot. If the owner decides not to sell the stumpage, and not to sell the land, but instead to set up an ecoforestry woodlot, what is involved? First, an ecological description and an assessment of value must be made. This will cost no more than a "timber cruise," and can be elaborated as time goes on, mostly by the owner at no expense other than the cost of walking the forest. Part of this initial description and assessment will be to determine what harvesting is possible and what restoration work is desirable in each area of the woodlot. At this point an initial estimate of setup and harvesting costs and income from the sale of products can be made for various periods of time.

Unless the woodlot has been cared for very well for over 100 years, there will be considerably more expense than income in the initial stages; not expense really, but capital cost in roads, trails, bridges, and log yards. The owner of an ecoforestry woodlot must be willing to invest in the future. The payoff will come after the trail system is in place and harvesting can be done easily and quickly, with logs stored at special locations in the woodlot to be milled there by a portable sawmill. The only products removed from the woodlot will be lumber, posts, rails, fuelwood, and pulpwood. The slabwood and sawdust will stay in the forest for road building. The brush will be piled, or stacked in long rows called Benjes Hecken. These piles and walls increase the structural diversity of the woodlot, allowing for greater abundance and diversity of animals.

The harvesting costs, relative to the income generated, will vary depending on how mature and diverse is the forest. An all-aged, species diverse woodlot with a good road system and well-placed log yards will yield a very high rate of return. Up until the woodlot reaches this point, however, the owner will have to settle for somewhat lower returns, or, at the very beginning, perhaps no return at all.

One can identify three stages in the establishment of an ecoforestry woodlot. First is building the infrastructure: roads, trails, bridges, and log yards. Second—and this phase can begin before Phase One is completed—is the initiation of diversity restoration treatments. These often take the form of low-grading and patch cutting,[4] which result in marketable logs, posts, rails, fuelwood, and pulpwood. As the restoration progresses over the years, the woodland becomes more "natural" and its products become increasingly valuable. The third stage is the annual harvesting of large logs and the associated posts, rails, and pulpwood. The logs should be processed on site into high quality lumber. At this stage, the road system and log yards are in place, and the annual allowable cut has been optimized. The ecoforestry woodlot can continue to produce an abundance of high-quality product annually without degrading the forest environment or contributing to pollution and flow disruption downstream. Because the harvest is continual, and because it is labor-intensive, it will provide significant regular employment in the community. The 40 hectare sample woodlot can provide full-time employment for at least four people if the logs are sawn and the lumber dried and planed on site.

In discussing the economics of ecoforestry, one must consider several categories of value. One is the value of the forestland to the owner. In this case, the value (both dollar value and ecological value) of an ecoforestry woodlot is far greater than any other class of commercial woodland. Another consideration is capital investment, which is necessary, no matter which forestry methods are used. In the case of an ecoforestry woodlot, however, the investment is in slabwood/sawdust roads, wooden bridges, and in-forest log yards, *not* in heavy harvesting equipment. One kind of capital investment is ecologically supportive; the other is ecologically disruptive. In either case, the results of the capital investment accrue to the investor, and to society as a whole, which is waiting downstream. If all the costs and benefits are taken into account, there is no question that ecoforestry is the more lucrative investment. However, when society is forced to subsidize the industrial forester by paying a major portion of the restoration costs, the analysis gets a little murky. A third category of value is local community health and welfare, which is dependent, in large measure, on productive, rewarding local employment opportunities. An ecoforestry woodlot is the ideal in these terms. Our forestland in the Maritimes would support several times the present forest-related workforce if ecoforestry methods replaced clearcutting, high-grading, and other diversity-degrading forestry activities.

It might be easy to get carried away with enthusiasm for what seems like an answer to all our economic and environmental problems. However, we must not overlook the difficulties that will be encountered by a landowner wishing to establish an ecoforestry woodlot. The difficulties are three fold: first, ecoforestry is not well-understood yet, because it has not been taught in our forestry schools, and because it does not lend itself well to the large-scale industrial harvesting operations that are so profitable to large forestry corporations. Second, there is considerable up-front cost involved in the establishment of an ecoforestry woodlot. Third, there is a shortage of skilled people who know how to do this kind of woodswork.

These are major obstacles, and only a serious commitment to long-term economic and ecological sustainability will compel anyone to deal with them head-on. Although the principles and practices of ecoforestry are not well-known, there is good work being done in many places across Canada. The Ecoforestry Institute and SILVA Forest Foundation in British Columbia are leading in this new field. The Ecoforestry School in the Maritimes offers seminars, short courses, and a program leading to Certificates in Ecoforestry. There are some remnant woodlots still being managed according to the "old ways" of ecoforestry. The knowledge, experience, and examples are out there, but one has to search for them. The information does not come in the form of million-dollar advertising campaigns generating slick pictures in magazines or jingles on TV.

The initial cost of establishing an ecoforestry woodlot is a serious deterrent, but it probably is a better and more secure investment than most in these times. In other words, investing in forestry is not just buying the land, but also building the infrastructure that will provide low-impact ease of harvest in the future. This is the cost of building long-term sustainable value. For someone who owns the land already, but has no cash to invest in roads and bridges or diversity restoration, there may be creative ways to get the needed capital. Joint ventures or long-term operating agreements with established ecoforesters may be possibilities. Because of the tremendous benefits to society as a whole, governments should provide assistance for the establishment of ecoforestry woodlots, but so far they don't. This is partly due to the fact that governments are broke, and it is partly because they have already "bought in" so heavily to the industrial forestry model.

The shortage of woodsworkers skilled in ecoforestry techniques is a major problem. The situation is so serious that most woodsworkers don't even know they don't have the skills. However, the principles are logical and can be taught. The skills can be developed fairly quickly with practice under the guidance of experienced ecoforesters. Training programs have begun in British Columbia, and in Nova Scotia at the Ecoforestry School in the Maritimes.

So what about the economics of ecoforestry? Does it work? Yes. Are there examples? Yes. Does it cost anything to get started? Yes. Are there other problems? Yes. Are they surmountable? Yes. Is there somewhere one can go to learn more and

> **Our forestland in the Maritimes would support several times the present forest-related workforce if ecoforestry methods replaced clearcutting, high-grading, and other diversity-degrading forestry activities.**

to get assistance? Yes.

This discussion of ecoforestry economics would not be complete without mention of current trends and future possibilities. Among scientists and the public, awareness of forestry-created environmental and social problems is increasing daily. At the same time, the big trees that provide the most valuable lumber in this region are falling much faster than they can be replaced by smaller trees; the economic value of our forest resource is declining sharply while the ecological costs escalate. More and more woodsworkers, consumers, and woodlot owners are looking to the new field of ecoforestry as a sustainable alternative to the conventional practices of clearcutting and high-grading.

Certification of ecoforesters, of ecoforestry woodlots, and of the wood products from those woodlots has begun. The Forest Stewardship Council international certification will be the strongest of the various "sustainably produced" claims. It will be the consumer's assurance that her or his purchasing power is supporting forest restoration. For the foreseeable future, demand for ecoforestry products will exceed supply, so, although the initial costs of producing ecoforestry lumber may be higher, the price premium that already is developing may offset some of those higher costs. When governments come around to adopting the principles and practices of "full-cost accounting," and the clearcutters are made to pay all the costs of their harvest, ecoforestry will become the mainstream, and the whole value of our forests will begin the long steady process of restoration.

33

A Model for Community Economic Systems Based on Ecoforestry

Alan Drengson

THE ECONOMIC IMPLICATIONS OF ECOFORESTRY need more attention. The chart below illustrates the different dimensions and relationships that exist between the elements of a whole community ecoforestry system. The transition to ecocentric-based practices, i.e. those based on ecological values and principles, will be facilitated by developing all of the elements of a whole system as shown above. There are objectives and services that can be provided by nonprofit corporations or societies, and there are objectives and services that can be realized by profit-making entities in the form of small corporations, small businesses, individual consultants and contract workers and cooperatives for manufacturing and marketing. In addition, a land base is needed, which will include some private lands; community forest land trusts; ecoforestry land trusts; and some public lands—local, provincial, state, and federal. Finally, the whole system requires outlets for ecoforestry-related goods and services. *It is important to stress that we need a diversity of types of organizations to address the multi-dimensional nature of the ecological and environmental challenges we face.*

The whole system works as follows:

A. The nonprofit corporations provide three primary services:

    1. The Ecoforestry Institute, in cooperation with other ecoforestry-related nonprofits, sets up a system of certification for raw materials, demonstration forests, and secondary products. It provides educational programs on forest ecology and ecoforestry for a wide audience, but also offers specialized, professional training and retraining;

    2. an institute for ecology and economics generates support for community economic initiatives (helping workers set up a marketing co-op, for example), in the form of funding, advice and other services;

    3. the ecoforestry stewardship land trust provides a growing land base in

perpetuity for the practice of ecoforestry.

B. The profit corporations, small businesses and co-ops provide services and management arrangements to landowners and managers, provide marketing services for material gatherers, and manufacture and market secondary products, etc.

C. The ecoforestry land base will consist of private forest land that owners decide to set up with ecoforestry principles; public lands of various classifications that policy and administrative decisions allocate to ecoforestry practice; and all trust lands, including ecoforestry trust lands, that agree to participate in long-term ecoforestry programs.

D. The outlets will consist of three principal markets:

1. direct sales of raw materials to individuals, companies and cooperatives;

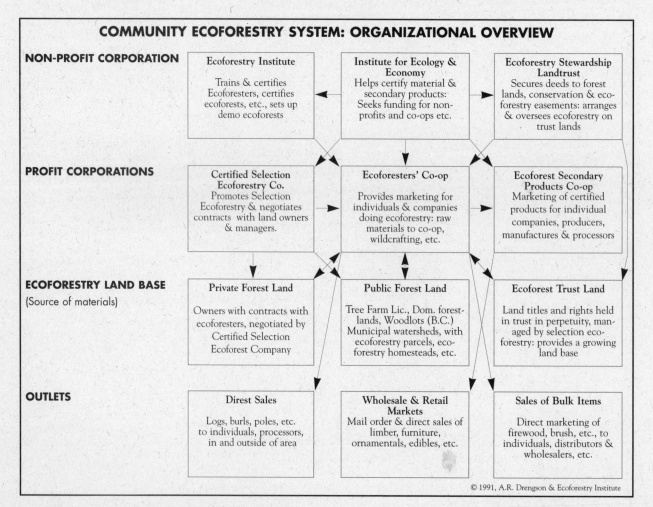

COMMUNITY ECOFORESTRY SYSTEM: ORGANIZATIONAL OVERVIEW

NON-PROFIT CORPORATION

Ecoforestry Institute
Trains & certifies Ecoforesters, certifies ecoforests, etc., sets up demo ecoforests

Institute for Ecology & Economy
Helps certify material & secondary products: Seeks funding for non-profits and co-ops etc.

Ecoforestry Stewardship Landtrust
Secures deeds to forest lands, conservation & ecoforestry easements: arranges & oversees ecoforestry on trust lands

PROFIT CORPORATIONS

Certified Selection Ecoforestry Co.
Promotes Selection Ecoforestry & negotiates contracts with land owners & managers.

Ecoforesters' Co-op
Provides marketing for individuals & companies doing ecoforestry: raw materials to co-op, wildcrafting, etc.

Ecoforest Secondary Products Co-op
Marketing of certified products for individual companies, producers, manufactures & processors

ECOFORESTRY LAND BASE
(Source of materials)

Private Forest Land
Owners with contracts with ecoforesters, negotiated by Certified Selection Ecoforest Company

Public Forest Land
Tree Farm Lic., Dom. forest-lands, Woodlots (B.C.) Municipal watersheds, with ecoforestry parcels, ecoforestry homesteads, etc.

Ecoforest Trust Land
Land titles and rights held in trust in perpetuity, managed by selection ecoforestry: provides a growing land base

OUTLETS

Direst Sales
Logs, burls, poles, etc. to individuals, processors, in and outside of area

Wholesale & Retail Markets
Mail order & direct sales of limber, furniture, ornamentals, edibles, etc.

Sales of Bulk Items
Direct marketing of firewood, brush, etc., to individuals, distributors & wholesalers, etc.

© 1991, A.R. Drengson & Ecoforestry Institute

2. wholesale and retail sales of items that have been processed, packaged, etc.;
3. direct sales of bulk items, such as firewood and brush, to distributors and wholesalers.

Under this system all work (whether tree selection, road construction, raw material collection, secondary processing) as well as forests, workers and consultants, will be certified, provided they meet the rigorous ecological and other requirements of ecoforestry certifiers. This means that the whole system will provide a range of economic benefits to local communities and to the larger society and global community. This certification system and the earned certification stamp of approval will advise all customers, community members, and marketers that the ecoforestry practices in question are carried out with the highest standards of ecological responsibility. In selecting these products and services, consumers and participants will be contributing to restoring and maintaining local community economic and ecosystem integrity.

This whole system represents a movement toward downsizing, decentralization, and democratization of forest economics. Studies have shown that communities that manage their resource activities so that they are consistent with the needs of the forest ecosystem have a natural, self-maintaining system that provides a wide range of products, services and values. As a result, an ecoforestry-based community economic system is as diversified as its forests' ecology. The bust-boom characteristics of old industrial forestry are a product of its large-scale application of industrial methods to biological processes. Ecoforestry community systems are not one-product, one-industry systems. The large-scale industrial system, on the other hand, removes the whole forest ecosystem, bringing with it a host of economic, ecological and community problems. In the ecoforestry approach, the natural forest ecosystem is never removed or degraded.

Mixed forest in spring
Alan Drengson

The transition to ecoforestry-based community economics is a necessary transition if we are to save rural communities and natural forest ecosystems. The critical element in this transition is training and education of ecoforesters and a credible certification system for management, manufacturing and raw materials. The Ecoforestry Institute and other NGOs are dedicated to seeing that these education and certification elements are provided, so that this transition can proceed smoothly.

It is important to note that such local systems will not be uniform. The above model is only a sketch of how to organize and structure the system so as to assure that all major functions are addressed. Preservation and restoration of biodiversity will help to protect and promote growth of cultural diversity. Diversity in an area depends upon many factors. Under a natural forest system such as temperate rainforest, great biological diversity gives rise to diversity of functions and structures, as well as processes and creative evolution. This in turn gives rise to a multitude of values. Human cultures that are ecologically wise add to the sum total of all values.

Ecoforestry is not just focused on selective removal of trees from forests. An ecoforestry-based system is one which recognizes diversity of products and values and uses those in an ecologically responsible way. The following categories of values are representative of the diverse and rich qualities supported and inherent in a natural forest. Both intrinsic and instrumental values can be found in most of the following categories.

Ecoforestry Categories of Value:

1. *Environmental*: biodiversity, climate moderation, clean air and water, wildlife, healthy soils;
2. *Productive*: timber, poles, medicines, chemicals, firewood, paper, ornamentals, wood fibre;
3. *Recreational*: boating, camping, hunting, fishing, hiking, skiing, canoeing, mountain climbing;
4. *Esthetic*: natural beauty, painting, drawing, photography, artistic inspiration, poetry, storytelling, natural history, craft traditions, florist supplies;
5. *Spiritual*: tranquillity, communion with nature, reconnection to our natural self, ecological wisdom from forests, connections with the whole community of living beings, contact with the free creative power of nature and the inherent values of the earth.

Preservation of maximum values depends on preserving functions and structures characteristic of stable, integral, whole, natural, wild forest ecosystems. The ambitious Wildlands Project started by Dave Foreman and others in the U.S. and Canada aims to preserve and restore large wildland areas that have minimal human impacts. These are important to ecoforestry since such wildlands are our necessary *reference* for our practices. It is in the wild forests that all natural values are created and preserved. Reference reserves should be designated for each area where ecoforestry is practised so that monitoring and research can be carried out. The aim is to preserve all values and to create new ecocentric ones. Total-cost accounting and multiple product assessments should be settled ecoforestry practices.

PART FIVE

Lessons from the Forest —
A Comprehensive Ecocentric Approach

In the heart of the forest, Bo Martin

34

The Movement to Ecologically Sustainable Forestry

Michelle Thom

TRADITIONAL WOOD HARVESTING PRACTICES, known as industrial forestry, are both economically and ecologically unsustainable. Industrial forestry often involves a centuries-old, vicious cycle of cutting down native trees in complex ecosystems; replacing them with fewer varieties; harvesting these at the same time, creating even-aged stands; and again replanting fewer varieties, leading to out-of-balance forests which are more prone to infestation and disease. Industrial forestry also favors clearcutting, which lends itself to the "efficiencies" of large machinery. Clearcutting not only extracts all the trees, but also wipes out most of the habitat logged. By some estimates, 90 percent of all logging lands in the world are being clearcut at a rate ten times faster than 20 years ago.

Forests exist as entire ecosystems, housing life-forms that rely on one another for survival. If treated with this in mind, they also have the ability to provide jobs over the long term, enabling the survival of surrounding human communities.

ECOFORESTRY AS THE ALTERNATIVE

In an attempt to counter some of the damage done to most of our national forests and their surrounding communities, a growing number of organizations are promoting the concepts and practices of *ecoforestry*. Two of these organizations are the Ecoforestry Institute/U.S. and the Ecoforestry Institute Society/Canada, groups that work with an expanding network of private forests and owners who seek to sustain their forests. The Institutes offer education and apprenticeship training programs to help people understand and work with the ecological patterns and processes of the entire forest ecosystem.

Ecoforestry is *ecocentric* forestry. It is based on an understanding that the complex communities of beings who make the forests their home have intrinsic value which needs to be recognized and respected. Ecoforestry seeks to protect, maintain and restore fully functioning, natural forests, while harvesting forest goods to meet vital human needs on a long-term, sustainable basis.

Ecoforestry places first priority on maintaining the ecological processes of the forests so that it *can then provide* for the economic needs of workers, their families, and communities, not the other way around, as industrial forestry has operated. Specifically, elements of ecoforestry include:

- Protecting all remaining ancient forests, which are refugia for countless species of wildlife as well as sources of oxygen (needed to absorb heat-trapping carbon dioxide linked to global warming) and clean water (habitat for fish and other aquatic life-forms).

- Protecting genetic diversity. Ecoforestry is based on a diversity of ecocentric practices that grow out of place-specific wisdom, learned by dwelling as a native in those places.

- Protecting wildlife populations for complete ecosystem functioning based on the principles of conservation biology. Industrial forestry has left us with declining northern spotted owl populations, at an estimated rate of 4.5 percent annually, and about 106 salmon populations already lost in the Northwest in recent years. Ecoforestry recognizes the importance of maintaining wildlife.

- Sustaining workers, their families, and forest-interdependent communities by working with all forest goods—timber, poles, medicinals, decoratives, edibles, etc.—and by employing these for their highest uses. Ecoforestry addresses the ecological/economic transition from industrial forestry and its short-term profit orientation to a decentralized, community-forestry from the local to the global scales. Ecoforestry recognizes that sustainable forestry practices are more labor-intensive, thereby creating the potential for job growth, if the wealth from the forests is shared equitably, circulated locally, and traded regionally and globally.

- Encouraging research by land grant universities on forestry methods that protect old-growth forests and promote ecological forestry practices while looking beyond the immediate, short-term economic gain linked to plywood and paper fibre production.

- Changing the current tax structure, which encourages companies to decimate forests; establishing a depletion tax as well as tax benefits for companies that practise ecoforestry.

ECOFORESTRY IN ACTION

The transition to ecoforestry requires a broader paradigm shift to an ecological society. While the U.S. Forest Service and Bureau of Land Management (BLM) have adopted an "ecosystem management" policy, they still primarily rely on conventional silvicultural practices, which are rooted in the reductionist science of the past. They have not yet adopted even demonstrations of ecoforestry on public lands.

> The transition to ecoforestry requires a broader paradigm shift to an ecological society.

Furthermore, encouraging private landowners and timber companies to log sustainably is not easy. The U.S. Forest Service does not provide research or financial incentives that encourage private logging interests to move to ecoforestry practices.

The Ecoforestry Institutes work with private forestland owners in the Cascadia bioregion of the northwest United States and British Columbia who are practising ecoforestry on their lands. Selective logging, based on natural selection indicators, is used, together with the harvesting of other forest products. Demonstration forests are being established so that the public can tour and see working forests where ecoforestry is practised.

The Institutes also promote "Ecoforestry Cooperatives" to practise both ecoforestry and a variety of secondary, value-added enterprises. For example, where timber is milled on-site, and on other sites, mushrooms, medicinal herbs, and other ornamentals are harvested and processed. Products from forests where ecoforestry is practised will be certified as "Ecoforest Products" so concerned citizens can support the protection of fully functioning natural forests where forest goods are harvested.

The future of forestry practices, if they are to be sustainable, must involve an appreciation for forests' intrinsic esthetic, recreational and even spiritual value over the long term. As Alan Drengson, an advisor to the Ecoforestry Institute, puts it, "We believe it is irresponsible to take trees that are hundreds of years old and turn them into Kleenex."

Norwegian forest-farm landscape
Alan Rike Drengson

35

Culture and Environment

Arne Naess

WHAT I AM GOING TO DISCUSS is certain relations between culture and the global process of increasing ecological unsustainability. One of the many factors that make it difficult to change the process into one of increasing sustainability is the required shift in ways of thinking from that of environment to that of ecology. The former term suggests something apart from humanity, something we regrettably are dependent upon. It is easier to mobilize people and money if we acknowledge the human tendency to self-destruction by policies that not only spoil our nests, but also lead us away from our own basic goal in life, whether it is called happiness or not. This increasing ecological unsustainability is something much nearer to our souls and selves than we have traditionally assumed.

It is often acknowledged today that overcoming the increasing ecological crisis—the increasing level of ecological unsustainability—means overcoming problems in the humanities, in sociology and political science. It even fosters new branches like "environmental diplomacy." The Canadian government proposed to stop complaining harshly about air pollution in Canada due to U.S. pollutants, provided the U.S. government agreed to a trade treaty favorable to Canada. It is accepted today that every major ecological problem has a social and political aspect. Furthermore, it is clear that technological invention, even of a revolutionary kind like solar energy, has had practically no influence on the curve of increasing unsustainability. Whether the use of an ecologically salutary invention is adopted on an appropriate scale depends upon social and political factors. Unfortunately, these factors are neglected in research and development programs. Natural science has a higher cultural standing than social science, and governments gladly spend money on studies of climate, the ozone layer, and similar nonpolitical issues.

Turning our attention to the situation in the Third and Fourth Worlds, we find that old, stable cultural traditions still play a decisive role. Among such traditions we very often find ecologically sophisticated and beneficial technologies and ways of life. The influence of industrial societies, including the pressure of mass tourism, has increased in this century and has, with few exceptions, been negative.

An example: The traditional Sherpa culture in Nepal contained strict rules regarding how to make use of trees and bushes for heating. Living in the Himalayas between 2,000 and 4,000 metres [6,562-13,123 ft.] above sea level, and with long winters, the Sherpas' vital need for wood was clear, but only dead trees were used. With tourism the Sherpas got jobs, especially as mountain guides and porters. Their mobility increased immensely. There was, to use an expression about the development in the European Community, an avalanche of transport across traditional borders.

The Sherpa ethics and practice of forest protection were local, not general. So, as soon as the Sherpas were far from home, they would cut and burn everything in order to secure hot showers for tourists every morning.

In short, wonderful ecological ethics and practice in many nonindustrial countries had mostly local areas of validity and dominance. It turned out that the tourists' way of life generally was conceived as one with very few ethical or other constraints but was nevertheless capable of securing a fabulously high material standard of living. Large-scale corruption has been a regular consequence, with few notable exceptions.

A very important development since the 1960s has been the emergence of a drive among people in the Western industrial nations to join the minorities in the Third and Fourth Worlds to re-establish ecologically sane technologies and ways of life. One group, called "social ecologists," includes subgroups such as one in Uruguay, living and working among the poor to support the few, mostly very old people, who still remember and make use of those old technologies.

The introduction of Western, mostly non-ecological, technology has a devastating influence on culture and upon the state of the economy, requiring imports and "help," and increasing the distance between rich and poor. (Example: the influence of the so-called "green revolution" based on Western agricultural technology.)

Unfortunately, Western colleges and universities do not favor Westerners working in the spirit of the above-mentioned subgroup of social ecologists. Effective cooperation with the "poor" people requires not only knowledge of cultural anthropology and the ability to live a life that is not provocative and strange in a foreign country, but also requires willingness to stay there for years. And Westerners want to be fairly sure that when they come back to their own countries they are either able to find a job, or are helped to be trained in available kinds of jobs.

If the devastating ecological trend in the Third and Fourth Worlds is going to be changed, it is necessary that the institutions in the West understand their responsibility either to decrease Western pernicious influence or to change the influence into a beneficial one.

Every year counts. To teach environmental ethics, as it is now accepted at many Western colleges and universities, is a very indirect help, especially because it is mostly "meta-ethics"; that is, academic discussion about various theories about ethics. Even in academic institutions ethics was what is now called "normative ethics": prescribing (and discussing) duties, obligations in various sorts of life situations, and wise guidelines. This also included discussing consequences and evaluating guidelines in the light of consequences. One of the reasons governments in many industrial countries now finance environmental academic ethics may be that it costs so much less than studies of social and political ways to fight the ecological crisis, and much less than doing, on a proper scale, doing anything about the crisis. One may compare the 50 years from 1830 to 1880 in Europe and North America when there was much talk about the misery of labor. Women of the aristocracy wove and sewed clothing for the poor, and there were constant fundraisings to help the poor, but on a scale that was completely insufficient. As now, economics was used as an explanation: more wealth among the wealthy must be accumulated in order to change conditions in a decisive way.

There are today two different basic attitudes toward nonhuman beings. According to the so-called anthropocentric view, no nonhuman being can have value in itself, it can only have instrumental value, that is, value as a means for humans. Among contemporary philosophers, Habermas has such a view. The other basic attitude holds that nonhumans may have value in themselves independent of what they can be for humans.

As long as there was a moderate number of humans with moderate means to interfere with the richness and diversity of life on Earth, it did not matter much for the planet how they conceived their relation to the Earth. But now, with an enormous number of people, with a practically infinite capacity for destruction, how humans feel about nature is of great importance. The simplest reason for this is our ignorance of the long-range effects of our interferences. A so-called "green society" is expected to be ecologically sustainable. The term is mostly used in such a way that a society deserves the name only if the peace and the distribution problem is also largely solved.

There is, unfortunately, a tendency to talk about the "environmental" crisis rather than the "ecological" crisis. Environment is conceived as something outside of humanity. Humans are clearly inside the ecological systems of the Earth, and the societies of humans have the same need and right to be protected as societies of other living beings. The rapid extinction of non-industrialist societies is an ecosystem degradation and destruction. The threat of the extinction of cultures has an ethical aspect, and belongs to the proper problematics of general ecology. Protection of human cultural diversity is a genuine part of the protection of biodiversity.

Writers who characterize a (future) "green society" sometimes make it clear that they describe a utopia; others attempt to describe a future society that will be a reality

> Now, with an enormous number of people, with a practically infinite capacity for destruction, how humans feel about nature is of great importance.

if the ecological crisis is overcome.

There is a regrettable tendency to talk and write about "green societies" as if they will be realizations of only one culture. In my opinion, the absence of deeply different future cultures would be a calamity. Richness and diversity of future cultures is for me a great ideal, perhaps the only way towards further developments of the human species. Diversity of subcultures as we see them today in big cities for instance cannot replace diversity of cultures. In at least a couple of decades there were thousands of new musicians in a certain part of New York City, thousands who lived "in and for music." As long as the children were exposed to very different lifestyles and value systems, no specific culture was created. No traditions, no completeness.

Most pictures of conditions in a "green society" suggest a rather uniform way of life. I reckon that some people will relish conspicuous consumption. Some will be victims of unsatisfied greed, some will delight in ecologically expensive gadgets. But in the latter case the owners of these gadgets will live rather inexpensively in other ways. The laws or mores should tolerate great differences of lifestyles. Today we know that some people may spend 90 percent of their income on purposes for which others would not even spend 5 percent.

Vancouver Island wilderness recreation
Duncan Taylor

The protection of richness and diversity of life-forms is compatible with a variety of political systems. But national socialist and fascist systems are intolerant of deep cultural diversity and therefore cannot furnish the basis for a "green society." There is great literature comparing communism, socialism, and capitalism. Also "vertical" versus "horizontal" societies are compared, and "tightness" versus "looseness." As long as only vague descriptions of countries are offered for comparison, next to nothing can be concluded about their relative merits on the way to ecological sustainability. The presumption among writers is that democracies are best. The argumentation is weak because it mostly relies on historical and contemporary evidence, that is, on actual ecological states of affairs. Authoritarian, hierarchical, Buddhist countries have often been used as examples of countries with great chances of remaining ecologically responsible in spite of not being democracies, but they are not industrial societies. If the democracies of the West do not within X years, for instance 50 years, change the ecological policies in the direction of decreasing unsustainability, the catastrophic situation may be reached when "strongmen" are able to acquire power and change policies by decrees. My guess is that ecological dictatorship has no better chance to be realized than "ecological democracy."

One may ask what is the relation of the various existing systems of economy, technology, family relations, reproduction habits, religion and so on, and what are the relative prospects of leading to ecological sustainability? The answers are in many ways hypothetical, because it is difficult to say to what degree a deplorable or less deplorable situation in a country is due to the system. So-called systems are changing all the time, even in the cultures called traditional. One cannot easily predict how a worsening ecological crisis will be met. People read that we, because of our irresponsible behavior, may cause a new ice age, or a metre-high rise of the water level of the ocean, even within a hundred years, and many get concerned. But when they read what might be the effect of continued population explosion, they often are reluctant to approve ethically acceptable, appropriate measures. There are or have recently been cultures with norms favorable to the stability of the size of the population. Among animals, biological processes that limit reproduction are fairly common when resources are small or dwindling. For example, certain insects produce fewer females every autumn, anticipating winter and springtime scarcity. Limited resources on remote islands have motivated appropriate customs. Malthus thought that Norway's agricultural population had customs that counteracted the blind drive for procreation. On the whole, cultures today do not have institutions favorable for early stabilization and reduction of population.

The small minority of 500 million who are responsible for most of the degradation of life conditions on Earth tolerate cultural patterns today that favor irresponsible reproduction. A 10 percent decrease of the birth of unwanted children would make richer European countries enter the process of population decrease before long. The increase of criminality among children ages 10 to 15 testifies to the presence of devastating cultural trends that prohibit adequate education.

Many people active in the fight against the ecological crisis look forward to "green societies" where children from the time they are able to walk have access to patches of free nature without crossing dangerous streets. But this requires architectural revolutions. As it is now, the street is a cultural center.

There is, in short, much to be learned from the study of cultures in the past and the present, but the global state of affairs is so complex that any fairly simple general conclusion about relative merits of different cultures is highly speculative. What we know as members of Western democracies, whatever our culture, is that we are heavily responsible for the increasing unsustainability.

The above notes have the modest aim of emphasizing the importance of increasing efforts in every country under every sort of political, cultural, etc., conditions to turn the tide from increasing to decreasing unsustainability.

This conclusion is compatible with a certain mobility in area of concentration:

some groups may concentrate on overcoming definite dominant ideological or spiritual aspects of their culture (in a wide sense of the word); others may concentrate on reforms of their economic systems; still others may concentrate on the fight against the implementation of an ecologically horrendous concrete plan or a source of horrible pollution. The frontier of this kind of work is long, and discussion about what is most needed should not degrade into polemics.

36

Forest Reflections

Gary Snyder

1. Watershed Perspectives

IT HAS BEEN RAINING FOR FOUR DAYS NOW. One can wonder: why does it rain one year, not rain so much another? But eventually the rains (or the dry days) return. This process of rain falling, streams flowing, and oceans evaporating gives us the water cycle: every molecule of water on Earth makes the complete trip once every two million years. And so the Earth is carved into watersheds, a kind of familial branching, a chart of relationship, and a definition of place. The watershed is the first and last nation, whose boundaries, though subtly shifting, are unarguable. Races of birds, subspecies of trees, and types of hats or raingear go by the watershed. The watershed gives us a home, and a place to go upstream, downstream, or across. The watershed is beyond the dichotomies of orderly/disorderly, for its forms are free, but somehow inevitable. And the life that comes to flourish within it constitutes the first kind of community.

For the watershed, cities and dams are ephemeral, and of no more account than a boulder that falls in the river, or a landslide that temporarily alters the channel. The water will always be there, and it will always find its way down. The Los Angeles River is alive and well under the city streets, running in giant culverts. It is amused by such diversions. But we who live in terms of centuries rather than millions of years might wish to hold the watershed and its communities together, to enjoy the clear water and fresh life of this landscape we have chosen. From the tiniest rivulet at the crest of a ridge, to the main trunk of a river approaching the lowland, the river is all one place, and all one land. To keep a river clear for the trout and salmon, you might have to stop a huge dam, or put in a water-bar on a high mountain trail, or challenge a timber sale with too many roads.

We hope to learn our watershed, and support it and sustain it in many ways. The water cycle and its stream-flow is, after all, our springs and wells, and is the spring peeper in the pond and the acorn woodpecker chattering in a snag. It's where our friends live, it is our friends. So let's jump into the whole process and see where it takes us.

2. AT HOME IN THE FOREST

One can choose to live in the forest as a sort of visitor, or become an inhabitant. We decided from early on to try to fully live here. This attempt was made partly from lack of resources and ignorant bravado. There was some sense of art and ecological morality that came into it, but mostly we learned by necessity: how to live in the woods as part of the natural community.

I'm talking about how one thinks about things like screens, fences, or dogs. These are often used for keeping the wild at bay. ("Keeping the wild at bay" sounds like fending off hawks and bears, but it is more often a matter of holding back beetles and deer-mice.) I am glad that I learned to live a permeable, porous life in the stands of oak and pine. Our house is entirely opened up for the entire long Sierra summer— Mud-daubers make their trips back and forth from inside the house to the edge of the pond like little tireless cement trucks, and pour their foundations on beams, in cracks, in rifle-bore holes, in the ends of hoses. They drop little daubs as they go. For the mosquitoes, which are never much of a problem, the house is just another place to enjoy the shade. At night the bats dash around the rooms, in and out of the open skylights, swoop down past your cheek and go out an open sliding door. In the dark of the night the deer can be heard stretching for the lower leaves of the apple trees, and at dawn the wild turkeys are strolling a few yards from the bed. It all does little harm.

The price we pay is the little extra effort to put all the pantry food into jars or other mouse-proof containers. Ground squirrels come right inside for fresh fruit on the table, and the deer step into the shade-shelter to nibble a neglected salad. You are called to a hopeful steadiness of nerves as you lift a morsel of chicken to the mouth with four meat-bees following it every inch of the way. You must sometimes (late summer) cook and eat with the yellowjackets watching every move. This can make you peevish, but there is a kind of truce that is usually attained when one quits flailing and slapping at the wasps and bees.

It's true; living and cooking in the outdoor shade-shelters someone occasionally gets stung. This is a price we pay for living in the porous world that is open to the wild. And that's about the worst that can happen. There's a faint risk of rattlesnake-bite as we stride around the little trails, and the ever-present standoffishness of poison oak. Life in the semi-open is not for everyone, but if you can get used to it, it's a great way to enjoy life in the forest.

As we increasingly come to inhabit the edges and inholdings of the middle-elevation forest lands, we have to look more and more closely at our impact. Carrying capacity, it should be obvious, is a highly flexible concept, and depends not just on the per acre density-figures, but also on the way that the density is lived. If the roads are few and of modest width and rough enough to slow cars down, if there

> **One can choose to live in the forest as a sort of visitor, or become an inhabitant.**

are no or very few fences, if the human inhabitants are not pumping heavily from the wells to irrigate pasture or orchards, if the number of dogs is kept small, if the houses are well-insulated and house temperatures are kept down in the winter, if feral cats are not allowed, if an attitude of tolerance is cultivated toward the occasional mischief of bears, raccoons, or *pekun* the cougar, we will cause almost no impact on the larger forest ecosystem. This, even as we take out firewood, cut some deliberately chosen sawlogs, gather manzanita berries for the cider, seek redbud for basketry supplies, or any of a number of other possible light economic uses of the forest. It is an old/new way to live, and we are learning it again. Coyotes and screech-owls make the night magic.

Permeability porousness works both ways. You are allowed to move through the woods with new eyes and ears, when you let go your little annoyances and anxieties.

3. CRAWLING

I was travelling the crest of a little ridge, finding a way between stocky deep red mature manzanita trunks, picking out a route and heading briskly on. Crawling.

Not hiking or sauntering or strolling, but *crawling*, steady and determined, through the woods. We usually visualize an excursion into the wild as an exercise of walking upright. We imagine ourselves striding through open alpine terrain, or across the sublime space of a sagebrush basin, or through the somber understory of an ancient sugar pine grove.

But it's not so easy to walk upright through the late 20th century mid-elevation Sierra forests. There are always many sectors regenerating from fire or logging, and the fire history of the Sierra would indicate that there have always been some areas of manzanita fields. So people tend to stay on the old logging roads or the trails, and this is their way of experiencing the forest. Manzanita and ceanothus fields, or the brushy ground-cover and understory parts of the forest, are left in wild peace.

My crawl was in late December and although the sky was clear and sunny, the temperature was around freezing. Patches of remnant snow were on the ground. A few of us were out chasing corners and boundary lines on the Bear Tree parcel (number 6) of the Inimim with retiring BLM forester Dave Raney, who had worked with that land many years before. No way to travel off the trail but to dive in: down on your hands and knees on the crunchy manzanita leaf-cover and crawl around between the trunks. Leather work gloves, a tight-fitting hat, long-sleeved denim workjacket, and old Filson tin pants make a proper crawler's outfit. Face right in the snow I came on my first of many bear-tracks. Along the ridge a ways, and then down a steep slope through the brush, belly-sliding on snow and leaves like an otter. You get limber at it, and see the old stumps from early logging surrounded by thick manzanita, still-tough pitchy limbs from old wolf trees, hardy cones, overgrown drag-roads, 4-foot butt logs left behind, webs of old limbs and twigs, and the periodic prize of a bear scat.

One of our party called us back a bit, "A bear tree!" And sure enough, there was a cavity in a large old pine that opened up after a fire had scarred it. A definite black bear hangout, with scratches on the bark. To go where bears, deer, raccoons, foxes, all our other neighbors go, you have to be willing to crawl.

So we have begun to overcome our hominid pride and learned to take pleasure in turning off the trail and going direct into the brush, to find the contours and creatures of the pathless part of the woods. Not really pathless, for there is the whole world of little animal trails that have their own logic. You go down, crawl swiftly along, spot an opening, stand and walk a few yards, and go down again. The trick is: have no attachment to standing; find your body at home on the ground, be a quadruped, or if necessary, a snake. You brush cool dew off a young fir with your face. The delicate aroma of leaf molds and mycelium rise from the tumbled humus under your hand, and a half-buried young boletus is disclosed. You can *smell* the fall mushrooms when crawling.

I began to fantasize on the larger possibilities of crawling. Workshops in Power Crawling? "Crawling to Achieve your Goals"? Self-esteem Crawls? Well, no. But at least, Crawl Away into the Wild. The world of little scats and tiny tracks. And, self-esteem, no joke! "I feel finally liberated, I have overcome my aversion to crawling, and I CAN GO ANYWHERE!"

It's not always easy, and you can even get lost. Last winter we took a long uphill cross country transect on some of the land just above the Yuba Gorge that soon turned into a serious crawl. We got into denser and denser old manzanita that had us doing commando-style lizard crawls to get under their low low limbs. It became an odd and unfamiliar ridge and I had no idea where we might be. For hundreds of yards, it seemed, we were scuttling along, and we came on a giant, totally fresh, worm-free Boletus Edulis, the *prize* of all the boletes. That went into the little day pack. And a bit further the manzanita opened and there we were! Suddenly it was just the opening below Suzanne Graham's old cabin built half on BLM land at the edge of Ananda, and a dirt road that led toward home.

Get those gloves and a jacket and a hat and go out and explore California.

37

The Heart of the Forest

Arne Naess

MANY CULTURES EXPRESS AWE of the "heart" of the forest. To be in the heart of the forest has been, and still is, considered to be something very special. Something quite different from merely walking along its outskirts, or where you know or feel the direction you should walk to reach the edge of the forest.

A forest that is not deep has no heart. It has to have depth, but that is not enough. Sometimes we may feel it is adequate to say we are deep in the forest, but we may lack the feeling or experience of being at its heart.

Development at or in the heart of a forest obviously changes everything. A poster saying: "Now you are in the heart of the forest" is ridiculous at the best. We who are brought up in an industrial country may, with some justice, be said to be oversensitive when we react negatively even to a little poster or to the cottage of a ranger, well hidden and built with exquisite ecological care. But painful experiences again and again have made us sore.

It is encouraging that people who endorse "progress" and continued economic growth often retain the heart metaphor and the respect which it entails. They react against utterances which seem to imply absence of any idea of the heart whatsoever, and compare it with the square kilometres of the whole forest. They say "you will understand that the road makes practically no difference. You say the road goes through the heart of the forest. You mean the center? We may let the road avoid the center, if you are happier that way." Even enthusiastic developers reject this kind of crude talk.

We who sense the heart clearly see that a forest with such a road really is divided into two forests: The "roadiness" area is broad; hundreds of times that of the road itself. The forest changes into two smaller ones.

To be in the heart of the forest *implies* distance from the road, but does not *mean* just "to be at a distance." To be there and be conscious about it is to spontaneously experience (and understand) a kind of quality or set of qualities that are unique. It transcends awareness of distance as such.

"How great a distance do we need?" In a practically impenetrable forest: small distance. In an open, subarctic forest with small trees: much longer. It would be a scholastic exercise to go into details because "distance" here has much to do with our imagination: You look one way, "forest, forest, forest...," you look another way, "forest, forest, forest, FOREST." The forest *fills* your mind; you are not a subject and the forest is not an object. The dualism is overcome.

To meet a big, wild animal in its own territory may be frightening. But it gives us an opportunity to better understand who we are and our limits of control: the existence of greatness other than human. The same applies to meeting the greatness of the forest. We are not in control. Our eminent eco-anarchist Kropotkin, in his *Mutual Aid*, tells us that people working in the vast Siberian forests have a tradition to shout loudly and repeatedly before starting to eat their lunch brought from home: There may be a fellow-human who has lost his or her way and would need the food more urgently. (An example of mammalian broad empathy or identification as an evolutionary force.)

A spontaneous experience of terror being alone in a great forest is an experience of something real, the-terror-alone-in-a-great-forest. But we don't cherish terror, so better reduce acquaintance with that part of reality. We should prepare ourselves and get informed, like we do when we go out on a glacier. The point I am trying to make here is that spontaneously experienced negative characteristics of nature, not just the positive, refer to something real. It is a task of wilderness enthusiasts to express their positive experiences.

Do contemporary forests in Europe have no heart? It would be misleading to answer "yes," but the rate of destruction has been heartbreaking and even if it is slowing down, invasion and fractioning of undeveloped areas continues.

Forest and lake intertwine
Sierra Club of Western Canada

When a new road made for big vehicles is constructed where a week ago one had a path for walking and skiing, a new path through the wood is often carefully prepared, but ridiculously near the gigantic monster of a road. The preparation of the alternative path presumes that there is no loss of deepness of the forest as long as developments are out of sight.

How old must we be to spontaneously experience being at the heart of a forest? Small children growing up in a wood, even in small patches of wood around their homes, may sometimes wander off straight into the "wild." They turn from time to time, looking back. "Is Mommy still in sight?," "Is big brother there?" When they trust enough to go further into the wood the little boy or girl, I suppose, may feel the greatness and independence of the wild, independence even of the power of mommy and big brother. Their body language tells a lot. They don't have, but they don't know they don't have, any control over the big world all around them. Don't underrate children!

The outlook for the near future is grim, but I feel it impossible to believe that destruction will continue until there is no forest with a heart.

38

Nature as a Reflection of Self and Society

Duncan Taylor

I.

MATHESON LAKE LIES IN THE HEART OF A SMALL WILDERNESS AREA on Vancouver Island. For untold centuries it has been the home for a complex array of animals and plants. Loons, bald eagles, turkey vultures, ravens, northwestern crows, warblers, yellow pond lilies, cattails, Douglas fir, lodgepole pine, arbutus, willow, snowberry, baldhip rose, salal, western painted turtles, red-legged frogs, snails, zooplankton, and phytoplankton, all of which have remained dynamically intertwined and interacting in an array of ecosystem communities, food webs, trophic levels, and nutrient cycles. Towards the more inaccessible end of the lake is a sheltered area, and it is there that the water often takes on a shimmering and mirror-like quality. Many times, I have looked into the water, at the algae, the beetles, the rough-skinned newts, and minnows, only to discover my own image, albeit one that is usually shadowlike and distorted. And then occasionally I have experienced those fleeting, yet paradoxically timeless, moments when the boundary between myself and the world has suddenly dissolved, and the lake and all its myriad creatures have become powerfully and indelibly incorporated into my own, into me, and the existence and fate of the animals and plants and insects have been felt as my own.[1]

But then, just as suddenly, as if implicit within the very act of attempting to understand the experience, the boundary between self and other is once more imposed, and I am cast again into the role of the proverbial prisoner in his cave of epistemological shadows: subject/object dualisms, and self/other projections.

Throughout Western literature, our descriptions of the natural world have reflected the values and biases of a given period in our history. Our perceptions of nature often tell us less about what is actually "out there" in the landscape, and more about the types of mental typography and projections that we carry about in our heads. It is natural, therefore, that as values change, so too do our views regarding nature. We might demonstrate this phenomenon with a number of examples from the past.

One fascinating illustration of the way in which people have projected upon nature their political and social biases is to be found in 17th century England. During the English Civil War the example of the beehive, with its queen, drones or "nobles," and its workers, was regularly employed by Stuart supporters to defend the concept of feudalism and social hierarchy. This tendency to project human values upon nature and then use such values to lend support to a particular worldview or social structure can again be witnessed throughout the 19th and 20th centuries. Thus, for some, the natural hierarchy of the biological world legitimized British class structure. For a number of the late 19th and early 20th century thinkers, such concepts as biological hierarchy and homeostasis were employed to validate and support those traditional values that were being eroded away in a rapidly expanding industrial world.

Similarly, throughout this period, Darwin's biological concept of "the survival of the fittest" was utilized to advocate a host of social, economic and political activities. For example, while Herbert Spencer in Great Britain sought to apply Darwinian theory to all aspects of social and political life, in the United States Darwin's line of reasoning was frequently used to justify wholesale economic growth and industrial expansion by means of unrestricted competition, including in Commodore Vanderbilt's maxim, "the public be dammed!" Thus, the political economist, William Graham Sumner (1840-1910), related the process of natural selection to the development of a society in which the ruthless and the industrious rose to the top.

While many persons were able to find in the processes of the natural world a justification for class privilege, cutthroat competition, and social Darwinism (the latter exemplified in the propaganda of German National Socialism), others were able to look to nature for a wholly different set of social values. For example, in contrast to Darwin's "survival of the fittest" doctrine, the Russian anarchist Peter Kropotkin (1842-1921) carried on researches and found in the natural realm the endorsement of such values as "mutual aid," cooperation, and social synergy and harmony. Recently, this line of reasoning has been taken up by environmentalists, ecofeminists, and New Age advocates, all of whom find in their study of ecology the justification for the establishment of a new society based upon the values of unity and diversity (the recognition of "one world" and yet at the same time appreciation of the need for political and cultural decentralization), limits to growth, egalitarianism, and interdependence. And much along the lines of the Counter-Enlightenment and the Romantic writers of the late 18th and early 19th centuries, a growing number of people are now perceiving in nature a set of values which, in many ways, is radically different from those that currently dominate our modern world.

> **A growing number of people are now perceiving in nature a set of values which, in many ways, is radically different from those that currently dominate our modern world.**

II.

It is for this reason that ecology, at least in its "deep" or radical sense, has been labelled a "subversive" science. And while ecology is regularly employed by mechanistically inclined purveyors of reductionism, for many it goes beyond the study of the relationships between organisms and their environments, and points in turn to a fundamentally new way of looking at our relationship to ourselves, to one another, and to the world. Indeed, ecology represents a wholly "new" type of consciousness that is emerging within the collective psyche of humankind. But while it is new, it is also perennial and timeless. It is a consciousness of synthesis, integration, and nondualism, and as such is increasingly able to discern those corresponding values in the world about us.

Ferns of forest floor
Bo Martin

To endorse this perception of the world is to reject many of the dualistic assumptions (body/mind; human/nature; knowing subject/known object) that underlie our traditional world view. Instead, this new perception regards the whole of nature as a complex but unified web of interdependent organisms, people, and events. It is the perception of the universe as an essential wholeness, but one which manifests itself in terms of countless diversities, expressions of behavior, and life-forms. And while this perception of the world does not in itself constitute a moral norm, an ecological interpretation of our place in nature does allow us to describe and acknowledge many of the multi-relational consequences of our activities. Hence, this makes it easier for us to adopt an ethical stance that is more in keeping with the universe recognized and appreciated as a unified whole. For example, I am more likely to acknowledge a sense of responsibility towards my environment and other people if I am convinced that "self" and "other" are not isolated categories, but instead form parts of an interrelated continuum. For if we, as individuals, perceive ourselves to be inextricably linked to the rest of the planet, and indeed our solar system and beyond, we are much more likely to be drawn to an ethic that relates our own self-interest both to other human beings and to the environmental community of which each of us is a part. In this regard, there is often a strong relationship between the way the world is imagined and the types of behavior and obligations people acknowledge and act upon.

Consequently, an ecological view of the world lends itself to the adoption of a set of values in which the boundaries of our morality are increasingly extended outwards from ourselves not only to include other humans and cultural traditions, but also to encompass nonhuman members of the earth's biotic community—

animals, trees, plants, and ecosystems. Such a perspective implies a relationship to the biotic community that goes beyond its usefulness as an economic commodity and an object of exploitation.

Yet ironically, we still find the majority of arguments for the protection of a natural area couched in, and therefore reflecting, the dominant economic and utilitarian values of our age. Hence, even for most conservationists the land is perceived as primarily an economic commodity to be exploited, albeit this time on a sustainable basis. In fact the very term "resource management" underscores the assumption that we are still somehow separate from nature and that our knowledge of the world "out there" must be used in Baconian fashion to manipulate and master its objects for our own use. It is noteworthy that Gifford Pinchot, the original proponent of "wise management" conservation, had equated conservation with "sustainable exploitation" and made it abundantly clear that this was not to be confused with "preservation." Similarly, its latest incarnation in the form of "sustainable development" has come to be synonymous with "sustained economic development," not with "developing sustainability."

Forest dependent Red squirrel
Jerry Valen DeMarco

Consequently, we find arguments for the protection of wilderness areas usually couched in economic or utilitarian terms. For example, if a cost/benefit analysis of a region can demonstrate that its value lies primarily in recreation and tourism, then it may be worth saving. If, however, its chief value is to be found in forest products and mining, then it goes. What is absurd here is to give a qualitative evaluation to something that cannot be measured solely on a monetary basis. Neil Evernden points out that this situation is much like saying that since the human body has been assessed at $12.98 in terms of the market value of its constituent parts, therefore that figure comprises its final worth.[2] Yet we still continue to argue on behalf of nature on such grounds, or at least in terms of some perceived use. Thus, we contend that wild areas must be protected because of their genetic worth or that we must protect the wolf population because of its value in weeding out the genetically inferior members of the deer and moose communities. The temperate rainforests of British Columbia are important for protecting the quality of our water, for climatic regulation, and as sinks for carbon dioxide, and so on. And while such arguments often prove to be expedient in terms of their accessibility to human self-interest, it is not always easy to provide plausible economic or utilitarian "uses" for everything in nature, and increasingly the justification for protecting snail darters and other such creatures becomes less and less convincing in terms of our traditional values.

III.

In the end, perhaps, the only justification for the careful protection of the land and life-forms from total exploitation and final destruction is our recognition that they possess intrinsic value and worth. Indeed, as we begin to acknowledge our own implicit value and even essential divinity, we shall begin increasingly to perceive these same qualities in the world around us. For ultimately the quality of my relationship to other people and to nature mirrors the relationship that I have to myself and the integration, or lack of integration, with my own psyche. So, if we treat our bodies as objects or commodities, we shall tend to treat others and nature in a similar fashion. If I have not acknowledged my own inner shadow, repressions, and fears, I will tend to project these upon others and the outside world. On the other hand, to the extent that I am able to affirm my own inner beauty, love, and wholeness, these qualities in turn will tend to be mirrored in my experience of the world.

Veteran, an important structural element
Bo Martin

If the world "out there" mirrors my inner one, then in a very real way its transformation begins with the transformation of myself. If this is the case, I must be willing to take responsibility for what I experience. If, for example, I perceive or experience a world filled with poverty, injustice, and pain, it is because these attributes are also within me. However, as I begin to heal myself and express my own inner wholeness, I shall be able in turn to help transform the external world as well.

It is not uncommon for a wilderness experience to act as a catalyst for an experience of one's own inner being and essential wholeness, and consequently for the experience of one's fundamental relatedness to, and inseparability from, other life-forms. Ultimately, it is in this experience of myself and therefore of my relatedness to the dragonflies, the birds, and the plants at such places as Matheson Lake that I recognize their intrinsic worth and need for protection. They are extensions of my ecological self, and if they are hurt or lost, a part of me is also hurt or lost.

Throughout history, people have journeyed into forests, deserts, and mountains and gained transpersonal experiences of one sort or another. It is in places such as these that we are less likely to be caught up in human conventions and readily definable social structures. Consequently, we are more apt to confront the contents of our psyches and acknowledge whatever may happen to lie within. More often than

265

not, we will retreat into the security of our internalized social structures and categories, and project these upon the world about us. However, one may find that it is at those moments when we manage to suspend our internal judgments, authorities, and daily rules that we are also most open to all the transpersonal experiences of Being, of wholeness, and of merging participation with the universe. But this implies being willing to be vulnerable and open to the moment, without recourse to the normal securities of intellectual categorizations and comparative values.

Traditionally, we have attempted to find security and order through the imposition of our own dualistic categories upon the world. As such, the form that our Western knowledge has taken has been predicated upon dualistic subject/object distinctions, and the objectification and control of other people as well as the natural environment. However, in the last years of the 20th century, we are at a stage in history when, if only for our very survival, it becomes necessary to realize that our ultimate security lies not in the ongoing separation of ourselves from one another and the environment, nor in a consciousness based upon fragmentation and manipulation, but rather in the relinquishment of such thought patterns in favor of a consciousness of wholeness and integration, one that is necessarily grounded in Being itself. So in order to step successfully into the future, we must find the courage to step first into the deepest recesses of ourselves. And perhaps significantly, the consciousness we shall be nurturing is already being reflected in outline form in our growing ecological perception of nature and its awareness of the profound integration of ourselves with all manifestations of life.

39

Beyond Empire Resourcism to Ecoforestry

Alan Drengson

A PERSON WHO SUPPORTS THE PLATFORM PRINCIPLES of the deep ecology movement is committed to working to bring about necessary fundamental changes in policies and practices. It is important to articulate the ecocentric implications of one's ultimate philosophy. By doing this, one becomes more aware of the practical implications of the platform for transforming one's work and lifestyle. For example, what is ecologically responsible agriculture and how ought it to be practised in particular places? What is ecologically responsible forestry, and how ought it to be practised in forest stands within a landscape? What is ecologically responsible fishing? And what about mining, energy and water use, and construction of shelter? How does one practise these so as to realize ecological harmony? These are examples of areas in which deep practical questioning must be undertaken.

Forestry and agriculture are particularly critical, since they have major impacts on landscapes, ecological communities, and global ecosystems. Forestry and agriculture provide most of the raw materials and food to meet our vital needs. It is important to consider them together, since they are historically, economically, and ecologically interconnected. Agriculture is often practised in areas that have been cleared of forest. Forests are almost always integral parts of watersheds that provide water for agriculture. Many agricultural plants and products, such as mushrooms and berries, have their origins in diverse forests. The human use of forests predates agriculture. Humans evolved in forests and forest savannahs. They gathered and hunted in them to meet their needs. Early agriculture was an extension and modification of both gathering and hunting; it involved domesticating wild plants and animals.

There are many forms of agriculture; some are sustainable because they are ecologically harmonious, some are not because they are ecologically dissonant. The same is true for forestry. In Western industrial forestry, which today is applied globally, the practices are based on an industrial agricultural model with a long history of ecological destruction. This model has its roots in the practices of the Romans, and as they applied it they destroyed much fertile land in Italy and North Africa. Their forest practices also led to wide-scale deforestation in the Mediterranean basin and elsewhere. These practices exemplify empire resourcism.

Rome was an imperial society. It was based on a top-down, patriarchal, ruling hierarchy. Its centralized government was enforced and extended through systematic application of managed force to attain control. This was facilitated by deforestation, since forest dwellers resisted conquest and were almost impossible to conquer as long as they had the security of the forests. Removing the forests exposed them, and also removed the basis of their lives. The hierarchical control of Rome was extended through management backed up by the military legions. Its systems of roads, transportation, and communication facilitated its rule. When Rome was converted to Christianity a new dimension of centralization was added, that of conformity of belief in a single, centralized doctrine backed up by the hierarchical power of the church which spoke for the one true God.

Imperialism is the imposition of external control by means of force over large areas, subjugating other humans and beings to a centralized power center. Such use of power is a form of management based on methodically subduing that which is managed for purposes of complete control. This system was applied to conquered peoples, the Roman populace, and also to the lands and forests. As Christianity developed on the pattern of the Roman Empire, it became an empire religion. Its dominion was the world as a whole; its scope was all beliefs and values. Pagans, who were country dwellers following nature religions of place, stood in the way of applying Roman Christian control, which sought to transform their dwelling places into the managed systems of the empire. These systems of control are present in today's military, governmental and corporate bureaucracies. They attempt to manage and control nature only as resources.

Nature religions grow out of long dwelling in specific places. In this long-term dwelling a spontaneous richness of understanding and harmony develops between dwellers and places of dwelling. Long-term dwellers become natives, indigenous to their places. They hear its many voices and know its spirits. Their practices are in harmony with what the forest can support through its abundance. Such cultures develop practices that enable them to sense intuitively what they can take respectfully from the places they dwell within. In this way, they fit in. They do not alter their places in major ways, or try to control nature as it is manifest in them. Their cultural practices focus on self-discipline and spiritual realization. Thus, they manage themselves. This is the wisdom of the Old Ways. Wise dwelling grows out of being in harmony with one's place, coming to understand it through identifying with it, so that one loves it. From such love comes a different understanding, one that gives rise to place-specific wisdom. Moreover, such dwellers are sensitive to the

> **Wise dwelling grows out of being in harmony with one's place, coming to understand it through identifying with it, so that one loves it.**

sublime mysteries of their places. This is not true of the abstract theories of modern management based on power-over models.

The large-scale monocultures used in industrial agriculture and forestry are based on the imperial model. They are based on an anthropocentric philosophy that treats nature as mere resource and instrument. Its aim is to control the natural world and remake it according to abstract ideas, so as to survive, be secure, and profit. This monoculturing control eliminates cultural, biological, and geological diversity. It arises from a monoculturing mind-set. For it, there is but one truth, one doctrine, one power, one centralized authority; thus, people who embrace it enact uniformity, standardization, and monocultures not only in "resource management," but also of human experience and culture. We travel the world in jets and get out in airports that have no place-specific wisdom in them. Electronic media beam this consuming monoculture into every hamlet. So it is with industrial agriculture and forestry. Their theories and practices are placeless. They destroy unique places. Everywhere we travel, the practices are the same. They are simple, based on abstract concepts and theories, and rely on power and external control. We see their large checkerboards spreading across forest and grasslands. They destroy diversity of contexts and their contents.

The farmers and foresters who apply industrial agriculture and forestry, which is the mechanization of the empire resource system of centralized management and control described above, get caught on a treadmill of ever-increasing growth and debt. They get caught in an international, urban, monetary system. The growth of this centralized financial system leads to declining local autonomy. It undermines the integrity of local communities based on forestry and agriculture. As industrial forestry and agriculture are used in place after place the land suffers, the local economies are destroyed, and land is controlled by centralized, corporate, public and private bureaucracies. These distant functionaries and institutions have no connection to or understanding of the needs of specific forests and lands. Nonetheless, their decisions have drastic, long-term, adverse effects on communities, human and nonhuman, that dwell in rural areas. We see this happening in both agriculture and forestry in North America and elsewhere.

There are counter movements to this mainstream application of centralized systems of management as control and power over people, lands, forests, and other beings. Because the words "agriculture" and "forestry" are closely linked to the empire industrial models described and are defined in terms of one another, it is helpful to use new terminology to foster a transition to practices that are wise and ecologically responsible (ecosophic). Our current practices are not sustainable. They are ecologically irresponsible and cause much damage and suffering. To mark the shift to ecologically responsible forestry and agriculture, based on ecocentric values, we now use the words "ecoforestry" and "ecoagriculture." These terms represent a diversity of practices that grow out of place-specific wisdom, learned by dwelling as a native in those places. This is reflected in cultural diversity, for cultural diversity arises from biological and topographic diversity.

How then is ecoforestry practised so as to realize ecological harmony and wisdom (ecosophy)? As observed above, we must begin by means of deep questioning that leads us to understand the values and mind-sets represented by the exploitative industrial management systems and practices. We must then explore the implications of the platform principles of the deep ecology movement. We must commit ourselves to learning from nature as it is in specific places by dwelling there to learn its inherent wisdom and intrinsic values.

Ecoforesters are open to learning from nature's wisdom, learning how to practise responsible forest use from the forest itself. There are many people in the world and in North America who practise this dwelling and learning. The practices of the aboriginal Turtle Islanders often manifested such place-specific understanding which was integral to their religion, art, and technology practices. More recent European descended dwellers in the forest have begun to relearn this indigenous wisdom of how to dwell in and use forests wisely and responsibly. The essence of ecoforestry is to learn to perceive what the forest can supply us without altering its basic ecological functions and intrinsic values.

Ecoforesters are committed to protecting and caring for the forest. Caring for the forest does not mean managing or controlling it. If I care for a dog or child, I love and nurture them; I also learn from them, so that I can honor their vital needs. Some of these needs are based on their own drives toward self-realization, and this is something I cannot do for them. In the case of forests with their many beings, ecoforesters who dwell therein care for them through love; practices have as little impact as possible. Ecoforesters recognize the integrity and self-creating processes of the forests with their many beings and communities of communities. Ecoforesters understand that forests are complex communities of multitudes of beings, each of which has intrinsic value, and each of which contributes values and serves functions that make the whole possible. All of these many beings coevolve in relationships that for all their complexity defy our imaginations. Ecoforesters appreciate this diversity, complexity, richness and integrity. Ecoforesters also have a sense of the whole and its processes of evolution and change. Ecoforesters have a sense of the forest's history, and what it is for that forest as a whole to flourish.

Trees are only part of a forest. The monoculturalist, who wants to centralize control and standardize methods, requires no place-specific wisdom, does not recognize that it exists, and instead bases practices on abstract theories and piecemeal information. The monoculturalist relies primarily on imposing his or her will on the land and forest to control it, taking over its evolutionary destiny to replace it with plantation trees in cornlike rows. This is part of the agenda of modernity, that is, the imposition of Cosmopolis (as Stephen Toulmin calls it in a recent book of the same name) as a "rational" geometric model, over the entire

> **Trees are only part of a forest.**

world. Ecoforestry rejects these aims of Cosmopolis. Nature shows us that diversity, complexity, and richness are good in themselves. They are also part of our own wildness and spontaneity.

Ecoforesters therefore do not ask, "How much can we take from this land and forest to maximize production and profits?" Instead, aware of their ignorance, ecoforesters humbly ask, "What must we leave?" Then they ask "What can we take from the forest, if we are not to interfere with its many functions and processes, and the intrinsic values of its many beings?" Ecoforestry is a process of adaptive learning which deepens as practice continues. It is guided at the watershed level by landscape ecology. Its stand-level practices are informed by conservation biology. And yet, it is vernacular in practice, since it learns from the wisdom of each place. This means that ecoforestry cannot be defined by any one set of practices, equipment, prescriptions, or desired future states. Instead, ecoforesters realize that they participate with nature and strive to make that participation as harmonious with the will of the forest and its wildness as possible. Just as the forest evolves through complex processes of natural selection, community creation, and self-realization, so the practices of ecoforestry evolve. A community based on the practice of ecoforestry engenders a rich culture respecting and reflecting the specific values and characteristics of the forest in which it dwells. These flow out of the arts of responsible ecoforestry.

The modern monoculture management model centralizes power. It destroys ecological, economic and cultural diversity. Ecoforestry decentralizes authority and preserves all forms of diversity. It must not be confused with sustainable development or ecosystem management. Both of these are based on translating the imperial, anthropocentric models into other terminology; they then use only palliative measures. They are based on the assumption that we must continue to control the forests and ecosystems and manage them for our benefit; we manage their functioning because we need and want them. This anthropocentric approach does not enable us to realize our larger ecological Self, so as to appreciate and practise ways of life consistent with the values inherent in the places in which we dwell.

The practitioners referred to above, who have dwelled in the forests for years, and who have let the forests teach them how to practise wise and responsible forest use, do abide by ecocentric values and principles. They constitute a growing worldwide movement of people who are reinhabiting the countryside in not only forestry, but also in agriculture. They are bioregional supporters of the deep ecology movement. They see the violence and destructiveness of the dominant Western development model and reject it. They also have an alternative to it. If they are indigenous peoples, who have been dwelling in their places for eons, they already have this wise dwelling and are defending their places and cultures. Newer dwellers regrow community from its roots in natural diversity.

The broad principles of ecoforestry are sufficiently refined to enable us to proceed to certification of materials removed from forests in ecologically responsible ways. Certification of raw materials and products manufactured from such material is developing. This will enable those who use forest-based products to make ecologically responsible choices. This is similar to the move to certification of organic agriculture.

Ecoforesters minimize the impact of forest use through minimizing road construction, using low-impact appropriate technologies, and by removing only trees that natural indicators reveal have been selected for removal by nature. Trees of the same species and age growing together will consist of some trees that have become canopy dominants. Those which reside under the canopy are those whose rate of growth has slowed. Some of these trees must be left to assure preservation of all of the functions that dead trees perform in a forest, as they support a multitude of many kinds of beings. They are part of forest mineral cycles. However, nature usually produces abundance, and ecoforesters take only some of that abundance. Ecoforesters gather many "goods" from the forests. Studies show that diverse, ecologically responsible forest use yields far greater economic benefits over the long term than short-term, industrial forest removal. Industrial agricultural forestry reduces a complex forest community to one value—monetary—and fells all trees for timber and fibre. All of the other values, accumulated wisdom, and genetic and functional diversity are lost.

The practice of ecoforestry leads to communities that have intimate, long-term relationships with the forests. The raw materials removed satisfy vital human needs. They are processed so that high value, durable products are manufactured locally. To have sustainable cultures and economies, there must be self-sustaining natural forests. Such forests sustain and teach us; we do not sustain them. However, we can, with foolish and irresponsible practices, destroy all of their values and in the process lose ourselves and communities.

The practice of ecoforestry is the practice of ecologically responsible forest use based on self-discipline, love of the forest, and deepening realization of the ecological Self. Today it can be seen as a *transitional* practice to perennial forestry. In many areas of the world, industrial forestry has destroyed the natural forests so extensively that ecoforestry becomes part of a necessary restoration transition to the kinds of practices possible with full-functioning mature natural forests. Under those conditions full biodiversity can re-establish itself, even if the original genetic heritage of an area has been lost as a result of industrial forestry. Industrial forestry is a major cause of the destruction of biodiversity and genetic heritage. This practice must stop immediately! Ecoforestry is a necessary element in a strategy of recovery and transition to sustainability.

We also need to develop an economic transition in areas of extensive forest destruction if we are to rebuild sustainable forest communities. The web of forest-dependent communities is quite large, including not only those who take material from the forest directly, but all other beings who depend on forest functions, which

> The practice of ecoforestry leads to communities that have intimate, long-term relationships with the forests.

includes oceanic, freshwater and riparian communities, both human and nonhuman. It is urgent that a strategy team be brought together to spell out a new ecologically responsible economics, not only for forest-based and -dependent communities, but also for a more comprehensive context. Economics and management practices cannot be separated from ecosystem requirements. A new vision of decentralized management must have bioregional and ecosystem guidelines. Management must depend upon the multivalued wisdom of all workers in a place, not on top-down, anthropocentric hierarchies. We need to downsize in all areas of life, from lifestyle to national policies and management practices. Above all, we must change our philosophy of management so that it is not based on resource empirism and anthropocentrism, but on ecocentrism and mutual respect.

We must draw back from destructive behavior, let go of denial, accept the fact that the large-scale, industrial, consumer-debt-driven monoculture, whose growth we have defined as progress, has been an experiment whose consequences we can no longer afford. Even if we had more time, as far as the integrity of natural systems is concerned, we would have to change our lives now that we realize that destruction of forest ecosystems is morally and spiritually wrong. It is an offense to all values: spiritual, moral, social, communal, esthetic, and economic. We must change the tax laws and policies that make it possible to conduct ecosystem destruction and call it "business." As it now stands it is difficult for ecoforestry, ecoagriculture, sustainable fishing, ecologically responsible mining, and other ecosophic practices to go on. The cards are stacked against these superior practices. As the playing field is now tilted, it leans toward the creation of global corporate feudalism in which all practices are monocultures and a single consumer TV society permeates the Earth.

As ecoworkers, we must heal our own pain and reconnect with the wild that is within and the larger world of all beings that is our living context. If we are ecoforesters, this requires that we learn to manage our own practices by letting the forests teach us what we can do. Ecologically responsible place-wise practices have none of the arrogance and violence that characterize the industrial management models and practices. They are not imperialistic or monoculturing. They sustain, enrich and ennoble their communities and practitioners. Thus, ecoforesters are committed to an oath of ecologically responsible forest use, as endorsed by the Pacific Cascadia Ecoforestry Working Group in September 1993 at Wave Hill Farm. (See the epilogue below.)

EPILOGUE

The Ecoforester's Way:
An Oath of Ecological Responsibility

IT IS FITTING TO CONCLUDE THIS BOOK with the following statement of philosophy and the Ecoforester's Way taken from the documents of the Ecoforestry Institute. The document is a fitting testament to the vigorous growth in awareness and practices that has been part of the recent history of forest use.

THE ECOFORESTER'S WAY

The emergence of ecoforestry coincides with the deepening of the environmental crisis. The manifestations of this crisis are all around us and well known. The environmental movement has roots in earlier times, but has become a worldwide grassroots movement. There are two main forms of environmentalism, one is the *status quo, mild reform movement*. The other, the *deep ecology movement*, is based on the awareness that we cannot go on with business as usual. We must make fundamental and sweeping changes in our values, philosophies and practices. From the platform of the deep ecology movement, it is clear that the crisis we face is a crisis in culture, character and consciousness.

George Sessions and Arne Naess formulated a version of the platform principles of the deep ecology movement in 1984. These principles recognize that we must make cultural and individual changes based on respect for the intrinsic worth of all natural beings. Since mild reform continues to treat nature as a source of only instrumental values for human support, profit and enjoyment, it cannot end the destruction of nature.

Acceptance of the platform principles leads to new practices that respect and work with the values *inherent* in ecological communities, natural beings and their processes. In the case of forestry, this new practice is called *ecoforestry* to signify its break with traditional forestry. Traditional Western forestry is based on an agricultural *industrial* model that views natural forests as something to be replaced with technologically designed and managed tree plantations. It is now obvious that this approach has failed, and that its continuing practice will destroy all natural forests; it plays a major role in global ecological destruction and species extinction.

And finally, it is wrong to destroy ecological contexts, the basis of life for all beings.

Ecoforestry realizes ecologically responsible forest use by means of commitments and new practices based on *ecocentric* values. Its practices follow from accepting the platform principles of the Deep Ecology Movement in conjunction with leading-edge knowledge of forest ecology, evolution, landscape ecology, conservation biology, stand-level practical knowledge and the vernacular wisdom found among forest *dwellers*, primarily but not only indigenous peoples. Ecoforestry is perennial forest use, based on respect for the wisdom and intrinsic values of the forest. In conjunction with the platform principles, the Ecoforestry Institute urges that we immediately take all of the necessary steps to recycle, and reduce use and waste of all resources. We must find substitutes for wood fiber in most applications. Timber taken from forests must be used for high-quality products that are durable.

The Institute endorses diversified forest-based economies made up of small businesses, workers' co-ops, nonprofit organizations, small corporations, private land, and land trusts. Finally, the Institute in cooperation with SILVA Forest Foundation and other organizations is building a certification system that informs users of wood products how to choose those obtained and manufactured by ecologically responsible standards and practices.

Because of the deep responsibilities of ecoforesters, an oath that they strive to live up to has been developed. It distils and summarizes the philosophy and values of ecoforestry practices. It is hoped that the oath stated below inspires general agreement and will be adopted by all organizations and individuals devoted to ecologically responsible forest use, whatever their activities and products.

THE ECOFORESTER'S WAY:
AN OATH OF ECOLOGICALLY RESPONSIBLE FOREST USE

1. We shall respect, hold sacred, and learn from the ecological wisdom (ecosophy) of natural forests with their multitudes of beings;
2. We shall protect the integrity of full-functioning forests;
3. We shall not use agricultural practices on the forest;
4. We shall remove from forests only values that are in abundance and only to meet vital human needs;
5. We shall remove individual instances of values only when this removal does not interfere with full-functioning forests: when in doubt, we will not;
6. We shall minimize the impacts of our actions on the forest by using only appropriate, low-impact technology practices;
7. We shall use only nonviolent resistance (e.g. Gandhian methods) in our protection of the forests;
8. We shall do good work and uphold the Ecoforester's Way as a sacred duty and trust.

AFTERWORD

Bill Devall

A GROUP OF JOURNALISTS went to visit Gandhi at his ashram in a rural district of India. At that time Gandhi had spent over three decades as a social activist. The journalists asked him what motivated his altruism, his passionate service to the poor in India. Gandhi replied, "I serve no one but myself."

His Self, however, was broad and deep. He manifested deep and broad identification with the suffering of the poor, the outcasts, the oppressed. His life was dedicated to social transformation based on the principle of "truth force" and based on nonviolent direct action.

Like Gandhi, the ecoforester serves no one but him/herself. But the ecoforester has broad and deep identification with salmon, salamanders, fungi, fallen trees, rivers, streams, bears, mountain lions and the great ecological processes—fire, wind, rain and decay—that sustain the life of the forest/watershed/mountains.

An ecoforester is called to the Way by the erotic/sentient/living gestalt that we call a forest/watershed/mountain. An ecoforester is called to serve his/her greater Self as part of the landscape.

As part of the flow of the great processes of the landscape, the ecoforester is always mindful. Practicing mindfulness, as the Buddhist teacher Tich Nhat Hanh says, involves us in joy-filled, full breathing during each moment of life.

The poet and philosopher Robinson Jeffers identified the process of incorporating oneself in the landscape as "falling in love outward," away from the narrow ego into the greatness of life and death.

Love, commitment, compassion, ecological understanding—all of these inform the ecosophy of an ecoforester.

Like living waters flowing from a spring, deep in the forest, the intuition of the ecoforester draws from and lives with the life force of the forest/watershed/mountain.

The ecoforester asks, "How much value can I leave in this forest?" He/she never asks, "How much value can I take from this forest—to make a profit, pay my bills, service my debt?" The ecoforester recognizes that trees are not a forest. Most of the landscape in which an ecoforester participates will never be logged. The ecoforester always respects the integrity of the land.

The ecoforester works with public regulatory agencies to protect the habitat of threatened and endangered plants and animals, protect riparian zones, protect areas of potential geological activity (such as slides) and protect the soil and living streams. For an ecoforester, private property ownership is a responsibility and a trust. As a private landowner or consultant to private property owners, the ecoforester cooperates with neighbors, with government agencies, and cooperates with private organizations dedicated to the welfare of plants, animals, rivers, forests and mountains.

The ecoforester embraces the dynamic forces in the landscape. Fire, for example, returns to the forest as part of the landscape processes as the ecoforester embraces the order out of chaos, embraces events that naturally occur in the evolution of the forest ecosystem.

After fire or flood or windstorm, the ecoforester does not rush to salvage but watches and waits, always mindful of the processes and events occurring on the parcel of land/watershed/mountain of which he/she is the guardian.

The ecoforester approaches trees, wild creatures, rivers and rocks as aspects of unfolding answers to questions he/she has not yet begun to ask.

In his essay "Modesty and the Conquest of Mountains," Norwegian ecophilosopher Arne Naess writes, "As I see it, modesty is of little value if it is not a natural consequence of much deeper feelings, and even more important in our special context, a consequence of a way of understanding ourselves as part of nature in a wide sense of the term. This way is such that the smaller we come to feel ourselves compared to the mountain, the nearer we come to participating in its greatness. I do not know why this is so."

Like the mountain climber participating in the life of the mountain, the ecoforester participates modestly in the life of the forest. The smaller the ecoforester comes to feel as part of the forest, the nearer he/she comes to participating in its greatness. We do not know why this is so.

Natural forest, spiritual sanctuary
Bo Martin

NOTES AND REFERENCES

Introduction:

1. Phil Carter, "The Summer of Clayoquot," *Borealis* Vol. 5, No. 1, Issue 15 (Spring, 1994): 8-17; Ron MacIsaac and Anne Champagne, eds., *Clayoquot Mass Trials* (Gabriola Island, B.C.: New Society Publishers, 1994); Tzeporah Berman, Maurice Gibbons, et al., *Clayoquot and Dissent* (Vancouver: Ronsdale Press Ltd., 1994); Howard Breen-Needham, Sandy Francis Duncan, eds., *Witness to Wilderness: The Clayoquot Sound Anthology* (Vancouver: Arsenal Pulp Press, 1994).

2. Some good discussions of Muir and Pinchot are found in: Roderick Nash, *Wilderness and the American Mind* (New Haven: Yale University Press, 1979); Carolyn Merchant, ed., *Major Problems in American Environmental History* (Lexington, Massachusetts: D.C. Heath and Company, 1993); Stewart Udall, *The Quiet Crisis* (New York: Avon Books, 1963).

3. Thomas L. Burton, *Natural Resource Policy in Canada: Issues and Perspectives* (Toronto: McClelland and Stewart, 1977).

4. These points are a synthesis of principles found in ecoforestry literature; see such writers as Merv Wilkinson, Orville Camp, Chris Maser, and Herb Hammond in the bibliography.

Chapter 2: Forest Practices Related to Forest Ecosystem Productivity

R. Constanza, H. Daly and J. Bartholomew, "Goals, Agenda and Policy Recommendations for *Ecological Economics*," in Ecological Economics, ed. R. Constanza (N.Y.: Columbia University Press, 1991).

C.J. Hagen, et al., "Incorporating the Earth," *Pan Ecology* Vol. 6, No. 8 (1991).

R. Margalef, *Perspectives in Ecological Theory* (Chicago: University of Chicago, 1968).

J. Needham, *Time, the Refreshing River* (London: Alan & Unwin, 1941).

E. Odum, *Fundamentals of Ecology* (Philadelphia: Saunders, 1971).

E.C. Pielou, *Population and Community Ecology* (New York: Gordon and Reach, 1974).

A.G. Tansley, "The Use and Abuse of Vegetational Concepts and Terms," *Ecology* 1, 6 (1935): 284-307.

James W. Toumey, *Foundations of Silviculture Upon an Ecological Basis*. Second ed. rev. C.F. Korstian (New York: John Wiley & Sons, 1947).

A.E. Wittbecker, *The Poetic Archaeology of the Flesh* (Wilmington: Mozart & Reason Wolfe, Ltd., 1976).

A.E. Wittbecker, *The Ethics of Ecosystem Interference* (being reviewed).

Chapter 3: The Battle for Sustainability
1. E.g. Bill Mollison, *Permaculture: A Practical Guide to a Sustainable Future* (Covelo, CA.: Island Press, 1990).

Chapter 9: The Role of Coarse Woody Debris
Literature Cited
Amaranthus, M., J.M. Trappe, L. Bednar and D. Arthur. Hypogeous Fungal Production in Mature Douglas Fir Forest Fragments and Surrounding Plantations and its Relation to Coarse Woody Debris and Animal Mycophagy. *Can. J. For. Res.* 24 (1994): 2157-2165.

Carey, A.B. and M.L. Johnson. Small Mammals in Managed, Naturally Young, and Old-growth Forests. *Ecological Applications* 5 (1995): 336-352.

Casa, C.L. *Woody Debris in the Forests of British Columbia: A Review of the Literature and Current Research.* B.C. Ministry of Forests, 1993.

Crites, S. and M. Dale. Relationship Between Stand Age, Stand Structure and Nonvascular Species in Aspen Mixedwood Forests in Alberta. In *Relationship Between Stand Age, Stand Structure, and Biodiversity in Mixedwood Forests in Alberta*, ed. J.B. Stelfox. Vegreville, AB: Alberta Environmental Center [AECV95-R1], and Edmonton, AB: Canadian Forest Service [project no. 0001A], 1995.

Daniels, L., J. Dobry, K. Klinka and M.C. Feller. Death and Decay *of Thuja plicata*. Vancouver, B.C.: Forest Sciences Department, U.B.C. In prep.

Gregory, S. and L. Ashkenas. Riparian Management Guide: Willamette National Forest. Dept. Fish. and Wildl., Oregon State Univer., 1990. 120 p.

Gyug, L. Timber Harvesting Effects on Riparian Wildlife and Vegetation in the Okanagan Highlands of British Columbia: Part 1. Trees and Coarse Woody Debris. Final Project Report. Penticton: B.C. Environment, 1996. Unpublished.

Hansen, A.J., T.A. Spies, F.J. Swanson and J.L. Ohmann. Conserving Biodiversity in Managed Forests. *Bioscience* 41 (1991): 382-392.

Harmon, M.E., J.F. Franklin, F.J. Swanson, P. Sollins, S.V. Gregory, J.D. Lattin, N.H. Anderson, S.P. Cline, N.G. Aumen, J.R. Sedell, G.W. Lienkaemper, K. Cromack Jr. and K.W. Cummins. Ecology of Coarse Woody Debris in Temperate Ecosystems. *Advances in Ecological Research* 15 (1986): 133-302.

Harmon, M.E., W.K. Ferrell and J.F. Franklin. Effects on Carbon Storage of Conversion of Old-growth Forests to Young Forests. *Science* 247 (1990): 699-702.

Harmon, M. Woody Debris Budgets for Selected Forest Types in the U.S. In *The Forest Sector Carbon Budget of the United States: Carbon Pools and Flux Under Alternative Policy Options*, ed. D. Turner, J. Lee, G. Koerper and J. Barker. Corvallis, Oregon: U.S. Environmental Protection Agency, Environmental

Research Laboratory, 1993.

Harmon, M., J. Sexton, B.A. Caldwell and S.E. Carpenter. Fungal Sporocarp Mediated Losses of Ca, Fe, K, Mg, Mn, N, P, and Zn from Conifer Logs in the Early Stages of Decomposition. *Can. J. of For. Res.* 24 (1994): 1883-1893.

Harvey, A.E., M.F. Jurgensen and M.J. Larsen. Effects of Soil Organic Matter on Regeneration in Northern Rocky Mountain Forests. Portland, OR: USDA Forest Service, Pacific Northwest Research Station, GTR-PNW-163, 1983. pp. 239-242.

Harvey, A.E., M.F. Jurgensen, M.J. Larsen and R.T. Graham. Decaying Organic Materials and Soil Quality in the Inland Northwest: A Management Opportunity. Ogden, UT: USDA Forest Service, Intermountain Research Station, GTR-INT-225, 1987. 15 p.

Harvey, A.E., M.J. Larsen and M.F. Jurgensen. Forest Management Implications of Improved Residue Utilization: Biological Implications in Forest Ecosystems. In *Harvesting and Utilization Opportunities for Forest Residues in the Northern Rocky Mountains*, pp. 259-269. Ogden, UT: USDA Forest Service Intermountain Forest and Range Experimental Station, GTR-INT-110, 1981. 294 p.

Harvey, A.E., M.F. Jurgensen, M.J. Larsen and J.A. Schlieter. Distribution of Active Ectomycorrhizal Short Roots in Forest Soils of the Inland Northwest: Effects of Site and Disturbance. Ogden, UT: USDA Forest Service Intermountain Forest and Range Experimental Station, Res. Pap. INT-374, 1986. 8 p.

Keenan, R., C. Prescott and J. Kimmins. Mass and Nutrient Content of Woody Debris and Forest Floor in Western Red Cedar and Western Hemlock Forests on Northern Vancouver Island 1993.

Kurz, W.A., M.J. Apps, T.M. Webb and P.J. McNamee. The Carbon Budget of the Canadian Forest Sector: Phase I. Northwest Region, Forestry Canada, Information report NOR-X-326, 1992.

Lattin, J.D. and A.R. Moldenke. Moss Lacebugs in Northwest Conifer Forests: Adaptation to Long-term Stability. *The Northwest Environmental Journal* 6 (1990): 406-07.

Lertzman, K., G.D. Sutherland, A. Inselberg and S.C. Saunders. Canopy Gaps in the Landscape Mosaic in a Coastal Temperate Rainforest. *Ecology* (in press).

Little, S.N. and J.L. Ohmann. Estimating Nitrogen Loss from Forest Floor During Prescribed Fires in Douglas Fir/Western Hemlock Clearcuts. *For. Sci.* 34 (1988): 152-164.

Maser, C., S.R. Cline, K. Cromack Jr., J.M. Trappe and E. Hansen. What We Know about Large Trees that Fall to the Forest Floor. In *From the Forest to the Sea: A Story of Fallen Trees*, ed. C. Maser, R.F. Tarrant, J.M. Trappe and J.F. Franklin. USDA Forest Service, General Technical Report PNW-GTR-229, 1988. pp. 25-45

Moldenke, A.R. and J.D. Lattin. Dispersal Characteristics of Old-growth Soil Arthropods: The Potential for Loss of Diversity and Biological Function. *The Northwest Environmental Journal* 6 (1990): 408-09.

Nadel, H. Abundance and Diversity of Soil Microarthropods. 1994 Draft Report,

B.C. MOF Sicamous Creek Silvicultural Systems Project, A11 (IR42), 1995.

Parsons, G.L., G. Cassis, A.R. Moldenke, J.D. Lattin, N.H. Anderson, J.C. Miller, P. Hammond and T.D. Schowalter. *Invertebrates of the H.J. Andrews Experimental Forest, Western Cascade Range, Oregon. V: An Annotated List of Insects and Other Arthropods.* USDA Forest Service. General Technical Report PNW-GTR-290, 1991.

Samuelsson, J., L. Gustafsson and T. Ingelog. Dying and Dead Trees: A Review of their Importance to Biodiversity. Uppsala, Sweden: Swedish Threatened Species Unit, 1994.

Schreiner, E.G., K.A. Krueger, P.J. Happe and D.B. Houston. Understory Patch Dynamics and Ungulate Herbivory in Old-growth Forests of Olympic National Park, Washington. *Can. J. For. Res.* 26 (1996): 255-265.

Setälä, H. and V. Marshall. Stumps as a Habitat for Collembola During Succession from Clearcuts to Old-growth Douglas Fir Forests. *Pedobiologia* 38 (1994): 307-326.

Sinclair, A.R.E., D.S. Hik, O.J. Schmitz, G.G.E. Scudder, D.H. Turpin and N.C. Larter. Biodiversity and the Need for Habitat Renewal. *Ecological Applications* 5 (1995): 579-587.

Soderstrom, L. The Occurrence of Epixylic Bryophyte and Lichen Species in an Old Natural and a Managed Forest Stand in Northeast Sweden. *Biol. Conserv.* 45 (1988): 169-178.

Soderstrom, L. Regional Distribution Patterns of Bryophyte Species on Spruce Logs in Northern Sweden. *Bryologist* 92 (1989): 349-355.

Torgersen, T. and E. Bull. Down Logs as Habitat for Forest-dwelling Ants—The Primary Prey of Pileated Woodpeckers in Northeastern Oregon. *Northwest Science* 69 (1995): 294-303.

Walker, B. Conserving Biological Diversity Through Ecosystem Resilience. *Conservation Biology* 9 (1994): 747-752.

Personal Communications

M. Harmon, Department of Forest Sciences, Oregon State University, Corvallis.

S. Taylor, Pacific Forestry Center, Victoria, B.C.

Chapter 10: Water and Connectivity

R.T.T. Forman. The Ethics of Isolation, the Spread of Disturbance, and Landscape Ecology. *In Landscape Heterogeneity and Disturbance*, ed. M. Goigel Turner. New York: Springer-Verlag, 1987.

J.F. Franklin. Old-growth Forests and the New Forestry. In Forests, *Wild and Managed: Differences and Consequences*, ed. A.F. Pearson and D.A. Challenger. Vancouver, B.C.: Students for Forestry Awareness, University of British Columbia, 1990.

L.D. Harris. *The Fragmented Forest.* Chicago: The University of Chicago Press, 1984.

M.L. Hunter et al. Paleoecology and the Coarse-filter Approach to Maintaining Biological Diversity. *Conservation Biology* 2 (4) (1988): 375-385.

T. King. Water, *Miracle of Nature*. New York: Collier Books, 1961.

J.W. Thomas, technical editor. *Wildlife Habitats in Managed Forests: The Blue Mountains of Oregon and Washington*. USDA Forest Service, Agriculture Handbook No. 553, 1979.

A. Vittachi. *Earth Conference One*. Boston: New Science Library, 1989.

Chapter 12: Fire in Our Future

J.K. Agee. *Fire Ecology of Pacific Northwest Forests*. Covelo, CA: Island Press, 1993.

J.K. Agee and R.E. Edmonds. Forest Protection Guidelines for the Northern Spotted Owl. In *Recovery Plan for the Northern Spotted Owl*: App. F. Washington, D.C.: USDI Fish and Wildlife Service, 1992.

J.K. Agee and M.H. Huff. Structure and Process Goals for Vegetation in Wilderness Areas. In *Proceedings: National Wilderness Research Conference*. USDA For. Serv. Gen. Tech. Rep. INT-212, 1986. pp. 17-25

J.K. Agee and D.R. Johnson. *Ecosystem Management for Parks and Wilderness*. Seattle: University of Washington Press, 1988.

L. Bancroft, T. Nichols, D. Parsons, D. Graber, B. Evison and J.W. van Waglendonk. Evolution of the Natural Fire Management Program at Sequoia and Kings Canyon National Parks. In *Proceedings: Symposium and Workshop on Wilderness Fire*, tech. coords. J.E. Lotan et al. USDA For. Serv. Gen. Tech. Rep. INT-182, 1985. pp. 174-180.

T.M. Bonnicksen. Ecological Information Base for Park and Wilderness Fire Management Planning. In *Proceedings: Symposium and Workshop on Wilderness Fire*, tech. coords. J.E. Lotan et al., USDA For. Serv. Gen. Tech. Rep. INT-182, 1985. pp. 168-173.

N.L. Christensen, J.K. Agee, P.F. Brussard, J. Hughes, D.H. Knight, G.W. Minsall, J.M. Peek, S.J. Pyne, F.J. Swanson, J.W. Thomas, S. Wells, S.E. Williams and H.A. Wright. Interpreting the Yellowstone Fires. *Bioscience* 39 (1989): 678-85.

F.E. Clements. Experimental Ecology in the Public Service. *Ecology* 16 (1935): 342-63.

Department of Natural Resources. *Washington Smoke Management Program Annual Report*: 1991. Olympia, WA: Division of Fire Control, Washington Department of Natural Resources, 1992.

M.D. Flannigan and C.E. Van Wagner. Climate Change and Wildfire in Canada. *Can. J. for Res.* 21 (1991): 66-72.

J.F. Franklin, F.J. Swanson, M.E. Harmon, D.A. Perry, T.A. Spies, V.H. Dale, A. McKee, W.K. Ferrell, J.E. Means, S.V. Gregory, J.D. Lattin, T.D. Schowalter and D. Larsen. Effects of Global Climatic Change on Forests in Northwestern North America. *Northwest Envir.* J. 7 (1991): 233-54.

J.F. Franklin. Scientific Basis for New Perspectives in Forests and Streams. In *Watershed Management: Balancing Sustainability and Environmental Change*, ed. R.J. Naimen. New York: Springer-Verlag, 1992. pp. 25-72.

W.R. Gast Jr., D.W. Scott, C. Schmitt, D. Clemens, S. Howes, C.G. Johnson, R. Mason, F. Mohr and R.A. Clapp Jr. *Blue Mountains Forest Health Report: New*

Perspectives in Forest Health. USDA For. Serv., Pacific Northwest Region, Malheur, Umatilla, and Wallowa-Whitman National Forests, 1991.

C.S. Holling. *Adaptive Environmental Assessment and Management.* London and New York: John Wiley and Sons, 1978.

D. Hopwood. *Principles and Practices of New Forestry.* B.C. Ministry of Forests Land Manage. Rep. 71, 1991.

J. Leverenz and D.J. Lev. Effects of Carbon Dioxide-induced Changes on the Natural Ranges of Six Major Commercial Tree Species in the Western United States. In *The greenhouse Effect, Climate Change, and U.S. Forests,* ed. E.W. Shands and J.S. Hoffman. Washington, DC: Conservation Foundation, 1987.

N. Maclean. *Young Men and Fire.* Chicago: University of Chicago Press, 1992.

S.J. Pyne. The Summer We Let Wildfire Loose. *Natural History* (August 1989): 45-49.

W.H. Romme and M.G. Turner. Implications of Global Climate Change for Biogeographic Patterns in the Greater Yellowstone Ecosystem. *Conserv. Biol.* 5 (1991): 373-86.

D.G. Sprugel. Disturbance, Equilibrium, and Environmental Variability: What is "Natural" Vegetation in a Changing Environment? *Biol. Conserv.* 58 (1991): 1-18.

C. Walters. *Adaptive Management of Renewable Natural Resources.* New York: Macmillan, 1986.

Chapter 13: The Worth of a Birch
Suggested Readings

Van Cleve, K., F.S. Chapin III, P.W. Flanagan, L.A. Viereck and C.T. Dyrness, eds. *Forest Ecosystems in the Alaskan Taiga.* New York: Springer-Verlag, 1986.

Viereck, L.A. and E.L. Little. *Alaska Trees and Shrubs.* Washington, D.C.: Forest Service, U.S. Department of Agriculture, 1972.

Sampson, George R. et al. *Alaska's Agriculture and Forestry,* Forestry in Alaska. Cooperative Extension Service, University of Alaska and U.S. Dept. of Agriculture, 1983.

Burns, Russell M. and Barbara H. Honkaka. *Silvics of North America, Volume 2, Hardwoods.* Washington, D.C.: Forest Service, U.S. Department of Agriculture, 1990.

Scagliotti, Lisa. "The Sweet Science." *Anchorage Daily News,* 30 May 1993.

Woodring, Jeannie. "Big Bowl Business." *Alaska Business Monthly,* November 1993, p. 40.

Chapter 14: The Effect of Nature-oriented Forestry on Forest Genetics
Note

1. A single birch and its descendants can produce so many seeds in 28 years that the entire mainland of the Earth could be thickly forested with them (Rohmeder and Schoenbach 1959).

References

Malhotra, Kailash. Social Forestry and the Arabari Experiment. In *Forests as Living Space and Economic Factor*. Bombay: Max Mueller Bhavan, 1989. p. 51-54.

Rohmeder, E. and H. Schoenbach. *Genetik und Zuechtung der Waldbaeume*. Hamburg und Berlin, 1959. 383 pp.

Chapter 18:
Sustainable Forestry at the Crossroads: Hard Lessons for the World
Notes

Thanks to Christoph Wiedmer, forest campaigner, Greenpeace Switzerland, Zürich, Andres Rohner, forest engineer and Michael Dipner, both Basel, Switzerland for background information on the Swiss forest industry. The principal author acknowledges support by grant number 82100-04025 from the Swiss National Foundation (Schweizer Nationalfonds). Photographs by Eidgenössische Anstalt für das Forstwesen (EAFV), Monika Jäggi.

1. This article is a substantially revised version of an article published in the *International Journal of Ecoforestry* 10, 4 (1994): 166-173.
2. This number applies for the canton of Baselland and might be different in other cantons according to the cantonal law.

References

Angus, J.T. *A Deo Victoria: The Story of the Georgian Bay Lumber Company*. Chapter 14. Thunder Bay: Severn, 1990.

Berkes, Fikret et al. Comanagement: The Evolution in Theory and Practice of Joint Administration of Living Resources. *Alternatives* 18(2) (1991): 12-18.

Brugger, Ernst A. et al., eds. *Zur Ökoeffizienz multinationaler Unternehmen in Entwicklungsländern*. Kurzfassung NFP 28. Geographisches Institut Universität Bern, 1994.

Bundesamt für Statistik et al. *Nachhaltige Holznutzung*. Press release nr. 65/94, 10 August 1994.

Bundesamt für Statistik. *Schweizerische Forststatistik* 1993. Press release, 10 August 1994.

Burnand, Jacques et al. *Waldgesellschaften und Waldstandorte im unteren Baselbiet*. Verlag des Kantons Baselland, 1991.

CH-Forschung. Forschung auf Windwurfflächen (3) (1996): 1-6.

Dunster, Julian A. Forest Conservation Strategies in Canada. A Challenge for the Nineties. *Alternatives* 16 (4)/17 (1) (1990): 44-51.

Flader, Susan, ed. *The Great Lakes Forest. An Environmental and Social History*. Minneapolis: University of Minnesota Press, 1983.

Forestry Canada. *The State of Canada's Forests* 1992. Ottawa, Ontario: Forestry Canada, 1993.

Forstwart/Förster - Berufsbild. Waldwirtschaft Verband Schweiz. Biberist, 1991.

Gubler, Thomas. Die strukturelle Krise der Schweizer Waldwirtschaft. *Basler Zeitung*, 3 November 1994.

Hasler, Barbara. Leise rieselt der Wald.... *Tagesanzeiger*, 16 August 1994.

Jahrbuch der schweizerischen Wald-und Holzwirtschaft 1992: Das Wichtigste in Kürze. Bern: Bundesamt für Statistik, 1993.

Jahresstatistik. Schweizerische Aussenhandelsstatistik. Bern: Zweiter Band, 1993.

Jimmie, Chief Roger. Timber Supply from a First Nations Perspective: 'Maybe Squirrel He Climb that Tree,' pp. 164-70. In *Canada's Timber Resources*, ed. D.G. Brand. Hull, Quebec: Forestry Canadam 1991.

Jordi, Beat. Ökolabel: Schweizer Holzwirtschaft steht abseits. *Basler Zeitung*, 5 Juni 1996.

Köhl, M. Vom Ersten Landesforstinventar zur Permanenten Waldbeoachtung. *Schweizerische Zeitschrift für das Forstwesen* 146 (12) (1995): 991-1013.

Marchak, Patricia. *Logging the Globe.* Vancouver: McGill-Queens University Press, 1995.

M'Gonigle, Michael and Ben Parfitt. *Forestopia: A Practical Guide to the New Forest Economy.* Madeira Park, B.C.: Harbor, 1994.

Nelles, H.V. *The Politics of Development: Forests, Mines and Hydro-Electric Power in Ontario, 1849-1941.* Toronto, Ontario: MacMillan, 1974.

Nesper, L. and Pecore, M. 'The Trees will Last Forever,' The Integrity of their Forest Signifies the Health of the Menominee People. *Cultural Survival Quarterly* (Spring 1993): 28-31.

Netting, R. McC. *Balancing on an Alp.* Cambridge: Cambridge University Press, 1981.

Niesslein, Erwin. Can Historical Research Be of Help in Forest Policy Decisions. In *History of Sustained Yield Forestry*, ed. H. Steen, pp 16-20. Santa Cruz, California: Forest History Society, 1984.

Ontario Round Table on Environment and Economy. *Native People's Circle on Environment and Development.* Toronto, 1992.

Patterson, Doug. Consumers, Certification and Changing Patterns. *International Journal of Ecoforestry* 10 (1) (1994): 5.

Pratt, Larry and Ian Urquhart. *The Last Great Forest. Japanese Multinationals and Alberta's Northern Forest.* Edmonton, AB: NeWest Press, 1994.

Raphael, Ray. *More Tree Talk: The People, Politics, and Economics of Timber.* Washington: D.C. Island Press, 1994.

Richardson, Mary et al. *Winning Back the Words: Confronting Experts in an Environmental Hearing.* Toronto: Garamond Press, 1993.

Schweizerisches Bundesgesetz über den Wald. Art. 20-24, 1992.

Sedjo, Roger. Global Consequences of U.S. Environmental Policy. *Journal of Forestry* 91 (4) (1993): 19-21.

Sullivan, James. Why Should I Care About Criteria and Indicators? *International Journal of Ecoforestry* 10 (2) (1994): 76-80.

United Nations Conference on Environment and Development (UNCED). 1992. Bericht der Schweiz. Konferenz. Bundesamt für Umwelt, Wald und Landschaft BUWAL, Bern, 1992.

Wagner, Murray. Footsteps Along the Road. Indian Claims and Access to Natural Resources. *Alternatives* 18 (2) (1991): 22-28.

Western Canada Wilderness Committee. *A New Leaf. Real Sustainability for the Boreal Forest.* Video, Edmonton, 1993.

WWF (World Wildlife Fund) Switzerland. Wald. *Panda,* 2, 1984.

Chapter 20: The Bradley Method of Bush Regeneration
Notes

For more on the Bradley Method, see Joan Bradley, *Bringing Back the Bush, The Bradley Method of Bush Regeneration,* Sydney: Lansdowne Press, 1988.

References

Commoner, Barry. *The Closing Circle.* New York: Bantam, 1972.

Jeffers, Robinson. *Selected Poetry.* New York: Vintage, 1965.

Leopold, Aldo. *A Sand County Almanac.* New York and London: Oxford, 1949.

Chapter 22:
"The Earth's Blanket:" Traditional Aboriginal Attitudes Towards Nature

The author expresses her sincere gratitude to the many wise and knowledgeable aboriginal people who have taught her about traditional plant use. She especially acknowledges the late Annie York (Nlaka'pamux), the late Edith O'Donaghey (Stl'atl'imx), the late Jorn Thomas (Ditidaht), Mary Thomas (Secwepemc), Kenneth Eaglespeaker (Blackfoot) and Kim Recalma-Clutesi (Kwakwaka'wakw) for the information contained here. Robert D. Turner, Alison Davis and David Bosnich provided helpful editorial council.

Boas, Franz. *Religion of the Kwakiutl Indians.* Columbia University Contributions to Anthropology, Vol. 10, Part 1, Texts; Part 2, Translations. New York: Columbia University Press, 1930.

Gottesfeld, Leslie M. Johnson. The Importance of Bark Products in the Aboriginal Economies of Northwestern British Columbia, Canada. *Economic Botany* 46 (2) (1992): 148-157.

Kuhnlein, Harriet V. and Nancy J. Turner. *Traditional Plant Foods of Canadian Indigenous Peoples. Nutrition, Botany and Use.* Volume 8. In Food and Nutrition in History and Anthropology, ed. Solomon Katz. Philadelphia, Pennsylvania: Gordon and Breach Science Publishers, 1991.

McAllister, Don E. and Erich Haber. Western Yew—Precious Medicine. *Canadian Biodiversity* 1 (2) (1991): 2-4.

Turner, Nancy J. and Richard J. Hebda. Contemporary Use of Bark for Medicine by Two Salishan Native Elders of Southeast Vancouver Island, Canada. *Journal of Ethnopharmacology* 29 (1990): 59-72.

Turner, Nancy J., Laurence C. Thompson, M. Terry Thompson and Annie Z. York. *Thompson Ethnobotany: Knowledge and Usage of Plants by the Thompson [Nlaka'pamus] Indians of British Columbia.* Royal British Columbia Museum Memoir No. 3, Victoria, 1990.

Chapter 29: The Bioregional Basis for Certification: Why Cascadia?

1.   Robert Putnam, *Making Democracy Work: Civic Traditions in Italy,* Princeton,

N.J.: Princeton University Press, 1993.

Chapter 30: Certifying Ecologically Responsible Forest Use and Restoration: Future Direction for the Ecoforestry Movement
1. C.A. Bowers, *Educating for an Ecologically Sustainable Culture*, Albany, NY: SUNY Press, 1996.
2. Ibid., p. 12.

Chapter 31: An Ecoforestry Land Stewardship Trust Model
For further information, legal documents or technical advice please contact:
Tyhson Banighen, Turtle Island Earth Stewards, Box 3308, Salmon Arm, B.C. V1E 4S1. Phone (250) 832-3993, Fax (250) 832-9942, e-mail: ties@jetstream.net
Barbier, Edward. "The Concept of Sustainable Economic Development." *Environmental Conservation*. Vol. 14, No. 2 (Summer 1987), p. 101-110.
Clague, Michael. Community Economic Development in British Columbia. Vancouver: SPARC Status Report IV, August 1986.
Hardin, G. "The Tragedy of the Commons." *Science* 162 (1968): 1234-1248.
ICE (Institute for Community Economics). *The Land Trust Book*. Emaus: Rodale, 1988.
Leopold, Aldo. *A Sand Country Almanac*. New York: Ballantine Books, 1966.
Raphael, Ray. *Tree Talk: The People and Politics of Timber*. Island Press, 1981. p. 235.
Rusland, Peter. "Lasqueti Feuds Tax." *The Parksville-Qualicum Beach News*. Tues., April 18, 1989.
World Commission on Environment and Development (WCED). *Our Common Future*. Oxford: Oxford University Press, 1987.

Chapter 32: The Economics of Ecoforestry
1. J. Drescher, "The Heavy Healthy Forest and the Sickness of Heavily Mechanized Harvesting," New Germany, Nova Scotia: Windhorse, 1995.
2. J. Drescher, "The Battle for Sustainability," A talk given to the Ecoforestry Institute in Victoria, British Columbia, 13 November 1993, New Germany, Nova Scotia: Windhorse (reprinted in this anthology); J. Drescher and A. Scott, "Mimicking Natural Patchiness," 1994.
3. J. Drescher, "Clearcut Death for Atlantic Salmon," A report prepared for the LaHave River Salmon Association, November, 1994.
4. J. Drescher, "Three Systems of Forest Harvesting in the Maritimes," *International Journal of Ecoforestry*, Fall, 1994.

Chapter 38: Nature as a Reflection of Self and Society
1. One of the best descriptions to date of this type of "free flow" experience is to be found in John A. Livingston's *The Fallacy of Wildlife Conservation* (Toronto: McClelland and Stewart Ltd., 1981), Chapters Four and Five.
2. Neil Evernden, *The Natural Alien: Humankind and Environment* (Toronto: University of Toronto Press, 1985), p. 10.

SELECT BIBLIOGRAPHY

I. Philosophical Context

Bowers, C.A. *Education, Cultural Myths, and the Ecological Crisis*. Albany, N.Y.: SUNY Press, 1993.

Devall, B. *Simple in Means, Rich in Ends: Practicing Deep Ecology*. Salt Lake City, UT: Gibb Smith, 1988.

Devall, B. and Sessions, G. *Deep Ecology: Living as if Nature Mattered*. Salt Lake City, UT: Gibb Smith, 1985.

Drengson, A. *Beyond Environmental Crisis: From Technocrat to Planetary Person*. N.Y.: Peter Lang, 1989.

Drengson, A. and Inoue, Yuichi, eds. *The Deep Ecology Movement: An Introductory Anthology*. Berkeley: North Atlantic Books, 1995.

Fox, W. *Toward a Transpersonal Ecology: Developing New Foundations for Environmentalism*. Boston: Shambala, 1990.

Mathews, F. *The Ecological Self*. Savage, MD: Barnes and Noble, 1991.

McLaughlin, A. *Regarding Nature: Industrialism and Deep Ecology*. Albany, N.Y.: SUNY, 1993.

Naess, A. *Ecology, Community, and Lifestyle*. London: Cambridge University Press, 1991.

Snyder, G. *The Practice of the Wild*. San Francisco: North Point, 1990.

II. The Theory and Practice of Ecoforestry

Camp, O. *The Forest Farmer's Handbook: A Guide to Natural Selection Management*. Ashland: Sky River, 1984.

Hammond, H. *Seeing the Forest Among the Trees: The Case for Wholistic Forest Use*. Vancouver: Polestar Press, 1991.

Head, S. and Heinzman, R., eds. *Lessons of the Rainforest*. San Francisco, CA: Sierra Club Books, 1990.

Kaza, S. *The Attentive Heart: Conversations With Trees*. N.Y.: Fawcett-Columbine of Ballantine Books, 1993.

Maser, C. *The Forest Primeval*. San Francisco: Sierra Books, 1990.

Maser, C. and Sedell, J. *The Forest to the Sea: The Ecology of Wood in Streams, Rivers, Estuaries and Oceans*. Delray, FL: St. Lucie Press, 1994.

Pilarski, M., ed. *Restoration Forestry: An International Guide to Sustainable Forestry*

Practices. Durango, CO: Kivaki Press, 1994.

Robinson, G. *The Forest and the Trees: A Guide to Excellent Forestry*. Covelo, CA: Island Press, 1988.

Wilkinson, M. and Loomis, R. *Wildwood: A Forest for the Future*. Gabriola, B.C.: Reflections, 1990.

III. Critiques of Industrial Forestry and Related Topics

Banuri, T. and Marglin, F.A., eds. *Living With the Forests: Knowledge, Power and Environmental Destruction*. London: Zed Books, 1993.

Devall, B., ed. *Clearcut: The Tragedy of Industrial Forestry*. San Francisco, CA: Sierra Club Books and Earth Island Press, 1994.

Drushka, K., Nixon, B., Travers, R., et al. *Touch Wood: B.C. Forests at the Crossroads*. Madeira, B.C.: Harbor Books, 1993.

Ervin, K. *Fragile Majesty: The Battle for North America's Last Great Forest*. Mountaineers. Seattle, 1989.

Maser, C. *The Redesigned Forest*. San Diego, CA: R. and E. Miles, 1988.

M'Gonigle, M. & Parfitt, B. *Forestopia: An Urgent Guide to the Economic Transition of the B.C. Forest Industry*. Vancouver, B.C.: Institute for New Economics, 1994.

O'Toole, R. *Reforming the Forest Service*. Covelo, CA: Island Press, 1988.

Perlin, J. *A Forest Journey: The Role of Wood in the Development of Civilization*. N.Y.: Norton, 1989.

Raphael, R. *Tree Talk: The People and Politics of Timber*. Covelo, CA: Island Press, 1981.

IV. The Larger Environmental and Cultural Context

Berger, J. *Restoring the Earth*. New York: Knopf, 1985.

Berger, John, ed. *Environmental Restoration*. Covelo, CA: Island Press, 1990.

Berry, W. *The Unsettling of America: Culture and Agriculture*. New York: Avon, 1977.

Blackburn, T. and Anderson, K. *Before Wilderness: Environmental Management by Native Californians*. Menlo Park, CA: Ballena Press, 1993.

Boone, A. *The Language of Silence*. New York: Harper and Row, 1970.

Bowers, C.A. *The Cultural Dimensions of Educational Computing: Understanding the Non-Neutrality of Technology*. New York: Teachers College Press, 1988.

Boyd, D. *Rolling Thunder*. New York: Delta, 1974.

Brown, L. et al. *State of the World 1993*. New York: Norton, 1993.

Bruntland, G. *Our Common Future*. London and New York: Oxford University Press, 1988.

Cairns, J., ed. *The Recovery Process in Damaged Ecosystems*. Ann Arbor, MI: Ann Arbor Science Publications, 1980.

Cajete, G. *Look to the Mountains: An Ecology of Indigenous Education*. Durango, CO: Kivaki Press, 1994.

Commoner, B. *The Closing Circle*. N.Y.: Bantam Books, 1972.

Carter, V. and Dale, T. *Civilization and Soil*. Norman: University of Oklahoma Press, 1974.

Daly, H. and Cobb, J. *For the Common Good: Redirecting the Economy Toward Community, the Environment and a Sustainable Future*. Boston: Beacon, 1989.

Drengson, Alan. *Doc Forest and Blue Mountain Ecostery*. Victoria, B.C.: Ecostery House, 1993.

Drengson, Alan. *The Practice of Technology*. Albany, N.Y.: SUNY Press, 1995.

Duncan, D. *The River Why?* N.Y.: Bantam, 1983.

Dunster, J. and K. *Dictionary of Natural Resource Management*. Vancouver, B.C.: UBC, 1996.

Durning, Alan T. *This Place on Earth*. Seattle: Sasquatch Books, 1996.

Ehrlich, P. and A. *Extinction: The Causes and Consequences of the Disappearance of Species*. New York: Random House, 1981.

Goldsmith, E. *The Way: An Ecological Worldview*. Boston: Shambala, 1993.

Gore, A. *Earth in the Balance: Ecology and the Human Spirit*. New York: Houghton Mifflin, 1992.

Gradwohl, J. and Greenburg, R. *Saving the Tropical Forests*. Washington, D.C.: Smithsonian Institute, 1978.

Harrison, H.P. *Forests: Shadow of Civilization*. Chicago: Univ. of Chicago Press, 1992.

Harker, D. and K., and Evans, S. and M., eds. *Landscape Restoration Handbook*. Boca Raton, FL: Lewis Publications, 1992.

Harner, M. *The Way of the Shaman*. New York: Bantam, 1986.

Henderson, H. *Creating Alternative Futures: The End of Economics*. New York: Harper and Row, 1978.

Hughes, D. *American Indian Ecology*. El Paso: Texas Western Press, 1983.

Hyams, E. *Soil and Civilization*. New York: Harper and Row, 1976.

Jackson, W., Berry, W., and Colman, B. *Meeting the Expectations of the Land: Essays in Sustainable Agriculture*. San Francisco, CA: North Point, 1984.

Jordon, W.R., Gilpin, M.E., and Abers, J.D., eds. *Restoration Ecology: A Synthetic Approach to Ecological Research*. London and New York: Cambridge, 1987.

Kusler, J. and Kentula, M., eds. *Wetlands Creation and Restoration*. Covelo, CA: Island Press, 1990.

Leopold, A. *A Sand County Almanac*. New York and London: Oxford, 1949.

Macy, J. *World as Lover, World as Self*. Berkeley, CA: Parallax Press, 1991.

Mander, J. *In the Absence of the Sacred: The Failure of Technology and the Survival of the Indian Nations*. San Francisco, CA: Sierra Books, 1991.

Mander, J. and Goldsmith, E. *The Case Against the Global Economy, and for a Turn to the Local*. San Francisco, CA: Sierra Club Books, 1996.

McRobbie, G. *Small is Possible*. London: Abacus, 1989.

Meadows, D. and R. *The Limits to Growth*. Universe, New York: Club of Rome, 1972.

Naess, A. *Gandhi and Group Conflict: An Exploration of Satyragraha, Theoretical Background*. Oslo, Norway: Universitetsforlaget, 1974.

Norberg-Hodge, H. *Ancient Futures: Learning from Ladakh*. San Francisco, CA: Sierra Books, 1991.

Orr, D. Ecological Literacy: *Education and the Transition to a Post Modern World*.

Albany, N.Y.: SUNY Press, 1992.

Pianka, E. *Evolutionary Ecology*. New York: Harper and Row, 1978.

Ponting, C. *A Green History of the World*. New York and London: Penguin, 1993.

Quinn, D. *Ishmael*. New York: Bantam, 1993.

Savory, A. *Wholistic Resource Management*. Covelo, CA: Island Press, 1988.

Scherer, D. and Attig, T. *Ethics and the Environment*. Englewood Cliffs, NJ: Prentice Hall, 1983.

Schumacher, E.F. *Small is Beautiful: Economics as if People Mattered*. New York: Harper and Row, 1973.

Schumacher, E.G. *Good Work*. New York: Harper and Row, 1979.

Shepard, P. and McKinley, D. *The Subversive Science: Essays Toward an Ecology of Man*. New York.: Houghton Mifflin, 1967.

Shiva, V. *Monocultures of the Mind: Biodiversity, Biotechnology and the Third World*. Penang, Malaysia: Third World Network, 1993.

Soulé, M. & Wilcox, M. *Conservation Biology*. Vol. 1, New York: Sinauer, 1980.

Soulé, M. Conservation Biology. Vol. 2, New York: Sinauer, 1986.

Smith, J.R. *Tree Crops: A Permanent Agriculture*. Covelo, CA: Island Press, 1950.

Taylor, D.M. *Off Course: Restoring Balance Between Canadian Society and the Environment*. Ottawa, ON: IDRC, 1994.

Wilson, E.O. *The Diversity of Life*. Cambridge, MA: Harvard Press, 1992.

CONTACTS

The following is a list of organizations that practise or promote to a greater or lesser extent various ecoforestry ideas and principles. This is but a small sampling of such groups and is by no means meant to be a complete or exhaustive listing of ecoforestry practioners.

Canada

1. SILVA Forest Foundation
    Box 9, Slocan Park
    British Columbia, Canada V0G 2E0
    Tel: (250) 226-7222, Fax: (250) 226-7446

2. Ecoforestry Institute Society
    P.O. Box 5070, Stn. B
    Victoria, British Columbia
    Canada V8R 6S8
    Tel: (250) 477-8479, Fax: (250) 721-5579

3. Wildwood Forest
    RR 3
    Ladysmith, British Columbia
    Canada V0R 2E0
    Tel: (250) 722-2853

4. Haliburton Forest and Wild Life Reserve
    RR 1
    Haliburton, ON
    Canada K0M 1S0
    Tel: (705) 754-2198, Fax: (705) 754-1179

5. Weathervane Institute
    R.R. 2, New Germany
    Nova Scotia, Canada B0R 1E0

6. Ecoforestry School in the Maritimes
    R.R. 2, New Germany
    Nova Scotia, Canada B0R 1E0

7. Turtle Island Earth Stewards
    Tyhson Banighen
    Box 3308
    Salmon Arm, B.C.
    Canada V1E 4S1
    Tel: (250) 832-3993, Fax (250) 832-9942
    e-mail: ties@jetstream.net

U.S.A.

1. Ecoforestry Institute
    785 Barton Rd.
    Glendale, Oregon, U.S.A. 97442
    Tel./Fax: (541) 832-2785

2. Institute for Sustainable Forestry
    P.O. Box 1580
    Redway, California, U.S.A. 95560
    Tel: (707) 923-4719, Fax: (707) 923-4257

3. Rainforest Alliance Smart Wood Certification Program
    270 Lafayette St., Suite 512
    New York, New York
    U.S.A. 10012
    Tel: (212) 941-1900, Fax: (212) 941-4986

4. Rogue Institute for Ecology and Economy
    Box 3213
    Ashland, Oregon, U.S.A. 97520
    Tel: (503) 482-6031

5. Forest Trust
P.O. Box 519
Santa Fe, New Mexico, U.S.A. 87504
Tel: (505) 983-8992

6. Nature Conservancy
1815 N. Lynn Street
Arlington, Virginia, U.S.A. 22209
Tel: (703) 841-5300

7. Forest Reform Network
Ned Fritz
5934 Royal Lane, Suite 223
Dallas, Texas U.S.A. 75230
Tel./Fax: (214) 352-8370

8. American Wildlands
7500 E. Arapahoe Road, Suite 355
Englewood, Colorado, U.S.A. 80112

9. Protect Our Woods
P.O. Box 352
Paoli, Indiana, U.S.A. 47454
Tel: (812) 723-2430

10. Headwaters
P.O. Box 727
Ashland, Oregon, U.S.A. 97520
Tel: (503) 482-4459, Fax: (503) 482-7282

11. Michigan Forest Advocates
7015 Thilhorn Rd.
Sheboygan, Michigan, U.S.A. 49721
Tel: (616) 627-6691

12. Native Forest Action Council
P.O. Box 2171
Eugene, Oregon, U.S.A. 97402
Tel: (503) 249-2958

13. Center for Woodlands Culture and Alternative
Forestry Research
1 Main St., P.O. Box 73
Strafford, Vermont, U.S.A. 05072
Tel: (802) 765-4337, Fax: (802) 765-4262

14. Northwoods Citizens for a Sustainable Forest
8333 Bemidji, Minnesota, U.S.A. 56601
Tel: (218) 751-7676

15. Society for the Protection of New Hampshire
Forests
54 Portsmouth St.
Concord, New Hampshire, U.S.A. 03301
Tel: (603) 224-9945

16. Waldee Forest
Walton R. Smith
221 Huckleberry Creek Road
Franklin, North Carolina, U.S.A. 28734
Tel: (704) 524-3186

17. Ecotrust
1200 NW Front Ave.
Portland, Oregon, U.S.A. 97209
Tel: (503) 227-6225

18. Forest Land Management Committee
8400 Rocky Lane SE
Olympia, Washington, U.S.A. 98513
Tel: (206) 459-0946

19. Forestcare Company
P.O. Box 38
Lorraine, Oregon, U.S.A. 97451
Tel: (503) 942-5424

20. Institute for Sustainable Forestry
P.O. Box 1580
Redway, California, U.S.A. 95560
Tel: (707) 923-4719, Fax: (707) 923-4257

21. Olympic Peninsula Foundation
1200 W. Simms Way, Suite 201
Port Townsend, Washington
U.S.A. 98368
Tel: (206) 385-9421

22. Wood Forum
P.O. Box 2012
Bellingham, Washington
U.S.A. 98227
Tel: (503) 856-4947

23. Woodworkers Alliance for Rainforest Protection
Box 133
Coos Bay, Oregon, U.S.A. 97420

24. Yuba Watershed Institute
    17790 Tyler Foote Road
    Nevada City, California, U.S.A. 95959
    Tel: (916) 478-0817

25. Camp Forest Farm
    2100 Thompson Creek Road
    Selma, Oregon, U.S.A. 97538
    Tel: (503) 579-4313, Fax: (503) 579-4044

26. Cerro Gordo Forestry Cooperative
    Dorena Lake, Box 569
    Cottage Grove, Oregon, U.S.A. 97424

27. Smilin'O Forest Farm
    70417 Follett Rd.
    Elgin, Oregon, U.S.A. 97827
    Tel: (503) 437-5252

28. Wild Iris Forestry
    Box 1423, Redway, California, U.S.A. 95560
    Tel: (707) 923-2344

29. Pacific Forest Trust
    PO Box 879
    Boonville, CA 95419
    Tel: (707) 895-2090, Fax: (707) 895-2138
    e-mail: pft@pacific.net

Finland

1. Timo Helle, President
   Finnnish Association for Nature Conservation
   Rovaniemi, Finland
   http://www.sll.fi/trn/index.html

Sweden

1. Swedish Society for Nature
   Box 245 S-401 24 Goteborg
   Sweden
   Tel: 46-31 803835, Fax: 46-31 153305

2. Tiaga Rescue Network
   AJJTE Box 116
   S-96223 Jokkmokk, Sweden
   Tel: 46-971-17037, Fax: 46-971-12057
   email: tiaga@jokkmokk.se

Norway

1. Natur og Umgdom
   Attn: Frode Pleym
   Torgatta 34, 0183 Oslo, Norway
   Tel: 47-22-36-42-18, Fax: 47-22-20-45-94
   http://www.grida.no/ngo/nu/

2. Naturvernforbundet I Oslo og Akerhus
   Attn: Gjermund Anderson
   Maridasveien 120, 0461 Oslo, Norway
   Tel: 47-22-38-35-20. Fax: 47-22-71-63-48
   http://omni.uio.no/noa/

3. Agriculture University of Norway
   Norwegian Institute for Forest Research
   Attn: Joerund Rolstad
   N-1430, Aas, Norway

Russia

1. Biodiversity Conservation Center
   G-270, a/ya. 602
   119270, Moscow, Russia
   Tel: (095) 111-41-80

2. Siberian Forests Protection Project
   Pacific Environment and Resources Center
   (PERC)
   Fort Cronkhite Bldg. 1055
   Sausalito, California, U.S.A. 94965
   Tel: (415) 332-8200, Fax: (415) 331-2722

Scotland

1. Reforesting Scotland
   5 Holyrood Road
   Edinburgh, Scotland EH8 8AE
   Tel: (0131) 557-6997, Fax: (0131) 558-1550

2. Trees for Life
   The Park, Findhorn Bay
   Forres, Scotland, IV36 0TZ
   Tel: 01309-691292,
   Fax: 01309-691155 or 690933

3. Millennium Forest for Scotland
   P.O. Box No. 16063
   Glasgow, Scotland, G12 9YE

Germany

Luebeck City Forest
Office of the Head Forester,
23896 Ritzerau
* Foresthaus, Germany
Tel: 49-4508-1072

India

1. Sunderlal Bahuguna
   Chipco Information Center
   P.O. Silyara Via-Ghansali
   Tehri-Garhwal, U.P., 249155
   India
   Fax: Delhi 91-11-4364914 or 91-11-4360784

2. Save the Seeds Movement
   Tehri Garhwal District
   Uttar Pradesh, India
   Contact: Parveen Sikand
   parveen@slblr:frlht.ernet.in

Africa

1. The Forestry Association of Botswana (FAB)
   P.O. Box 2088
   Gaborone, Botswana
   Tel: (267) 35-1660, Fax: (267) 30-0316

2. Friends of the Trees Society of Ghana
   P.O. Box A227
   La, Accra, Ghana

3. Green Belt Movement
   P.O. Box 14832
   Nairobi, Kenya
   Tel: 254-24634

4. Africa Tree Center
   R.T. Mazibuko
   P.O. Box 90
   Plessislaer, 4500, Natal
   Republic of South Africa

Central and South America

1. Arbofilia
   Apdo 512 Tibas, 1100, Costa Rica
   Tel: (506) 35-54-70

2. Proyecto Desarrollo del Bosque Latifoliado
   P.O. Box 427
   La Ceiba, Honduras
   Tel./Fax: (504) 43-1032

3. INIFAP - Mexico Forestry Research
   Patricia Negreros Castillo, Director
   Calle 62, No. 462-205
   Merida, Yucatan, Mexico
   Tel: 99 24-77-64 Fax: 99 23-93-03

4. Union de Comunidades y Ejidos Forestales
   Zapotecas y Chinantecas (UCEFO)
   Domicilio Conocido
   Capulalpan de Mendez
   Ixtlan, Oaxaca, Mexico
   Tel: (52-951) 69233

5. Ayacara Project
   Pablo Sandor
   Avenida Suecia 567
   Provedencia, Santiago, Chili

6. Fundacion Lahuen
   Orrego Luco 054
   Providencia, Santiago, Chili
   Tel: +56-2-234-2617

New Zealand

1. Native Restoration Trust
   P.O. Box 80-007
   Green Bay, Auckland 7, New Zealand
   Tel: (04) 724-250

2. Maruia Society
   P.O. Box 756
   Nelson, New Zealand

Japan

1. World Wildlife Fund Japan
   Nihon Seimei Bldg., 3-1-14
   Siba, Minato-ku
   Tokyo 105 Japan

GLOSSARY

This glossary is compiled from contributions submitted by Herb Hammond, Alan Drengson and Alan Wittbecker. Those who want a more complete lexicon relevant to the topics discussed in this book should consult the *Dictionary of Natural Resource Management*, edited by Julian and Katherine Dunster, University of British Columbia Press, Vancouver, 1996.

Abiotic The nonliving component of the environment (from the Greek "not living").

Access road A road built into isolated stands of commercial timber so the forest can be reached by loggers, firefighters and others.

Acre A unit of land measurement: 43,560 square feet or 10 square chains.

Actual cut The amount of timber cut from a forest at one time, as opposed to the amount planned or offered for sale.

Afforestation The planting of trees where they have been absent.

Agroforestry Land-use practice where trees are integrated with crops and animals in the same area.

All-aged Applied to a stand in which, theoretically, trees of all ages up to, including, and beyond those of the felling age are found. See also even-aged and uneven-aged.

Allowable Annual Cut (AAC) An estimate of the timber volume that can be cut from an area on an annual basis, allegedly in perpetuity.

Allowable Sale Quantity (ASQ) A target level for harvesting a maximum amount, especially in U.S. National Forests.

Annual ring A ring of wood put on each year by a growing tree, composed of spring and autumn wood. Viewed in cross-section, the age of the tree may be determined.

Anthropocentrism has two forms. The trivial one arises from the truism that all humans think and feel as humans. It is said we cannot get out of this species-centered condition. This is akin to saying that a male can only speak and see as a male, which is true, but this does not entail patriarchal bias for all males. In the nontrivial sense, anthropocentrism is a bias which holds that only humans have intrinsic value; everything else is of instrumental value to them. All nature is a resource for human use. In contrast with anthropocentrism, ecocentrism recognizes and seeks to appreciate and respect the multitude of intrinsic values found in the natural world.

Appropriate technology is designed and used as if humans and nature matter. It is technology based on ecocentric values. It is low-impact, thermodynamically sound, ecologically balanced, locally controlled, knowledge-rich and labor-intensive, in contrast to the megatechnology systems of our dominant culture. The appropriate technology movement started in the Third World, but it is rapidly growing in industrial nations.

Autopoeisis Literally self-making and self-organizing (F. Varela, from the Greek), as a natural forest is autopoeitic.

Back fire A fire intentionally set along the inner edge of a control line located ahead of an advancing fire. The back fire is set against an unwanted fire to exhaust the fuel, so that when the two fires meet, both go out.

Backcut The final cut made in a tree to sever the wood and allow it to fall.

Bark The active layer of tissues (inner) between the cambium and recent periderm, or the dead layer of tissue outside the recent periderm.

Biological diversity The variety and variability in living organisms and the ecological patterns of which they are part.

Biological productivity The capacity to concentrate biomass.

Biomass The weight of organic matter.

Biome An extensive community of organisms, e.g., the northern coniferous forest, determined by and determining climate and soil.

Biotic Composed of living beings.

Board foot (b.f.) The volume of wood contained in an area with outside dimensions of 12 x 12 x 1 in.

Board measure (b.m.) Signifying measurement in board foot or feet.

Bole The stem or trunk of a tree, usually the lower, usable or merchantable portion of the trunk.

Broadcast burn A controlled fire over the entire surface of a designated area.

Broadleaf A tree with two cotyledons, or seed leaves; it usually is deciduous, that is, it sheds all its leaves annually. Broad-leaved trees, such as maple and oak, have relatively broad, flat leaves, as contrasted with the conifers, which have needles.

Buck To saw felled trees into logs or bolts. The person who does it is a bucker.

Buffer forest A forest that separates two areas, such as a wild forest and an agricultural field, usually to protect one.

Burl A hard, woody growth on a tree trunk or on roots, more or less rounded in form, usually the result of entwined growth of a cluster of buds. In lumber, a burl produces a distorted and unusual (but often attractive) grain.

Cambium The innermost living bark or a laterally disposed sheath of generative tissues usually found between the xylem and phloem, giving rise to secondary xylem (wood) and phloem.

Canopy The upper level of vegetation in a forest.

Cant A log partially or wholly square cut.

Carbohydrate A chemical compound, such as sugar, starch, or cellulose, that contains carbon, hydrogen, and oxygen.

Carbon An abundant, basic, nonmetallic element that occurs in all organic compounds and many inorganic ones.

Carbon reservoir An area, e.g., coal beds, where carbon has accumulated due to the activity of a carbon sink, which is an area where the rate of uptake exceeds the rate of release.

Carrying capacity The number of individuals in any one species that can live in a habitat without degrading it.

Cellulose A major constituent of woody cell walls. A carbohydrate of long-chained polymers combined in microfibrils. Paper is made up of tiny matted wood fibres or cellulose.

Certification Endorsement or verification by a forest foundation or other agent that timber is grown and managed according to certain standard procedures. Certification systems are based on a range of social and ecological requirements. Ecologically responsible forest use represents the most stringent level of certification.

Chaos theory The formal thought that small changes can lead to major effects, as when the extinction of a fungus could destabilize an ecosystem (or butterfly cause a hurricane).

Character (of a forest ecosystem) A description of how a particular forest ecosystem works, from the largest landscape level to the smallest stand or patch. For example, forests that have frequent fires have a different character from forests where wind and root decay are the primary agents of disturbance. Some forests are characterized by steep slopes, shallow soils, and well-defined drainage patterns, while other forests have gentle slopes, cold soils, and diffuse drainage patterns. Forests of a different character will have different composition and structure. (See composition and structure.)

Choker A length of cable with a pair of knobs and a bell that is wrapped around logs so they can be skidded; connects the logs to a winch line or the skidder.

Clearcutting A method of cutting that removes all (or all merchantable) trees in the area, generally 20 acres or more, in one cut.

Climax An old classification for a plant community that does not change unless there is a change in conditions (e.g., from climate, logging, or fire), that is, the culminating stage in natural plant succession or a final stable stage. See maturity.

Closed crown A full, closed forest canopy that excludes sunlight.

Community Groups of plants, animals, and other forms living together in a place.

Composition (of a forest ecosystem) The parts that make up a particular forest area, such as the different species of plants and animals, the type of soils, and the slope gradient of the terrain.

Condition (of a forest ecosystem) A description of how human uses have modified forest functioning from the landscape level to the stand or patch level.

Ecologically responsible forest use respects the ecological limits of forests for various human uses. Ecological limits to human use are determined by describing and interpreting the character and condition of, first, the forest landscape, and then the forest stand or patch.

Conifer A tree belonging to the Coniferales, an important order of the group Gymnospermae, usually evergreen, with cones and needle-shaped leaves, and producing wood known commercially as softwood.

Conk Large, protruding, firm fruiting body of a fungus on a tree.

Conservation Biology An application of science centered on biodiversity and the processes that produce and sustain it.

Contour planting Planting so that the rows run around the hill or slope on the same level, rather than up and down.

Controlled burning A burn started intentionally and overseen for a definite purpose.

Coppice A method of encouraging reproduction by sprouting.

Cord A volume measure of stacked wood. A standard cord is 4 x 4 x 8 ft. or 128 cu. ft. of space. A long cord (unit) contains 160 cu. ft. of space and is 4 x 5 x 8 ft. Since round wood cannot be stacked to give solid volume, actual wood volume varies between 70 and 90 cu. ft. per cord.

Crop trees Trees that are designated to make up the final or rotation timber crop in industrial forestry.

Cross-valley movement corridors Travel routes for animals and plants to cross the ridges that separate one riparian ecosystem from another. Cross-valley corridors are not "natural"; before human beings began extensive modifications of forest landscapes, animals moved freely throughout, and occupied all of the landscape. However, with human modification of forests, cross-valley corridors have become a necessary component of forest landscape plans in order to provide protected travel corridors between human use zones.

Crown The upper part of a tree, including the branches with their foliage.

Crown fire A forest fire that extends to and sweeps along the tops and branches of trees.

Cruise A survey of forest lands to locate and estimate volumes and grades of standing timber; also, the estimate obtained in such a survey. A person who does it is a cruiser.

Culture The ways of living built up by a community of beings and passed on through generations. By this definition, wolves have culture, also.

Cut The yield, during a specified period, of products that are cut, as of grain, timber, or sawmilling lumber.

Decadent A term used in conventional timber management to describe a forest stand that includes a relatively large number of snags, fallen trees, and partially decayed, large, old trees. Conventional timber managers view decayed and dead trees to be waste. In fact, however, decadent forests are ecologically rich and an absolutely vital forest phase for maintaining fully functioning forest ecosystems.

Decay The decomposition of wood by micro-organisms resulting in progressive loss of strength and weight, with changes in color and texture.

Deciduous A term applied to trees that shed their leaves annually. The wood from such trees is generally called hardwood.

Deep ecology movement is a grassroots, worldwide, political movement that embraces radical environmentalism. It is defined by support for anything like Arne Naess' eight platform principles. Supporters agree that we cannot go on with business as usual; human numbers and technology are destroying the ecological systems; we must make fundamental changes in our values and practices; these require recognizing that there are values inherent in nature, and in thinking, speaking and acting ecocentrically. People support this platform from a number of different philosophies or religions. Supporting the platform principles leads to different sorts of policies and practical actions, depending on one's own context.

Deforestation Clearing an area permanently for another use, such as agriculture or road-building.

Degrade Diminish productivity or diversity; reduce quality or yield.

Den tree A dead or deteriorating tree containing cavities resulting from decay or holes created by birds or other animals. Compare wildlife tree.

Dendrology The science of systematic classification of trees.

Desertification The process of making deserts, often from grasslands or forests, as the result of exceeding critical limits.

Dieback Death of branches associated with changes in soil moisture or explosion of pathogens. Applied to trees, canopy, stand, and forest also.

Diversity The relative number of kinds per unit area; kinds may be species, genes, ecosystems, or cultures.

Dominant The trees in the forest that are tallest, largest, and often most valuable.

Duff The uppermost layer of the forest floor, made of organic debris.

Ecocentric refers to a value framework and approach that humans are part of larger ecological processes and communities. Natural and human communities are folded into one another. We participate (and cannot avoid doing so) in these communities. Our primary mission as moral agents is to take responsibility for ourselves. The environmental crisis is a result of collective and personal failure in responsibility. We must live as ecologically responsible members of the ecosphere. To do so requires appreciating all ecological values, so far as this is possible.

Ecofeminism is feminist scholarship and activism focused especially on the ecological dimensions of human activity. Ecofeminists say that industrial society is dominated by patriarchal structures of top-down control. These structures embed masculine values as good, feminine ones as bad. The result is a society that exploits nature, as she, and women as shes. Ecofeminism also involves visionary breadth, and practical actions aimed at deconstructing these older domination hierarchies, while working for social justice, ecological harmony and world peace.

Eco- Ecoforestry and ecoagriculture use the prefix "eco" to emphasize that their foundation is ecological paradigms and ecocentric values. In forestry this means rejecting the current industrial agricultural model that endorses large-scale clearcutting of natural forests and their replacement by human-designed plantations of a few tree species.

Ecoagriculture involves applying the same philosophy to farming. There are many ways to practise ecoforestry and ecoagriculture.

Ecoforestry is based on learning to use forests in ecologically responsible ways based on the wisdom of the forests. Ecoforestry manages human activities so as not to interfere with fully functioning natural forest ecosystems.

Ecological balance A controversial term referring to the dynamic equilibrium within a community subject to continual change.

Ecological integrity A description of the quality of an ecosystem (wild or managed) that leads to sustainability, continuity, diversity, and health.

Ecological health A property of an ecosystem; not dominated by disease, but able to adapt to it, continue, and flourish.

Ecological limits Physical and biological factors that indicate that various human uses may result in unacceptable levels of modification or degradation of forest ecosystem functioning. Common ecological limits include shallow soils, very dry or very wet sites, very steep slopes (greater than 60% slope gradient), broken slopes (abrupt slope gradient changes occuring regularly across a small landscape), very dry climates (less than 25 cm/10 inches of precipitation annually), cold soils, snow-dominated forests characterized by open, canopied forest stands (i.e. parkland forest ecosystems), and riparian ecosystems.

Ecological Self is the larger Self of which each of us is a part. In most spiritual traditions it is recognized that natural maturation processes take us beyond identification with our own narrow self-interest (egoism) to a larger sense of obligation, to family, to place, and to the larger community. The widest extension of caring is love for the ecos as a whole with its many beings; this is ecocentrism realized as ecosophy, wisdom to dwell with unconditional love for a place. The realization of the Ecological Self involves the flourishing of compassion and relationships that are spontaneously supportive and caring. The egoself is the separate, small, boundaried self. What is our main self of identification; with whom or what do we identify?

Ecologically responsible forest management A system developed by Herb Hammond based on general standards across several levels, including social, landscape, and stand. Also called wholistic forest use.

Ecologically responsible forest use An ecosystem-based approach for planning and carrying out human uses that gives first priority to the protection, maintenance, and (where necessary) restoration of whole ecosystems. The principles of ecologically responsible forest use apply to all human uses of the forest, including tourism, recreation, nontimber forest products, and hunting and fishing, as well as timber management.

Ecologically responsible timber management One aspect of ecologically responsible forest use, referring to timber management plans and activities that are developed and carried out in ways that protect, maintain, and restore (where necessary) a fully functioning forest ecosystem at all temporal and spatial scales. Forest composition, structures, and functioning are maintained, from the largest landscape to the smallest forest community, in both short and long terms.

Ecology is the science of the interrelationships, distribution, abundance and contexts of all organisms and their interconnections with their living and nonliving environment. It takes two forms: systems ecology that relies heavily on computer modelling and inventory data, and field ecology that studies organisms, communities and their processes in their natural settings. Ecology as a study is not restricted to biology. Most disciplines now have a branch using the word ecology or the eco-prefix. Sociologists study human ecology; eco-economists apply ecological principles and values to the study of economics, and so on.

Ecophilosophy is philosophizing as if nature matters. Its aim is to bring philosophy to the larger context of the natural world. Modern Western Philosophy has ignored this context in its mainstream value theories. An ecophilosopher is dedicated to understanding the spiritual and philosophical dimensions of the environmental crisis so as to contribute positive understanding and ecological paradigms and values that involve ecosophic practices. It synthesizes new visions through narratives out of which grow cultural practices appropriate to an Age of Ecology. The ultimate aim is practical realization of ecosophies. It is practised by people who have become ecophilosophers through examination (deep questioning) of the philosophical foundations of their own disciplines and lives as these relate to the natural world.

Ecosophy means literally the wisdom of the household place. It implies the wisdom to dwell harmoniously in a place. It involves being receptive and responsive to the needs of a place and the wisdom that nature has enfolded into it, with its many beings and communities. Communities that live ecosophically evolve unique practices of forest and land use that are called *vernacular technologies*. For example, shelters are built to fit the place to take full advantage of the natural heating and cooling characteristics there. Ecosophy deepens throughout one's life, and throughout a culture's life. To develop one's personal ecosophy is to articulate one's ultimate values and philosophy of life as an Earth dweller. Often a person's ecosophy is based on a traditional religion, such as Christianity or Buddhism.

Ecosystem The interacting unit of all beings in a physical environment. According to A.G. Tansley, any complex system or organisms that we "isolate" mentally to study, from a rotten log to the planet. Forest ecosystems have tree canopies covering more than 20 percent of an area.

Ecosystem management A program designed to achieve specific goals in an ecosystem; includes protection and manipulation.

Edge effect The edge effect in ecology refers to an ecotone in which species from two different ecosystems share space with the ecotone species. One misguided ecologist recommending cutting a high percentage of the Amazon rainforest just to multiply the apparent diversity of the edge effect. The effect is valuable, but it cannot be multiplied by destroying most of an ecosystem (remember island biogeography principles). Worldwatch estimates that for every 10-hectare clearcut, the edge effect degrades an additional 14 ha of old-growth forest.

Entomology The science that deals with insects and their relation to forests and forest products.

Environment All living and nonliving components of a place.

Environmental Ethics is a subdiscipline of applied values studies in philosophy.

Ethics is the study of moral values and good. The word also refers to a person's values.

Environmental ethics has two main forms: the first is based on axiology, that is, the development of a system of "thou shalts" and "shalt nots", or a code, usually supported by an ethical theory. The other form involves the realization that values are embedded in nature and that one cannot separate moral and human values from the whole spectrum of values.

Erosion The mechanical moving of soil by processes such as weathering, abrasion, corrosion, transportation, or flooding.

Even-aged A term applied to a stand in which relatively small age differences exist between individual trees. The maximum difference in age permitted in an even-aged stand is usually 10 to 20 years, although where the stand will not be harvested until it is 100 to 200 years old, larger differences, up to 25 percent of the rotation age, may be allowed. Methods of even-aged management include clearcutting, shelterwood, and seed tree cutting.

Exotic Not native; foreign. Those trees, plants and animals introduced from other climates or countries.

Falldown A reduction in the quantity of timber than can be cut in the future caused by miscalculating or exaggerating sustainable cutting levels.

Faller Person who cuts down trees. Also called Cutter, Sawyer, Chopper, or Flathead.

Fell To cut down a standing tree. Sometimes "fall."

Forb A herbaceous plant.

Forest An ecosystem characterized by trees or a plant community in which trees predominate (from the Latin word meaning outside the door).

Forest capital The whole, self-renewing forest, from which goods, in the form of interest, can be removed.

Forest ecosystem types Relatively homogeneous forest areas delineated by their biological and physical characteristics, and by their ecological limits or lack of ecological limits. Stands or patches frequently contain several ecosystem types.

Forest functioning How a forest works at a full range of scales over long time frames.

Forest restoration Assisting natural processes to re-establish forest composition and structures necessary to re-establish fully functioning forests at all scales. A key part of this definition, from the standpoint of ecological responsibility, is that people assist natural processes, as opposed to fixing natural processes.

Forestry The art, science, business, and practice of managing forests for human benefit (business seems to predominate). Four principles of ecology from Commoner: that (1) nature knows best, (2) there is no free lunch, (3) everything goes somewhere, and (4) all things are interconnected. These principles can be used to develop guidelines for planning and design. For example, if nature knows best, then we should learn sustainable forestry from the forest, not from abstract models and theories based on the assumption that humans know best, and that plantations are superior to natural forests.

Fully functioning forest ecosystem A forest ecosystem where biological diversity is maintained at all levels (genetic, species, ecological community, and landscape levels) and at all temporal and spatial scales. Maintaining biological diversity does not imply an absence of change; a fully functioning forest ecosystem includes natural disturbances and may include carefully designed human-induced changes.

Fungus A plant without chlorophyll that derives its nourishment from the organic matter of other plants.

Gene The material unit of inheritance; part of the deoxyribonucleic acid (DNA) molecule that encodes a single enzyme or protein unit. There is flow, exchange, and an ecology of genes.

Gene pool The genetic information in an interbreeding population, or the genetic resources of a species in its geographical distribution.

Gigatrend (ìgigaî, from the Greek for very large or giant) A long or very long-term trend, usually ignored by science and economics, e.g., global deforestation.

GIS (Geographic Information Systems) refers to the discipline, the software, and the databases for electronic mapping.

Grade The designated quality of a log, based on its possible end use, e.g., sawmill or peeler, according to species and scaling and grading rules.

Groundwater Water that stands or flows beneath the ground surface in soil or rock material that is thoroughly saturated. The upper surface of this saturated zone is called the water table.

Habitat A unit area of environment, (sometimes synonymous with site) or a place with a particular kind of environment where a community of organisms lives (home).

Hardwood Generally, one of the botanical group of trees that have broad leaves, in contrast to the needle-bearing conifers; also the wood produced by broad-leaved trees.

Harvest A general term for a cutting method that removes mature trees.

Heart rot A decay characteristically confined to the heartwood, usually originating in the living tree.

Heartwood The inner core of a woody stem, composed completely of nonliving cells and usually differentiated from the outer enveloping layer (sapwood) by its darker color.

High-grading The removal of only the best trees from the stand.

Humus The plant and animal residues of the soil, litter excluded, that are undergoing decomposition.

Hydrological cycle The path of water from the atmosphere through plant, animal, and water bodies and back into the atmosphere.

Indigenous Native to the locality.

Industrial forestry A business with a corporate structure, which limits liability (and common sense), usually having large land holdings and doing forestry on the industrial agricultural model.

Instrumental values are means to an end. They are the actions, beings, materials, etc., that we value for their functional use in attaining other valued things and states. We explain instrumental value choices as related to our understanding of our lives, who we are, what meaning there is in life for us, and our intrinsic values. Instrumental values depend ultimately upon intrinsic values for their sense. A person might value running only for its health benefits, that is, instrumentally, but could also value it as good in itself. Many values come into play in our activities and pursuits.

Intrinsic values are actions, states, beings, conditions, relationships, etc., valued for their own sake, and not just for what they lead to or produce. A person can value mountain walking for its own sake, not because it conditions the body, not because it gets him or her somewhere, but just for its inherent goodness. Of course one could also value it for all its instrumental benefits as well. If one has no intrinsic values, then all instrumental values are merely means to other means which are means to yet other means. Values lose their sense. All value systems presuppose a context. An egocentric value system presupposes a context that only extends as far as one's ego. An ecocentric value approach includes all beings. Intrinsic values are ends in themselves. Our committed intrinsic values help define who we are.

Knot The portion of a branch enclosed in the wood of the trunk. Live, tight, or green if the branch was alive; dead or loose if dead. Knots also vary in shape: splay (or spike), arris, edge, margin, and face.

Landscape ecology The study of how ecosystems change and interact on a large scale; useful in forestry for zoning and preservation.

Large protected reserves Whole draining basins of watersheds of about 5,000 hectares/12,500 acres or more, maintained as genetic, species, and ecological community reserves in forest landscapes. Protected reserves need to be large enough to accommodate the largest natural disturbance in a landscape and maintain ecosystem integrity.

Lignin An encrusting substance, a polymer of phenylpropane units, densely packed in the middle lamella. An organic substance which, with cellulose, constitutes the woody cell walls of plants and the cementing material between them; the essential part of woody tissue.

Litter The uppermost layer of the organic debris composed of freshly fallen or slightly decomposed organic materials. Commonly designated by the letter L.

Logging The process of taking tree stems from the forest: biomass removal on a grand scale. On a smaller scale biomass removal happens in a wild forest. Chris Maser notes that trees end up in the ocean; elk transfer biomass to grasslands.

Management Plan A written plan for the operation of a forest property, using forestry principles to prescribe measures to provide optimum use of all forest resources.

Mean Annual Increment (MAI) The average annual growth rate for a tree.

Moderately stable ecosystem types Terrain that consists of a mixture of ecologically sensitive ecosystem types and stable ecosystem types (areas that have not been designated as ecologically sensitive).

Monoculture A crop of a single species.

Multiple-use Forestry The practice of forestry that combines two or more objectives, such as production of wood or wood derivative products, forage and browse for domestic livestock, environmental conditions for wildlife, landscape effects, protection against floods and erosion, recreation, production and protection of water supplies, and national defence.

Natural Selection Forestry An all-age, all-species management system as popularized mostly by Orville Camp, in which he takes the weakest trees and leaves the stronger dominants.

Needle The stiff, narrow, chlorophyll-bearing leaf of conifers.

Net annual growth The net increase in the volume of trees during a specified year. Components include the increment in net volume at the beginning of the specific year surviving to its end, plus the net volume of trees reaching the minimum size class during the year, minus the volume of trees that died during the year, minus the volume of trees that became rough or rotten during the year.

New Forestry A form of industrial forestry that starts to acknowledge ecosystem processes, and considers forests in terms of larger systems.

Niche Habitat necessary for the existence of a species (its "work address").

Nursery An area where young trees are grown for forest planting.

Old growth Timber stands dominated by mature trees and other organisms in which little or no cutting has been done. Also known as first growth timber, mature forest growth, or virgin timber.

Paradigms are organizing gestalts or models that center and guide a practice. Worldviews use paradigms to exemplify human ideals (the saint), knowledge ideals (scientific method), and life-value ideals (salvation or enlightenment). A shift in paradigm is a revolutionary change in outlook. Usually this occurs when existing paradigms have reached their moral, physical, social and ecological limits and new root metaphors are emerging. Some say that the shift from sexist to nonsexist language represents a paradigm shift away from patriarchal paradigms to gender neutral ones, for example. The Modern world view culminates in the Industrial Paradigm which organizes all life according to economic measures and mechanistic models, in other words, production, consumption and increasing rate of growth are the dominant values.

Permaculture A permanent agriculture based on self-maintaining systems based on genetic and ecological diversity and emphasizing perennials (Bill Mollison 1980).

Phenotype The external characteristics of an organism, as a result of the interaction between its genetic constitution and the environment.

Photosynthesis The transformation of carbon dioxide and water into carbohydrates by plants using solar energy.

Pitch The resin of certain conifers, such as Ponderosa pine.

Plantation An area artificially reforested by planting or direct seeding.

Preserve An area in which species are allowed to create their own conditions apart from human interference. There can be many kinds, with different levels of protection or management.

Pulpwood Wood cut primarily for manufacture into wood pulp for subsequent remanufacture into paper, fibre, or other products, depending largely on the species and process.

Reforestation The natural or artificial restocking of an area with forest trees; most commonly used in reference to the artificial.

Resistance The ability of a plant to develop and function normally despite adverse environmental conditions or the attacks of disease or insects. Resistance can also involve human communities.

Resource industry An operation, such as forestry or fishing based on a primary resource.

Ring A growth layer seen in the cross-section of wood; may be related to annual growth.

Riparian ecosystem (riparian zone and riparian zone of influence) The wet forest adjacent to creeks, rivers, lakes, and wetlands (the riparian zone) and the drier upland forest (the riparian zone of influence) found next to the riparian zone. These upland sites are important buffers that protect the riparian zone, and also provide drier, more open habitat that is used as a movement corridor by upland species. Riparian ecosystems are the most common and most important landscape connectors.

Root metaphor refers to the dominant model that underlies a paradigm. For example, in the Modern Western Industrial Paradigm the root metaphor is the machine. Things are explained by analyzing them into their parts and by means of reduction to individuals obeying mechanistic principles. Thus, "the world is like a machine" (an analogy) becomes a root metaphor when literalized and used as a way of constituting our thought about something. The world is a machine, and so is the human body. These are not scientific claims. They are based on the application of an analogic mode of thought that becomes a taken-for-granted root metaphor defining the nature of reality as we experience it. The power of root metaphors cannot be overemphasized since they are often implicit and encoded through learning to use language from birth onward. Cultures reproduce themselves through encoded metaphors and analogies by means of which the unknown is related to the known in stories with shared contexts and values.

Rot A state of decay in wood. Dry rot is a brown rot from a fungus that conducts moisture to dry wood. Heart rot is a decay of the heartwood originating in living trees.

Rotation age The age at which average annual timber volume increase is the highest; also known as culmination age. In conventional timber management, trees are cut at rotation age, and the AAC or ASQ is determined based upon timber volumes at rotation age. This concept is useful only in conventional timber management, which attempts to maximize timber volume as opposed to maximizing timber value and maintaining overall forest functioning. Rotation age may also be defined as the age at which timber managers desire to cut trees, based upon ecological, social, and economic factors. This approach to rotation age is more useful in ecologically responsible forest use.

Runoff The rate at which water is discharged from a drainage area, usually expressed in cubic feet per square mile of drainage area; surface or subsurface.

Salvage cut A cutting method to remove dead trees with merchantable wood.

Sapling A young tree, older than a seedling, younger than a pole, usually 2-4 inches dbh.

Saprophyte A plant that gets its food from plants or animals that have died.

Sapwood The light-colored wood that appears on a cross-section of wood. The sapwood is composed of living cells and serves to conduct water and minerals to the crown.

Second growth Timber growth that comes up after removal of the old stand by cutting, fire, or another cause. Typical second-growth conditions may come about in a forest that is untouched by cutting.

Secular worldview is said to describe the Modern Industrial approach. For it, nothing is sacred. Its activities are placeless and contextless. They are free of religion, desacrilized of the holy. Everything must conform to uniform standards for industrial paradigms. The only values are the result of human making. Farming, fishing, forestry, etc. should all be industrialized and automated; the aim is total control from the top down by secular organizations.

Seedling A tree grown from seed. The term is restricted to trees smaller than saplings.

Seed tree A tree that produces seed; usually trees reserved in a cutting operation to supply seed. Also a cutting method that leaves seed trees.

Selection cutting The removal of selected mature, large, or diseased trees as single, scattered trees or in small groups of trees to maintain an uneven-aged forest.

Shelterbelt A wind barrier of living trees and shrubs maintained for the purpose of protecting farm fields. As applied to individual farmsteads, it is termed a windbreak; also called a belt.

Shelterwood cutting A method of removing mature timber in a series of cuttings to encourage natural reproduction.

Shrub A woody perennial with low stature and low habits, e.g., branching from the base.

Silviculture The science and art of producing and tending a forest; the application of the knowledge of silvics in the treatment of a forest; the theory and practice of controlling forest establishment, composition, and growth.

Skid To pull logs from the stump to the skidway, landing, or mill.

Skidder A vehicle for pulling logs. Also skidder grappler.

Skid road A road for skidding timber, formerly made of logs.

Skyline A cable logging system in which logs are carried through air rather than skidded.

Snag A standing, dead tree from which the leaves and most of the branches have fallen, or a standing section of the stem of a tree broken off at a height of 20 ft. or more. If less than 20 ft. high, it is properly termed a stub; if close to the ground, a stump. Snags are standing dead trees.

Social ecology is the study of the ecological context of human societies, including the ideological and other dimensions of culture, as well as the biological and geological relationships and settings. Social ecology also involves a critique of human systems based on artificial forms of domination and control from centralized power bases, or that favor one group over another. It involves a positive side that applies ecological knowledge to the design of human communities that are decentralized, democratic, diverse, and in harmony with their local places.

Softwood One of the botanical group of trees that generally have needle or scale-like leaves such as the conifers; also, the wood produced by such trees, regardless of texture or density.

Soil Geological material modified by physical, chemical, and biological processes to support rooted plants.

Species (of trees) Subordinate to a genus; trees having common characteristics. In common language, a kind such as sugar maple or white pine. Species may be endemic (indigenous or native) or exotic (alien or foreign).

Stable ecosystem types Areas that have not been designated as ecologically sensitive.

Stand A continuous group of trees or other growth occupying a specific area and sufficiently uniform in composition (species), age, arrangement, and conditions as to be distinguishable from the forest or other growth on adjoining areas.

Stem The trunk of a tree; the principal axis from which buds develop.

Stewardship The responsible and accountable management of resources (originally referred to the herding of sheep).

Structures (of a forest ecosystem) The arrangement of the parts of an ecosystem. Forest structures include large old trees, large snags (standing dead trees), large fallen trees, the arrangement and depth of soil organic layers, and the pattern of forest ecosystem types across large forest landscapes.

Stump The part of a tree left in the ground after the stem has been felled.

Stumpage Standing timber that has commercial value, and/or the fee paid to the landowner for harvested timber.

Succession The progressive development of the vegetation toward its highest expression of maturity. The replacement of one plant community by another. Changes in species composition.

Successional patterns The stages of forest growth and development that follow natural disturbances.

Super trees Industrial term for fast growing, high-yield, genetically-engineered trees. A superior phenotype, plus-tree, or select-tree.

Sustainable development A process of change leading to increased order, in which the exploitation of resources is considerate of future needs. "Meeting the needs of the present without compromising the future's needs."

Sustainable selective logging A set of alternative forest practices demonstrated by Merv Wilkinson and others.

Sustained yield As applied to a forest management plan, the term implies continuous production, with the aim of achieving an approximate balance between net growth and harvest, either by annual or somewhat longer periods.

Symbiosis The relationship of two or more organisms living in close association, usually with benefits for each and often obligatory.

Thinning Cutting in an immature stand to increase its rate of growth, to foster quality growth, to improve composition, to promote sanitation, to aid in litter decomposition, to obtain greater total yield, and to recover and use material that would be otherwise lost.

Topography The physical features of an area.

Total-cost accounting An accounting of all the values, benefits, costs, and effects of an activity, including subsidies, free goods, social and ecological costs. Also full-cost accounting (J.B. Cobb et al. 1988).

Transpiration The process by which water moves up through the living plant and vapor leaves the plant and enters the atmosphere.

Tree farm A farm on which trees are the crop; may also include hedgerows, orchard trees, agroforests, plantations, and associated organisms.

Type conversion The change from a diverse, all-age forest to a plantation dominated by one species of tree.

Ultimate Religion or Philosophy refers to the largest narrative we can present that explains our life as a whole in relation to nature and the cosmos. For most people this story is grounded in a particular religion such as Christianity or Taoism. For others the ultimate premises are based on a personally developed philosophy, such as Naess' Ecosophy-T. Most cultures are identified by their ultimate beliefs and meanings. Ultimate meanings and values are usually communicated in a culture through myths, religions, stories, spiritual disciplines, rituals, art, artifact design and use, to mention a few ways these are encoded.

Undercut The wedge-shaped piece cut in a tree to set direction of fall. See face.

Understory That portion of the trees in a forest stand below the overstory.

Uneven-aged A term applied to a stand in which there are considerable differences in age of trees and in which three or more age classes are represented. A management technique. See also all-aged.

Value-added Processing of a raw material, such as timber, by skilled labor to make finished items with more economic value, such as cabinets, musical instruments or furniture.

Virgin forest A forest not modified by humans or domestic livestock.

Waste Material no longer usable by an organism; it may be usable by another organism, however.

Watershed An area drained by a system of streams.

Wetland An area seasonally or permanently covered by shallow water or where the water table is close to the surface, characterized by hydric soils and hydrophilic (water-loving) plants and animals.

Whole forest certification Endorsement or verification by a forest foundation or other certifier that timber is grown and managed according to the principles of ecologically responsible forest use; applies to land where the land steward or forest manager has decision-making control over the landscape or part of the landscape and has decision-making control over the forest stands or patches that make up the landscape in question.

Whole tree harvesting A logging system that removes the trunk and all of the tree top, including branches, from where the tree was felled. The branches and top are cut off (bucked) at the central landing, where they are usually burned or buried.

Wild That which is not part of human systems. Beings and places that have a will of their own. Not identical with natural, since everything is natural, including human systems, although the artificial is a subset of the natural.

Wildcrafting Harvesting of nontimber forest products.

Wilderness Area not managed by human methods, sufficiently large to be self-regulating.

Wildlife tree A tree designated to be left as habitat. Also called a reserve tree.

Windfall Timber blown down by the wind.

Windthrow Destruction of trees by the wind.

Wisdom is the ultimate aim of philosophy, which literally means the love of wisdom and its pursuit. Ecological wisdom, or ecosophy, is the ultimate aim of ecophilosophy. In Western tradition, Socrates noted that wisdom begins when we realize our ignorance, and it requires that we examine our lives deeply to gain deep insight into self and world. Humans can live wisely without having complete knowledge, if their values and practices are sound. Once we realize our radical ignorance, we understand that data, information, and knowledge must be embedded in a larger sense of life that can only be gained by active experience and reflection on life as a whole. For wisdom we must have comprehensive understanding of our selves, context and relationships, the values that guide us, the commitments we honor, the respect we show, and the compassion we can live.

Wholism (or holism) refers to the idea that a whole is more than the sum of its parts. As applied, wholes are the basic "units" of understanding, rather than their parts. Whole and part are relative terms in some respects, especially in recent ecological paradigms. Wholes are usually enfolded in larger wholes, etc. Wholes exhibit self-organization, self-replication, and self-integrity. Just as a word, sentence and theme make sense by reference to a larger story and its setting, so wholes are understood in relation to their internal and external relationships within their larger ecological setting.

Woodlot A unit of forest (Canada); an enclosure near a house (for firewood or domestic livestock).

Xerophyte A plant of a dry habitat able to endure drought.

Xylem Vascular tissue that makes up the bulk of the stem and all of the roots. Wood.

Yard Place where logs are collected. Also, a landing.

Yarding Removing trees from stumps to a landing area.

Yield determination A calculation of forest products that can be harvested annually.

Zone An area characterized by distinct physical conditions and populated by organisms adapted to those conditions. Forestlands can be zoned using landscape-level, ecologically-based criteria as in ecoforestry.